JACKIE, JANET & LEE

This Large Print Book carries the
Seal of Approval of N.A.V.H.

JACKIE, JANET & LEE

THE SECRET LIVES OF JANET AUCHINCLOSS AND HER DAUGHTERS JACQUELINE KENNEDY ONASSIS AND LEE RADZIWILL

J. RANDY TARABORRELLI

THORNDIKE PRESS
A part of Gale, a Cengage Company

Farmington Hills, Mich • San Francisco • New York • Waterville, Maine
Meriden, Conn • Mason, Ohio • Chicago

GALE
A Cengage Company

Thorndike Press® Large Print Biographies and Memoirs.
The text of this Large Print edition is unabridged.
Other aspects of the book may vary from the original edition.
Set in 16 pt. Plantin.

LIBRARY OF CONGRESS CIP DATA ON FILE.
CATALOGUING IN PUBLICATION FOR THIS BOOK
IS AVAILABLE FROM THE LIBRARY OF CONGRESS.

ISBN-13: 978-1-4328-4794-4 (hardcover)

Published in 2018 by arrangement with Macmillan Publishing Group,
LLC/St. Martin's Press

Printed in Mexico
1 2 3 4 5 6 7 22 21 20 19 18

To my parents,
Rocco and Rose Marie Taraborrelli

CONTENTS

I have fought the good fight. I have
finished the course. I have kept the faith.

— PAUL THE APOSTLE

PROLOGUE

March 15, 1961. The White House.

It was an evening Janet Auchincloss would never forget, the kind that made her wonder whose life she was living, because it certainly didn't seem like her own. Wearing a beige silk dress with a delicately jeweled bodice, pearls at her neck, and a fine emerald pin on her shoulder, Janet, with her husband, Hugh, walked into the State Dining Room and stood in stunned silence. Before them was a sea of people in formal wear seated at round tables, seven at each, in chairs covered in yellow, brown, and raspberry-colored silk. The tables were draped in gold cloth with simple yet elegant centerpieces of yellow-and-white hydrangeas, freesia, peonies, a sprig of tangerines, and two perfectly placed, tapered white candles. The flatware was antique vermeil. The room itself was also stunning, adorned tastefully in an eighteenth-century Louis XVI style with pale yellow walls, gold silk drapes, and crisp white molding. As a small string quartet softly played, people milled about searching for their place settings while chatting happily among themselves.

As Janet would later recall, it took a minute or so for her to focus on the seventy-plus guests before she realized that most of them were relatives and personal friends. Continuing to survey the room, she saw one animated young woman trying to flag her down. It was her daughter Lee. Janet made a beeline for her. After an embrace, Lee took her mother by the hand to the table where she was seated with her husband, Prince Stanislaw Radziwill — known to all as "Stas." Hugh, impeccably tailored in a gray-and-white tuxedo, greeted his stepdaughter with a warm hug and Stas with a firm handshake.

As everyone enjoyed one another's company, the anticipation in the cavernous dining room continued to build. Finally, a stately-looking gentleman went to a microphone and, with great pomposity, announced, "Ladies and gentlemen, the President of the United States, John Fitzgerald Kennedy, and the First Lady, Jacqueline Kennedy." At that point, everyone rose and applauded as the first couple made their way slowly through the dining room, smiling, shaking hands, and graciously greeting guests.

Janet's oldest daughter, Jacqueline — Jackie — was a real beauty, her ink-black short hair in a glossy yet simple coif, her angular face clear and luminous as if carved from polished marble. She had prominent cheekbones and dark eyes set far apart. Her teeth weren't perfectly aligned, but her smile was appealing just the same, as if that one flaw lent humanity to her goddess-like quality.

Love and pride lit up Janet's face as Jackie reached out to her and kissed her on the cheek. Jackie then embraced Hugh and Stas, saving her sister for last. Smiling, she and Lee joined hands, holding each other at arm's length to compliment their fashion choices — Jackie in white sleeveless organza, Lee in flowing red silk — before finally hugging each other.

Janet knew the evening was one Jackie had planned especially for Lee because Lee hadn't been well. She'd had a difficult time giving birth about six months earlier, which had debilitated her to the point where she'd not even been able to attend the inauguration of President Kennedy. Making things all the more difficult for her, Lee was now living in Europe with Stas, an ocean separating her from her beloved family members. These days, she seemed muted, sad. She was certainly gorgeous, though, with a slender and willowy frame. Her eyes, large and intelligent, were maybe her greatest feature. Some people thought she was actually prettier than Jackie. She didn't comport herself with the same authority, though. Jackie's beauty was more than skin deep; it emanated from within because of her unwavering self-confidence. Lee just wasn't as vital and arresting a person, at least not these days. Therefore, out of concern for her, Jackie decided to host this dinner-dance in Lee's honor.

Of course, it had to have felt a little to Lee like it was *Jackie's* night, especially given the grand entrance she'd just made. Lee was used to it, though. After all, Janet's girls had been in competition since they were youngsters — mostly one-sided, Lee's side, unfortunately. Now that Jackie was First Lady, there was scant hope that Lee would ever be able to top *that*.

Though the Kennedys had moved into the White House only a few weeks earlier, it already felt to a lot of people as if they'd taken the country by storm. Jackie was, at thirty-one, a new kind of youthful, elegant First Lady, especially coming after the conservative, sixty-five-year-old Mamie Eisenhower. Her husband, John — better known to friends and family as Jack — was forty-three and handsome in a rock-solid sort of way, fairly bursting with vitality, or what the Kennedys liked to call *"vi-ga!"* His extended family was fascinating, too; tonight, though, they were scarce. In fact, if one were to peruse the official White House guest list, on top would be found "The President and Mrs. Kennedy," of course. Next was "Prince and Princess Stan-

14

islaw Radziwill" (that would be Stas and Lee), followed by "Mr. and Mrs. Hugh D. Auchincloss" (Hugh and Janet), after which was "The Atty. General and Mrs. Kennedy" (Bobby and Ethel, naturally), and then all of the other guests, mostly friends of Jackie's, Janet's, and Lee's. Though Jack's brother-in-law Sargent Shriver was present, that was only because, less than two weeks earlier, Jack had announced a ramping up of his plans for a Peace Corps with Sargent as its director. Jackie thought he should be present out of respect for Jack, but his wife, Eunice, was nowhere to be found. There were no other Kennedys.

If anything, Jackie's decisions relating to who would be invited to this particular dinner-dance underscored her pride in her own side of the family. Looking back all these years later, some might view the Auchinclosses as the other side of "Camelot," the romantic term Jackie would one day use to describe her husband's administration. After all, Jackie really did have a full life that had nothing to do with the Kennedys; for instance, she had a half brother and half sister the world didn't seem to know a thing about: Janet Jr., fifteen, and Jamie, fourteen, born to Janet and Hugh and both at boarding school.

Though many people didn't realize it, Jackie had modeled herself after her mom, Janet Lee Bouvier Auchincloss. Janet was remarkably stylish in her own right. At the age of fifty-three, her face was barely lined or scored by the years. She was petite and in shape thanks to her dedication to long walks, horseback riding, and isometric exercises. Self-assured, she held herself with a bearing that could best be described as regal. It made sense. After all, she'd been raised in an entitled world of privilege and money. Her first marriage to a scoundrel named Jack Bouvier in 1928 would result in their two daughters, Jacqueline Lee Bouvier — Jackie — and Caroline Lee Bouvier — known simply as Lee — now twenty-eight.

Of course, mother and daughters didn't always get along, each headstrong, passionate, and, at times, temperamental. However, they were bound not only by a deep affection for one another but, like most families, by a shared history of triumphs and disappointments. Incredibly enough, their journey had somehow led them to this astonishing moment — one that found Jackie as America's First Lady, Lee as a princess, and Janet the proud mother of two accomplished, intelligent young women of substance.

The party was great fun, Jackie's exquisite taste on full display, as always. "Come with me," she whispered conspiratorially to Janet at one point in the evening. "I have something I think you should see. Let's get Lee." Eventually, they found Lee and Stas in front of the fireplace, under an imposing oil painting of Abraham Lincoln, talking to Oleg Cassini, Jackie's dress designer. They pulled Lee aside and asked her to join them. Sensing a matter of possible urgency, Stas and Oleg wanted to come along, but Jackie said no. What she had in store was just for her sister and mother.

Jackie then walked Janet and Lee out to the hall, where they boarded an elevator that took them down one floor. They then walked through a seemingly endless maze of rooms to the West Wing and then into a foyer area utilized by the President's personal secretary. Before them was a large, imposing, glossy white door, which Jackie opened with a flourish. After Janet and Lee had walked about a foot into the room, they stood in place beaming with pleasure, their mouths wide open.

It was the Oval Office, the executive headquarters of the President of the United States. The three women took a few careful steps onto the large, round green carpet, still in place from the Eisenhower administration. There were statues, busts, and figurines not yet in their proper places; most of the décor was still just as President Eisenhower had left it. Jackie said she eventually intended to change out the green drapes on the three large south-facing French windows behind the President's desk to ivory to match the walls. She said that Jack was thinking about going with red carpeting instead of the present pale green, but she thought it might be "too obvious," as she put it. The President and First Lady were free to implement their ideas; each new administration was given the opportunity to redecorate the Oval Office to its own taste. For now, though, Jackie's only concern was to share this one special moment with the two most important people in her life, her mother and her sister. The three Bouvier women stood in the middle of the Oval Office for a long time, wondering how in the world they'd ever arrived at this incredible and also solemn moment. "It took my breath away," Janet would later recount to her friend Oatsie Charles. "I simply could *not* believe my eyes," she exclaimed.

Janet walked over to the President's desk. It was Eisenhower's, not the Resolute Desk that Jack would eventually use, made from wood of the HMS *Resolute* and a gift from Queen Victoria to President Rutherford Hayes. Jackie would later have that particular piece of furniture brought out of storage and placed in this office for her husband. But now, before Janet was Eisenhower's big and imposing desk, a symbol of great strength and power if ever there was one.

"Go ahead, Mummy," Jackie told her. "You know you want to."

Janet paused a moment. Dare she? Then, according to what she would recall, she held her breath and slowly sat down in the President's chair, taking her place behind the large desk. Once she was seated, she exhaled and tried to relax. "Is this real?" she asked her daughters, both of whom were beaming at her. They would later agree that seeing their mother sitting behind the desk that belonged to the Leader of the Free World somehow seemed to make all the sense in the world. After all, Janet had ruled the family with an iron fist for many years, and would continue to do so. The moment didn't last long, though. After about a minute, Janet had to stand up and walk away from the desk, saying, "It's just too much to take!"

The magnitude of the moment hit Janet hard, so much so that she made a decision. "I must call him Mr. President from now on, mustn't I?" she asked Jackie as the three women took seats on the beige couches in front of the fireplace. According to one account, Jackie said, "Of course not, Mummy. He's still Jack." No, Janet decided as she gazed about the hallowed circular room. She noted that the important decisions likely to be made in this space in years to come would be so urgent that never should they be shouldered by a mere man named "Jack." She offered, "We can no longer think of him as the *man*, we have to think of him as the *office*." Therefore, from that time on, out of respect not only for the office but for the officeholder, Janet would always refer to her son-in-law as "Mr. President."

Mother and daughters spent about a half hour in the Oval Office, much of their discussion remaining private between them, the details lost to the ages and all but wondered about by their relatives for years to come. "I can't believe I missed out on that moment when those three stepped into the Oval Office," Oleg Cassini would recall many years later. "To think, I was standing right there when Jackie asked her mother and sister to join her! Later, when Lee told me about it, I must admit I was filled with envy."

"It was such a proud moment," Janet later remembered of her and Lee's first and only time in the Oval Office. "It was something I'm so happy to have been able to share with my girls." She said it felt to her, during that special evening in March of 1961, as if everything was right in their world, as if nothing could ever go wrong. Jackie and Lee would have agreed; this was the good life, all right. Surely, they thought, it would only get richer and more fulfilling with the passing of time, the promise of tomorrow.

Unfortunately, as fate would have it, mother and daughters could not have been more wrong. In fact, Jackie wouldn't even get to see how that "obvious" red carpet Jack so badly wanted would look in the Oval Office, nor the realization of many of her other ideas relating to his inner sanctum. Those final renovations wouldn't be completed until November of 1963 while the Kennedys campaigned in Texas. However, that was the trip from which Jackie would return a widow. She would then walk into the Oval Office only to find it already torn apart to suit the taste of the next administration. Swift decisions made by those newly in power would serve as harsh reminders that what had once been held sacred would now be laid to waste. Soon one sister would be forced to forgive the unforgivable while the other would make life choices based on fear and desperation. Indeed, before long, the lives of Janet and her daughters Jackie and Lee would change so abruptly — so unexpectedly — that it would take their breath away.

■ ■ ■ ■

PART ONE:
THE BEGINNING

■ ■ ■ ■

"My Lee"

November 1952.

Janet Lee Bouvier Auchincloss, forty-four, came sweeping down the hall wearing a waistcoat jacket with a mink collar over a white silk blouse and matching cotton skirt. Her spike heels made staccato clicking sounds as she approached an office at the end of a long hallway. Peeking inside the small room, she found a young woman working behind a typewriter. "Excuse me. I wonder if you can help me?" she asked. "I'm looking for my Lee." At the mention of the name, from around a corner came a familiar voice: "Mummy, is that you?" Lee suddenly appeared, also looking elegant in a smartly tailored black pantsuit with a wide leather belt. (In black-and-white photographs taken on the day, the belt appears to be gray but Lee would later call it "shocking pink.") *Lee,"* exclaimed Janet as she sized her up. "For goodness sake! Why are you wearing *pants*?" For a moment, Lee's glowing smile disappeared; her shoulders drooped dejectedly. She recovered quickly, though, as Janet pulled her into an embrace.

It could be said that Janet Auchincloss's life up until this point had unfolded pretty much the way she'd expected. She always knew, for instance, that she would marry "up," as she had ten years earlier with her second husband, the well-heeled Hugh Dudley Auchincloss Jr., affectionately known as "Hughdie." "Hughdie's not perfect and neither am I," she would tell intimates, "but we suit each other." On the whole, she was content, even though, as a young woman of thirty-four, she had made certain sacrifices in marrying Hugh — not the least of which had been forfeiting the kind of passion she'd once shared with her first husband, Jack Bouvier. However, she was a pragmatic woman who, once she made a choice in life, made an effort to never look back. While the marriage to Bouvier had produced two daughters, Jackie, now twenty-three, and Lee, nineteen, with Hugh she had Janet, seven, and Jamie, five.

Janet had not been happy with some of Lee's decisions of late, but her daughter seemed to have landed in a good place. For the last month, she'd been working at a new job as assistant to fashion icon Diana Vreeland at *Harper's Bazaar*. It was going well for her. Because Janet had a full itinerary of business meetings with Hugh in New York,

26

where Lee was now living, the opportunity for a mother-daughter visit at the new job presented itself. As she looked around at the *Harper's* workplace, Janet took in the chaos of busy writers and photographers popping in and out of each other's offices, all with so much to do. The creative energy in this place captivated her just as much as it had Lee when she first applied for the job.

Deena Atkins-Manzel worked at *Harper's* at the same time as Lee, as a designer in the art department. "Lee and I started the exact same week, she a few days before me," she recalled. "She was model thin, had a great complexion, a beautiful smile, a way about her that was elegant and smart. She had long dark hair and big, inquisitive brown eyes that sometimes looked hazel. She was eager, loved fashion and design. We spent hours talking about the latest styles and trends. I thought she was marvelous.

"I well remember the day Lee's mother first came to visit," she added. "Mrs. Auchincloss was a small-framed woman with a large personality. Much to Lee's dismay, she invited herself into each office to ask the employees, 'So what is it *you* do here?' Lee would say, 'Mummy, you can't just barge into people's offices.' Mrs. Auchincloss said, 'But I think it must be nice for these poor people to get a break from their humdrum jobs.' She was a real character and I could tell that Lee was embarrassed by her, the way daughters sometimes are of their moms."

Landing the job as Diana Vreeland's assistant had been a real coup for Lee, and she didn't have many victories in her life up until this time. She also never felt the warmth of her mother's approval. Five months earlier in June, at the end of her sophomore year at Sarah Lawrence, Lee had gone to Rome with Janet for a holiday. While there, she decided to take vocal lessons. Janet couldn't believe it when Lee told her about this sudden new desire to be a singer. In her mind, it was just another in a long list of impulsive decisions that made no sense; Lee was always coming up with new plans and schemes. When Janet discovered that Lee's "Italian" vocal coach actually hailed from Mississippi, that was all she needed to hear to know that singing was just another one of Lee's pipe dreams. It didn't matter, though, because after a couple of weeks, Lee was finished with it. She then said she was going to take textile design courses because "I love to draw and paint." "Fine, Lee," her exasperated mother said, "draw and paint, then."

Meanwhile, mother and daughter were scheduled to return to America at the beginning of July after a week in London. Lee wanted to stay on in Europe, however, and continue on to Paris. When she was abroad, she was just happier, the distance between her and her mother somehow influencing her mood in a positive way. Therefore, the two parted company after London with Lee promising she would be back to the States in time for the beginning of the new school year in September. However, when she finally returned, she found that she wouldn't be able to continue at the tony Sarah Lawrence College where she'd left off in her studies. Instead, she would have to repeat some of her sophomore courses. "So, I dropped out and just never went back," Lee would remember. Again, Janet was maddened. "Quite a lot was expected of one," Lee would recall many years later to Charlotte Ford for *McCall's*. "We [she and Jackie] were expected to do what we did well and to be decent. But we were never decent enough. We never did well enough. Always, we weren't working hard enough for Mummy's taste."

Making her life all the more complex for her, Lee always felt she was in her elder sister Jackie's shadow. As they got older, it had become a template of their lives that Jackie was the sister living a happy and carefree existence, always able to not only adapt to every new situation but find good in it and make the best of it. Lee was the one who found herself out of sorts, unable to cope, always in search of contentment. "As a young woman, Jackie had a definite look of destiny, as if she was inevitably going to be someone unique," said her half brother, Jamie Auchincloss. "Lee was an attractive girl who seemed like she was struggling to keep up. Whereas Jackie was always sure life would unfold for her with good fortune, Lee had a more pessimistic attitude. Despite this stark difference in their personalities, they truly did love one another. They were constantly whispering to one another conspiratorially as if it was them against the world."

When she returned to the States, Lee still didn't know what she wanted to do with her life, but she was smart enough to realize that she should make contacts in as many fields as possible. "After a job opened up on Vreeland's staff at *Harper's,* Lee had no trouble snagging it," recalled Anna DeWitt, a friend of hers from those early Manhattan days. "Suddenly, Lee was all about fashion," said DeWitt. "Now *this* was her latest passion, but this time she really committed herself to it. It was actually a good fit. She had style, she understood design, she was current with all the trends, and she had a critical eye."

Laura Pyzel Clark, one of Diana Vreeland's fashion editors at that time, said, "Lee was a little bit, not fey, but a fantasy girl. Her fantasy life wasn't evident in anything she said, though. It was just her air, the way she moved, the way she dressed. She had a little extra something from the other girls, what the French call *cachet,* all kinds of lovely ideas about life and how it should be. Quality was important to her. Lee loved quality things — handmade shoes, beautiful fabrics. If she could only have one chair in her home, that chair would have to be the best and have the best fabric on it."

Of course, since *Harper's* was at the very heart of the fashion world, working for Diana Vreeland was a dream-come-true job for Lee. "Anyone who had any contact with Diana caught something special," added Laura Pyzel Clark. "In the morning she would sweep off the elevator and the whole floor would change. Diana gave off an electric charge. There was a mood you would catch. She would sweep into the office looking absolutely fantastic. She smelled wonderful — the scent that she wore trailed after her — and then she would go and sit in this marvelous office of hers with its wonderful photographs of, say, some socialite or model wearing a fabulous necklace, and she would start calling us in one at a time. We all got such a charge out of this."

"Diana Vreeland was a mad, fashion genius," Lee would later recall. "I idolized her. I loved her style, the way she walked and talked. In some ways, I patterned myself after her. She was *finished,* if you know what I mean. And, of course, she was creative and daring. I wanted to walk into a room and feel

31

just the way I imagined she felt, with all eyes on her."

Like her daughter, Janet also admired Diana. Therefore, after Lee had introduced Janet to everyone else in the office, she excitedly took her to meet her boss. Unfortunately, Vreeland was brusque and unfriendly; maybe she was having a bad day. While she complimented Janet on her rearing of Lee, allowing that she was "charming," she seemed patronizing and definitely had no time to chat. "Walk with me," she commanded. As Lee, Janet, and Deena kept a steady pace with her, Diana barked instructions while her two employees took rapid notes on legal pads. "No time for lollygagging," she concluded as she dashed off without so much as even shaking Janet's hand. "Get to work, ladies!" A red-faced Lee covered for her boss by reminding Janet that she was a busy woman. As far as Janet was concerned, though, a tight schedule was no excuse for bad manners; she instantly changed her opinion of Diana Vreeland.

ABOUT MICHAEL

After Janet, Lee, and Deena left the Manhattan high-rise that housed *Harper's,* they caught a cab to the Oyster Bar, which is on the lower level of Grand Central Station. Already seated in a corner in the back of the restaurant at a table covered with red checkered linen was Jacqueline Bouvier. She jumped up to greet them: "Mummy! Lee!" Again according to a photograph taken that day, she was wearing what appeared to be a chartreuse wool day suit with a long skirt that flared from the calf, along with a matching tailored jacket over a white silk blouse; she was model thin and gorgeous. Her glossy chestnut-colored hair was cut quite short with bangs. She had met Deena Atkins-Manzel earlier while visiting Lee at *Harper's*. After the two shook hands and exchanged pleasantries, everyone sat down.

Jackie was immediately full of questions for Lee: Was she enjoying her job? Was Diana Vreeland "still just awful"? Had she put aside any interesting fashion magazines for her? "Their closeness was immediately obvious," recalled Deena. "They would even finish each other's sentences! For I would say fifteen minutes, it was as if there was nobody else in the room. Their eyes were filled with such admiration for each other. Mrs. Auchincloss just sat quietly studying her menu as the two sisters went on and on and on."

"So, have you made a decision about Michael?" Jackie wanted to know.

Janet perked up. "Michael?"

The sisters shared a secret look.

"Mummy, you know Michael," Lee said. "Michael Canfield."

Twenty-seven-year-old Michael Temple

Canfield was a six-foot-three, brown-haired Harvard graduate. He'd served in the Marine Corps in World War II and had been wounded at Iwo Jima. With his chiseled features and elegant comportment, he could easily have passed for a model. He also had all of the appropriate social graces necessary to squire Lee about town. The author George Plimpton once described him as "a paragon of good taste. His clothes were different from ours, the consistency of the material. He was probably the most elegant figure I've ever seen." Moreover, he was a sincere person, empathetic and a good friend; few could find a reason to be critical of him. "He spoke *le mot juste,* a phrase that he fancied," said his stepbrother, Blair Fuller. "He wrote very good letters and was always seeking the exact word for things, and it gave his speech, which was sometimes complicated by a stammer, a great deal of distinction. Michael didn't sound like anyone else."

Jackie, who had met Michael on several occasions, thought he was, as she put it, "stunning and smart, yet somehow quite sad." She and Lee had apparently already discussed Lee's interest in him.

Further distinguishing Michael, who now lived in Manhattan, was the fact that he had an intriguing, albeit bizarre, backstory about possibly being of a royal bloodline. Even though Janet had met him in the past as an acquaintance of Lee's when they were younger, she couldn't really remember him and certainly didn't know the details of his storied family history. As lunch was being served, Lee attempted to explain as much of it as she could remember. She said that, as a baby, Michael was adopted by the famous publisher Cass Canfield and his wife, Katsy, when the couple lived in England. In recent years, Michael had come to believe that his biological father was really Prince George, the Duke of Kent (younger brother of the Prince of Wales), and that his mother was an American woman named Kiki Preston, the niece of Mrs. Cornelius Vanderbilt II. Kiki was an outrageous lady with a terrible drug habit who'd previously had a passionate romance with Rudolph Valentino, after which she seduced Prince George. As it supposedly happened, after Kiki became pregnant by Prince George, she went off to Switzerland to have the baby in secret. By coincidence, Kiki's brother, the writer Erskine Dwynne, was a friend of Cass Canfield's and he asked him to adopt the baby. That's how Michael ended up being raised by the Canfields.

"Oh, my," Janet said. "Now, that's *quite* the story, isn't it?"

"But I *also* heard," Lee continued with an excited glance at Jackie, "that, *maybe,* Michael is the son of the Lord of Acton . . . and his maid." Now Janet looked skeptical. She asked which was the case: was he the son of Prince George or the son of the Lord of Acton? Lee said she didn't know and, apparently, neither did Michael. What difference did it make, though? Either way, Lee noted, he was British nobility. "Or he's just an American with a vivid imagination," Janet concluded with a smirk.

"Mrs. Auchincloss said she couldn't remember him," Deena Atkins-Manzel recalled. "Jackie then told her that they — the sisters and Janet — once ran into him in London. She reminded her that Michael was an editor at Hamish Hamilton, a division of Harper & Brothers [later to become Harper & Row]. 'Wait. Is that the man we ran into at the theater?' Janet asked, turning to Lee. Lee said yes, that was him. 'But Lee, he's a *homosexual*,' Janet exclaimed. When Lee said that it wasn't true, Janet held up a silencing hand. 'Oh my goodness, Lee, *of course* it's true,' she said. 'He's *a fairy*, Lee,' she concluded. 'My God! You can't see that?'

"The discussion quickly escalated into an argument over whether or not this man — Michael Canfield — was homosexual," Deena Atkins-Manzel recalled. "I just sat there and watched the three of them go at it, my head turning from one to the other to the other. 'I know Michael quite well,' Lee said as she nervously twisted her hands together, 'and he is *not* light in the loafers, Mummy.' Janet said,

'Fine. It doesn't matter to me, anyway.'

"Lee said she felt it was unkind of Janet to come to any conclusions about Michael without knowing him," continued Deena Atkins-Manzel. "She dreamily added that wherever they were in the world, their stars kept crossing and she felt there had to be *some* reason for it. She also said she believed Michael was going to ask for her hand in marriage and, if so, she planned to say yes. At this, Jackie was surprised. 'Really?' she asked. Lee nodded. However, she seemed a little unsure; I thought maybe she was just trying to get under Janet's skin."

Perhaps with the same goal in mind for Lee, Janet then concluded that she knew what was *really* going on. She noted that Jackie had recently been dating a senator named Jack Kennedy. Obviously, at least as Janet now saw it, Lee was just trying to top her. "Jackie has a senator," Janet observed, turning to Lee. "So now *you* have to have a prince? It's so transparent, Lee! You know very well that I do *not* approve of this kind of competition!"

"For the rest of the meal, Lee was quiet and withdrawn," recalled Deena Atkins-Manzel. "Her eyes darted about nervously any time she spoke. The rapport she had with Jackie had all but disappeared. She just went into a shell. Jackie and Janet continued with an animated conversation about something else and brought me in from time to time, but Lee was left on the outside of it."

Finally, Lee spoke. "If I were trying to compete with *her*," she said, gesturing toward her sister but not even glancing at her, "I should have started at about the age of five."

"I thought you *had*," Janet deadpanned.

VERY DIFFERENT SISTERS

Jackie and Lee Bouvier couldn't have been more different from each other, even from the start. Jackie, a little more than three years Lee's senior, always somehow seemed the more precious of the two. For instance, when she and Lee were little girls and played "make-believe," Jackie would always be the princess and Lee her dutiful handmaiden, her lady-in-waiting. Lee didn't mind the role, at least not at first. Ironically, though, it would foreshadow the nature of their complex relationship as they got older.

Whereas Jackie enjoyed her childhood for the most part and seemed to cope well with any problems, Lee was more sensitive. She wasn't able to grapple with tough issues, especially after Janet divorced the girls' adored father, Jack Bouvier. Today, it's rare for Lee Radziwill to have a memory of her childhood that isn't dark or troubled. It could be argued that she didn't know how good she had it because she was so shielded from the Depression. However, an entitled life was all she knew and, despite her many blessings and advantages, she still leaned toward escapism. "I created a realm of fantasy and lived in it," Lee would later explain. "At about six, I had three imaginary friends with the utterly inexplicable names of Shaday, Dahday, and Jamelle. They were girl spirits who wore ethereal floating dresses — nothing down-to-earth about them — and they lived in the house with me except when we took trips together. They said, 'Come, Lee. We'll take you away!' I only remember that we flew and danced and everything was beautiful. They took me out of reality."

Janet raised the girls to be exceedingly polite, their patrician manners always on full display, their social refinement uppermost among their mother's concerns. They were taught to speak with perfect diction, pronouncing their words slowly and deliberately. They'd learned to read at an early age and were personally schooled by Janet in the arts. Constantly, they were escorted by her to museums and libraries, and then quizzed at the dinner table about what they'd learned and experienced that day. While it may seem a burdensome life for a child, it really wasn't. The Bouvier sisters had fun and were exceedingly close; Jackie's nickname for Lee was "Pekes"; Lee's for Jackie was "Jacks." When Janet wasn't lecturing them about one thing or another, it didn't take much for the girls to break out in a game of tag at a museum — all Jackie had to do was tap Lee on the shoulder, announce, "You're it, Pekes!" Lee would counter with, "Oh, no, I'm not!" And the two were then off and running, racing all over the museum, chasing each other and squealing with delight while their chagrined mother hid in a corner telling others, "I don't know those girls. They do not belong to me."

One happy memory for Jackie and Lee had to do with the Christmas play they performed every year for Janet. They sang Christmas carols as Jackie played Joseph and Lee portrayed the Virgin Mary. "The final carol we sang was always 'One Night, When Stars Were Shining,' which touched my mother so much that she was always reduced to tears," Lee would recall. "No one else seems to have heard of this carol, but it was her favorite."

Both Bouvier girls were pretty, with soft brown eyes and silken brunette hair, which Janet routinely washed by cracking three raw eggs over their heads and rubbing the yolk into their hair. She said she did so because the eggs had protein in them — which she pronounced as "pro-*ti*-en."

Jackie was the thinner of the two, more chiseled and classic-looking, much like her father, Jack Bouvier. While Lee was a good-looking youngster, she was more ordinary in appearance, like her mom. She was also a little chubby, with the kind of cheeks people loved to squeeze. Jackie was a tomboy; Lee more girly in nature. Maybe because of their differences, by the age of twelve — the summer of 1941 — Jackie was protective of Lee. For instance, once, when Lee was about nine and being picked on by a student in school, Jackie rushed to her defense. She would not engage in any physical altercation, though, lest she muss her crisply starched, emerald-green school uniform. Typical of the decorum she would demonstrate as an adult, Jackie engaged in a grown-up conversation with the child's mother, explaining in explicit detail just how the boy's actions had hurt her sister. The bullying stopped.

What Janet took the most pride in was the fact that nothing could come between her daughters. They would sit reading books to each other for hours at a time, or become completely absorbed in their arts and crafts, complimenting each other on their creativity. If one was punished by Janet, the other would go into the bedroom and comfort her. Or if Janet would send one to her room, the other would insist on going, too. "Then it's not a punishment," Janet would argue. In the end, she would almost always relent. "They have each other as sisters, and as they get older they will *need* each other as sisters," she would say. "She loved their closeness," said one of Janet's relatives, "I think maybe because she'd always been more at odds with her two sisters, Marion and Winifred. She really worked hard to make sure her daughters had a real bond."

Because of the difference in their ages, the sisters would both be separately educated at the elite and strict Miss Chapin's School for Girls on the Upper East Side — the same school Janet had attended — whose academic motto was *Fortiter et Recte* (Bravely and Rightly). At Chapin's, the girls kept a regimented schedule and were expected to excel in their studies. Miss Chapin, who taught poetry, Latin, and history, would accept nothing less from them; she was extremely active in the school's day-to-day regimen and was steadfastly determined that each and every student well represent her school. It was tough and challenging for Jackie and Lee, but it taught them order, discipline, and tenacity. They worked hard to keep their grades up. Though Jackie sailed right on through with ease, Lee had a lot of trouble. "I will never forget," she said. "I was terrible at sports and I was always the last to be chosen for a team which was *so* embarrassing and made me feel *pathetic*." (Today Lee has a habit of accentuating words for the sake of drama; to hear her tell it, "I've *always* been *quite* dramatic.")

Though exceedingly close, there was also a distinct whiff of competition between the girls, which, as it would happen, would be a lifelong issue for them. An early hint could be detected during that same summer of '41. Jackie was scheduled to give a piano recital at school, playing "The Blue Danube" for an assembly. She had a difficult time with the composition and really wasn't good at all as she pecked away at the keys. Still, she practiced every day on the piano at home. One day, she came to Janet in tears and told her that Lee had added her name to the list of those who would be performing at the recital. Janet didn't take it seriously, noting that Lee couldn't even play the piano! When Janet asked Lee about it, she just shrugged and looked up at the ceiling as if she didn't have much to say.

The next day, Jackie played her song at the assembly, and failed miserably. Then, sure enough, the teacher announced, "And now little Lee will play the same song." Lee then proudly sat in front of the piano and played "The Blue Danube" perfectly and to great applause. Jackie was mortified and, later, ran crying to Janet, who was not in attendance. It turned out that Lee had been privately practicing the whole time at school. Janet was astonished, and not happy about it. Though she would inadvertently foster a sense of competition between the girls just by virtue of preferring one over the other depending on the circumstance, she felt strongly that they should stick together. "You two are all you have," she would often tell them. "I will not have you arguing. I will not have you fighting. You will get along because once I'm gone, you will only have each other." The two girls would smile and hug each other, taking comfort in the security of their sisterhood. It wouldn't be long, though, before Lee would start to feel that she was once again in Jackie's shadow and seek to balance the scales.

It's worth noting, though, that their sisterly competition seemed to be completely one-sided. Jackie never thought to compete with Lee. In fact, she'd actually lost count of the number of times she told Lee that there was no need for such rivalry and that they should both shine at their own interests. "I think the way Lee took that advice, though, was as if Jacqueline had implied that they shouldn't compete because she [Lee] could never win," Janet would later say. "Jacqueline was in her own little world, though. She excelled at everything, she just had an easy ride, to tell you the truth. She was blissfully unaware that other people had it harder. But how much can a child be expected to recognize of the world around her?"

To hear Lee tell it years later, she would have done pretty much anything to distinguish herself from Jackie, especially when she got to Miss Porter's boarding school in Farmington, Connecticut (grades nine to twelve).

Again, Jackie had sailed through with good grades while Lee struggled. "I always hated school, but I *really* hated Miss Porter's," she would say. "It was very *rah-rah-rah* and their teams must win." She was constantly unfavorably compared by teachers to her sister. "All I ever heard was how *Jackie* had been a better student than I," she later recalled. "It does tend to wear one down."

"With the passing of not a lot of years, Lee began to develop a real complex about Jackie," their cousin John Davis once observed. "Jackie, even as a teenager, dominated over Lee. People paid more attention to Jackie than they did Lee. Even her father and her grandfather. Her father was in love with Jackie. It was so patently obvious that there was a strong bond between those two. She was older and more on his level intellectually. I know that Lee always felt that her mother, too, loved Jackie more than she loved her. Lee was always just the little girl on the sidelines, and I believe she suffered because of it."

"Lee had a real quality, but she always felt Jackie got the recognition," added Rue Hill Hubert, who knew Lee as a youngster. "Jackie was much more obvious, and Lee a more subtle person. Lee certainly looked up to Jackie for a lot. But it's what she felt deep down inside. She always felt Jackie had something she didn't have, something that she so desperately wanted. It would be true all of her life."

Jill Fuller Fox, who was a year ahead of Lee at Miss Porter's, recalled, "The thing that all of us at school were aware of then was Lee's extreme envy of Jackie, her feeling of being so much the paler of the two. The problem of being Jackie's kid sister emanated from within Lee. I remember one time she said to me, 'How would you like to have a sister like *that*?' It was something she and I empathized about because I have an older sister who was also a great belle, but it was more painful for Lee because she and Jackie were so close."

Another classmate, Lisa Artamonoff Ritchie, added, "I remember Jackie would come occasionally to school from Vassar to visit Lee, and there would be such light flashing out from her. She was so dazzling. Next to her, Lee looked so washed out. Somehow, at fifteen, she seemed as if she were thirty. There was no sense of youngness or freshness about her. There was a fatigue about her that was not so much jadedness as a kind of apathy. Lee was lovely, gracious, intelligent and she was not dull, but she was just in a veil. She didn't have any verve."

Janet couldn't help but worry about Lee's feelings of inadequacy when it came to Jackie. She joked now and then about the competition she so clearly saw going on between the girls and tried to make light of it. In her

46

heart, though, she didn't approve of it. Ironically, she made things so much worse by being so unrelentingly critical of Lee and praising of Jackie. She always thought Jackie was the smarter of the two and would probably have a career, and that Lee would just have to settle for a husband and a lot of children. Janet didn't see a problem with her estimation of Lee, either. She was blunt, always had been, and thought it best that Lee be equipped with an accurate appraisal of her potential from her own mother. There was nothing wrong with being a homemaker anyway, Janet would argue. Not every woman could hope for more. However, Lee didn't at all see things that way and she fought her mother every step along the way. "Oh, that's just Mummy being Mummy," Jackie would say. For Lee, though, the constant badgering only served to underscore her ever-growing insecurity complex. She just wished Janet would ease up on her, but the possibility of that happening didn't seem to be in the offing.

"If she was okay before she went home for a break from Miss Porter's," said one of her classmates, "she was ten times worse when she got back. Her mother would wear her down. You'd see it on Lee's pretty little face when she got back to school — she was just worn down to the nub by her mother.

"So many times I would be in the girls'

company when they would break out into an argument about some petty thing only to be chastised by Janet, who would say, 'You do *not* fight with each other. I won't allow it!' Then she would go off with Jackie, the two hand in hand, leaving poor Lee behind with a sad face. She wanted them to be close as sisters, but it was hard when she so clearly preferred one over the other."

A SAD KIND OF LOVE

Most people didn't understand what was going on between Lee Bouvier and Michael Canfield. Though they officially announced their engagement at the end of 1952, they sure didn't seem well suited. The first sign of incompatibility could be detected when the two were in London together before Lee had even started her job at *Harper's.* There just wasn't a spark between them. They acted like siblings, definitely not a couple with passionate intentions.

Michael's stepbrother, Blair Fuller, recalled, "Michael and I were roommates all through Harvard. I can tell you that he was impotent at a young age. I know because he told me. However, Lee was patient about this, and she did not give up on him." In fact, Michael wrote a letter to Blair's sister Jill Fuller Fox in which he stated, according to her, "Lee had been rather pursuing him, and they didn't know each other that well. I don't think she meant anything to him."

"He confided in me over beers that he probably would not be able to make love to her," said Terrance Landow, who worked with Canfield at Hamish Hamilton. "I asked him why he wanted to be with her, then. He said, 'First of all, she has enormous intelligence. She's also beautiful, tough, and strong. She seems to need me as much as I need her. Maybe I will grow to want to be with her in that way. We'll see, I guess.' He told me that he'd explained to Lee that he wanted to wait for marriage before being intimate."

"The story handed down in the family was that, while in the service, Michael had some-how been disfigured on his backside with an exploding grenade," said Jamie Auchincloss. "I can't say this was true. I can only say that this was what we had heard in the family."

"He and Lee got along great, though," continued Terrance Landow. "They seemed like they were the best of friends, if nothing else. They laughed a lot, getting a real kick out of each other. You have to understand that people back then, at least at that level of society, seldom married for sexual attraction, anyway."

Jill Fuller Fox also recalled a telling conver-sation she and her brother, Blair, had with Michael. "As we walked through the woods at Crowfield [a village in Suffolk, England],

49

he told us that Lee had proposed to him," she said. "The last we heard about Lee from Michael was that she was pursuing him, and what was he to do about it? So we just laughed and said, 'Oh, well.' But then Michael said, 'I'm going to accept.' Blair and I almost fell sideways off the path. I said to him, 'But, Michael, you can't do that! You don't love her.' And Michael replied, 'Oh, but the dear girl, she loves me so!' "

Some people in Michael Canfield's life speculated that there were mercenary intentions behind his interest in Lee Bouvier. They figured he assumed Lee had family wealth, and he wanted in on it. In fact, the family of her stepfather, Hugh Auchincloss, *was* extremely wealthy. However, Janet had made it clear that none of the Auchincloss money was ever going to trickle down to Lee or Jackie. Since Hugh had his own children from two previous marriages plus two with Janet, Lee and Jackie could expect nothing from him. The girls always knew that the only money they might one day stake claim to was whatever "Grampy Lee" (Janet's father, Jim T. Lee) left them in his will. Maybe when Janet passed away, there would be some money for them there, too, but hopefully that was years off. A primary reason Janet didn't want her daughters to have any illusions about wealth was because she wanted them to consider a potential suitor's bank account before marrying. She didn't want them to be under the impression that it didn't matter because it most certainly did.

When Michael told Lee that he had a trust fund to augment his publishing business income, she was happy about it. However, she didn't seem to care as much as one might think she would given the way she was being raised. While she didn't want to be without security, she also didn't place nearly as much of a premium on marrying well as her mother.

Another valid question was why Lee, a gorgeous young woman of a socially upstanding family, would want to spend her life with a man who seemed not to be attracted to her, especially given what other men viewed as her appeal. Chauncey Parker III, who was the son of Hugh's business partner, Chauncey II, and who knew Lee from the time she was eleven, said of her, "She had a *douceur* about her. *Douceur* is a French word that implies more than gentleness, something stronger than just sweetness. She had a sense of wonderment, a lilt in her voice, and a wonderful smile. She was someone you really just wanted to take in your arms and hug. She had a delicious aura."

Maybe because of her low self-esteem, Lee felt she couldn't do any better than Michael. Then, of course, her competition with Jackie probably came into play; royalty always *did* make for a good catch, after all. Chauncey

Parker recalled, "I have long thought another reason Lee wanted to marry Mike — besides the fact that she was determined to get as far away from her mother as possible — was that she was absolutely hell-bent-for-leather determined to beat Jackie to the altar. At least beat her at that!"

It's also worth noting that Lee and Michael shared the same forlorn temperament. Though Michael was witty, charming, and good-looking, like Lee he had a deep pathos about him. Always sad and melancholy, he seemed to suffer from what would today be considered depression. Maybe it was understandable. After all, he never knew where he fit in: was he a vaunted royal from an exclusive bloodline or just an American from a successful publishing family? This confusion and uncertainty about identity ate away at him and was, no doubt, one of the reasons he drank so heavily. Like a moth to a flame, Lee seemed drawn to him and his downhearted persona. "She told me that she loved his sensitivity," said one close friend of hers at that time. "She knew that he didn't want to sleep with her. *Of course* she knew! But she felt that sexual attraction between them would grow in time."

Maybe Michael said it best about his relationship with Lee at the couple's engagement party, which was at the home of Pat and Jerry Hill, parents of Lee's roommate at the time, Rue Hill. In front of several guests, he pulled Lee into his arms and, with no small measure of vulnerability, observed, "A guy like me doesn't get a girl like you, Lee. It just doesn't happen." Lee was visibly overcome; any witness could see her heart go out to him. "Yes, Michael, it *does* happen," she said, kissing him on the cheek. "It really does."

They had a beautiful yet, at the same time, sad kind of love, one most people didn't think had a chance. While a great many observers had a great many opinions about it, probably none were as vocal or as vociferous as Janet. She put her foot down; there would be no wedding to Michael Canfield, not as far as she was concerned, anyway. She ticked off her reasons to Lee one night over dinner with the family: "He's not in love with you. You're not in love with him. He drinks too much. He's homosexual. He's broke." Janet said she was endeavoring to shield the family from gossip and innuendo, but, more important, she said, she was also trying to look after Lee. "Say what you will about my mother," said her son, Jamie, "she was tough, yes, but also fiercely protective of my sisters. Maybe it could also be said that she didn't know when to let go or to back off, but that was just who she was as a parent."

The discussion quickly turned into an argument, with Lee raging on that Janet was meddlesome and critical. "Enough, Lee!" Janet said, raising her voice. "I have made my decision. This is not up for debate." One witness to the disagreement recalled, "Lee was so upset, she refused to even look at her mother. The next thing we knew, Janet was saying, 'Eyes on me, Lee! *Eyes on me!*' It was quite the spectacle. Those two could be very dramatic."

Why, Janet wondered, did it always have to be such a battle of wills between her and Lee? It certainly wasn't that way with Jackie. In fact, when Janet had concerns about the suitability of a man named John Husted for Jackie, the two had been able to work through them as mother and daughter. Janet not only managed to get rid of the guy, she got Jackie to agree with her about it!

JOHN HUSTED

As much as she craved an exciting life for herself that included a career of some sort, by the time she was twenty-two Jacqueline Bouvier also felt a strong pull toward domestication. As was the custom for young women at that time, Jackie, like Lee, wanted to get out from under her mother's domination, too. While her relationship with Janet was nowhere near as contentious as Lee's, she still felt that Janet was overbearing and overprotective. Therefore, getting married and becoming her own woman appealed to her. She knew that whomever she chose would have to meet with Janet's high standards, though, and many of the men she'd dated recently didn't even come close. However, through connections made by Hugh Auchincloss in New York high society, Janet was introduced, in 1951, to a man she thought would be just perfect for Jackie. He was a stockbroker named John G. W. Husted Jr., whose family, much to Janet's pleasure, was listed in the Social Register. His father was a friend of Hugh's, a partner in Brown Shipley, which was the British arm of Brown Brothers Harriman on Wall Street. Janet knew his mother and liked her.

Born John Grinnel Wetmore Husted Jr. in 1926 in Hartford, this tall and urbane stockbroker spent much of his youth in England, where he attended the preparatory Summer Fields School in Oxford. An eventual Yale graduate, he also served in World War II. "On our first date we went to the Dancing Class in Washington, which was a proper, social thing to do in those days," he recalled of himself and Jackie. "I was immediately attracted to her, and we began seeing each other every weekend."

Any relationship with John would have to wait, however, until after Jackie returned from a much-anticipated European vacation with Lee in June of 1951, which Janet paid for —

London, Paris, Venice, Rome, and Florence. "We were so young," Jackie recalled. "It was the first time we felt really close, carefree together, high on the sheer joy of getting away from our mother; the deadly dinner parties of political bores, the Sunday lunches for the same people that lasted hours, Lee and I not allowed to say a word. My dream was France, but Lee's was really Italy, as art was all she cared about through school." The sisters were probably closer during this trip than they'd ever been, loving Europe together, enjoying its many exotic sights, and learning all about art history there. It was a happy time, a period that they would both remember with great fondness. When they returned in September, they gave Janet a homemade scrapbook they called "Our Special Summer." It was composed of anecdotes from the trip along with photos they'd taken, captions and memories designed to thank Janet for allowing them to go on a vacation they'd never forget. (Years later, this book would be packaged and released by a major publisher.)

Back in the States, Lee began attending school at Sarah Lawrence College in Bronxville, New York, while Jackie tried to figure out what she might do now that she'd graduated. In Janet's mind, the decision was an easy one; Jackie should just settle down with John Husted. However, Jackie was a little lukewarm on the idea. She kept saying she wanted to live happily ever after with *some-one,* but she just wasn't sure John was the one.

The idea of "happily ever after" was just a tad naïve for Janet's taste. The subject came up during a "Mother-Daughter Tea," a tradition of the Bouvier women for many years. Whenever possible — and when the girls were in boarding school it was a little more difficult — Janet made sure to take her daughters to high tea at one of the better hotels in New York, usually the Plaza. This special occasion became known among the three as a Mother-Daughter Tea. They would dress to the nines, and spend the entire day together, shopping before tea and then afterward, and maybe even see a Broadway show that night. All three looked forward to this time together; they really enjoyed being in one another's company. Mostly, it was typical mother-daughter conversation — boy-friends, clothes, school. Janet would always reiterate her wish that the two girls remain close, that they not compete with each other — usually this dictate was directed to Lee, of course — that they not fight. As they got older, the subject matter became more about the men in Jackie's and Lee's lives. Sometimes, the occasion was to discuss a pivotal decision one of the girls had to make. Other times, it was just an opportunity for Janet to impart some motherly advice or wisdom, as it was on this day. "Do you know what the secret to happily-ever-after is?" Janet asked Jackie and Lee during their teatime, according to what she later confided in her socialite friend, Oatsie Charles. "Money and power," she said, answering her own question. Janet was raised to believe that the two often went hand in hand, money acting as a means to power if only just for its ability to finance a life well lived. Years later, when recounting this particular anecdote, Janet would say of her daughters, "They looked at me as if I was the devil, especially poor Lee. God love her, she was such a little romantic." Janet said she saw Jackie's wheels turn as if she truly got it. However, Lee was taken aback. "She almost choked on her finger sandwich," Janet said, laughing. "Fine. If it made her think, *good*. She *should've* been thinking."

John Husted was a nice-enough gentleman, but it was clear that there was no real attraction for Jackie. However, Janet had heard that he was successful and believed him to have money; she was certain Jackie would learn to love him in time. Jackie had already experienced real passion with a man, though, a year earlier when she was in France. She had a one-night stand with John P. Marquand Jr. — everyone called him Jack — son of the famous writer John P. Marquand Sr. The two had quick sex in an elevator. It wasn't exactly romantic, but it was exciting. It took her months to get over it, though, not sure how she should feel about it, whether or not it had compromised her morality since she'd been a virgin. In the end, she decided it had been good experience and that she wanted to feel that way again one day, only with the added element of true love. She also decided not to tell anyone about it, not even her sister, Lee.

During the girls' most recent trip to Europe, though, Jackie had wanted to see Marquand again. She then confided in Lee about him and the sexual interlude they'd had, swearing her to secrecy. Lee promised to keep her confidence. Much to Jackie's dismay, though, Lee then turned right around and told Janet all about it by transcontinental phone call. Why? Because Lee had information Janet didn't have, and she decided to use it to curry favor. It worked. On that day, anyway, Lee was definitely Janet's favorite. Though Lee apologized, Jackie was heartbroken. "But we had a deal!" she reportedly exclaimed. *We had a deal!* It would take her some time to get over the betrayal, though in a strange way she seemed to understand it. She would never have done the same thing to her sister, but she certainly knew what it was like to want to win points with "Mummy."

After Janet made some quick calls to her high-society friends in Paris, she learned that John Marquand's finances were in disarray;

he was pretty much broke. When the girls got home, Janet made it clear that she was deeply disappointed in Jackie for having kept the relationship with Marquand a secret from her. The fact that she'd been intimate with him was more than Janet could bear; she couldn't even discuss that part of the story, preferring to act as if it had never happened. She made it clear, though, that Jackie was never to see Marquand again. When Jackie tried to protest that she was old enough to make decisions about who to date, Janet smacked her across the face — twice. That was the last time mother and daughter ever talked about John Marquand. Instead, Janet now preferred John Husted for Jackie.

Meanwhile, at this same time, Jackie landed a job at the *Washington Times-Herald,* taking over a column that had originally been called "The Inquiring Photographer." Jackie was hired to pen what was a daily question-and-answer "think piece" in which readers were able to state their opinions on current events and then have those remarks be published, accompanied by their photographs. Jackie would write the column and also take the respondents' pictures. Though she wasn't a professional photographer, she did have an eye for composition and design and, in just a few days, learned to use the professional cameras provided her by the newspaper. Soon, the column was renamed "The Inquiring Camera Girl," and Jackie was earning a little over forty bucks a week composing it. Therefore for the next year and a half, she would be asking innocuous questions of strangers about life and love such as: "Is your marriage a fifty-fifty partnership?" "Do the rich enjoy life more than the poor?" and "What do you think women desire most?" John Husted, who sometimes helped Jackie with her work, would call it "an insipid little job, but kind of fun."

One snowy evening in December of '51, John Husted asked Jackie to meet him at the Polo Bar in the Westbury Hotel. He took a leap of faith and said that if she was interested in marrying him she should show up at a certain time. That night, he then waited for her, fretting she would not appear. At the last second, she showed up. She wasn't exactly swept away by his proposal. "You can do a lot worse, Jackie," Janet told her later that evening as they talked things over. The problem with John, as Jackie saw it, was that he was just so dull and pedantic. Janet was persuasive, though; Jackie eventually agreed to marry John, and told him so the next day. Now, in Janet's mind, everything seemed to be working out — Jackie not only had the career she had wanted for herself, but more important, she also had the kind of spouse Janet wanted for her. The wedding was set for June of 1952.

Unfortunately, things took a bad turn just before the engagement party in mid-February '51 at Janet and Hugh's Merrywood estate in McLean, Virginia. At Janet's behest, Hugh had begun to dig a little deeper in the Manhattan business world about John's financial situation. Through these inquiries, he came to understand that Husted and his family were not at all well off. While they had some money, it wasn't much. Janet was upset and felt that Husted had been purposely covering up the truth just to snare Jackie. She therefore decided to learn more about whatever was going on with him at, of all places, the couple's engagement party.

At the party, Janet asked the right questions of the right people and learned that John only made $17,000 a year (about $160,000 in today's money). This was a surprise. She had it in her head he was worth a lot more, even given Hugh's recent inquiries. Once Janet knew the truth, she turned on John with a vengeance, no longer gracious to him, his friends, or his family members. She just wasn't one to hide her feelings, no matter how hard she tried. During the party, John presented Jackie with a sapphire-and-diamond ring in front of all of the guests. As Jackie accepted it, Janet turned to Hugh's son Yusha and, with a real edge to her voice, said, "She must have fallen off her horse and hit her head."

At one point during the festivities, Janet and Helen Husted, John's aunt, had a difference of opinion over the simple placement of a large floral arrangement. Helen relocated it in order to make way for a platter of food. However, Janet didn't want it moved. This insignificant moment led to harsh words. Jackie was mortified. A rising panic took hold of her when she realized that people were whispering all around her about the outburst, calling it "undignified." She pulled Janet into another room and demanded to know, "Why are you trying to ruin this day?" Janet angrily shot back, "Because he's not for you, not unless you never want to be able to afford to travel again! I'm trying to *protect* you, can't you see that?"

Janet then told Jackie what she had learned about John's finances, and she also noted that Jackie's father had earned almost three times as much when Janet married him — "And that was more than twenty years ago!" Now Jackie was the one surprised. "How did I not know this?" she asked. *"You* tell *me,"* Janet countered.

A couple weeks later, members of the Auchincloss and Bouvier families — Janet, Hugh, Jackie, Lee, Janet Jr., and Jamie and a few others — were having dinner at Merrywood when, according to one relative present, the subject of John Husted came up. As the uniformed waitstaff solemnly served beef

Wellington, Jackie said she was worried about hurting John's feelings by ending it with him. "Why care about him when, in a week, he won't be in our lives?" Janet asked. "We won't even remember his name," she added.

After dinner, Janet tried to talk to Jackie about John, but Jackie seemed more invested in a stack of fashion magazines she had brought down from her bedroom. "Eyes on me," Janet reminded her daughter. *"Eyes on me!"* Jackie looked up, annoyed. She then said that if she was going to end it with John, she wanted to do it with kindness and consideration. She didn't want to hurt his feelings. "But it's not your job to take care of his feelings," Janet said. "That's what *his* family is for."

Janet said that she had invited John Husted to Merrywood in a few days' time and that she would then find out all there was to know about his suitability for marriage. While Jackie begged Janet not to embarrass her, Janet felt that any awkwardness would be the least of Jackie's problems if she married someone who couldn't afford to give her a good life. Then, staring at her daughter with a stern expression, she told her that this was not the time for sentiment. She, as the mother, knew what was best. By this time, Jackie couldn't take another second of Janet. "I know, Mummy," she exclaimed petulantly as she rose and stormed from the room. Hugh, who

64

was sitting at the head of the table, just smiled and shook his head. He was used to such scenes and almost always stayed out of the line of fire.

Shortly after that conversation, John Husted spent the weekend at Merrywood as planned. With Jackie not present, Janet asked him directly how much money he earned. He told her the truth — $17,000 annually — which, of course, she already knew. "My prospects for making more money were reasonable but not assured," he would later recall, "and I had no great family fortune, at least not the kind she wanted for Jackie. Consequently, Janet did not approve."

After talking to John, Janet told Jackie what she had learned. Mother and daughter knew what had to be done. Later, when Jackie took him to the airport for his return flight, she simply slipped the engagement ring off her finger and dropped it into his jacket pocket. "She was ice cold," John would remember. "Like we never knew each other. I understood that the end had come. I never heard from her again. Not ever."

In the weeks to come, Jackie would experience pangs of guilt about the way it had ended with John. She'd even gone to church to pray for guidance. Had she done the right thing? Yes, Janet reassured her, she had, and, in fact, she would one day thank her for her counsel. She was looking out for her by protecting her and their family from a marriage to the wrong kind of man. Janet had even put a correction in the local newspaper announcing that the engagement was off "by mutual consent." As far as she was concerned, that was the end of it. When she found out that Husted was still sending letters to Jackie asking what had happened, she took it upon herself to answer one of them herself. She told him the time had come for him to move forward with his life without Jackie, and to do so immediately.

It's worth noting that Janet's prediction that the family wouldn't remember John Husted's name seemed to come to pass when the first in-depth biography of Jackie was published in 1961. It was an authorized book written by a good friend of Janet's, Mary Van Rensselaer. In it, John Husted isn't even mentioned, totally written out of history.

LEE AND MICHAEL MARRY

Less than two years after Janet put the kibosh on Jackie's romance with John Husted, she had to contend with Lee's affection for someone she viewed as being just as unsuitable, Michael Canfield. She had to wonder why she and Lee couldn't just sit down as mother and daughter and work out the problem of Canfield in the same way she and Jackie had dealt with Husted. "I am not the enemy," she kept telling Lee. "I am on your side."

To Janet, this was the part of raising daughters that mattered most — the part where she was able to weigh in on their choice of mates and how they would then fit into high society. Her prior responsibilities as a mother were pretty much limited to hearing their stories about life at boarding school, making certain they had time for a Mother-Daughter Tea when they were home, and then keeping them entertained during the summer months by sending them off and paying for trips abroad. It wasn't as if Janet — and, later, her daughters — was a hands-on mother all year round. When her girls were old enough to make decisions about marriage, *that's* when the experienced mother's opinion and guidance really mattered. For years, Janet had looked forward to this time. For her, it wasn't supposed to be a battle but, rather, the natural course of things. It was also her responsibility. Or, as she liked to say, "This is what a mother is for! Otherwise why even *have* a mother?"

"I think that Jackie was always grateful to her [Janet] because she felt that she had intentionally enlarged her world — our world — for our sake as much if not more than for her own sake," Lee would have to admit. "I think she was always far more grateful than I was for that kind of guidance. She appreciated it so much."

Lee didn't see things quite the same way, though. She didn't want her world "enlarged" as much as she just wanted to make her own choices in it. There would definitely be no talking Lee out of a marriage to Michael, especially if the reasons against it all felt to her like criticisms of her and her judgment. Whereas Jackie tried to agree with Janet when it came to matters of the heart and would almost always bend to her will, Lee vehemently disagreed. She was headstrong and determined to live her own life her own way. If this meant Janet loved Jackie more because Jackie would acquiesce to her — and Lee certainly thought this was the case — then so be it. Lee was satisfied just knowing she was her own woman, and that would never change.

Janet fully understood that a primary reason Lee wanted to marry at just nineteen was to escape her influence. She was self-aware enough to know that, yes, she could be imperious and that this trait was sometimes difficult for her daughters to accept. After all, she'd been through the exact same thing with her own father, Jim T. Lee, who never approved of anything she ever did. In fact, one of the reasons she married Jack Bouvier at Lee's age was to escape her father's dominance over her and, at the same time, to defy him. Though the notion of being in love wasn't foremost on her mind when it came to her daughters' selection of spouses, if Janet thought Lee actually felt that way about Michael, she might have been a little more accepting. She realized, though, that Lee just wanted to make her own statement of independence, and that Michael represented a means to that end.

Janet was willing to give Michael a chance, though. She decided to take him to lunch in New York at Le Pavillon, one of her favorite French restaurants, "just the two of us, my treat," she told him, this according to what Tom Guinzburg once recalled; he was a publicist at Viking Press (where Jackie would one day work) and a close friend of Michael's. Of course, Lee didn't want this tête-à-tête to take place without her, but Michael felt sure he could handle Janet, and asked Lee to allow him to do so. "Michael was an innocent," said Guinzburg. "He didn't know what he was in for." First, Janet plied her future son-in-law with liquor to see just how much he would imbibe and, unfortunately, she found that it was quite a lot. He definitely didn't pass that particular test. When she wanted to know about his relationship history, he told her about this girl and that one, but he wasn't convincing about any of them. Then he said something like, "There are a lot of things I am confused about, but not the way I feel about your daughter." His comment did nothing to make Janet feel any better. In fact, all she took from it was his admission that he was "confused" about "a lot of things."

In the end, Michael did warm Janet up a little, though. Something about him always managed to bring out the maternal instincts in a woman, and Janet wavered a little after their luncheon. If anything, she began to think that maybe the reason he and Lee shouldn't marry was because he was too weak-willed to take on such a strong-minded woman. She felt that any man Lee married would have to be tough on her in order to get her to comport herself in a more disciplined way, and she didn't believe that was Michael. Therefore, she left the luncheon thinking the poor guy might be in way over his head.

Also at this time, Janet was frustrated when she learned that Lee had decided to quit her job as Diana Vreeland's assistant. Janet thought this decision only served to underscore her daughter's maddeningly indecisive nature. She had truly believed Lee had finally found a good place for herself at *Harper's*. However, true to her mercurial nature, Lee was ready to move on after just four months. Of course, Janet had to mention to Lee that Jackie was quite happy at her job as "The Inquiring Camera Girl" at the *Washington Times-Herald,* and she, once again, wondered

70

why Lee couldn't be more like her sister. Why did Lee have to be so, as Janet put it, "wishy-washy"?

Some people thought Lee was just so happy with Michael that she no longer needed a job to feel fulfilled. A lifelong challenge for her, though, would be to avoid looking to outside influences for inner happiness. "She did sort of glom on to Michael," Jill Fox recalled, "and, yes, it did seem to make her happier. I thought that being in love with Michael had brought about a great change in her, though. She was giggly, outgoing, and rambunctious, so different than the person I had last seen at Farmington that it was breathtaking."

"They were such a gorgeous couple, I thought, my goodness wouldn't it be fun to leave Seventh Avenue and all this stuff behind?" recalled her colleague at *Harper's,* Laura Pyzel Clark. "I wouldn't stay at *Harper's* for five minutes if I was getting married to someone like Michael Canfield. I thought he was the most attractive man I had ever met."

So what was Janet to do about Michael Canfield, especially given that Lee was so determined to be with him? She gave it a lot of thought. She knew that when she was Lee's age, she, too, was defiant and determined to be her own woman, to make her own decisions, no matter what. There was a lot to be said for such independence, and

Janet recognized it and respected it in Lee, even if it did vex her. "In the end, she remembered how important it was that she disobey her father by marrying Jack Bouvier, Lee's dad," said Janet's former assistant, Adora Rule. "Years later, she told me, 'Defying my father was truly a defining moment for me. It gave me a self-confidence I'd never known before. I felt that if I could take on my father, mean old bastard that he was, I could take on the world. So, I made the decision to let Lee have the same kind of victory.'"

Janet said she decided that Lee's marrying Michael might actually serve a good purpose and that, perhaps, it was to make her feel empowered enough to come to her own important decision and then, "for once in her darn life," maybe stick to it! The idea that she was marrying before Jackie also appealed to Janet; she thought perhaps it might be good for Lee to have that achievement for herself, to have finally done *something* before her sister. "I decided maybe it wasn't so bad," Janet would recall.

"Did you tell her you had changed your mind about Michael Canfield?" Adora asked.

"No," Janet said. "That would have completely ruined it."

Janet actually wanted Lee to be under the false impression that, in choosing Michael, she was defying her mother and making a decision to live life on her own terms. "It seems a little twisted, but if you knew Janet, you understood that, despite all of this manipulation, she was really *trying* to do something good for Lee," said Adora Rule, "trying to give her a sense of independence and self-confidence. She figured the marriage wouldn't last anyway, she said, so there may as well be some good attached to it."

Janet sat down with Lee at a special Mother-Daughter Tea (without Jackie) and told her that she could marry Michael if she insisted upon it, that it was her mistake to make. However, she also said she couldn't give the union her blessing. Therefore, it would be Lee's move. She waited for Lee's reaction. It could have gone in one of two ways: Lee could have said, "No, Mummy, I won't marry him," or "I'm marrying him, anyway." If it had been the former, Janet would have been disappointed. Of course, it was the latter — chip off the ol' block that Lee was.

The marriage of Lee Bouvier to Michael Canfield took place at Holy Trinity Catholic Church in Georgetown on April 18, 1953. Lee looked stunning in a high-necked, short-sleeved and bouffant ivory-toned wedding dress. She wore an Irish lace, floor-length bridal veil handed down to her by her maternal grandmother, and then by her own mother. Model thin with angular features that

73

were somehow softer than Jackie's or Janet's, she was gorgeous. Jackie was her maid of honor, of course.

Jackie didn't share her mother's disapproval of Michael. While she wasn't certain he was the perfect mate for her sister, she was determined not to second-guess Lee's decision. "He's lovely" is how she described him to Lee's friend from *Harper's,* Deena Atkins-Manzel, who was also at the wedding. "I hope Lee will be very happy. She's my sister," Jackie said. "What happens to her happens to me. If she's happy, I'm happy." When Lee tossed her bouquet, she directed it at her sister, who eagerly nabbed it.

Despite the fact that she had pretty much orchestrated and manipulated the entire thing, Janet was out of sorts at the wedding reception, held at Merrywood. Had she made the right decision to let this marriage go forward? Now that it was all over, she had mixed emotions. "I think maybe I should have stepped in and stopped this," Janet told Deena Atkins-Manzel at the reception.

"But could you have stopped it?" Deena asked.

Janet looked at her as if she was out of her mind. "What do *you* think?" she asked.

"But they're so *in love,*" Deena said, dreamily.

Janet shook her head. "You think that's love?" she asked, staring at Michael and Lee.

74

The newlyweds were sitting on settee in a corner, each one looking blankly in an opposite direction and seeming a little lost. "That's not love," Janet said, squinting at them. "I don't know what that is, but it's not love."

"BLACK JACK"

Flashback to 1927.

There he stood in the main dining room of the popular East Hampton Maidstone Club in New York, about six feet tall, lean and trim, and with a deep, summer tan. He wore a white shirt, a crimson silk tie, and a dark blue suit made of the finest imported raw silk, flawlessly cut and unerringly tailored. At thirty-six, John Bouvier III — known as "Jack" or "Black Jack," because of his swarthy, dark good looks — had a classically handsome face with expressive dark eyes, a high forehead, chiseled cheekbones, and a pencil-thin mustache. He was so vital and arresting, Janet Lee, nineteen, couldn't stop looking at him.

Though Janet Lee wasn't necessarily a pretty girl in the accepted sense, she was thin and slender of frame and did possess a certain grace. She had an elongated face, a strong jawline, and a long, straight nose. Her dark eyes were her best feature. She sometimes wore her short auburn hair parted on one side. What she may have lacked in looks, she more than made up for with her outgoing personality. She was funny, smart, and a good conversationalist, but it would be overstating it to say she was warm. She had a patrician way, speaking in a soft pitch and slowly in an inordinately polite manner, as did many young women of her background and time. She could appear aloof, sometimes disconnected and chilly. Still, she had a great many friends, was social and well liked.

Upon this fateful meeting, Jack and Janet stared at each other, their eyes locked in an intense gaze that neither was able to break. Janet would later admit that, to her, it felt like love at first sight. Fate had cast its die; these two would become inextricably tied to each other.

James T. Lee had certainly set the bar high as far as a suitor was concerned for his daughter Janet. An enterprising businessman, he would make a million dollars in real-estate development in Manhattan, losing that fortune in the panic of 1907 but then earning it back and much more. He was not only smart, he took chances. "Better a bad decision today than a good one three weeks late," he liked to say. He was as headstrong as he was rich, though. When his daughter told him — after a quick courtship — that she wanted to marry Jack Bouvier, he said, "Absolutely not," and that was the end of it for him.

One might have thought Jim would have been impressed with Jack Bouvier. The Bouviers — of French ancestry — were of "old money" and had lived in great splendor in a number of Fifth Avenue residences before settling into a magnificent twenty-four-room apartment at 765 Park Avenue. The family also owned two impressive estates in East Hampton. "Black Jack" was earning almost $100,000 a year, which in today's currency would be almost $1.5 million. Supposedly he also had almost a million dollars in savings — almost $15 million in today's world. On the surface, Jack looked pretty good. Dig a little deeper, though, and problems became evident, and Jim knew it. Typical of Jack's laissez-faire attitude about business, he was in tremendous debt. "He put on a good show" is how his nephew John Davis put it in a 1999 interview, "but he was heavily leveraged, and Jim knew it. His family had bailed him out many times. Despite appearances, he was always on the brink of financial ruin."

That Jack Bouvier dressed as he did, so elegantly and without so much as a loose thread anywhere, and that his manner was so courtly and sophisticated didn't fool Jim at all. It just made him more suspicious. "Not only does he not have solid money," Jim told his attorney, Lyndon Davis, this according to Davis's son, Barry. "He doesn't have power.

That's what worries me most. You need not only money in this life, but power. This man has neither."

Janet's immediate acceptance of Jack's proposal of marriage caused another deep rift in a family that was already troubled. Janet's mother, Margaret, felt that Jim was being unreasonable, withholding his approval simply because he didn't believe Jack to be "good enough" for Janet. Moreover, Margaret held fast to the notion that Janet and her sisters, Marion and Winifred, should not only marry well but, hopefully, be happy, too. Her own marriage was in a shambles, and had been for years; she and Jim practically never even spoke to each other. Embittered by her own marital experience, she famously told Janet, "The only thing I know about relationships is that they don't work." Margaret also knew that Janet just wanted to get out of the house, that she was tired of being under the thumb of her domineering father. She wanted the same for her.

In the end, Janet openly defied her father and married Jack on July 7, 1928, in the small, quaint St. Philomena's Church in East Hampton.

For a while, the Bouviers lived a fun, extravagant lifestyle, spending much of it at Lasata, their summer home, where Janet was able to improve her horseback-riding skills while also lording over a house full of obedient servants. Meanwhile, in Manhattan, her social status soared as a result of her well-connected marriage. A big problem was clear, though, almost from the outset: Jack couldn't stop cheating on Janet, and there was nothing she could do about it. "It hurts being cast aside," she would say years later about this time in her life. She realized early on that he wasn't going to change. Complicating things was that, regardless of how much he cheated on her, when she was with Jack in bed there were always fireworks. Their intimacy remained strong and powerful, and Janet was hooked by it. She wasn't willing to let it go.

At twenty-one, Janet would become a young mother with the birth of Jacqueline Lee Bouvier, on July 28, 1929, her name Jackie honoring both her father and grandfather. Three and a half years later, on March 3, 1933, she gave birth again, to Caroline Lee Bouvier — Lee, of course. It was interesting that both Bouvier daughters carried Janet's maiden name, Lee, as their middle name. Clearly, Janet wanted to make sure their identities were as linked to her family's name as to their father's.

In years to come, Janet and Jack would separate and reconcile so many times, people in their lives had lost track. Every time Janet decided to leave him, Jack would come by and sweep her off her feet. There would then be the unfolding of another sexual marathon, soon to be followed by another reunion and then breakup. This was unusual. In these circles, at that time, sexual compatibility was generally not something people in high society cared about one way or the other. For Janet and Jack, though, it was definitely something that kept them bound.

Despite their problems, Jack didn't want to separate from Janet, either. He loved his daughters so much he couldn't bear the idea of being away from them. "Jackie meant everything to Jack," said Kathleen Bouvier, his niece, "and, to a certain extent, Lee did, too. He devoted himself to making sure every day was special for them, whether it was gifting them with a new dog — and there were plenty in the household already — or taking them to the park, just spending time with them, there was no limit to what he would do for them. Janet was more of a disciplinarian than Jack so, naturally, they gravitated toward him. Janet felt he spoiled the girls. Maybe so, but it was out of love."

"The fights with Jack Bouvier were non-stop," said Danine Barber, whose mother, Theresa Gambit, had been one of the governesses hired by Janet for her daughters. Danine Barber recalled to her daughter a time when little Jackie was in the parlor playing with her stuffed animals while her parents argued in front of her about an affair he was apparently having. Her resentment spilling over into rage, Janet gave Jack an angry shove. As he fell backward, his head hit a doorknob. He began to bleed. Jackie began to cry. Janet scooped her up and got her out of the room. "When her mother — Margaret — came to visit, Janet cried, resting her head in her mother's lap," said Danine Barber. " 'Men are complicated,' she told her daughter, 'but it's your *children* that matter,' she said, 'and you must never allow them to witness another fight between you and Jack. You must promise me.' Janet did make that promise. There was nothing she cared about more than those girls. They both meant the world to her."

At the beginning of '36, Janet finally had enough; she wanted out of her marriage. Surprisingly, her father, Jim, did not support her in her decision, though, telling her that if she went through with a divorce she would be on her own.

Jim's reaction was consistent with the mind-set of many people of their time; after all, less than two percent of women in this country were divorcées. Plus, it was against their Catholic religion. Also, there had never been a divorce in the family. Moreover, it was a decision Janet had come to without her father's counsel — therefore, as far as he was concerned, it was a bad one. To make matters worse for her, he reminded her that she had no money of her own. He had not set up trust funds for any of his three daughters and had no intention of ever doing so, either. He believed that Janet and her siblings should inherit his survival instincts, definitely not his money. "No free rides here" is how he liked to put it.

"Would it kill you this one time to be on my side?" Janet asked, according to her later recollection. Jim had no response. "Fine," she said, gathering her things. "At least now I know where I stand with you." She would not cry, though. She would later recall "that's the one thing I would not do." Instead, she straightened her shoulders and reportedly told her father, "Maybe one day you'll climb down off your pulpit and understand what I've been going through."

What would it take for Janet to stick to her convictions and end her marriage? It would take courage, she knew that much. Maybe she actually *had* inherited something from Jim, that being his survival instinct. Because her parents had tolerated their own unhappiness for years didn't mean, in her mind, that she should have to do the same. She couldn't help but be angry at Margaret for staying with Jim for so long, thereby setting a bad example for her daughters. While she loved her mother, she also viewed her as weak. In Margaret's view, *her* mother was weak, too, as evidenced by the way she allowed herself to be treated in the household. Poor Maria Merritt, Margaret's mother, was allowed to live with the Lee family, but because of her Irish brogue not allowed to speak in front of company. When people came by, she would dart in and out of her room, a strange, shadowy figure. The Lees said she was the family maid; it had been that way for as long as Janet could remember. How could Margaret tolerate this indignity of her own mother? Obviously, it was because both women were weak, at least in Janet's opinion. She hated weakness in people — especially in herself. "Weakness isn't something you're born with," Janet would observe in years to come. "*You learn it.* And I learned it from my mother. And she learned it from hers."

The question of religion was a significant one for Janet. Though she was a devout Catholic who attended church every Sunday, she would never be the kind of woman who would be vocal in her beliefs; in other words, she would never proselytize. However, she did value her faith. When she went to see a priest about a possible divorce, he was adamant that it would not be accepted by the Church, that she would be excommunicated if she divorced Jack Bouvier. Of course, this made her decision all the more difficult. It would not, however, change her mind.

The separation between Janet and Jack finally became official in late '36 with Jack agreeing to pay Janet about a thousand dollars a month — roughly $17,000 a month, today — as well as take care of his daughters' medical and dental bills and education. Janet would continue to live with Jackie and Lee in a Park Avenue duplex.

Now that he was separated from Janet, of course Jack felt at liberty to date other women. However, Janet, unrealistically enough, still expected faithfulness from him — at least, she said, until after a final divorce decree. True to form, he would lie about his dalliances, she would find out about them anyway, and the subsequent fight would occur, all of it in front of her girls. The two would then tumble into bed again together, despite their legal separation. "The one thing I learned from my relationship with Jack," Janet would later tell her friend Oatsie Charles, "is knowing when someone is being dishonest with me. I can smell dishonesty a mile away, and I owe all of that to Jack Bouvier."

To Oatsie, Janet would many years later recall an incident that happened one evening in early 1938 as she and Jack were on their way home from a production of *The Greatest Show on Earth* at the Playhouse Theatre. At the time, Janet was thirty; Jack was forty-six. On the night in question, it was pouring rain, the weather almost freezing cold. The Bouviers had been arguing for hours about a woman Janet knew he'd been dating. Jack told the driver to pull over to the side of the road, and then he ordered him out of the vehicle despite the stormy weather just so that he and Janet could argue in private. "You have to choose," Janet told Jack as the two sat in the car. "It's me. Or her."

"It would probably be best if you didn't make me choose," Jack warned her.

Oatsie recalled, "As the rain pounded on the rooftop of their vehicle, Janet told Jack, 'I dislike you so much.' He smiled and said, 'No, actually you don't, Janet.' He was so goddamn smug, that guy. She told me it was maddening."

In that moment — at least to hear Janet tell it — she could feel her affection for Black Jack begin to lift from her. Janet bundled up her coat and, without warning, exited the car into the driving, lashing rain. She slammed the door closed behind her. When she turned around and looked into the vehicle's backseat window, she saw Jack's startled expression staring back at her. Then she spun around and walked away.

It was so cold, Janet later recalled, she began to shiver convulsively. She hunched her shoulders against the driving wind. She walked and walked and walked, without an umbrella, in what had to be one of the worst storms of the year. She cried the entire time. By the time she got back to her apartment, she was soaking wet from head to toe, and all cried out. Apparently, she was also finished with Jack Bouvier. "It was as if the rain had washed me clean of that no-good son of a bitch," she would recall.

When Janet walked into the apartment, her maid rushed to her, alarmed to see her so bedraggled, her clothes soaking wet, her makeup running down her face. "Madam, what in the world happened?" the maid asked.

"I came to my senses," Janet answered as she stood in the entrance hall, dripping wet. "That's what happened. I came to my senses."

"This is the only way for me to get on with my life and the lives of my daughters, Jacqueline and Lee," Janet Bouvier later explained to the judge who finalized the divorce in 1939. "All I care about are my girls. That's it."

After she left the courthouse victorious, she telephoned one of Jack Bouvier's sisters and, during their conversation, couldn't help but gloat just a little. "I didn't think it was possible for Satan to be overthrown," she said, "but I darn well did it, didn't I?"

JACK KENNEDY

It was the summer of '53. Fourteen years had passed since Janet Lee Bouvier secured her hard-earned independence from Jack Bouvier. Her daughter Jackie was now twenty-three, and the question of romance was on the minds of both mother and daughter. "I'm just so *frustrated* by this man," Jackie told Janet, according to what Janet would later recall to Joan Braden for her oral history at the JFK Library. She said the two were sitting on Jackie's bed at Merrywood talking about Senator Jack Kennedy. This certainly wouldn't be the last time she would find herself exasperated by him. They'd been dating for about a year, after having been introduced at a party by the journalist Charles L. Bartlett, a friend of Jack's.

John Fitzgerald Kennedy — known to most of those in his life as Jack, just like Janet's first husband — was a good-looking, charismatic war hero. Now thirty-five, he was an extremely engaging man. He was just a tad over six feet tall and about 170 pounds, with hair that was almost red but mostly brown. His eyes seemed either gray or green depending on the light. Lighthearted and funny, his sense of humor appealed to Jackie. He was also, obviously, intelligent; when he spoke of history, she couldn't help but fall under his spell.

"He's a Democrat, you know," Janet warned Jackie of Jack. It seemed as if she was looking for reasons to disapprove. Though she was Republican, as was the whole family, citing politics was pushing it. Jackie was not a political animal and wasn't even registered to vote.

"But you didn't mention the word 'Democrat' in my mother's house," Lee would say, "or even in my father's."

As Lee suggests, there was some long-standing grievance against Democrats like the Kennedys, especially from the Bouvier side of the family. Back in the 1940s, President Franklin D. Roosevelt had appointed Jack Kennedy's father, Joe, as the chief operating officer of the newly created Securities and Exchange Commission. This commission was formed to monitor stock trades and prevent the kind of wild speculating that had put money in the pockets of the wealthy while wiping out pretty much everybody else. Since this was exactly how Joe had made a great part of his fortune, it was ironic that he was now charged with policing such activity. He immediately enacted dozens of restrictions on speculative trading, all done with an eye toward ruining anyone who'd ever crossed him in the past — and their number was legion.

Black Jack had made a lot of money buying and selling large blocks of stocks for other brokerage firms. However, with Joe Kennedy's new regulations in place, he was unable to continue this lucrative practice. With his hands now tied by Kennedy, he lost big in the stock market — $43,000 in 1934 alone. In fact, he would earn barely $5,000 that year in dividends, and half that much in brokerage commissions. "Because of what Kennedy had done, men like Black Jack loathed him," said John Davis, "so Jackie and Lee knew from an early age that the name 'Kennedy' was never to be so much as whispered in their household. Black Jack would earn and lose a lot more money from this time in his life and onward, but he would never really bounce back from the downslide caused by Joe Kennedy and his running of the Securities and Exchange Commission."

"I was a chubby, somewhat snobby six-year-old in black velvet shorts, silk shirt, lace cuffs, and black patent-leather shoes with brass buckles," recalled Jamie Auchincloss of his appearance when JFK first came to call. "The day Jackie brought him home, I already had an opinion of him. A Catholic, Democrat, perhaps liberal, Irish, and a politician, he was, in every way I had heard anyway, definitely an outsider. I stood at the top of the long staircase, glaring down the flight of red carpet at him as he entered the house. I coughed loudly to draw attention to myself and then snorted in my haughtiest voice, 'Hello, Kennedy.' Jack looked up at me and retorted in exactly the same tone, 'Hello . . . *Auchincloss.*' "

Though he had a great sense of humor and terrific charisma, Jack was still usually a bit reserved when with Jackie. Maybe he sensed it best that he hold back. There's little doubt

89

that if he had been aggressive and demonstrative, he would have scared her away. Jackie, like her mother, was anything but effusive with her emotions; Lee was more impulsive. Though Jack didn't represent head-over-heels love at first sight for Jackie, she didn't really want that kind of passion in a new relationship, anyway. Some felt she had never really reconciled that "quickie" she had with John Marquand in an elevator so long ago. Now she seemed to be looking for something deeper. As she learned more about him — a Harvard graduate from a close-knit family, his maternal grandfather the former mayor of Boston, his father the former ambassador to Great Britain — Jackie became even more interested in Jack. The Kennedys were noteworthy, exciting, and, apparently, also tragic — she soon learned that Jack's brother and sister were both killed in plane crashes.

"Are you sure about him, Jacqueline?" Janet asked her daughter in front of her family members at Merrywood. She found him charming if not exactly polished. She said that he certainly had an impressive pedigree, but that he seemed rather unkempt. Jackie had to agree. He did appear to need a good haircut, she said, and maybe a nice meal because he was so thin. However, she was drawn to him, just the same.

In so many ways, Jack Kennedy was a study in contrasts. He was strong, vital, and smart, alive with ideas for the future, ambitious in his political goals — he'd been a congressman for five years and had his eye on a Senate seat. However, he also suffered from a bad back partly as a result of war injuries as well as a deficiency of the adrenal glands called Addison's disease. Despite these health challenges, he always seemed hearty and full of life. He was also wealthy, as Jackie soon found out (and she did ask around, as did Janet). The Kennedys were worth at least $500 million thanks to Kennedy patriarch Joe's investments in the stock market (and no small share of bootlegging operations over the years). Jack had a $10 million trust fund from which he received a nice annual income.

As Jackie began to travel with Jack, joining his senatorial campaign in Boston and listening to his speeches in small surrounding towns, she continued to feel herself drawn to him. She had known, though, pretty much from her first conversation with Jack that he was not interested in settling down. Her intuition told her that he was probably just a playboy. However, he was also fun and exciting and even took her to the Eisenhower inauguration, which was pretty thrilling. But, afterward, he wouldn't return her phone calls. Then they had another date; he took her to meet his family in Hyannis Port, Massachusetts. After that, there was even more silence from him. She was beginning to feel that maybe he just wasn't interested in her. "Well, you are too *available* to him, Jacqueline," Janet said, "*that's* the problem. You need to disappear for a while, and if he still pursues things, *then* you'll know he's interested. If he doesn't, you'll know where you stand there, too."

Earlier, in the spring of '53, Janet happened to have a conversation with one of her social-ite friends, Emily Foley, during which Emily said that her daughter Aileen was going to London in June to watch the coronation of Queen Elizabeth II. "Why don't you suggest that Jackie go along with her," Emily said. Janet thought it was a good idea, especially since Jackie was now working for the *Washington Times-Herald* as a columnist. "I should think the newspaper would be happy to send you and another reporter to write up the coronation," Janet told her daughter, "and if they don't want to, I'd like to give you the trip because it would be a great experience for you."

Jackie didn't want to go. The more Janet pushed, the more Jackie pushed back. "Mummy, I *said* no," she said, annoyed. "I really do *not* want to go."

"But why?" Janet wanted to know. Then it hit her. "You don't want to be away from Jack, do you?"

Jackie nodded.

"Do you love him?" Janet asked.

Of course, that was not the kind of question Jackie would directly answer; she was just not that open a person. However, Janet knew from her expression that it might be the case. She was surprised, but if this was what was going on with her daughter she would accept it. "If you're so much in love with Jack Kennedy that you don't want to leave him," she told her (and, again, all of this is per her memory as she recalled in her JFK Library oral history), "I should think he would be much more likely to find out how he felt about you if you were seeing exciting people and doing exciting things instead of just sitting here waiting for the telephone to ring."

Finally, Jackie agreed to go to London after convincing her newspaper's editor to let her cover the royal event there. "Her drawings of the coronation appeared on the front pages of the *Times-Herald* three or four times, and they were very good, very clever," Janet would recall. Janet felt that, surely, Jack had seen them and been impressed by them. Hopefully, they made him wonder about Jackie and maybe even want to see her.

Janet's hopes were confirmed when, on the exact same day Jackie was returning to the United States, her telephone rang — Jack calling from the Cape. He wondered if she knew what flight Jackie would be on, and what time. Janet gave him the information and told him that she would be landing in New York and then flying down to Washington. Jack said he happened to know that this particular flight had a stopover in Boston. He said he was going to meet Jackie there, and surprise her. "It was the first time that I felt that this was really a serious romance," Janet would recall, "at least on his part. I had suspected Jackie cared a lot, although she had never really said so because she is the sort of girl who covers her feelings. Anyway, he did meet her at Boston."

Happily, Janet approved of Jack Kennedy in a way that she'd not of John Husted or Michael Canfield. At least Kennedy had a promising future. He also had money; Janet had checked out his family's finances thoroughly. For her part, Lee thought Jack was "terrific." She said Jackie should snap him up and added that if she didn't, "I might!" She was kidding, of course. (Or was she?)

It was difficult for Janet to raise too many objections about Kennedy — that is, until she began to ask around about his father, Joe. What she learned about him gave her pause. Joe was widely known to have been unfaithful to his long-suffering but tough-as-nails wife, Rose. As Janet dug a little deeper, she learned that Jack was also known for his many assignations with women, which was to be expected since, after all, he was young and handsome and also single. The fact that some of those ladies with whom he was known to have been involved were married is what caused Janet concern.

Of course, money mattered to Janet. However, because of what she'd been through with Jack Bouvier, she also had some pretty strong views about unfaithful husbands. Rose — and, it would seem, at least from what Janet could gather, her daughters and even daughters-in-law — felt that as long as philandering behavior wasn't flaunted, it was acceptable. Janet vehemently disagreed. In her mind, it simply wasn't tolerable. If a man could not be faithful, as far as she was concerned, he should not be married, especially not to one of her daughters, no matter how much he and his family had in the bank. There was no latitude in her thinking; it was absolute.

About a month before his planned wedding to her daughter, Janet was upset to learn that Jack Kennedy had gone sailing in the Caribbean with his friend Senator George Smathers. The trip had been planned months in advance, and the two were not about to cancel it. "Throughout the time we were gone," Smathers later recalled, "we were bombarded with telegrams from Mrs. Auchincloss wondering when we would be back, all in the guise of asking questions about the planning of the wedding — none of which Jack would have had the answers to, anyway. I remember that Jack said, 'She's not going to be easy, that one.' "

In fact, Janet was gravely troubled. Why would a man who was in love take a vacation without his fiancée so shortly before their wedding? She saw trouble on the horizon. Therefore, she couldn't in good conscience completely endorse the marriage, her default mechanism being to protect her eldest daughter. She didn't know what to do. She decided to go to St. Mary's Catholic Church in Newport, Rhode Island, where the wedding was to take place. (Though unable to receive the Catholic Church's sacraments because of her divorce, she still belonged to St. Mary's.) She would recall that she went early in the morning before there were any parishioners present, lit a candle, and then sat in the empty church for about an hour, thinking about her daughter's happiness and wondering what was best for her. After prayer, she would feel more certain that Jackie was making the right decision, and that she should not stand in her way.

Jackie felt she had the coping skills in place to deal with someone as unpredictable in fidelity as Jack. Jack had the potential to be something great and maybe powerful (and maybe richer), and Jackie saw it in him and was willing to overlook everything else. She didn't want anything to get in the way of her future as a Kennedy, not Jack's reputation and certainly not Janet's concern about it. The fact that the Kennedys loved Jackie from the start also helped things along. Was she of French ancestry? They thought she was, with a name like Bouvier. They weren't quite sure, though, the mystery of it all somehow seeming more exotic to them than the truth. (In fact, breaking it down, she was just one-eighth French, three-eighths English, and half Irish, the Irish strain being what she most had in common with the Kennedys.)

"Jackie had impressed them all — especially the powerful Joe — with her great beauty, rare humor, and keen intellect as well as what they viewed as her distinguished background," recalled her half brother, Jamie Auchincloss. "When they combined what they knew of her education at Miss Porter's and Vassar with the fact that she'd once been Debutante of the Year, as well as with her many travels abroad along with what appeared to be her wealth, she was the perfect aristocratic fit for the role of senator's wife. Of course, Jackie had no wealth of her own. Our family lived well, but she had little to no money in her bank account."

The Kennedys would be in the dark as to the specifics of Jackie's financial situation for quite some time to come. They would believe that Jackie's father, Jack, was wealthy and that Jackie would stand to inherit half of his estate. They also thought her grandfather Jim

T. Lee would make her wealthy at his passing. None of it was true, though. Jackie wasn't well off at all — which is why, while she knew she could've stopped the wedding if she'd elected to do so, Janet made the decision to abandon her reservations. After all, she knew what it was like to worry about day-to-day expenses. She never wanted to revisit that trying time, and she most certainly didn't want such a life for her daughter.

JANET'S TOUGH TIMES

Flashback to January 1941.

Janet Lee Bouvier would tell anyone who asked that she was exhausted by her penny-pinching existence after her divorce from her husband, Black Jack. In truth, while she thought she had it tough, most people likely would have disagreed.

Janet would awaken to breakfast in bed of toast and jam, sometimes eggs, with coffee and freshly squeezed orange juice served by the maid. Then she would sit at the antique French Louis XV–style oak fall-front writing desk in her bedroom and try to cope with a stack of bills. Shaking her head in bafflement while pounding away on a small adding machine, she would do her best to balance her account while meeting her fiscal duties. Jack was paying her a little over a thousand dollars a month. Still, it was never enough, especially given that Janet had a full-time personal maid and a governess for the girls. (She wanted a cook, too, but couldn't afford one, which was why the governess served breakfast in the mornings.) There were all sorts of financial responsibilities with which to deal, from the regular household bills to her personal maintenance — hairstyling, manicures and pedicures, new clothing, always couture — to the girls' ballet classes, art classes, piano and horseback-riding lessons, as well as dental expenses. In that last regard, because Jackie's teeth were coming in misaligned, Janet had a battle with Jack — who was supposed to cover dental — over braces, which were quite expensive in the 1940s; in the end the couple split the cost. Somehow, Janet always found a way to pay for everything, even if it meant swallowing her pride and borrowing from her father, which she had to do many times. She even appealed to her mother to talk to him about a weekly allowance so that she wouldn't have to keep going back to him. "But when has your father ever gone out of his way to help anyone," Margaret asked, "especially one of his children?" She had a point.

Earlier in the year, Janet got desperate and took a job as a model at Macy's department store. Jackie wanted to take horseback-riding lessons from an expensive trainer and Janet wanted nothing more than for her to have them. She took the job to earn enough money to pay for the training, and maybe have a little extra to do something for Lee, as well. It was demeaning work; she would don a dress in the morning and then stand in a corner all day long twirling the skirt for women who would appraise it critically. She found it undignified, saying she would never personally wear any of the clothes she was forced to model. It just lasted a few months, but she hated it; she did get the money she needed for Jackie's lessons but, sadly, nothing for Lee. Then, after taking a nurse's aide course at a local school, she started volunteering at Presbyterian Hospital. This, too, wasn't satisfying. But, then again, she wasn't really going to find any job fulfilling. She wasn't meant to earn money, she was meant to spend it! Right now, on this day in the winter of '41, she didn't have a job. All she had were unpaid bills. And a maid. And a governess.

At the end of her daily bill-paying session, a frustrated Janet would usually cry out for a cup of tea. Moments later, her maid would appear from the pantry with the hot beverage — imported from the famous gourmet tea company, Mariage Frères in Paris. The employee would place the pot and cup on a small, matching oak table next to the desk before scampering away. After drinking her tea, Janet would then take to her bed for an hour, exhausted from the morning ritual, though it was only ten o'clock. Sometimes she would take a couple of sleeping pills, wash them down with liquor, and not wake up until the girls came home from school — if then. At night, she would go out on dates with men, looking for a possible wealthy suitor, returning later, alone and disappointed.

Making things all the more difficult for Janet was the fact that her daughters clung so tightly to their father. He never disciplined Jackie or Lee. Whereas Janet was extremely critical, Jack was always praising. He was also full of sentiments that they would carry with them for the rest of their lives, many of which would shape their little, entitled personas. For instance, he once told them, "You never have to worry about keeping up with the Joneses, because we *are* the Joneses. Everyone has to keep up with us!" John Davis, Jack's nephew, said of him, "He told the girls, 'Style is not a function of how rich you are, or even who you are. Style is a habit of mind that puts quality before quantity, noble struggle before mere achievement, honor before opulence. It's what you are. It's your essential self. It's what makes you a Bouvier.' They never forgot it."

The dynamic between father and daughters was made even more complicated by the fact that Jack so obviously preferred Jackie to Lee. "*Of course* he did," Lee would say. "That was clear to me, but I didn't resent it." She said she understood that he had been with Jackie for more than three years before she was born, which had bonded him to her. Also, Janet had told them both that Jack had wanted a son, which is why they called their firstborn Jacqueline, as close to naming her after her father as possible. Also, the two looked very much alike, which made Jack all the more proud.

Even if he did prefer Jackie, *both* sisters would rather have been with their father than their mother. "He was a wonderful man, you'd have loved him," Lee told the writer Nicky Haslam in February of 2013. "He had such funny idiosyncrasies, like always wearing his black patent evening shoes with his swimming trunks. One thing which infuriates me is how he's always labeled the drunken black prince. He was never drunk with me, though I'm sure he sometimes drank, due to my mother's constant nagging. You would, and I would!"

"Little girls need to believe that their father is a hero," Janet said, according to Jack's nephew John Davis. "But even the best heroes are far from perfect." She said that, the way she saw it, Jack was just "seducing them the way he has seduced every other woman in his life."

In fact, the original reason behind Janet's Mother-Daughter Tea occasions was that she felt that she needed to carve out special time with her daughters. It hurt her that they preferred their father, and so she went out of her way to also have time with them that they would cherish. This was one of the reasons she also made sure that they attended church together. Even though she had been excommunicated because of her divorce, she continued to go to the Church of St. Ignatius Loyola on Park Avenue every Sunday, and made sure both Jackie and Lee accompanied her. When others in the congregation would receive the Holy Eucharist at the end of the Mass, she would sit with her girls in the back of the church and feel such a great sense of sorrow. In fact, she made the decision to not have the girls take the required catechism classes in order to also receive the church's sacraments since she knew they would not be able to do so as a family. She reversed her position on that, however, when a priest told her she was being selfish, that just because she had sinned and was banned from those sacraments didn't mean she should refuse to allow her daughters, both of whom had been baptized in the Catholic Church, the opportunity for grace. Filled with what she much later called "Catholic guilt," she finally did allow Jackie and Lee to take the necessary classes. (Jackie and Lee would always consider themselves Catholic, not Episcopalian, and their children would all be baptized and receive the other sacraments.) When they were young, their Sundays in church together were important to Janet, yet another opportunity for her to be able to bond with her daughters.

"But then Black Jack would swoop in and the girls would be all his again," said John Davis. "There was this constant tug-of-war always being waged as to who was the favored parent. Janet worked hard to be the chosen one, but the girls did love their daddy an awful lot. Spending the allocated time required by their custody agreement was fine, but after that Janet really didn't want to hear them talk about him anymore," continued Davis. "Therefore, she would tell the children's governess [Berthe Kimmerle] that if they started prattling on about Black Jack she should stop them. If they persisted, she should lock them in their bedroom."

During this time, Lavinia Jennings, the niece of Berthe Kimmerle, sometimes stayed with the Bouviers on weekends. She was eight, the same age as Lee. "I would be with my aunt on Saturdays, immersed in my schoolwork while she did the family's laundry, and all would be fine while Jackie and Lee were with their father," recalled Jennings. "Then, at the end of the day, he would drop them off, they would come upstairs, and all hell would break loose. Jack had spoiled them with a visit to the Central Park zoo, lunch at

104

the Plaza, ice-skating at Rockefeller Center, tea at the Waldorf. Naturally, they didn't want to come home to 'mean ol' Mummy.' Once they did, it was 'Daddy this' and 'Daddy that.' Janet would tell my aunt, 'I don't want to hear another word about their no-good father. Put them in their room and lock the door!' The girls' bedroom door locked from the other side, which I thought was disturbing even at that age," Lavinia Jennings recalled. "The three of us would end up getting locked in there together — me, Jackie, and Lee. I would be screaming for my aunt to let us out while Jackie and Lee would be screaming for their mother."

One afternoon in the spring of '41, after visiting her father and then getting locked in the bedroom with Lee and Lavinia, Jackie screamed at the top of her lungs, "Let me out! I hate you, Mummy! *I hate you!*" According to Lavinia, Janet stormed into the bedroom. "What did you just say to me?" she asked, her eyes blazing. Jackie was quiet, shaking in her little shoes. Dismayed, Janet looked at Lee, then at Jackie, then at Lavinia. "You," she said, pointing to Lavinia, "go into the closet over there and close the door." The scared youngster did as she was told. From inside the closet, Lavinia could then hear the sound of two loud cracks. Janet had, apparently, slapped Jackie across the face with the palm of her hand, and then the back of it. Of

105

course, Jackie cried out in anguish. "I slipped open the closet door just in time to see poor Lee scurry under the bed like a scared little rabbit," Lavinia Jennings recalled.

Jackie only allowed Janet to see her in pain for a brief moment before she suppressed it. She would not allow Mummy to see her cry. Instead, she just stared at her with big brown eyes, practically willing herself to remain composed. "If something unpleasant happens to me, I block it out," Jackie would say many years later as an adult. "I have this mechanism."

"I have sacrificed everything for you girls," Janet said as she steadied herself against a chair. Her voice cracking with emotion, she demanded to know, "Why don't you two ever appreciate it?" With that, she whirled around and bolted from the bedroom, slamming the door behind her.

"It's okay, Lee," Jackie said once Janet was out of the room. "You can come out from under the bed now." When Lee emerged, Jackie hugged her tightly, reassuring her that everything would be all right. Then she tapped her on the shoulder and announced, "You're it, Lee!" Without missing a beat, Lee countered with, "Oh, no, I'm not!" With that, the girls started chasing each other, happy to play their little game of tag as Lavinia watched, just content just to be with each other, as always.

As for Janet, it certainly seemed as if she was losing her grip. She needed some sort of salvation, someone to rescue her and her children from a life that wasn't making any of them happy. Luckily for her, that person was about to enter her life with the means necessary to give her and her daughters precisely the lifestyle she felt they well deserved.

HUGH AUCHINCLOSS

Back in 1939, when Janet Lee Bouvier went to Las Vegas to obtain freedom from her philandering husband, Jack Bouvier, she met a woman named Esther Auchincloss Nash. Esther happened to be in the same city to divorce her own husband. The two women struck up a lively friendship, and it was during dinner one night that Esther first brought up her brother, Hugh. She described him as a decent, honorable person, someone she felt Janet might want to get to know one day. "He could be a good husband for you," Esther said, only half joking. It would be another couple of years, though, before Janet's path would cross with Hugh's. Soon after that, she would, indeed, find herself married to him — and she would remain at his side as his loyal wife for the next thirty-nine years.

Born in 1897, Hugh Dudley Auchincloss — or "Hughdie," which was short for Hugh

D. — was descended from an old, noble Scottish family. Extremely conservative and old-fashioned even as a young man, he was the product of an entitled, privileged Newport, Rhode Island, background. His father, Hugh Sr., set into motion the family's upward mobility in 1891 by taking Emma Brewster Jennings of Fairfield, Connecticut, as his wife. Emma was related to Aaron Burr, the third vice president of the United States under President Thomas Jefferson. She was also the daughter of Oliver B. Jennings, William Rockefeller's brother-in-law and one of John D. Rockefeller's partners. Jennings also happened to be a chief investor in Rockefeller's Standard Oil, which generated many millions of dollars for his family. In fact, most family historians agree that it was because of the rich Standard Oil–infused dowry that Emma brought into her marriage to Hugh Sr. that he was then able to expand his dry-goods business into many lucrative banking, mining, and manufacturing enterprises, all of which would cement for generations to come the Auchincloss fortune.

By the time Hugh met Janet in the summer of 1941, he was forty-three and had already been twice married. Back in 1925, he'd married the former Maya de Chrapovitsky. Two years later, they had a son, Hugh Dudley Auchincloss III, nicknamed "Yusha" — Russian for "Hugh." When Yusha was about a year old, Hugh started his own investment firm with a million-dollar loan from his mother. Called Auchincloss, Parker & Redpath, it was headquartered in Washington, D.C., and, later, also in New York. In late spring of '31, Hugh bought his own seat on the New York Stock Exchange in order to serve on his company's board, paying roughly $300,000 (equivalent to almost $5 million today) for it.

In 1932, Hugh divorced Maya. Three years later, he married Nina Gore Vidal, who came into the marriage with a young son, Gore. (Of course, Gore Vidal would go on to a successful career as a premier novelist and playwright.) The couple had two children, Nina — who was nicknamed "Nini" — in 1937 and Thomas, known as "Tommy," in 1939. By 1941 the marriage was all but over after Hugh learned that Nina was cheating on him. It was then that Hugh decided to take a Caribbean cruise to clear his head, which would turn out to be fortuitous not only for himself but also for Janet Bouvier. By sheer coincidence, it was on that sea voyage that Janet would meet the man her friend Esther had raved about two years earlier.

Though Hugh Auchincloss was profoundly conservative, a serious person with not much of a sense of humor, he was exceedingly charming, a very intelligent man with a natural curiosity about others that made those in his life feel valued. Janet immediately brought a sense of gaiety into his world that was much needed, especially at this time when he was smarting over his unfaithful spouse. Janet had her own battle scars in that regard, of course, and was eager to share her stories with him. The two became close quickly. Of course, Hugh's wealth helped distinguish him in Janet's eyes, especially when he told her about his two massive estates, Merrywood in McLean, Virginia, and Hammersmith Farm in Newport, Rhode Island. Plus, there was the deluxe apartment he maintained at 950 Park Avenue in Manhattan.

Considering her entitled background, her recent financial frustrations, and her craving for security for not only herself but also her daughters, one might have thought Janet would have jumped at the chance to wed a suitor as wealthy as Hugh when he asked for her hand in marriage. After all, the Auchinclosses could be found in that year's Social Register — a listing of names of families who claim to be of the social elite — with forty-seven entries, compared with forty-two for the Rockefellers, eight for the Vanderbilts, and two for the Astors. Despite his family's prestigious pedigree, Janet actually had reservations about Hugh. For her, it was a question of compatibility.

Hugh was a gentle, amiable fellow who

presented not much of a challenge to Janet — "a magnum of chloroform" is how Gore Vidal once famously and unkindly described him. Janet was used to the fiery personalities of her father, Jim, and ex-husband, Jack. Simply put, she feared she would become quickly bored with Hugh.

Looking past his calm demeanor, Janet Bouvier was also deeply concerned about the physical attraction between herself and Hugh, or lack thereof. What she and Jack shared in their private moments had been the glue that kept them together long after they should have parted. They couldn't get enough of each other. Hugh was actually about six years younger than Jack, but he was a completely different kind of man, at least in Janet's eyes. He was stable and sensible whereas Jack was unpredictable and volatile. Hugh was a nice guy whereas Jack was a "bad boy," and, unfortunately enough for her, Janet wanted the "bad boy." Still, she was open to the possibility of a life with Hugh, if only she could sense some interest in her from him. He was a good-looking, large-framed man at over six feet tall, with dancing blue eyes, a silvery mane, and a ruddy complexion. She was certainly attracted to him. However, he wasn't very affectionate; there was virtually no spark between them. It wasn't as if she wanted to be intimate with him before marriage, but she wanted to at least know it was headed in that direction. After a few months of uncertainty about his intentions toward her, she decided to confront him about it when he asked for her hand. What kind of relationship was he proposing, anyway?

Hugh was honest with her. He sadly confessed that he was chronically impotent, and that this had been the case for many years. He said it was why his second marriage to Nina ended. "Well, what about the first one?" Janet wanted to know. He explained that the marriage to Maya collapsed after a freak accident that involved her accidentally walking right into the whirling propeller of an airplane. (She would recover, but never be quite the same, always suffering psychological issues afterward.) Had the mishap not occurred, she probably would have left him anyway because of his persistent problem. Because he felt it only fair to her, he wanted to be quite clear with Janet: the two of them would not have a sexual relationship. He had accepted this painful, unfortunate limitation in himself long ago and said he was too old to try to hide it, or act as if it wasn't the case.

Janet was stunned not only by Hugh's admission, but also by his acceptance of it. Why would he be willing to allow this kind of emasculation? She suggested he consult with doctors, maybe even psychiatrists, but to just accept it seemed unfathomable to her. She never accepted the status quo in any aspect of her life, always certain there was more and better for her if she just kept going for it. However, Hugh had tried everything, he told her, and there was simply nothing to be done about it. The decision was now hers: did she want to be with him, or not?

Of course, Janet knew she had to find a man with the kind of wealth she required not only for her own stability but for that of her two daughters. But was she willing to sacrifice passion in the process? Could she live in a sexless marriage? She said she needed to think it over. "I'm too young to just give it up," she confided in her friend Myrna Lloyd, this according to Myrna's daughter, Trina. "I'm in my prime!"

"Many people felt that the sexual revolution happened in the 1940s, not the 1960s, and Janet Bouvier was definitely of that era," said Trina Lloyd. "Janet was so unusual in this respect. My mom thought she'd lost her mind, that there should have been no debate about it. Sexual compatibility? *Are you kidding me?* Women back then didn't make choices based on sexual compatibility! They made choices based on love and romance, *maybe* . . . money and stability, *definitely* . . . but not sex. My mother said, 'Marry that man! What is wrong with you, Janet? What happens in the bedroom is no one's business. Who cares?' So, after a great deal of thought about it, Janet just came to terms with it. She was that kind of woman, a person who would look at a situation, make up her mind about it, and then not look back. 'I can do this and I will do it for my Jackie and Lee,' she said. 'If I just put my mind to it, I can close off that part of myself. I've had two wonderful children. Now, that's that.' It was very much like Janet to handle it that way. She was that pragmatic."

Janet told Hugh that she was sorry about his problem but that it would not stand in the way of their relationship. He was a wonderful man, she said, with much to offer in place of physical intimacy. Therefore, yes, she said, she would eagerly marry him. "He couldn't believe his luck," said one of his relatives, "because he really did love Janet but was fully prepared to let her go if she would not have him. When she said yes, it was as if he was now given a whole new lease on life. He thought she was beautiful, smart, and someone who would be a great partner in his life. It was like a merger was about to happen, really, more than a marriage. However, he was happy about it, just the same."

In December 1941, Hugh invited Janet, Jackie, twelve, and Lee, nine, to Merrywood so they could get to know one another. "It was a nice visit," Hugh's son Yusha, who was fourteen at the time, once recalled. "The girls were polite, yet still fun. The mother was strict, a no-nonsense kind of woman." (Yusha would end up with a bit of a crush on Jackie. They were always content to be in each other's company, usually to the exclusion of poor Lee, to whom they tried to give the slip at every opportunity.)

Six months passed. If they were going to marry, it had to happen fast, Janet and Hugh decided, because Hugh had just enlisted in the U.S. Navy; he was about to be shipped off to Jamaica with the British intelligence. Therefore, in early June, Janet sent her girls off to spend the summer with their grandfather "Grampy Lee" — Janet's father, Jim — in East Hampton. On June 21, 1942, while they were away, she married Hugh. Apparently, Janet suspected the girls would never allow a peaceful transition from their beloved father to the new man in Janet's life, so she decided to do the deed while they weren't around. "We were at our grandfather's house in East Hampton," Lee would recall. "My mother telephoned to say she had married Hugh Auchincloss. I felt my world crashed." After it was all over, Janet sent for her daughters so that they could all then move into Merrywood. Soon after, Hugh was unexpectedly reassigned to the War Department in Washington, which meant that he was, for the most part, living at home.

Jackie would recall Merrywood as an "exciting and lovely place." She would say, "Every day was wonderful. Horses and other animals and so many people all over, so much to do and learn. It was a special time with Mummy." She and Yusha flirted, too, though it was all harmless. One night, according to what Yusha told his friend Robert Westover many years later, she came into his room and said, "Yusha, I have such big lips. Who would ever want to kiss me?" He said, "But *I* want to kiss you, Jackie!" And he did. "So I think Jackie got her first kiss at the age of about thirteen from Yusha," says Westover. "It was a sweet, innocent, and fun time for her."

Not so for Lee: "I was left alone at this *enormous* house of my mother and stepfather in McLean, Virginia. They were off deep-sea fishing in Chile. I was just so lonely, all I did was play in the woods with my dogs day after day. [Jackie was at boarding school.] A very fat cook called Nellie was my only friend. And so I decided I couldn't stand it any longer and I looked up in the yellow classified pages 'orphanages.' And I took my *pathetic* allowance, called a taxi from the yellow pages, nearest to our house. And so the taxi came, we went to the orphanage. I asked him to please wait and walked in and said to the Mother Superior at the desk, 'My name is such-and-such and I have come to adopt an orphan. And I have a *lovely* place where she would be *terribly* happy. Horses and dogs and walks and she would really love it.' And she [the nun] looked at me absolutely stunned and she said, 'I'm so sorry, my dear, but you're just too *young* for us to allow you to adopt a *child.*' When my mother came back about a week later, I just got *such* hell for this — *'How you could upset me . . . how you could torture me the way you have . . . we were so worried about you!'* I couldn't figure out quite *why* that was the case since they were in *Chile* the entire time on a *motorboat*!"

Lee's unhappiness aside, it must have felt like a sweet victory to Janet when she invited her parents to Merrywood for the first time. As he grew older, Jim — now sixty-six and still wildly successful in real-estate development with properties all over Manhattan and, also, the director of the Chase National Bank — had become more distant in his relationship to Janet and her two sisters. Janet kept waiting for the day when he would soften, when he would want to repair their relationship. She liked to tell people that there was more to him than met the eye, that deep down he was a good man who loved his daughters but didn't have the capacity to express it, like many men of his generation. Perhaps that was true of Jim. The sad reality, though, is that Janet never knew for certain because never did he change, never did he open up to her — never did he in any way endeavor to mend the strained relationship he had with her or her sisters. "I keep waiting for that armor to crack," she told Hugh, "but

117

I guess people have armor for a reason."
When Jim met Hugh shortly before he and
Janet married, he wasn't impressed. "The
breeding is there, but not the stamina," he
said, as if describing an aging stallion.

Merrywood was considered among the
country's preeminent estates. It was fifty
bucolic acres of rolling hills upon which sat
an enormous two-story, ivy-covered mansion
that had been constructed in Georgian-style
architecture. Its terraces wrapped around the
back of the property and overlooked the Potomac. Amid the gently splashing fountains
and formal gardens, Janet pointed out to her
parents that the caretakers, who lived in a
five-bedroom cottage out in the distance, kept
the grounds meticulously cared for with no
concern about expense, money not being
anyone's worry, let alone the help's. She took
pride in explaining all she had learned about
the property's history from the estate superintendent (who lived in a separate guesthouse), such as the fact that George Washington had once surveyed it. Near the main
house was a four-car garage, above which was
a large five-bedroom, four-bathroom apartment. Beneath it was a full indoor gym and
badminton court. There was also a shooting
range, tennis court, Olympic-sized swimming
pool, and, of course, stables for the horses.
There was even a dog kennel. Inside the main
house it seemed as if there were powder

rooms every few feet. There was also a paneled library, an enormous banquet-style kitchen, with two garbage disposals — a device that had just been introduced that year — a butler's pantry, and two large dining rooms, one for the family and their guests and one for the help.

"Just how big is this place?" Jim asked as he, Margaret, Janet, and Hugh played pinochle after dinner at Merrywood. Janet said she had no idea, considering the many guesthouses and other structures. In totality, there were just too many rooms to count! After a moment's thought, Jim then said he imagined Janet would no longer be coming to him for money. Janet agreed that this was probably true. Then, according to family history, Jim fixed his daughter with a crippling stare. "You may have money now," he told her, "but not power. You don't have power. Don't forget that."

As he sat watching the scene unfold, Hugh Auchincloss probably couldn't help but smile to himself, as if he knew what was coming. "Yes, but *Hughdie* has it," Janet told her father. She then reached over and took her husband's hand. "Therefore," she concluded, "so do I."

AN UNCONVENTIONAL PREGNANCY

A couple of years after Janet Bouvier became Janet Auchincloss, she started having a longing for more children. She was surprised; she'd truly thought she was finished with kids. She had to ask herself, at least according to her relatives, if she would have still married Hugh had she known she would've wanted more children, given what she knew about his sexual dysfunction. If she was being honest with herself, the answer was still yes. After all, he had provided her with a marvelous lifestyle, was extremely indulgent of her, and treated her like a queen. He was also kind to her daughters. Still, she had her mind made up about having more children and, in fact, now said she wanted two boys. She hoped for sons, she said, because she felt that maybe she would be a better mother to them than she'd been to her girls. She always felt a strange sort of competition with her daughters, she'd confessed. It was difficult for her to have complete clarity about it, but she felt that maybe the reason she was sometimes at odds with Jackie and Lee was because both girls were always so defiant. She felt that sons might be more easily pliant, not as complex to raise. Being a good mother mattered to Janet; she wanted another chance.

Obviously, having children with Hugh was not going to be easy, if even possible. When Janet told Hugh of her desire, his position was that he'd been clear and honest with her about his problem and that there was no way he was going to father children. His children from previous marriages — Yusha, Tommy, and Nini — had been conceived, he said, during a time when he was willing to try. He had long ago, he told Janet, abandoned the idea of even trying; he simply was not open to it. He'd had years of psychoanalysis to try to figure out his problem, and nothing worked. Just the mere idea of sex was humiliating, he said, and he would not go through it, even for Janet.

Anyone who might have imagined Janet Auchincloss allowing Hugh's personal problem to get in the way of her goal to have children would not have known her very well. Janet did her research and investigated the possibility of artificial insemination, which was relatively new at the time; babies born of this procedure were commonly called "test-tube babies." She was fascinated to know that there were, as she put it, "ways to get around Mother Nature." The more research she did into it, though — and she also consulted two doctors at the New York University School of Medicine who were just developing a fertility program there — the more she viewed it as unnecessarily complex. In her mind, it was quite simple: Even though Hugh was not able to sustain an erection, he was able to produce sperm, though Janet had no idea how viable it was. As long as she got it into the right place in her body, though, she felt she would get pregnant. Therefore, she did what a growing number of women were doing at the time in experimenting with artificial insemination in the home: she used a kitchen utensil along the lines of a turkey baster — though it would be incorrect to say that this was the specific instrument she used; no one can quite remember. What is known is that one doctor suggested that a syringe might be more efficient, but she decided she preferred her own way. Though Hugh felt the process would be too embarrassing, Janet viewed it as strictly a clinical experiment in the bedroom. It worked. She wasn't even surprised, actually; she somehow knew it would work, and it did. The only thing that didn't pan out as planned was that, after a relatively easy pregnancy, she gave birth to a girl, not a boy, Janet Jennings Auchincloss, known as Janet Jr., born on June 13, 1945.

While Janet obviously loved her daughter, she still wanted a son. Therefore, she and Hugh did the procedure again and, after numerous times, it seemed clear that this time it would not work. Somehow, though,

Janet became pregnant, anyway. No one was sure how it happened, only that it wasn't by the previous means. Though Janet wouldn't discuss it, Hugh did tell a close friend that he and Janet were intimate "once and one time only," and that the happy result of what was likely not the best experience for them was the son Janet had wanted, James Lee Auchincloss, born on March 4, 1947.

Of course, Janet considered the way she had conceived to be private between herself and her husband, though many people in the family — in particular, Hugh's first two wives, Maya and Nina — suspected artificial insemination. Nina spread the word throughout the family that Janet had used a spoon to inseminate herself. In fact, Nina was, apparently, speaking from experience, since she told her son Gore Vidal that this was how *she* had been inseminated with each of her two children — Nini and Tommy — during her own marriage to Hugh. (Vidal would then publish the anecdote in his memoir, *Palimpsest*.)

Janet's children with Jack Bouvier, Jackie and Lee, were baptized Catholic. However, her children with Hugh Auchincloss, Janet Jr. and James Lee — Jamie — would both be baptized Episcopalian.* Along with marrying

---

* Jamie's christening would fall on the same day as his half sister Jackie's "coming out," with engraved

Hugh came a happy revelation for Janet regarding religion in her life. During a Sunday service at the Episcopalian church Hugh and his children had always attended, Janet had stayed behind when they went up for Communion. When Yusha asked why, she explained that she had been excommunicated from the Catholic Church because of her divorce from Jack. Much to her surprise, Yusha told her that all Christians were allowed to receive Communion in an Episcopalian church, even those who have been divorced. Janet was elated. Given this new information, she decided to learn more about the Episcopalian religion and, for the rest of her life, would attend churches of that faith. This did not mean, however, that she didn't consider herself to be Catholic; she would *also* attend Catholic Church services quite often, especially on Holy Days such as Christmas and Easter.

It's also worth noting that Jackie and Lee never referred to Janet Jr. or Jamie as their "half" siblings, or even to Hugh's children from his previous marriages — Yusha, Tommy, and Nini — as their "steps." All of

---

invitations sent to all announcing the party for "Miss Jacqueline Lee Bouvier" and, in smaller type, "Master James Lee Auchincloss" at Hammersmith Farm on "Friday, the first of August [1947]."

them always thought of one another as just brothers and sisters, and referenced each other that way in conversation.

■ ■ ■ ■

PART TWO:
A MOTHER'S DUTY

■ ■ ■ ■

WHAT MUMMY DID

It was September 12, 1953. Early morning dawned as Janet Auchincloss walked alone on a stretch of pebble-covered sand along the shoreline of the second of the Auchinclosses' grand estates, Hammersmith Farm. Her arms wrapped tightly around herself, she steeled her small frame against a crisp southwest ocean breeze. This was her daily morning ritual, which she would describe as "exercise to keep the body fit and the mind nimble." Facing the bay, she tilted back her head and arched her spine, a part of her daily isometric exercise, a regimen to which she was now completely devoted. Sometimes she would find a sand dune, lay down with her back on it, and do sit-ups. Not on this day, though. It was too cold for her to take off her coat, and trying to do sit-ups with it on was too cumbersome. Staying fit was important to her. Now forty-five, Janet had a good life, one of privilege and entitlement, the kind to which not many Americans during the Cold War could stake claim.

Hammersmith Farm was quite the showplace. It was almost one hundred acres of scenic rolling green hills that rose up in an undulating sweep upon which the Auchinclosses had built enormous barns, stables, and guesthouses with names like the Castle, the Windmill, and the Carriage House. It was located on the site of the first farm in Newport, established in 1639 by William Brenton, one of the city's founding fathers. (Brenton called the farm Hammersmith after his birthplace, Hammersmith, England. The main house was originally called "The House of Four Chimmnies" [sic].) John Winthrop Auchincloss, Hugh's uncle, purchased the property and built the main structure in 1887 and then, a couple of years later, sold it to his younger brother, Hugh Dudley Auchincloss, Hughdie's father. Hughdie would then inherit the estate after the death of his mother, Emma Brewster Jennings, in 1942.

The main house — called the Big House — was a sprawling, brick-stone-and-wood Victorian mansion typical of classic New England architecture with its artfully shingled roof, its aesthetically pleasing gables, its towering turrets, and its large picture windows overlooking Narragansett Bay. With its twenty-eight rooms and thirteen fireplaces, the Big House sat atop an elegantly manicured sloping lawn amid rolling pastures. It was surrounded by stables for horses and ponies and, since it was the oldest working farm in Newport (which supplied milk and eggs to a local naval base), all manner of animals were present, from sheep and goats to chickens. Years ago, Hugh's mother, Emma, had affixed to the front door a plaque that featured the family's coat of arms with the language *Spectemur agendo,* which translates from the Latin to "Let us be judged by our actions."

While they enjoyed Merrywood, Hammer-smith would be the preferred home for Janet's daughters, both of whom had grown into beautiful women. Jackie was now twenty-four, Lee twenty. The girls had been living a pampered life ever since their mother married Hugh. The family's staff was loyal and capable; no one ever wanted for anything.

Among those in Janet's employ at this time was the newly hired Adora Rule, just eighteen. She'd been sent to Janet from Russell Kelly Office Services, a company that provided temporary secretarial office help, called Kelly Girls. Though she'd just started with Janet that very week, Janet already appreciated Adora's work ethic — the fact that she had a tablet always at the ready and constantly took notes no matter what was going on around her. "Jackie and Lee weren't fond of me simply because they felt I was spying on them," Adora would recall. "Oh, they hated me, those two," she would say many years later with a chuckle.

This day — September 12 — was a joyous one for the family. After all, Jackie was marrying Senator Jack Kennedy today at Newport's St. Mary's Catholic Church. Though the story of what Janet did at Jackie's wedding has been told often, it does bear some repeating in order to further understand the relationship between mother and daughter.

It comes down to this:

Janet Auchincloss knew full well that Jackie's father, Black Jack Bouvier, had never liked Joe Kennedy. Therefore, because of her own long, conflicted history with Jack, Janet didn't trust him around Joe or any of his family members. She didn't want him at Jackie's wedding. "My mother had written to him [Bouvier] telling him she hoped he realized that he was *far* from welcome and that he might then change his mind and decide not to come," Lee Radziwill recalled, "and she felt that this would be a *far* more appropriate thing for him to do." Jack didn't agree. This was Jackie's big day; there was no way he was going to miss it.

After seeing him at the wedding rehearsal earlier in the day, Janet didn't like the way Jack looked. She suspected that he'd been drinking. Though a party was planned that night at the Clambake Club, Janet decided that she didn't want her ex-husband there.

132

She would be too busy to keep an eye on him, she said, and she had no idea what kind of embarrassment he might cause her. Therefore, she dispatched Yusha to the Viking Hotel, where Jack was staying in Newport. His mission: to tell Jack he wasn't invited to the dinner.

"Yusha had to go into Jack's room and sit on the bed with him and give him the bad news," Yusha's friend Robert Westover would recall. "Years later, Yusha would still become distraught talking about it. He begged Jack not to show up and make a scene. Then he left and cried in the car all the way back up to Hammersmith. Later, when he told Jackie what Janet had him do, she was upset about it, as well. She felt that her father should have been allowed to attend the dinner. She also felt that if Janet wanted to exclude him she should have done so herself, rather than send poor Yusha as her emissary."

Dismayed by Janet's dictate, Jack, apparently, spent the night alone drinking in his hotel room. Lee would say that his absence from the party "made him feel incredibly low, depressed." It was a shame, especially because, just a couple months earlier, Lee had sent Michael Canfield — no slouch in the drinking department himself — to accompany Jack to a detox center. She and Jackie were determined to help their father deal with his alcoholism before the wedding, and found

133

what they thought was just the right place in the South of France. It had been difficult to convince him to go, but they managed to do so. They promised that Michael would stay close by for the thirty days he was in treatment. Of course, thirty days wasn't nearly enough time to deal with Jack's long-standing problem. However, back then, treatment for alcoholism was such that doctors believed it was sufficient.

The morning after the party, Jack was too hungover to function. Therefore, he had a few more drinks. "He got completely drunk," Lee would recall, "from misery and loneliness. It was not his fault. I am sorry but I am a realistic person, not a woman given to revisionist history: it was my mother's fault." Lee would also recall, "I just remember my mother screaming with joy, 'Hughdie, Hughdie, *Hughdie,* now you can give Jackie away!' " Lee would chalk up Janet's decision to take the honor from Black Jack to the fact that "a woman's revenge is relentless."

"Unfortunately, Jackie would never quite be able to forgive Mummy for any of it," Jamie added. "She blamed her and would never get over it. She believed that Mummy's intention all along was to have Daddy, not Black Jack, be the one to walk Jackie down the aisle. Mummy thought Daddy deserved it. Daddy was a good man, a wonderful father, and a fine husband, whereas Jack was none of the above. Therefore, her mind was made up about it. That said, this sudden replacement of my father for Jackie's would result in a family grudge that Jackie would hold against our mother for pretty much the rest of her life."

"I am sure my father, despite his reserve, felt he was put in an awkward position and regretted it," recalled Yusha Auchincloss. "Formally attired, he was ready, if not prepared, to accompany Jackie down the aisle of St. Mary's Church. Privacy had become public," Yusha added, referencing the fact that everyone present seemed to know what was going on, "possible conciliation turned confrontational, and as an usher, brother, brother-in-law, and friend, I hoped the event would end quickly."

Despite whatever angst she felt that day, Jacqueline Lee Bouvier was a beautiful bride in her ivory-colored silk taffeta gown. She wore an heirloom veil of rose point lace that Lee had worn before her, and that was handed down from Janet's mother. The bridal party included Lee (matron of honor), Nini (maid of honor), the groom's sister Jean, and sister-in-law Ethel, as well as his brothers Bobby (who was best man) and Teddy, along with brother-in-law Sargent Shriver. Michael Canfield was one of the ushers. Jamie was the ring bearer and Janet Jr. the flower girl. It was a religious and ceremonial High Mass wedding, followed by a grand reception at Hammersmith, where — seated at tables with umbrellas that dotted the hillside in close proximity to roaming ponies and cattle — about 1,200 guests enjoyed the bucolic atmosphere.

A few weeks after the ceremony, Jackie would send a heartfelt letter to Black Jack completely exonerating him of any wrongdoing, saying she understood and she loved him. If anything, what had happened on her wedding day colored the way she viewed her mother, not her father. Though it had always been a pattern of her life in the way she looked at her parents that Jack could do no wrong whereas Janet was more suspect, the misadventure of her wedding elevated her father even more in her eyes.

Many years later, at Janet's sixty-sixth birthday party, the topic of Jackie's wedding day would be raised, as it often was over the years. "It all worked out for the best," Janet told her family members. With the passing of the years, she couldn't even be sure of the details anymore. All she knew was that whatever had occurred was Jack's fault, not her own. She noted that Jack had ultimately been allowed into the church, that he had sat in the back where he belonged and at least got to see his daughter marry from that vantage point. Lee insisted, though, that what Janet had done that day had been "perfectly awful" and, she charged, "You *know* it's true, Mummy!" Janet shrugged. "What is also true," she observed, "is that no matter how hard we fight it, we somehow always revert back to our true natures." Lee shook her head with resignation. "Indeed," she said with an arched eyebrow. "We somehow always do, *don't we, Mummy?*"

"To Your Good Times"

Though the Kennedys seemed to be off to a good start in their new marriage with no complaints from either one, the Canfields had a different story. By the time they celebrated their first wedding anniversary in April of 1954, they were already dealing with serious issues. "First of all, Michael was frustrated in his job; he hated publishing," recalled Michael Guinzburg. "He tried to fool people into believing otherwise, but he really had no passion for books or their authors and was completely bored by the business. Unfortunately, his dissatisfaction caused him to drink more, which had already been a problem for him."

Lately, Michael had been musing about possibly opening a "nice little antique shop" in the Village — which brought up the second issue in his marriage. Lee had long ago become accustomed to a certain way of life at Merrywood and Hammersmith, and the idea of being the wife of the owner of "a nice little antique shop" did little to excite her. Even though she had been willing to forfeit extravagance for a time while working at *Harper's* and living with a roommate at the Dakota, she thought that once she got married, her penny-pinching days would be behind her.

Lee kept up a pretense of happiness for the first year, not allowing anyone — especially Janet — to see how bothered she'd become not living the high life on Michael's salary. At this time, in the spring of 1954, she and Jackie were featured wearing sweaters in a splashy fashion spread for *Vogue* for which they were photographed by Horst P. Horst, a preeminent photographer of the times. Though Lee was excited to see herself on the pages of such a prestigious fashion magazine, she knew it was only because of Jackie and her connection to the Kennedys that she'd been asked to pose. She didn't fancy herself a fashion model, even though some people thought she could have a successful future in that field.

As the second year of marriage unfolded, Lee became less eager to hide the truth about her dissatisfaction. "We can't even afford nice linens," she complained to Janet during one of her mother's visits to her and Michael's apartment near the East River in New York. Janet didn't want to hear it. "Don't complain to me. Complain to Michael," she told Lee. "Tell him he needs to make more money!" Lee said she had already complained to Michael, but that he just didn't know what to do about it. Lee said she felt they just needed a fresh start. Therefore, she came up with a plan of her own: she wanted to move to England. She'd been thinking about it for some time, she said, and while she knew it was a dramatic change, she hoped it might be for the best. She wasn't exactly sure of anything, though. "I'm afraid that I knew what I didn't want better than what I wanted," Lee would admit many years later. "The world I grew up in — of family business and bridge playing and special schools — that was something I wanted out of, although I was grateful for having had it. Oh, it couldn't have been more pleasant, more agreeable, you understand, and yet it had no meaning for me. Nothing I was doing had any meaning. I got married and got out quite early, but still floundered. I knew what I was running from, but not to."

Michael was intrigued by Lee's suggestion that they relocate. He'd long fancied his British link to royalty and had never really felt at home in the States, anyway. Therefore, he spoke to his father, Cass Canfield, and managed to get a quick transfer to Harper's in London.

More than anything, Michael wanted to

make Lee happy, and he felt that the move to the United Kingdom might do it. One day he decided to take up the matter with someone who knew Lee better than anyone, Jackie. Jackie couldn't believe her sister's good fortune; she'd always wanted to live in Europe and now Lee had the opportunity to do just that. "Can you give me any advice as to how I can make your sister happier?" Michael asked Jackie. Because she was never critical of him, he felt he could trust her for an honest answer. Jackie thought it over for a moment and said, "Well, Michael, I think the best thing is for you to get her some real money."

"But listen, kiddo," Michael said, "I make a perfectly good living. I've got a certain amount of money of my own and Harper's pays me well."

Jackie shook her head. "I mean real money, Michael. *Real* money!"

Jackie's few words of advice did little to encourage her brother-in-law, though. How was he to make "real money" on his publishing salary? That remained to be seen.

Lee announced her and Michael's new plan to move to England during one of the ladies' Mother-Daughter Teas in Manhattan at the Plaza. Though Janet was worried about Lee being on her own in a foreign country, she understood the reasoning behind it and supported it. Jackie was excited for her sister.

140

Therefore, on February 1, 1955, after a farewell party hosted by Janet and Hugh at Merrywood, Michael and Lee were off to Europe on board the SS *United States.*

Once they arrived, the Canfields rented a house on Chesham Place in Belgravia in London. Immediately, they began to socialize with London's movers and shakers as they tried to carve out their own place in British high society, especially given Michael's possible royal lineage. When Lee appeared in a pensive pose on the cover of a social publication called *The Tatler and Bystander* with the headline AN AMERICAN HOSTESS IN LONDON, Janet was proud enough of it to keep it among her most prized possessions. Because they were young, good-looking, and engaging, it wasn't difficult for Lee and Michael to move about in influential circles, which is how they eventually met the American ambassador to the Court of St. James's, Winthrop Aldrich, at a cocktail party.

When Lee found out that Ambassador Aldrich was in need of a social secretary at the embassy, she felt the position would be perfect for Michael. She encouraged him to interview for it; he was quickly hired. Not only was he happy to leave publishing, he realized that the job would afford him and his wife the opportunity to meet new, influential people. "Michael's job was to basically squire around the ambassador's visitors and make sure they got into the best restaurants and nightclubs," said Lois Aldrech, who also worked as a social secretary at the embassy at this time. "He was given entrée to the best places in London, the most select private clubs, which worked out well for Lee. So, even though this was nothing more than a secretarial job for Michael, he seemed to enjoy it. I'm not sure that Lee had much respect for it, though. There was definitely growing tension between them."

Michael's drinking continued to be a problem. "A drunk needs a reason to get sober," he told Lee, according to Tom Guinzburg, "and I don't have one." Lee had to wonder how this had happened to her; she'd grown up with an alcoholic father, and now she was married to an alcoholic husband? Jackie said she felt it was Lee's duty to stand by Michael and try to help him. However, it was one thing to have an opinion about a drunk, Lee said, and quite another to actually be married to one. Maybe if the Canfields had lived in America in closer proximity to Jackie, Lee might not have felt so alone in her troubles. With her sister so far away, though, she felt sadder than ever.

Lee couldn't help it; her eye started wandering. She soon became attracted to someone who actually *was* a royal — David Somerset, 11th Duke of Beaufort. Did she have a fling with him? If so, it was brief. Whatever was going on between them ended in July of 1956 at Deepdale Stadium in Preston after the two watched a football game. The specifics of the argument are unknown, but as she stormed away from Somerset, Lee said, "And don't you *ever* call me." He shot back, "Don't worry, I seldom do." With that, she turned around, walked up to him, and slapped him right across the face. "He is such a *small* measure of a man," she later said of him.

Shortly thereafter, Lee and Michael entertained Terrance Landow and his wife, Betty, at their new home at 45 Chester Square. This was a spacious four-story complex in a row of homes on Chester Square, which Lee had decorated so beautifully one had to be impressed by what she could do on a limited budget. By this time, she knew all of the best high-end furniture dealers in London as well as the most preeminent art dealers and was able to barter well with them. "The place was full of antiques and only the best of the best," Betty Landow recalled. "You would look around and marvel at what Lee had done. She was an excellent interior designer. Terry and I were bowled over. They even had two servants. How could they afford servants on his salary? We were gobsmacked."

As a cook served helpings of roast beef and potatoes onto their plates, the Landows and the Canfields chatted happily at the dinner table until the awkward subject of David

Somerset was raised by Michael. He noted that Lee had a new friend, "David Somerset, the *Duke* of *Beaufort,*" he said, pronouncing the title with dripping sarcasm. He also slurred his words. Obviously, he'd had too much gin.

From the look on her face, Lee was embarrassed. Was Michael trying to humiliate her in front of guests? Fine, she seemed to decide, if he wanted to play that game, she was up for it. Even though whatever she had with David was over, she looked at Michael with cold eyes and said, "Oh yes, David is perfectly lovely." Not only was he rich, she said, he "unlike some others I know is a *true* royal." They were having loads of fun together, she added.

As the Landows squirmed in their seats, the Canfields stared at each other for an awkward moment. "Finally, Michael raised his glass in Lee's direction," recalled Betty Landow. " 'Cheers, my dear' he said. 'To your good times, then. Long may they continue.' Lee then lifted her own glass. 'And to yours as well, my husband,' she said, glaring at him."

UNCONSCIONABLE

"My Jacqueline is having *such* a difficult time adjusting," Janet was saying to friends at Hammersmith Farm over cocktails.

Julian Balridge, who was twenty in 1955, recalls visiting Hammersmith and Merrywood many times with his parents, Carolyn and Edward. Carolyn was one of Janet's bridge-playing girlfriends; Edward worked in the finance business with Hugh. "As a uniformed butler served us," he recalled, "Janet said that Jackie had moved into an enormous estate called Hickory Hill, a fifteen-room mansion on ten acres, and that she was now just lost." She noted that at Hammersmith and Merrywood there were always people coming and going, but at Hickory Hill there was no traffic — the only people she could talk to were the servants, Janet said, because Jack was so busy at the Senate.

Tasting her drink, Janet shuddered and turned to the butler. "This is not dry," she said. The functionary looked at her blankly. "Dry. Dry. *Dry!*" Janet repeated as she handed her cocktail back to him. "Made with *vermouth.*" The butler quickly disappeared with Janet's drink.

Janet said she'd spent many hours at Hickory Hill teaching Jackie how to run an estate. Of course, Jackie was used to such living at Hammersmith and Merrywood, but she never had to think about how anything worked. Everything was just done for her. Now, however, she was the mistress of her own massive domain. Janet made lists for her, drew diagrams, outlined every detail from

145

which servant should serve the meals to how those meals should be served and then how the dishes should be cleared. She had what she called "a formula for good living," and she delighted in sharing it with Jackie. "Mummy was the chief architect behind all of that," Jamie Auchincloss said. "I don't think she ever got the credit she deserved. My sister [Jackie] would never have become the great hostess she was known for being at the White House if not for my mother's coaching."

It wasn't long before Jack and Jackie decided that Hickory Hill was too big and too remote a location for them, especially with Jack at work at the Senate most of the time. They therefore sold it to Jack's brother Bobby and his wife, Ethel. Jackie and Jack would then settle into a new home in Georgetown on N Avenue.

Jackie couldn't have been surprised by Jack's preoccupation with politics; after all, he had told her shortly after they met that his ambition was to one day be President. As history has shown us, he and his powerful family would stop at nothing until that goal was achieved. He came close to that office in 1956 when he campaigned to be the vice presidential nominee for the Democratic Party. He'd only grown in stature in the Senate and many observers felt he had a strong chance when presidential nominee Adlai Stevenson let the convention select the VP nominee that year. Unfortunately, Jack finished second in the balloting, with Senator Estes Kefauver winning the nomination. The good news for Jack was that the national exposure he received during this time was the greatest of his career thus far. His father, Joe Kennedy, figured that there was still time, that the Eisenhower ticket would have been too great to overcome, anyway. As far as he was concerned, they were still on track.

As a politician, Jack was on the rise. However, as a husband, he left a good deal to be desired. Jackie had made her peace with the fact that he was going to be unfaithful to her and that there wasn't much she could do about it. Despite that realization, Jackie still felt that Jack was a good man who was usually there for her when she needed him. Plus, she enjoyed the power and prestige that came along with being a senator's wife. Also, she had money — "*real* money," as she would call it — and was living well. She felt certain that when children came into their lives Jack would become even more committed to her and to their family. Therefore, when she became pregnant, she was overjoyed.

Jackie shared the news of her pregnancy with Janet during a visit to Merrywood while Jack was in Manhattan on business. Of course, Janet, too, was elated. The two then called Lee in London with the news. This baby would be Janet's first grandchild, and she'd longed for one ever since her daughters had gotten married. She suspected that Jackie was having problems in her marriage, but true to their relationship, she would not pry. She would wait for Jackie to come to her.

As it happened, Janet didn't have long to wait. Having just lost the vice presidential nomination, Jack decided to go on a Mediterranean cruise around Capri and Elba with a few friends, some of whom were women. Janet had to wonder why a married man would go on a cruise with his friends while his wife was home, almost seven months pregnant. It sounded fishy. It was at least some consolation to her that Jackie would now be spending quality time at Hammersmith with her, Hugh, Janet Jr., ten, and Jamie, eight. On the afternoon of August 23, however, Jackie was napping when she was awakened by terrible pain. Alarmed, Janet rushed her to Newport Hospital, where Jackie then had to undergo an emergency cesarean section. Tragically, the baby she delivered was dead. It was a crushing blow to everyone, but no one suffered, of course, more than Jackie.

With the unfolding of such tragedy, Janet fully expected Jack to return to comfort his wife. He did not, however. Janet couldn't understand it. How could he be absent from Jackie's side in such a dire time of need? When Lee said she wanted to fly to the States to be with Jackie, Janet talked her out of it. She said that if Jackie woke up to find Lee at her side, it would be too alarming. She promised to put Jackie on the phone with Lee as soon as she was able to talk. However, Jack was another story; she definitely felt he should have been present.

After a couple of days of stewing over the situation, Janet got on the phone with Bobby Kennedy and let him have it. She would never be afraid to confront the Kennedys, never the least bit intimidated by any of them. "You tell your no-good brother to get here, *now,*" she demanded. Bobby promised to get back to her. When he called her a few hours later, he told her that Jack said he didn't see much reason to return to the States. "What's done is done," Bobby said, quoting his brother. "The baby is lost." Jack was sure, Bobby said, that Jackie was under the best medical care possible. Janet found this reasoning to be inexcusable.

By the 26th, Jackie was finally well enough to hear the terrible news of the stillbirth, but who was going to tell her? One might have thought Janet would have wanted to give her daughter the bad news. However, she decided to stand on ceremony and insist that it be Jack, maybe in hopes that it would compel him to return.

Janet called Rose Kennedy to see if there was anything she could do about her son.

149

Back in September of '53, after the wedding, Rose had written Janet, "Joe and I want to thank you again for Jackie. She was so beautiful to look upon. So charming to meet, that she again captured our hearts. I am sure she and you know by now how deeply we all love her — and with what affection we shall always cherish her." Based on that correspondence and on her other pleasant interactions with Rose, Janet felt certain the Kennedy matriarch would empathize with her and maybe even do something about her wayward son. It was not to be, however. "I'm quite sure Jack knows what's best," was Rose's dispassionate response. "We have had tragedy in our own lives, you know?" Janet thanked her and hung up, deeply disappointed.

When Janet called Bobby again, he wasn't home. She ended up commiserating with Ethel, who said she was going to send Bobby to be with Jackie as soon as she had a chance to talk to him. After getting off the phone, Janet then went to church to pray not only for her daughter but for the soul of her grandchild. She would say that she then felt at peace with the baby's passing, that she realized that, as she put it, "it was part of God's plan and there's no point in even questioning it. We'll never understand it."

Later that evening, Janet went to the hospital with Bobby, barely saying a word to him on the way lest she make a statement about his brother, or even worse, his mother, that she would later regret. She stayed outside Jackie's room when Bobby went in to tell her what had happened. Jackie wanted to know whether the baby was a boy or girl. Bobby told her it was the latter. "I had decided that if I had a girl, I wanted to name her Arabella," Jackie said through her tears. (Though the baby was never christened or legally named, in years to come Jackie would often refer to her as "Arabella.") Bobby lied and told Jackie that they were having a difficult time reaching Jack, "but Eunice is trying her best to locate him." When Bobby left the room, Janet replaced him. Jackie looked up at her mother from her bed and asked about Jack's whereabouts. He would be arriving shortly, Janet assured her. Now Janet was truly angry at Jack. "Mummy saw her job as being Jackie's protector," said Jamie Auchincloss, "and she felt she had failed miserably where this man was concerned. Miserably!"

Ultimately, Jack didn't return to the States until the 28th, and that was only after his friend Senator George Smathers and his father, Joe, warned him that if he ever wanted to run for President and hoped for support from female voters, he'd better get back to his wife. Upon his return, Jack was asked by a reporter if he'd spoken with Jackie. He said he hadn't and then weakly theorized that she hadn't been in touch because she didn't want to ruin his vacation. According to one of her maids, when Janet read her son-in-law's comment in the paper, she folded it and smacked it angrily on the kitchen table. "He is unconscionable," she said. Upset, she then got up and walked to a cabinet, found a bottle of pills — it's not known what they were — and quickly downed a couple with a glass of water. "I'm not sure what Mummy was taking but a lot of women back then had different diet pills that were amphetamines," recalled Jamie Auchincloss, "and they didn't even realize the harm it was doing." It was true that, when depressed, Janet would sometimes lament, "I think my diet pills are wearing off!"

Because Jackie was so distraught about the loss of the baby, at first Janet couldn't bring herself to have an in-depth conversation with her about Jack. The closest they came to it was when Jackie was released from the hospital and was in the company of some trusted relatives at Hammersmith. She wept at the breakfast table and said, "How could I have been so stupid?" Janet reached out and took her daughter's hand. "You're not stupid," she told her. "You just put your trust in the wrong person." Janet told Jackie that she blamed herself. After everything she had gone through with Jackie's father, she said, she never should have allowed Jackie to marry Jack. She was completely to blame, she fretted, not Jackie. Janet also knew what Jackie had to do, which was to end her marriage. However, she was tormented by the idea.

"She was a little frantic about the whole thing," Janet's longtime Newport friend Eileen Gillespie Slocum once recalled. Slocum lived in the Harold Carter Brown House, a Gothic Revival–style mansion built in the 1890s. Married to journalist and diplomat John Jermain Slocum, she was hosting a dinner for the Republican State Central Committee at her home when Janet pulled her aside to talk about Jackie's dilemma. "She said, 'She doesn't have any children and she doesn't have any money of her own. I told her she should divorce Jack, and now I don't know that this was the best advice.' She was concerned not just about Jackie's marriage but by the notion of maybe giving her more bad advice. 'What do *you* think?' she asked me. I told her to stick to her guns. If she thought Jackie should end her marriage, she should encourage her to do so. 'Jacqueline will always find a way to end up on her feet — just like her mother,' I told her."

DIFFERING VIEWS ABOUT INFIDELITY

In November 1956, because Jackie had been feeling depressed about the loss of her child and by her husband's recent betrayal, she went to London to visit Lee. Biting her nails to the quick and chain-smoking, Jackie seemed on the verge of a breakdown. She said what she really needed was just some quality time with her sister. Lee could be comforting and a good listener, no matter the sisters' "little competition," as they sometimes called it. Lee wanted to be present for her sister during this extremely difficult time. However, when Jackie told her that she'd been thinking of ending her marriage, Lee wasn't convinced that it was such a good idea. Jack had so much going for him, she reminded her sister. He had power, money, was good-looking, and had, thus far, afforded her a good life. Lee said she wished *she* had a spouse like Jack, someone in whom she could have total faith that he would do something big with his life and, by extension, hers. It didn't matter to Lee that Jack was unfaithful in his marriage. "Daddy did it to Mummy and it all worked out fine," she told Jackie.

It all worked out fine? For who? It could be argued that *none* of it had worked out "fine" for anyone. Jackie was astonished by Lee's logic. It was the first time she'd ever heard her sister say that adultery was acceptable. In Jackie's mind — as in Janet's — it was completely verboten. Jackie did go through a strange phase in college at Vassar, where she tried to make light of her father's penchant for women. She would point out the mothers of different classmates — most of them married — and ask Black Jack whether he'd had sex with them. "That one, Daddy?" she would ask. He would say yea or nay. "Well, how about that one over there?" In the end, though, she realized that she didn't approve of it at all, and that she didn't think it was funny, either.

How could two women who'd been raised by the same mother and exposed to the same cheating father have such differing views of infidelity? Obviously, Jackie took after her mother in this regard, and Lee her father. It caused Jackie to wonder what kind of marriage her sister had with Michael Canfield. She wouldn't have to wonder about it for long, though.

One afternoon while Jackie was visiting, the Canfields received an invitation to go shooting at the estate of Lord and Lady Lambton, who had a country home in Wooler, Northumberland. A jolly group was organized, which included, as well as Jackie, Lee, and Michael, two people Lee and Michael had just met through the Lambtons, Prince Stanislaw Radziwill and his wife, Princess Grace. They were all to travel by railway car together to the Lambtons' for the weekend. Once at their estate, everyone had a restful and fun weekend. Lee was immediately attracted to the courtly Prince Radziwill, though she

155

would later admit to also being intimidated by him. "Stas [pronounced "Stash," as he was known to his friends and family] was so brooding, so serious, I was absolutely terrified," she would recall. "I didn't say one word to him the whole weekend. But then our hostess organized a game of charades and dressed him up in one of her old slips. He wasn't so terrifying anymore — this dignified, masculine figure in all of those pink lace frills. I discovered he had a marvelous sense of humor, a great sense of the ridiculous."

Despite the fact that Lee recalls she didn't "say one word" to Stas, others present remember it differently. They remember them as having a natural rapport while isolating themselves and getting to know each other. Jackie couldn't help but notice Michael's unhappy reaction to his wife's growing fascination with Radziwill. She was troubled by it; something didn't seem quite right.

After the weekend was over and all had returned to London, Jackie had a conversation with Michael about his marriage. It was then that she learned that he believed Lee was cheating on him. "She couldn't believe it," said one Bouvier relative. "She got into an argument with Michael, saying that her sister would never do such a thing. 'That's not how we were raised,' is what she told him even though she'd certainly started having some doubts about Lee by this time. Through his tears, Michael said, 'Well, I don't know how Mummy raised you, I only know that Lee has been unfaithful, and more than once.' He was devastated."

Jackie and Lee never really aired their differences relating to Michael Canfield. They were beginning to fall into a pattern of not discussing issues between them, just glossing over them. Though this behavior would cause them to harbor resentment and suppress anger, it was becoming their way. By the time Jackie left London, she wasn't speaking to Lee. She returned to the States feeling more uneasy than she had when she left, but now not only about her marriage but her sister's as well. At a Mother-Daughter Tea with Janet she told her that she was angry with Lee, but decided not to go into detail about the reasons. If Lee wanted to confide in Janet about what was going on in her marriage, it would have been fine with Jackie. She just knew that she didn't want to have to be the one to tell their mother that Lee was probably cheating on her husband.

At the beginning of December '56, Lee and Michael flew to the States to spend the holidays with the family at Merrywood. The environment at the Auchincloss homestead was about as chilly as the weather, what with the two sisters freezing each other out. By this time, Michael and Lee were also not speaking. Janet didn't know what was going on, why everyone was so upset. She didn't like it one bit, though, especially for this week. At great expense to her and Hugh, she had sent for a favorite chef from France to come to prepare holiday meals for the family. He had planned an extravagant menu for every night of the week, beginning with tonight's feast of beef bourguignon and chocolate soufflé. It seemed a shame to ruin the evening. Therefore, Janet gathered everyone into the parlor and told them that she, Hugh, and the rest of the family — Janet, Jamie, and any other relative who came to call — only had the opportunity to see the sisters once in a while, and that whatever was troubling them would have to wait until after the holidays. She wasn't going to allow it to interfere with their time together, especially given the expense of flying the chef over from Europe, paying for his services for a week, and keeping him at Merrywood. She then poured all of the adults a glass of wine and, standing in the middle of the living room, ceremoniously raised her glass and asked everyone to do the same. "We are all we have," she said, "and, thusly, it's always going to be us against the world. So . . . *to family*," she proclaimed. Hugh agreed. "To family," he repeated. Jack Kennedy raised his glass and repeated, "To family. God bless America." Michael then added, "Oh, and God save the queen, too. Let's not forget

158

about her!" Though everyone laughed, there was still something about the moment that seemed forced and halfhearted.

Even without the familial upheaval, Janet was already on edge; she had just quit smoking in deference to Hugh, who'd been forced to stop due to his asthma. She'd been a chain-smoker, so it wasn't easy. Sometimes she would take a cigarette and hold it under her nose horizontally and inhale deeply, just to breathe in its scent. Jamie would say that he believed his mother began to drink more after she stopped smoking, and others in the family have agreed. Of course, as always, there was a lot of pill-popping going on, too.

Later that same evening, Janet found Michael out on the beach, diving into the river while lit only by the moon. As he got out of the water to greet his mother-in-law in his baggy, checkered swim trunks with a big smile on his face, his hair slicked back, he must have looked like a teenager. Janet would later say it was in that moment that her heart went out to him. He was barely thirty and didn't have a clue as to who he was or what he wanted to do with his life. Ordinarily, this kind of man would infuriate her, but for some reason Michael brought out the motherly instincts in her, as he did for most women. As they sat on a blanket together she bummed a smoke from him.

"You can't imagine how much I need this

right now," Janet told Michael as she took a deep drag on the cigarette. As he would later recall it in separate accounts to his friends Michael Guinzburg and Terrance Landow, it was then that Janet had a good talk with her son-in-law. She told him she genuinely liked him, but that she felt he was going to have to work much harder to keep "my Lee" interested. "You're probably the best thing that's ever happened to her," Janet allowed. "We're all so glad you are around." Michael would recall that Janet smiled at him as he put his head on her shoulder. He said that as the two then sat quietly with each other, they watched the stars shoot across the horizon.

Prince Stanislaw Radziwill

"I have always wanted to really visit Poland," Lee Canfield dreamily observed. "I mean, *really* visit it, you know? Get to know its culture, its art." She was curled up on a sofa in her home at 45 Chester Square with Prince Stanislaw Radziwill lying on the floor in front of her, his head on the couch just inches away from her lap. Meanwhile, sitting next to him was his wife, Grace. Next to her, also stretched out on the floor, was Michael Canfield. On a nearby chair were seated their friends Terrance and Betty Landow, Betty on her husband's lap. Lee looked down into Stas's eyes and observed that one really doesn't know a country until one lives there. She added that when she had the opportunity to live in Paris she began to understand its culture and its ways. She said that she now wanted to live in Poland. Looking at her with admiration, Stas said it was a lovely thought. All of this romanticism was a little more than Michael could take, and he could usually take a lot! "Not once, in the entire time I've known you have you *ever* mentioned wanting to live in Poland, of all places," he said, not even glancing at his wife. "You're so full of shit, Lee," he added. "Poland? Please. *Poland?* Oh my God! *Poland?*" Lee took umbrage at his condemnation of her. She angrily told him that she'd said in the past a hundred times — *"a million times, even!"* — she wanted to live in Poland. Then, turning to Stas, she told him that Michael didn't know what he was talking about: "I'd *adore* to live in Poland." Stas just smiled. It didn't really matter, he said, since he'd been exiled from Poland, "and we'll likely never be living there."

Betty Landow recalled, "Michael just shook his head and rolled his eyes. 'That's it. I'm done with you now,' he told Lee before taking off. Terry and I then watched Lee and Stas and wondered how long it would take before we'd hear that they were together. It was just in the air. Everyone knew it. Stas's *wife* knew it, you could tell by looking at her. It was as if we were all playing a bizarre parlor

161

game, which was, 'Let's act as if this thing we all know full well is about to happen is not about to happen.' "

Lee had been fascinated with Stas from the beginning and, as she and Michael began spending more time with him and Grace, she became determined to know him even better. Prince Stanisław Albrecht "Stas" Radziwiłł was from one of the wealthiest, most powerful dynasties of the fifteenth and sixteenth centuries. Born on July 21, 1914, he was fifty-two, nineteen years Lee's senior. Grace, whose full name was Grace Maria Kolin, was Stas's second wife. She, too, had come from old money, her father a wealthy shipping magnate from Yugoslavia.

Hailing from Volhynia, Poland, and raised in Warsaw, Stas was one of four children born to Janusz Franciszek, Prince Radziwill, and Anna, Princess Lubomirska. After World War I, his father led the Polish Conservative Party in restored Poland. His mother (also from a Polish noble family) would eventually die in a Soviet labor camp. The former deputy governor of the province of Stanislawow, Stas was left in dire financial straits after the Nazi invasion of Poland in 1939. With only the clothes on his back, he drove to the Swiss border and tried to find accommodations at a hotel once favored by his royal family. When it was learned that he had no money, he was turned away. He then spent months living in shelters in Switzerland before meeting a woman who had wealth of her own, Rose de Monléon. They married in 1940 and divorced five years later, but not without a little of her money becoming his own. He then married Grace Maria Kolin, in 1946.

That same year, Stas and Grace went to London in hopes of using the family's connections there to embark on business ventures that would replenish the family's dwindled fortune. "They really had to start over," said their son, John Radziwill, who they had in 1947. (His full name is Jan Stanislaw Albrycht Radziwill.) "They rebuilt from zero. But my father was determined and formidable. He had a lot of charm, was amusing. People liked my father."

"It didn't take Stas long to begin making his own fortune in real estate after forming a partnership with property developer Felix Fenston," explained Chauncey Parker III. "Eventually, he applied for and was afforded a British citizenship. However, in doing so, he would forfeit his right to be called a Prince of the Holy Roman Empire, a title his family had carried since the sixteenth century. Still, he continued to demand that he be addressed as Prince Radziwill, even though the idea of it raised more than a few eyebrows in the UK."

Stas was a round, short man with a large personality. His pencil-thin mustache did little to distinguish a face that was anything but handsome in the classic sense. There was something about him, though, that fascinated Lee. Part of it had to do with the aristocratic way he comported himself — "I have never seen someone with so many manners and so many good habits" — but, of course, the biggest attraction had to do with his royal background. It didn't matter what people thought; as far as Lee was concerned, he was a true Polish nobleman with an ancient title, and he had the unquestionable pedigree to prove it, unlike Michael, who may — or may not — have been a descendant of Prince George or, *maybe,* Lord Acton.

Stas made his money by being smart on his feet and finding ways to be in the right place at the right time. He had an accent so thick one had to concentrate to understand him. While he was not articulate, he talked and talked and talked and could be completely engaging and persuasive. He had an aura about him, and Lee couldn't take her eyes off him. It quickly became clear that there was no way Michael could compete with Stas, on any level.

By this time, the beginning of '57, poor Michael Canfield, only thirty, was beaten down and pretty much out of the game. He was tired of trying to be someone Lee would respect and love. His cushy job was also at its end now that his boss, Winthrop Aldrich, was retiring. Michael would be able to stay on at the embassy long enough to train his replacement, the incoming ambassador's assistant, but would then be forced to return to Harper's. The thought of that drove him straight to the bottle.

For her part, Lee was frustrated by Michael's basic disconnect from what she craved, which was real passion. "Women want to feel desired," she kept telling him. He didn't get it, though. For example, around this time the Landows were at Heathrow Airport with Michael, seeing off Lee, who was going to Paris for a week. When Lee went to kiss Michael on the lips, he turned away. She ended up brushing him on the cheek. Everyone noticed. "My God, Michael, when will you learn to kiss me like a man? Why must you insist on humiliating me?" As Michael left the airport terminal, he turned to Terrance and grumbled, "That bitch. Who would want to kiss her? Not me! Kiss like a man? Fuck her. Who does she think she is?"

By this time, everything about Lee seemed to annoy Michael, even her closeness to Jackie. For instance, it unnerved him that the sisters would whisper in each other's ears, to the exclusion of everyone else. Once, the three of them were in a rowboat, paddling along a lake. As Michael rowed, the sisters sat in the bow of the boat whispering to each other with great intensity. He figured surely they had to have been discussing some urgent family business. When he leaned in to hear what they were saying, he learned that they were talking about . . . *glove*s. "Perfect drivel" is how he later described it to Blair Fuller; "they have nothing on their minds but perfect drivel. They never have anything substantive to say about anything, and I've had it with the both of them."

Funny how things change. Michael had once been a perfect mirror reflection of Lee, who had also been accused of not knowing what she wanted to do with her life, who had often been thought of as joyless in Jackie's shadow. However, Lee had undergone a huge transformation since arriving in Europe. Now she presented herself as a completely free spirit with a real zest for new experiences. She was passionate about life and seemed to want to squeeze in as much as possible, whether it was art or design or fine foods or even sex. Something about Europe had invigorated her, made her come alive. Some felt that getting away from Janet was the best thing Lee ever could have done. "Oh my God, yes, that's very true," said Tom Guinzburg. "The distance between her and her mother changed everything for Lee. Also, I would venture to say that the distance between her and Jackie helped tremendously as well. She was able to become her own person in Europe, absolutely."

She was only twenty-three. Maybe Lee had married the wrong man, and now just needed a way out. If so, that could only happen after she found someone to take his place. She was not going to be alone in the world, not at her age; she needed someone to take care of her, or at least that's what she'd been raised to believe. Stas was a stocky, older guy who wasn't as handsome as Michael, nor was he graceful in the least; he was rather lumbering. However, he knew how to please a woman, apparently, or, at the very least, he knew how to please Lee. Sleeping with him behind Michael's back wasn't a difficult decision for her. She felt she had no choice. She wasn't getting it from Michael, and she was a young woman with desires. She wasn't going to tell Stas no. Once she was in it with him, she was in it with him for good. She didn't care about anything or anyone else. "I *deserve* this," she told her friends, "and goddamn it, I'm going to have it."

Therefore, by the beginning of the summer of 1957, Lee and Stas were in the midst of an all-out affair. However, she was still married and had commitments to keep, such as a cruise around Italy with Michael that had been planned earlier. Also on the books was an embassy reception for Adlai Stevenson, and then a party given by Mike Todd to celebrate the opening of his film *Around the World in 80 Days*. On August 3, though, Lee received a telegram from her cousin Michel Bouvier — her uncle Bud's son — which shook her to the core: her father, Black Jack, was in a coma.

JACK BOUVIER — R.I.P.

Lately, when Jackie and Lee spoke to their father, Jack Bouvier, on the telephone, he would ramble on in such a way that they believed his drinking was out of control. When Jackie saw him in East Hampton back in July, he didn't seem well but she assumed that his haggard appearance was a consequence of years of alcohol abuse. Yusha, who had also seen Jack, disagreed. He felt that Jack was seriously ill. It wasn't long before they learned that Jack was suffering from liver cancer, fast-moving and deadly.

As soon as Jackie heard that Jack was in a coma in New York, she rushed to be at his side. She and Jack Kennedy dashed into his room just after he passed away. He was sixty-six. Sobbing, Jackie stayed at her beloved father's side for a long while until, finally, a nurse asked her and Jack to leave. Lee and Stas arrived shortly thereafter.

The funeral took place on August 6 at St. Patrick's Cathedral in New York. Just a couple of dozen people attended, including, of course, his children and other relatives. A few women, strangers to the family, sat in the back of the church, each seeming quite upset.

Lee was beside herself with grief, whereas Jackie was more stoic, as was her wont. "I love you, Lee," she was overheard telling her sister when Black Jack was laid to rest at St. Philomena's Cemetery in East Hampton, "and we will get through this."

Janet was spared the decision as to whether or not to go the church funeral. It just so happened that she was on a cruise with Hugh, Janet Jr., and Jamie. "We got the call, somehow," Jamie recalled, "maybe when we hit a port. Was Mummy upset? To a degree. I think she would always have a lot of emotion attached to Jack Bouvier. However, she didn't like talking about it. She had made her peace with all of it when she married my father. She was sad for Jackie and Lee, though. She knew how much they idolized Jack. We all knew."

A few weeks later, when Janet and the family returned from their cruise, Jackie and Lee went back to Hammersmith Farm to welcome them home, along with many other loved ones, including Yusha and his fiancée, Alice, and Nini Gore Auchincloss, Hugh's daughter, and her new husband, Newton Steers (a financier worth almost $3 million). The family spent the entire evening talking and laughing and trying to enjoy their connection to one another, but it was strained because no one dared mention Jack Bouvier's recent death. However, Janet, always the perfect hostess, was still determined that everyone enjoy a nice night. She made sure the cook prepared an enormous amount of gourmet food for everyone's enjoyment. At one point, she and Hugh began dancing on the patio off the Deck Room to the music of Mel Tormé and Peggy Lee courtesy of Hugh's new stereo record player. Soon after, Jack and Jackie, Michael and Lee, Yusha and Alice joined in, and then everyone else began to partner up and dance together under a full moon and twinkling stars.

By about four o'clock in the morning, everyone was completely exhausted. It was time to retire. While the family members said good night to one another, they noticed Janet was nowhere to be found. With flashlights in hand, the Bouvier sisters walked down the sloping lawn out to the pier, where they found their mother sitting alone on the dock, where she often found peace of mind. They joined her. Janet, Jackie, and Lee then chatted almost until sunrise, the specifics of their conversation known only to the three of them.

BANISHED

After Jack Bouvier's funeral, Lee and Michael spent his thirty-first birthday on September 8 at Hammersmith. Janet could plainly see that things were no better between her daughter and the son-in-law of whom she had lately grown so fond. Around this time, someone told Janet that Lee was having an affair with Stas. It seems that it was probably Michael, but there is no clear proof that it was — it could also have been Jackie.

The blowup between Janet and Lee over Stas was as explosive as the mother and daughter had ever had with each other. Janet couldn't believe Lee would cheat on Michael. It was such a total violation of everything she believed she had taught her daughters about the sanctity of marriage, especially given what she'd been through with their father. She'd recently tried to counsel Jackie in the face of an unfaithful spouse, but in that case her daughter was the victim. To now find the tables turned in Lee's marriage, that it was Michael who was the wronged party, was upsetting to Janet. She had met Stas once, and it hadn't gone well. "Why, he's nothing but a European version of your father," she told Lee. Lee would later say that while she was indignant at the remark, it "made me love him all the more."

Making things worse, Janet had "let" Lee have Michael, hadn't she? She'd made the decision that if Lee thought she was defying her mother by marrying him, it would be actually good for her psyche. Lee didn't know that Janet had done so, but to Janet, the (arguably unreasonable) question was: "*This* is how she thanks me?"

However, Lee was Janet's child, and as much as Janet liked Michael, she now knew he had to go. The only way she could protect her daughter from herself, at least as she saw it, was to send poor Michael on his lonely way. In doing so, she would also be protecting her family from what promised to be a huge scandal. "I'm going to be very sorry to lose you, Michael," she told him, according to what he would later recall to Terrance Landow.

Landow remembered, "Michael said that he and Janet were sharing a smoke on the beach, as they often did, when she suddenly said, 'Michael, I want you to pack your bags in the morning and leave Hammersmith Farm.' He thought she was angry at him. 'But I didn't even *do* anything, Mummy,' he protested in that childlike way of his. She said, 'My point exactly. Here what's going to happen. You will walk away from your marriage and you will never look back. You have lost the fight, my boy. There's nothing left for you here,' she told him. 'If you don't leave now, I fear for what will happen to you, to my daughter, and to this entire family. It's quite simple, Michael,' she said, 'you don't belong here any longer.' Crying, Michael hugged her and said, 'No one has ever cared about me. Only you, Mummy. You're the only one. No one else.' He then went back to his and Lee's room, packed his things, and left, right then and there. He didn't even wait for sunrise. He called a cab and just left.

"The next morning, at least from what I later heard," said Terrance Landow, "Lee asked, 'Mummy, where's Michael?' Janet, as cold as ice, said, 'He's gone, Lee. I took care of it.' Lee didn't ask any questions. She just turned around and went back up to her room."

Lee and Michael would eventually divorce.

In June 1960, Michael would marry Frances Laura Charteris — who would, later in life, become Duchess of Marlborough. Michael was bitter, though. Around that same time, he ran into his former brother-in-law Jamie at a party in Manhattan. He was very drunk. He said that, once, while he and Lee were on vacation with Jack and Jackie, he overheard Lee having sex with Jack Kennedy in the next room. He then told Gore Vidal the same story, and added that Lee even bragged to him about it. Vidal would then write about it in his memoir, *Palimpsest*. Years later, Gore's sister, Nini, repeated the story, but with a twist. She insisted that Lee told her she had sex with Jack while she was staying with the Kennedys after Jackie gave birth to Caroline! Nini says that Lee told her she'd left the bedroom door open, and that Michael could, therefore, hear her and Jack going at it. Could any variation on this story possibly be true? Whatever its veracity, these damaging anecdotes are noteworthy only in that they were bandied about not by strangers or enemies or gossipmongers, but by family members! If Jackie heard these stories — and it's doubtful that she hadn't, considering that everyone else in the family seemed to be aware of them — they had to have made some impact on her, at the very least causing her to wonder if they were true.

In December 1960, Michael Canfield would die of a heart attack while on a flight to London, an overdose of alcohol and pills apparently precipitating his demise. He was only forty-three. Ironically, one of the men reputed to have been his father — Prince George — also had an airline-related death at a young age; he died in a plane crash at thirty-nine.

■ ■ ■ ■

PART THREE: HEADY TIMES

■ ■ ■ ■

LEE MARRIES HER PRINCE

By the beginning of 1958, Lee Bouvier Canfield, who was about to turn twenty-four, was feeling more alone and desperate than ever. Her marriage to Michael, a huge disappointment, was now over. Though she and Jackie had recently posed for a fashion spread in *Ladies' Home Journal,* she knew that she was still just basking in the refracted glory of her sister's growing popularity. The Bouvier sisters had both been bequeathed about $80,000 after taxes from their father's estate, which was a sizable amount. However, it was hopelessly tied up in probate court. Frightened for the future, Lee asked her Grampy Lee for an allowance of $3,000 a month, saying she could not live on less than that amount. He refused the specific request, giving her far less.

By this time, Jackie had given birth to her first child, Caroline Bouvier Kennedy. Jackie and Jack were, of course, overjoyed. The family — along with a nurse, cook, butler, and maid — would settle in a lovely four-story Federal house, an early nineteenth-century home in Georgetown, just a few blocks from Janet and Hugh.

Lee was happy for her sister and appreciated the gesture of having her niece named after her, but she couldn't help feeling melancholy at the same time. In her mind, Jackie always had it so good. First, she married a United States senator. Then she had a baby with him. In addition to the Georgetown home, she had an apartment in Boston with him and they had just bought a home in Hyannis Port in the Kennedy compound. Of course, there had been the tragic stillbirth, but Jackie was such a survivor, Lee mused, she'd gotten past it in the great tradition of Bouvier women. Jackie also seemed to have taken Lee's advice to try to overlook Jack's philandering. Not only that, but Lee felt that Janet was much more proud of Jackie than she was of her and, as she put it to one relative, "still loves her more than me, as always." All of this good fortune for Jackie just made Lee feel a little frustrated and unhappy. As if it wasn't bad enough living in a foreign country away from all of her friends and family members, she was now also involved with a married man.

While Lee believed Janet preferred Jackie over her, one person who didn't was Stas. As far as he was concerned, there could be no comparison. He viewed Jackie as more circumspect and guarded than Lee, more concerned about how she was being perceived. "[Lee's] bawdy in a way that many women these days aren't," he said, "yet she also has a certain kind of class, a certain refinement that's a paradox, really. It makes her more intriguing."

The prince was right about Lee. While she could swear and drink and have mad fun until all hours of the night, she also had more than a few habits that spoke to the kind of decorum to which even Stas's royal colleagues couldn't stake claim. For instance, after she flushed the toilet at home, her maid would always somehow appear from nowhere and rush into the bathroom to drop a gardenia into the bowl. "It keeps things fresh," Lee explained to Stas, who was completely dumbfounded by it. Typical of their relationship, though, he could get away with a gentle ribbing of her. Once in a restaurant when Lee rose from her seat to use the powder room, Stas asked, "Are you forgetting something, my dear?" as he reached into his vest pocket. From it, he pulled out a gardenia and handed it to her. She found it hilarious.

It would be a bit of a winding road to get to the altar, though. Before he took Lee's hand, the prince decided he wanted her marriage to Michael Canfield annulled. It was the only way Stas, a devout Catholic, would be able to marry his intended in the Church. Stas had been down this road before. He had tried to have his first marriage to Rose annulled so that he could marry his second wife, Grace, in the Church. However, when he had trouble securing that annulment, he went ahead and married Grace anyway in a civil ceremony. When the annulment finally came through, the marriage to Grace was already over. However, since that second marriage had never been recognized by the Church, and the first one had been officially annulled, Stas could now marry in the Catholic Church, provided Lee got an annulment of *her* marriage.

At this same time, Jackie and Lee finally had a meeting of the minds over Lee's marriage. Lee told her sister that she was disappointed that she had not been there for her when she was grappling with what to do about Michael. Instead, Jackie was, at least in Lee's estimation, judgmental and sanctimonious about Lee's affair with Stas. According to one of their intimates, Lee asked Jackie, "Haven't you ever done anything crazy for love?" Jackie answered quickly, "For love, yes. But not for this. This isn't love." Lee insisted that she *did* love Stas, though. She wanted her sister to accept it and just wish her happiness. What could Jackie do? Though she would never change her mind about infidelity, all she really ever wanted was for Lee to

180

be happy. The deed was done, anyway: the broken-down book editor was out of the picture and the dashing prince was in it. Therefore, Jackie said she would help Lee secure an annulment from Michael so that she would then be able to marry Stas in the Catholic Church. This gesture would, hopefully, set things straight between the sisters.

Jackie asked her father-in-law, Joe Kennedy, for advice as to how to proceed with an annulment. He suggested that Lee enlist a friend of the family's, Cardinal Spellman in New York. Therefore, in June of '58, Lee wrote to the cardinal to ask if he would begin the process. Lee then retained an attorney whose specialty was Vatican law. She stated that the marriage should be annulled because she was never really sure of the wisdom of marrying Michael and had questions as to whether or not they should have had children.

Then there was a surprising twist: Lee got pregnant with Stas's child. Now the situation had suddenly become even more complicated. How would it look if she had a child out of wedlock? The annulment papers had been filed, but who knew how long it would take to process them? Janet wouldn't hear of her daughter having a baby without the benefit of marriage, and Lee wouldn't have allowed it, either. "So, my dad left my mom for Lee," recalled John Radziwill, Stas's oldest by Grace Maria Kolin. "It was sad for the family because my father had been the love of my mother's life. But when Lee broke the news, he said, 'That's it. I'm going to marry you.' It's always a shame when a family breaks up, but Dad was with Lee long before she became pregnant. I was upset, yes, but I certainly didn't hold it against Lee. My father made his choice."

Since Stas, of course, was still a prince, marrying him would make Lee a princess. Again, there was some question about the authenticity of his princely title, just as there had been with Michael's lineage, but at least there was more historical and factual accuracy to Stas's claim. If she married him, Lee would become Princess Lee Radziwill.

Lee eagerly married Stas in a civil ceremony on March 19, 1959. They then had a small reception at Jack and Jackie's home; maybe twenty-five people attended.

After the wedding, Stas purchased a home at No. 4 Buckingham Place, a small street in London that is parallel to Buckingham Palace. Lee designed the place beautifully with eighteenth-century Polish, French, and Italian antiques long owned by the Radziwill family. (The home would be later be redecorated by the famous designer Renzo Mongiardino, who would use many yards of hand-blocked Indian fabrics to help create living spaces with a Turkish influence.) Then, on August 4, 1959, Lee gave birth to her and

Stas's first child, Anthony Stanislaw Albert, in Lausanne, Switzerland. For anyone inspecting the calendar while wondering about her pregnancy, the Radziwills said that the baby was born three months prematurely. She was now happier, Lee said, than she'd ever been. Those who knew her well, though, couldn't help but wonder how long would that last.

CAMPAIGN TRAIL

Still uncomfortable with politics, Jackie Kennedy seemed unable to find a way to balance her husband's public career with her own fierce and innate need for privacy. She did the best she could, though, while also stumping for Jack across the country in the fall of '58 as he ran for the Senate again, this time as the incumbent. He would win the seat handily, defeating his Republican opponent, Boston lawyer Vincent J. Celeste, by a wide margin.

When Jackie had enough of the Kennedys, she would retreat to Merrywood or Hammersmith with Caroline and use that time away to recharge her battery. Janet was proud of her. She knew how difficult it was for her daughter to live such a public life and was impressed by the many ways she rose to the challenge. In January of 1960, when Jack announced his intention to run for President,

Janet and Hugh (both still staunch Republicans) were present at his side along with Jackie. "This is a proud moment for our family," Janet said. Though she smiled broadly and put forth much enthusiasm for the public, secretly she found the prospects of a JFK presidency disconcerting. She would soon find the process of campaigning for office to be overwhelmingly invasive, foreign to her in every way. For instance, when Jackie began hosting teas in her home on N Street, Janet was perplexed. "Perfect strangers in the home sitting on your antique furniture?" she asked at the time. "It *is* a new world, isn't it?"

Julian Balridge was at Merrywood with his parents, Carolyn and Edward, for another party that Janet hosted for Jack and Jackie in the days after Jack announced his candidacy. Janet had spent the day making certain that, as she put it, "everything is just so." Always an exacting woman, Janet considered no detail too small to address, even after the guests had arrived. Julian recalls her walking by the dining room, stopping, and doing a double take. "Those candles are not right," she told one of the maids as she stared at a huge floral display in the middle of the table.

"But, madam, you *said* you wanted candles," the maid told her.

"Come with me," Janet said as she took the young woman by the elbow. They walked to the table and stood at its side in front of the elaborate centerpiece. Janet then told the maid that the wicks on the candles were too big at two inches. They should be no more than an eighth of an inch, "otherwise the whole centerpiece will go up in flames." She asked the woman to go into the kitchen, get a ruler and a pair of scissors, and cut the wicks down to size. The maid scurried off. At that moment, Janet saw Julian Balridge's mother, Carolyn, walk into the dining room. That's when she turned on the charm. "Oh, my *darling*," she exclaimed with a radiant smile. "How lovely to see you!"

Despite Janet's instant composure, Julian Balridge recalls her as being anxious not only about how well the party was going but about what the future might hold for her family. "This is just not us," Janet fretted to Carolyn. "We are not the Kennedys. I am private; Jacqueline is private; Lee is private; Hughdie, Yusha, Janet, Jamie — all of us in our family are very private people." She said that she wasn't sure how they would ever be able to become public personalities. "It's impossible," she concluded.

Janet then talked about her own contribution to the campaign; she said that she'd recently gone to Kentucky to stump for Jack. When asked if it was at JFK's request, Janet said no. Apparently, a college roommate of hers who hailed from Kentucky was a big

185

supporter of Jack's. She telephoned Janet and said she was concerned that Jack wasn't doing well in her state. She wondered if one of the Kennedy relatives might go to Kentucky to stump. Janet made some calls and was told that no one was available. Her former roommate then told her that it didn't matter who came, just as long as it was someone connected to Jack. She suggested that Janet might be the one to do it. "I was completely floored," Janet said. "Me on the campaign trail? Heavens no!" She called Jack and asked him what he thought. "He was very much amused," Janet recalled, and he encouraged her. "So I did it," she said, explaining that Lois Combs, the daughter of Kentucky governor Bertram Thomas Combs, drove her to the districts pinpointed for her participation. At each stop, she shook a lot of hands and attended a great many ladies' teas. In doing so, she felt about as uncomfortable as "I do when I have to make a tape recording of my voice. But, anyway, for Jack, I did it even though I felt very foolish." She proudly added that he carried two counties in which she campaigned. (In the end, JFK did lose the state, however.) She therefore understood how "intoxicating" politics could be. However, "a person simply can't do this every day, especially a woman!"

At that moment, Jackie swept into the room, wearing a simple black shift with white

186

pearls. She looked understated but glamorous with her bouffant hairstyle and meticulous makeup, including bright pink 1960s-style lipstick. Mother and daughter then engaged in a conversation about the new china being used at Hammersmith, Flora Danica, said to be the most expensive in the world, with each piece priced at between five hundred and a thousand dollars. Jackie's question was how could Janet trust that her guests wouldn't be careless and break one of the pieces. Janet explained that she does her research and plans the guest list accordingly. If she suspects someone might be careless with her expensive belongings, that person simply will not be invited. "Never have anyone in your home that you can't trust with your good china," she said. She added that this was precisely why she took issue with the teas Jackie was hosting at N Street. Jackie listened intently and nodded. "Mummy is so smart with these things," she told the others.

"My father was bowled over by both Janet and Jackie," recalled Julian Balridge. "He also believed JFK would make a great president. 'This country needs shaking up, anyway,' Jackie said. 'Jack has a great platform,' she told us. 'You should listen to what he has to say. He wants to make this country great and he knows just how to do it, too.' After she left our side, Janet told my mother she was concerned about Jackie's wardrobe. 'She needs to look more traditional, maybe like that woman on *Leave It to Beaver.* She was speaking of Barbara Billingsley. 'Now, *she* looks like a First Lady,' Janet said. 'Don't you agree?' "

On July 13, 1960, Jack Kennedy won the nomination of his party at the Democratic Convention in Los Angeles; later, Lyndon Johnson would be announced as his running mate. Jackie was in Hyannis Port at the time. Janet, Hugh, Jamie, and Janet Jr. were with her, keeping her company and watching the exciting events on TV. "This is when we knew that it was getting real," said Jamie Auchincloss, who was thirteen at the time. "I also remember one of the press conferences after Jack won. It was me and my sister Janet Jr. [fifteen] and Mummy and Daddy along with, of course, Jackie. Jack was in New York. I was standing there with flashbulbs going off and reporters shouting questions and I remember thinking, *Whose life is this?* Mummy was beside herself with pride that this was happening to us. She couldn't stop telling Jackie how proud she was of her. 'There's nothing you could do that would make me any prouder of you than I am in this moment,' she told her."

The excitement just continued to grow for the family, especially after Jackie officially announced that she was expecting her second child. The baby was due in November.

"THE BITTER AND THE SWEET"

By the summer of 1960, Lee and Stas had arrived in America from Europe for an extended visit in order to share in the family's excitement about Jack Kennedy's campaign. Stas eagerly became involved, strategizing with organizers about ways to secure the Polish vote. He stumped from Los Angeles to Boston, barely getting through each event while battling extreme performance anxiety. He almost fainted before giving certain speeches. Jack was extremely grateful; he could see how tough it was on Stas. "There are an awful lot of Poles in America," Lee told the Associated Press, "and Stas talked to most of them." As a result, Jack and Stas would go on to become great friends. Jackie would also be appreciative of her new brother-in-law's help and, after the election, presented him with a drawing she'd done of a map of the USA with a figure of Stas going coast to coast. She inscribed it with the words: "You really did do it, Stas!" She'd gotten over the way Stas had come into their lives, and was now just wanting to put any unhappiness about it behind them. Janet agreed. She hadn't been a fan of Stas because of the way he came into her daughter's life, but once she saw how devoted he was to family ideals and goals, she began to accept him.

Lee traveled with Stas as much as possible.

However, because — like Jackie — she was also pregnant with a baby due in November, Stas wanted to curtail her activity. Therefore, Lee enjoyed the Democratic Convention from the sidelines and then went back to her suite at the Beverly Hilton early to giddily call Jackie with her observations of the event. It was an exciting time for the sisters with no disagreements between them, just a sense that their lives were really working out for them.

Some observers found it unusual that, at this time, Lee asked the media to refer to her as "Princess Lee Radziwill." It was as if she wanted to ensure that the press understood that Jackie wasn't the only Bouvier woman of distinction. For instance, at Merrywood shortly after the convention, Janet and Lee were confronted by reporters at the front entrance to the property. One writer, Eddy Gilmore of the Associated Press, called out, "Any comments, Mrs. Canfield?" Lee corrected him. "It's *Princess* Lee *Radziwill,*" she said, "and, no, I have nothing to say!" Janet didn't think Lee's comment was appropriate. "This is *Jackie's* moment, not yours," she was overheard telling Lee. Lee flinched, Janet's rebuke obviously stinging. Standing corrected, Lee then went back to the reporter and said, "It's not that I want to appear elusive or uncooperative. It's just that I shrink from talking about myself. I believe that a person should have accomplished *something* on her own before she starts giving interviews." Janet stood by, pleased. "So . . . that's *Princess* Lee *Radziwill*?" the reporter asked, writing in her pad. "Yes, it is," Lee confirmed. "You see, I was born Caroline Lee Bouvier," she explained, "but I was always called Lee — and I absolutely *hate* it. I just detest it *so much*!" And that's when Janet's smile disappeared.

On August 18, 1960, Jackie was in Hyannis Port when the phone rang in the middle of the night. It was Stas. "Lee is in the hospital," he told her. "They had to call an ambulance and take her into emergency. It's the baby." Jackie was immediately frantic. She wanted to know what she could do; should she come? Stas told her that he was in Los Angeles and on his way, and suggested that she not make the trip because of her own pregnancy. "Just stay put and I will keep you posted," he told her. Jackie then called Janet to tell her the news. When Janet tracked Stas down in California, she found out that Lee had given birth prematurely to a girl and that, at three pounds, the baby wasn't doing well at all. Both mother and daughter were at New York Hospital. The next morning, Janet had a car drive her straight to Manhattan. She was there by ten o'clock and at Lee's side. She had with her the Book of Common Prayer, which contains the liturgy of the Episcopalian faith, and she brought it with her into Lee's room.

At just four years to the month since the stillbirth of Jackie's daughter, Janet found it hard to believe that Lee was now facing the mortality of her child, too. So bereft, Lee could barely speak to her mother through her tears. As it happened, the infant was dealing with a serious respiratory problem. Luckily, Janet knew of a specialist in the field, Dr. Samuel Levine, Professor of Pediatrics at Cornell University. He'd just retired a few years earlier. After his retirement, he continued as professor emeritus at CUMC and as a consultant pediatrician at New York Hospital, where Lee was now. Janet had met him at a cocktail party shortly after Jackie's stillbirth. The two had a conversation about what had happened to Arabella, and the doctor had a few theories that Janet found interesting. She took his card and put it in her wallet, thinking, for some reason, that she might need it one day. That day had come. She called his office only to find that, by coincidence, he was at the hospital already, looking in on another patient! He joined her in front of Lee's room and agreed to treat the baby.

By early afternoon, Stas finally arrived at the hospital, desperately wanting to see his wife and child. In the end, the baby, named Anna Christina — later known as just "Tina" — would be fine, though it would be touch and go for some time; she would actually have to remain in an incubator for months. It would take even longer for Lee to fully recover, not only physically but emotionally. In fact, she would suffer from postpartum depression for at least the next half a year, maybe longer. At the time, the condition wasn't treated as it is today; the medical profession didn't know much about the reasons for it, and some professionals thought of it as nothing more than "the blues." When Lee was finally able to leave the hospital and go to Merrywood with Janet to recover, she was muted, her personality dimmed. Everyone suspected it would take some time for her to return to her normal, spirited self.

On November 2, Janet hosted a tea at Merrywood with the Democratic Women's TV Committee for her son-in-law's campaign; by this time she was an official Democrat, finally having changed her voting status in honor of Jack. The guests enjoyed a viewing of a Kennedy documentary called *New Frontiers,* as well as the program *Coffee Hour with Senator and Mrs. Kennedy.* Jackie and Ethel Kennedy were both present to greet the guests. Lee was also there, but not at all well; for some reason, she seemed to be having trouble speaking. She just sat in a corner in a white wool sweater and matching straight-legged linen pants looking wan and unwell — so much so that Janet was afraid she might put off the guests and asked one of the maids to please take her up to her room. A couple of days later, Stas arrived. He took one look at his wife and decided he needed to get her back home to London as soon as possible, even though the baby was still in an incubator at New York Hospital. Janet would continue to check on her granddaughter as often as possible until the infant could be released and then transported to England.

Less than a week later, on November 8, John Fitzgerald Kennedy was elected President of the United States, defeating his Republican opponent, Richard M. Nixon, in one of the closest presidential elections of all time. Jackie and Jack had waited for the election results in Hyannis while Janet and Hugh watched from Merrywood. Meanwhile, Lee was in the UK with Stas, so anxious that she was now even having trouble breathing. She hadn't seen her baby since the day she left the hospital and was extremely worried about her. Stas had his hands full, trying to figure out what to say to her and how to say it. Everything he did set her off into crying jags. It seemed hopeless. "Still, the family had just experienced an incredible victory and, though everyone was worried about Lee, they had reason to celebrate," recalled Chauncey Parker III. "There was a lot of bitter and a lot of sweet at that time," he said, and then correcting himself, he added, "or maybe better stated, sweet and bitter."

On election night, Janet called Jackie to congratulate her, with Jamie and other family members standing by to get their exciting moment on the phone with her. "You are America's *First Lady,*" Janet exclaimed. "I just can't believe it, Jacqueline! I am just . . . I am just . . ." Janet couldn't find the words. She put her hand over the receiver, listened for a moment, and then told the others, "She said that I made her the woman that she is today!" She was truly moved. Apparently, Jackie then wondered if Lee had heard the news in England. Janet said she was going to call her. Jackie asked her mother to make sure Lee got in touch with her, saying that she really needed to talk to her sister.

A few weeks later, on November 25, Jackie gave birth to a healthy son, John Fitzgerald Kennedy Jr. It remained an extraordinary life for the Kennedys, Radziwills, and Auchinclosses, everyday occurrences such as the exciting births of new children set against what could only be viewed as a historical panorama. Correspondence from this time underscores as much. For instance, Janet invited Rose to lunch in January when she and Hugh planned to be in Palm Beach, and Rose responded on December 30 that she "should love to see you." However, "my schedule is very crowded and it would be much better for me to wait until a later date."

She added that "Jackie seems stronger and gayer every day, and John Jr. has put on two pounds." She closed, writing, "My love to you, dear Janet," and said that she and Joe "hoped to catch a glimpse of you and Hugh next week."

BETRAYAL

"Well, Jackie's going to be First Lady now," Lee Radziwill said, her eyes moist. "Why don't you just call *her* and talk to *her* if you love her and her husband so much." She was with Stas at their home on Buckingham Place. It was the end of the first week of the new year of 1961 and the Radziwills were hosting an intimate gathering. Because Lee had been too unwell to host a big New Year's Eve party, Stas organized an impromptu event in its place. Somehow, he and Lee had gotten off on the wrong footing and were arguing in front of guests. These days, Lee could be explosive one moment, depressed the next. She'd even said she didn't have the will to live, that's how bad it was for her. Everyone was concerned, but there didn't seem to be anything anyone could do. She wouldn't talk to Stas, and the subject of their lack of communication had been broached by Stas at the party, which was when she made that statement about Jackie.

Because of her various duties and the many

miles between her and her sister, Jackie wasn't able to be involved in the day-to-day concerns of Lee's emotional health at this time. When she talked to Lee by telephone, Lee seemed distant and disengaged. Many people in Lee's circle felt that her depression was a reaction to Jackie's ascension to First Lady, especially when Lee made statements such as "How can anyone compete with *that*? It's all over for me now." In John Davis's 1969 book, *The Bouviers,* he noted that Jackie's "accession to the White House promised to magnify a problem Lee had had to cope with for some time, the problem simply of being Jackie's sister. Although she was abundantly gifted herself . . . she had often been obscured by the shadow of her sister's prominence, and now that shadow threatened to eclipse her identity." Compounding things, Lee was also sure that in the competition for Janet's affection, she was still the loser. "*Of course* Mummy loves Jackie more than me," she again said at this time. "I understand it."

The depth of Lee's despair was greater than anyone knew. She truly felt alone. If one more doctor told her she just had "the blues," she said, she was going to scream. It was more profound than just sadness or melancholy, and she knew it. Something was seriously wrong with her; she just didn't know what it was or what to do about it. She felt fragile and defeated every day. Unfortunately, partly because of Lee's troubled state of mind, her marital happiness would be short-lived. From the birth of Christina onward, she and Stas would be at odds. Then the unthinkable happened.

According to family history, a young woman had often been coming to the Radziwill home and going off with Stas for a day of errands. There were so many people working for the Radziwills, it was difficult to keep track of them all, especially in Lee's present emotional disarray. However, something about this woman bothered her. One day, from her bedroom, Lee watched Stas as he opened the door of his car for this person, and that's when she knew. The observance of a simple act that would mean little to most people was all it took for her to know that Stas was having an affair. It was such a shock for her, to hear her later tell it, her heart started pounding and her knees turned to water. She had to immediately sit down and compose herself, she was just that shaken. Even considering the current rough patch in their marriage, Lee never would have imagined that Stas would be unfaithful to her. And while she was experiencing postpartum depression? What was he thinking?

For the next few days, Lee suppressed her anger and sadness until, finally, it boiled over and she confronted Stas. Caught red-handed, he was immediately remorseful. He didn't even try to deny it. However, it wasn't serious, he told her — just a young woman he'd "met along the way." For Lee, his explanation just made things worse. That he would jeopardize everything they had for someone who didn't even matter to him was difficult for her to accept. It was easy to rationalize her having cheated on Michael Canfield. She risked her entire marriage to him because she loved Stas. What Stas had just done wasn't at all the same, not in her mind, anyway. Plus, she felt stupid; her pride was hurt. "This doesn't happen to *me,*" she told one confidante at that time. Unfortunately, she couldn't confide in her mother or sister, since both had lectured her incessantly about her cheating on Michael. What she didn't need now was Janet saying what she often liked to say in such cases, "Finally, the chickens have come home to roost." It would never be the same, though, between Lee and Stas. This was a betrayal Lee would not be able to get past.

Like Jackie's, Janet's communication with Lee was sporadic at best; Lee stayed clear of her phone calls because she just didn't want to deal with her. Jackie and Janet were even more concerned when they learned that Lee would not be able to come to the States on December 12 to collect baby Tina from the hospital. Janet had scheduled one of their Mother-Daughter Teas on the 13th, and was disappointed that Lee wouldn't make it. She was worried about her and felt they needed time, with Jackie, to sort things out. Janet then said she would bring the infant to England, but Lee wouldn't hear of it. She said she wanted to send a nurse because she was so afraid that the baby might have an urgent health issue en route. Janet said that was fine, she would tag along with the nurse. No, Lee insisted, the nurse would be just fine on her own.

On the day the baby was to arrive, Lee and Stas got to London Airport two hours early simply because Lee couldn't stand the suspense another second longer. She paced nervously at the gate until, finally, the plane landed. One by one, passengers disembarked, meeting loved ones as Lee looked on anxiously. At last, an elderly woman appeared in a starched white uniform holding an infant in a blue blanket. Lee ran to her and took the baby into her arms. "She looks so much better," she said, tears streaming down her face. Tina was now six pounds, still small but at least able to make the long flight. Lee, Stas, the nurse, and the baby were then driven to Buckingham Place, where the nurse spent the night before departing the next morning. Though Lee and Stas had plenty of help — from nursemaids to cooks to maids and butlers — it would be Lee who would be primarily responsible for the care of little Tina.

It was therapeutic for her and, though it would be some time before she would return to her former self, it did seem as if she was on her way back. Her feelings for Stas had changed, though.

"Stas was filled with regret about the affair," said one of his relatives. "He worshipped Lee. It was a slipup. He felt pushed out by her and reacted badly. He promised her it would never happen again. However, from what he told me, she said, 'But what happens tomorrow when you wake up and don't want me? I don't trust you, now. I may never trust you again.' He became dedicated to making certain that this would not be the case. 'I broke her heart,' Stas told me. 'I can't change that. I can only try to win her back.' "

"Mummy was quite the equestrian when she was young," said her only son, Jamie Auchincloss. It was true; Janet Lee Bouvier won many trophies during her youth and even young adulthood. This picture is dated 1937, which would make her thirty. (JAMIE AUCHINCLOSS COLLECTION)

Janet Lee Bouvier and infant Jacqueline Lee Bouvier, 1929. (PHOTOFEST)

Janet and Jack "Black Jack" Bouvier with little Jacqueline. (PHOTOFEST)

Jackie, at about age six, and Lee Bouvier, age three. (PHOTOFEST)

Janet Lee Bouvier with Lee and Jackie, in 1941, walking in East Hampton. Once she divorced their father, Janet had to try to make ends meet for herself and her daughters and, given her entitled lifestyle, it wasn't always easy. (AP PHOTO)

Jackie always adored her father, "Black Jack" Bouvier. He could do no wrong in her eyes. Here they are in South-ampton on July 1, 1947, a few days before her eighteenth birthday. (PHOTOFEST)

Janet Bouvier finally found financial salvation when she married Hugh Auchincloss. Here is the newly blended Auchincloss family in 1946. From left to right, starting at the top: Jackie, Hugh Auchincloss III (Yusha), Nina, Lee, Janet, holding baby Janet Jr., Tommy (in the middle), and Hugh. Janet is pregnant here with her first and only son, Jamie. (WHITE HOUSE PHOTOGRAPHS/JOHN F. KENNEDY PRESIDENTIAL LIBRARY AND MUSEUM, BOSTON)

As they grew up, Janet and Lee became quite competitive but it was mostly one-sided—Lee's side. However, both were gorgeous, as well as charming and intelligent. (CECIL BEATON/CONDE NAST COLLECTION/GETTY IMAGES)

"You need to get her some money," Jackie told her brother-in-law Michael Canfield when he asked how he could keep her sister, Lee, interested in their marriage. "*Real money*, Michael!" (SLIM AARONS/GETTY IMAGES)

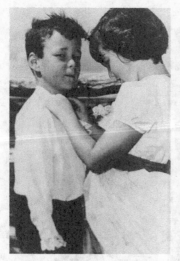

Janet Jr. adjusts her little brother Jamie's tie on big sister Jackie's wedding day, September 12, 1953. (JAMIE AUCHINCLOSS COLLECTION)

Jamie in 1954—around seven years old— with Senator John Fitzgerald Kennedy, his new brother-in-law, after marriage to his half-sister, Jackie. (JAMIE AUCHINCLOSS COLLECTION)

On the day of Jackie's wedding to Senator John Fitzgerald Kennedy. Here, on the happy day at Hammersmith Farm, are (left to right): Lee Bouvier Canfield, Jamie Auchincloss, JFK, Jackie, Bobby Kennedy, and Janet Auchincloss Jr. (JAMIE AUCHINCLOSS COLLECTION)

Lee finally found her prince and married him in March of 1959—her second husband, Prince Stanislaw Radziwill. (ASSOCIATED NEWSPAPERS/REX/SHUTTERSTOCK)

Jackie, Janet Jr., and Jamie watch Jack Kennedy win the nomination of his party at the Democratic Convention, July 13, 1960. "Mummy and Daddy were in the room too, but didn't want to be in the photo," Jamie, who was thirteen at the time, recalled. "This is when we knew that it was getting real, that our lives would be changed forever." (JAMIE AUCHINCLOSS COLLECTION)

Jackie and Lee ride a camel through the grounds of President Mohammad Ayub Khan's residence in Karachi, Sindh, Pakistan, on March 25, 1962, during their diplomatic trip abroad. (CECIL STOUGHTON/ WHITE HOUSE PHOTOGRAPHS/ JOHN F. KENNEDY PRESIDENTIAL LIBRARY AND MUSEUM, BOSTON)

Lee, Janet, and Jackie (with Lady Bird Johnson across the aisle) at JFK's State of the Union address, January 14, 1963. Hugh Auchincloss is seated behind Janet and next to Mrs. Charles Bartlett. (CECIL STOUGHTON/WHITE HOUSE PHOTOGRAPHS/JOHN F. KENNEDY PRESIDENTIAL LIBRARY AND MUSEUM, BOSTON)

JFK and his mother-in-law, Janet Auchincloss, arrive at Boston Hospital on August 8, 1962, deeply concerned about the well-being of his newborn son, Patrick. Sadly, the boy would die shortly after birth. (CECIL STOUGHTON/WHITE HOUSE PHOTOGRAPHS/JOHN F. KENNEDY PRESIDENTIAL LIBRARY AND MUSEUM, BOSTON)

Jackie (with binoculars) and Jack watch the first race of the 1962 America's Cup, on September 15, from aboard the USS *Joseph P. Kennedy Jr.* Behind them are Jamie (with the tie) and a very excited Janet. (ROBERT KNUDSEN/WHITE HOUSE PHOTOGRAPHS/JOHN F. KENNEDY PRESIDENTIAL LIBRARY AND MUSEUM, BOSTON)

JFK encouraged Janet Jr. to go ahead with her debutante party, even though there was such sadness over Patrick's death. (JAMIE AUCHINCLOSS COLLECTION)

It was Lee's idea to have Jackie join her and Aristotle Onassis on a Mediterranean cruise in order to help her get over Patrick's death. Here the sisters are, on October 9, 1963, sitting in the stern of a launch as they leave Iraklion, Crete, Greece. (LESLEY PRIEST/AP/REX/ SHUTTERSTOCK)

Unable to deny the strong attraction she felt for him, Lee couldn't help but become involved in an affair with Onassis in 1963. (GETTY PHOTOS)

Jackie and Aristotle Onassis with Franklin Roosevelt Jr. (right) aboard Onassis's yacht the *Christina* in the Mediterranean, in 1963. (AP/REX/SHUTTERSTOCK)

Vice President Lyndon Johnson with Janet Auchincloss, with Lady Bird in the background. (JAMIE AUCHINCLOSS COLLECTION)

When Jackie named her mother "Chairman of the Greater Washington Committee for the National Cultural Center," *Vogue* sent the famous photographer Bert Stern to take this lovely photo for *Vogue*. (BERT STERN/CONDE NAST COLLECTION)

■ ■ ■ ■

Part Four: The White House Years

■ ■ ■ ■

INAUGURATION

January 20, 1961. Inauguration day.

The weather was miserable, snow coming down in white sheets, the wind blowing harder than at any time in recent memory. The climate was sure to impact the number of people who could travel into Washington, D.C., for the inauguration of the country's new president, John Fitzgerald Kennedy. Janet and Hugh and the rest of the immediate family had to miss out on the pre-inaugural galas. Janet would never forget this unnerving time, its memory vivid in her mind for years to come. "We were snowed in the night before the inauguration," she would recall to the JFK Library for her oral history there. "I remember Hughdie getting stuck in the snow. Jamie flew down from school; he was attending the Fay School at Southborough, Massachusetts. The blizzard began at two-thirty in the afternoon and Jamie's plane was the last one that got in to the National Airport."

Driven by the family's butler, James Owen, Hugh went to meet Jamie at the airport. Afterward, on the way back to the Auchincloss home, they found that the George Washington Memorial Parkway was completely snowed in with no cars moving. Impatient about the whole mess, Hugh told Owen to just pull over to the side of the road and said they would walk the rest of the way. He suggested that Owen could pick up the car the next day, if he could even find it underneath all the snow. "Owen and Jamie tried to persuade Hughdie to stay in the car because with his emphysema he is not supposed to get pneumonia," Janet recalled. "But Hughdie did walk something like five miles through the deep snow that afternoon.

"Yusha, Nini, Tommy, Janet, Jamie, and Alice [Yusha's wife] — well, I don't know how many people we eventually had in our house that night — none of us got out because the two government cars that had been assigned to us to take us to the Inaugural Concert at Constitution Hall could not get up the driveway," Janet remembered. "I think if we hadn't had the government cars, we might actually have got there. But they blocked the driveway! So, the two soldiers [drivers of those cars] were also snowed in at Merrywood because they couldn't get out. So, none of us got out that night.

"The great thing was that Mr. Carper, the

local snowplow man, appeared at six o'clock in the morning with the snowplow and got us all out, including the government cars, so that we could finally get to the Capitol for the Inauguration."

This was a hallmark day in the family's storied history. Janet's son-in-law was being sworn in as President of the United States — the first Roman Catholic to hold that office — making her daughter the nation's First Lady and, at thirty-one, its third youngest. "It was hard to fathom," said Jamie Auchincloss. "Maybe people thought we took it for granted as a family or just went along with the flow without realizing how absolutely monumental the whole thing was. We didn't. We were acutely aware of the great honor, the great privilege, and, also, the great responsibility."

The many Auchinclosses all piled into two cars, the one with Janet, Hugh, Jamie, and Janet Jr. driven by James Owen, the butler. Though Stas, as Jack's close pal, was one of the first to donate to JFK's campaign, he and Lee would not be present at the Inaugural. Lee was too sick; Stas decided to stay at her side. "It was heartbreaking because I knew how much it meant to him," Lee would later say.

"In the car, we started looking at our tickets," recalled Jamie, who was thirteen at the time, "and we realized that, based on the numbers, all of us weren't going to be seated together. 'Don't worry about it,' Mummy said. She figured she and Hughdie would be in front with Jackie and we kids would probably be scattered throughout."

When the Auchinclosses got to the Capitol and started walking toward the inaugural stand, there was some confusion as to where everyone should sit. An usher took Janet and Hugh one way, another usher took Jamie, Janet Jr., Nini, and the other family members another way. After everyone sat down and got their bearings, Janet was in for a surprise. "Hughdie and I were in the stand in back of the President [Dwight D. Eisenhower] and the President-elect," she later recalled. "All of the children were in seats facing him." In other words, she and Hughdie were not sitting with Jackie or with any other dignitaries. Instead, they had seats in the peanut gallery *behind* JFK.

"I'm looking around and who do I see next to me? Eleanor Roosevelt," Jamie Auchincloss recalled. "So, clearly, I have great seats, as do my siblings, all of us facing Jack as he would be sworn in. I'm completely excited by this turn of events and I want to wave to Mummy and Daddy so they can see how terrific my seats are. I look way down front for them where I figure they would be seated, also facing the presidential podium. But they aren't there. Then I look all around the huge place for them, and can't find them anywhere. I actually think that, somehow, they haven't gotten in! Finally, way off in the distance, I see them. There they are, little dots out in the distance, facing the *back* of the President and Jackie. I couldn't believe their seats! I knew Mummy would be infuriated by this slight. It seemed so wrong."

How could this bizarre seating arrangement be explained? "We were at a loss when we all came back together after the swearing in," Jamie Auchincloss recalled. "Mummy didn't know what to think. Even later, Jack told me he was looking all over the place for Mummy and Daddy and couldn't find them. Mummy was deeply hurt, but it seemed like an unintentional slipup. So what could she do? This breach came close to ruining the day for her."

Janet could barely contain her disappointment about the obvious seating arrangement snafu. In turn, Jackie was completely horrified. She said couldn't understand it and promised to get to the bottom of it. Janet told her that if such a terrible situation could occur to her own mother, *anything* could happen during her time as First Lady. She told her that she would have to redouble her efforts to avoid further embarrassment. "Mummy felt it a responsibility to make sure that a lesson had been learned," said Jamie. " 'Despite the efforts of all of the people who work here, in the end, it falls upon *you*,' she told her. My sister may have been First Lady now, but her station in life would never preclude her from getting a thorough dressing-down from Mummy when necessary.

"This was maybe one of the first of many times in the years to come that something strange would occur, or Jackie would say something odd that would totally perplex Mummy. Jackie would then leave the room, and Mummy would stand there with an expression on her face that would be so comical. It was as if she was trying to figure out, 'What in the world is that girl *thinking*?' "

JACKIE IN THE WHITE HOUSE

Not surprisingly, the first month of the Kennedy administration was an extremely busy time for the country's new First Lady, Jacqueline Bouvier Kennedy. As soon as the Kennedys moved into the White House on February 4, 1961, Jackie became consumed by her duties. She'd not even had the time to stay in touch with her sister, Lee, who was still ailing in the United Kingdom. By March, though, Jackie was a little more settled into her new home and beginning to adapt to public life. She thought it would a good idea to host a dinner-dance in honor of Lee to bring her out of her doldrums. This she did on March 15, 1961, the night she also brought Janet and Lee into the Oval Office for the first time.

In the months to come, as First Lady, Jackie found herself in a new, highly pressurized situation, the responsibilities of which even Janet couldn't have completely fathomed when she first stepped into the Oval Office with Lee. Jackie responded to it by setting up so many barriers between her and her loved ones, it was almost impossible to reach her. First to go were the customary Mother-Daughter Teas. In fact, the Bouvier women wouldn't have a single one of their familial confabs the entire time Jackie was in the White House. "Jackie often thought of her mother as a nuisance," her secretary, Mary Barelli Gallagher, would say. Sometimes Janet would call and Jackie would tell Mary to say she wasn't present even though she was standing right at her side! "I hated lying to Mrs. Auchincloss when I had to but, of course, my first duty was to Jackie."

Maybe one reason Jackie wanted to distance herself from Janet at this time was that Janet, true to her nature, could be so critical about small things. "There is *always* room for improvement, Jacqueline," she would repeatedly remind her. For instance, she once noticed that Jackie's dress was too short, so much so that when she bent down, one could see the top of her garter. Rather than have a squabble with her about it, Janet asked Mary

211

Gallagher to mention it to Jackie. Jackie wasn't open to suggestions about her wardrobe, though, especially if she suspected they were coming indirectly from her mother. Janet later said, "I used to get a good many critical letters about Jackie's appearance. She was in a period of more exaggerated hairdos. I used to get a lot of letters from people saying, 'Don't you think it would be better if she did her hair this way or that way?' Sometimes, I made mild suggestions, and sometimes I didn't."

Occasionally, though, Jackie appreciated Janet's intrusion. For example, quite often Jackie would be at a White House function smoking. If Janet happened to see a photographer hovering about, she would snatch the cigarette from Jackie's hand and snuff it out in an ashtray lest Jackie ever be pictured smoking.

About six months into her White House years, Jackie realized that it made no sense pushing her family away, especially her mother. In fact, Janet was one of her greatest allies and Jackie was wise to depend on her. There would be many times in the next two and a half years when she would ask Janet to substitute for her at White House events Jackie couldn't bear, such as a coffee hour for the wives of members of the New York Stock Exchange. On that day, Janet dressed in a white linen dress with a matching hat and arrived earlier than anyone else, ready for her duty. "It was fun for her," said her son, Jamie, of Janet's White House duties, "and she was good at it, too. I remember she stepped in for Jackie at a meeting for the International Council of Women and it was successful. Jackie was grateful. But then there was some trouble afterward. Mummy asked Jackie if she could have free copies of the White House guidebook for her friends. Jackie didn't respond personally; she sent word to Mummy that she would have to purchase them, that there was no budget for complimentary copies. Mummy's feelings were hurt, but what could she do other than just voice her displeasure?"

Janet never had a difficult time expressing herself to her daughter when she felt disrespected. When she did so, Jackie was usually filled with regret. She would say that the pressure of being First Lady had once again gotten to her and forced her to act without thinking. She'd explain that she was always signing documents and barking instructions and, as a result, breaches in courtesy would often occur. For instance, Jackie once hosted a tea for her mother at the White House and was more than an hour late in arriving. "Where in the world is Jackie?" Janet's friend Eileen Slocum asked when she reached her in the receiving line. Janet said she didn't know; she'd heard, though, that Jackie was out walking Clipper, the dog given to her as a gift by Joe Kennedy. "Walking the dog?" Slocum asked, astonished. Janet shrugged. "Apparently," she said, annoyed. The next day she called Jackie to have it out with her about the breach in etiquette. As sometimes happened, Janet was told that Jackie was indisposed. "I am going to sit on this phone on hold all day long until you put me through to my daughter," Janet said, fed up. Finally, Jackie came on the line, complaining that she was busy and didn't have much time to talk. The two then had an argument, the specifics of which would only be known to the two of them — neither seems to have discussed it with friends or family.

When it came right down to it, though, Janet would always do whatever she could for Jackie and Jack during their White House years. She was so proud of them and had such respect for the power of the office, *of course* she would overlook any transgression. Sometimes it was the small gestures that would most matter, as when she offered Hammersmith to the President and First Lady when both seemed particularly stressed out. Since Janet and Hugh were out of the country and Jamie was away at boarding school, the Kennedys had the run of the property in September of 1961.

"You could never guess what this vacation has done for Jack," Jackie wrote to Janet on

October 1 from Hammersmith. "That said, it was the best he ever had." She added, "Here we sit for hours on the terrace just looking at the bay and drinking in the beauty, and all one's strength is renewed." She also wrote that Jack was much "tireder [*sic*] than I ever thought." Then, she closed with: "So, you can't imagine what you have done for the country in allowing Jack to come here for a rest." Though in retrospect that seems like a rather strange statement for a daughter to make to her mother, if one understands Janet's deep sense of patriotism, it becomes obvious that Jackie was paying her what she would have considered a supreme compliment.

Having Janet and Hugh available to her, as well as Jamie, Janet Jr., Lee, and the rest of her family, helped to make Jackie's time in the White House much easier for her to handle. "My life here, which I dreaded and which at first overwhelmed me is now under control and the happiest time I have ever known," Jackie would write to her friend William Walton in 1962, "not for the position," she added, "but for the closeness of one's family. The last thing I expected to find in the W. House."

215

JANET'S APPOINTMENT
BY THE FIRST LADY

In early 1962, Jackie was named honorary chairman of the national fund-raising committee for the building of a proposed cultural center in Washington, the National Cultural Center. Because Jackie immediately recognized that her mother would be a tremendous asset in the planning of the center, she quickly named her chairman of the Greater Washington Committee for the National Cultural Center. *The Washington Post* called it a "fortunate choice." Janet accepted the nomination at a tea she hosted for the committee's trustees at Merrywood.

"I have forgotten what I wanted to say . . ." Janet said when beginning her speech at Merrywood. Because she was so charismatic, she was immediately embraced by all who attended. (It should be noted that on a copy of her written speech, the first line was: "I have forgotten what I wanted to say!") Her charm wouldn't have gotten her far, though, if she didn't have good ideas to back it up. She noted that it was "terribly important for the building that we are planning to be of good design" and added that she had inherited a flair for architecture from her father, "who, as some of you may know, made quite a mark on New York City's skyline. Jackie has also been greatly influenced by him." Janet then outlined her intention to raise at least $7 million in the District of Columbia, and not just because the money was necessary to build the center, she said, but also "as incentive for the rest of the nation to understand that we must support the arts. After all," she noted, "if Washington's residents who will most stand to benefit from the center can't support it, then why would the rest of the country?" She said she was planning a number of fund-raisers and that she hoped to raise over a million dollars — a big commitment on her part. "That's a lot of money, Mummy," Jackie told her in advance. "Are you *sure* you want to make that promise?" Janet said yes, that she believed that if she set her intention clearly, she would somehow find a way to make it a reality.

A month later, in an article about Janet's appointment, *Vogue* noted that she was "a gentle, disarming woman of both enormous distinction and careful efficiency." The magazine even published a full-page picture of her. This kind of publicity concerned Janet, though. She wondered if she was generating attention for herself that perhaps should have been going to the First Lady. "Are you certain you want me to do this?" she asked Jackie. "Absolutely, I do," Jackie said. Jackie noted that a nationwide fund drive for a cultural center had failed in 1958 under Eisenhower, and she knew her mother wouldn't quit until she had the money needed to help finance the project, especially after her million-dollar oath. This endeavor was now quite a challenge for Janet, with a good deal of pressure attached to it. However, she was determined that she would not let her daughter, or the country, down.

A few weeks later, Jackie and Janet unveiled an architectural model of the arts center in the ballroom of the historic cottage The Elms in Newport. Janet was introduced and, with Jackie sitting next to her and listening intently, she told the crowd of about a thousand people, "There should be in our capital a symbol of the growing importance of the arts in American life. Washington has had almost no national or international influence [in the arts]." She said that she was planning a dinner and show at the National Armory for which 550 tickets would be sold at $100 each. There would also be $25 seats available for a buffet. She was also planning events at colleges and movie theaters across the country for tickets at $5. "If we get college kids involved, how wonderful would that be?" she asked. "For our youth to have an investment in America's culture, it's a dream not only of mine but, more importantly, my daughter the First Lady and son-in-law, the President."

Soon after, Janet chaired the promised gala at the Armory, which she called "An American Pageant of the Arts." As she had arranged, the show — hosted by Leonard Bernstein with performing artists such as Marian Anderson, Hal Holbrook, Bob Newhart, Robert Frost, Danny Kaye, and Jason Robards — was broadcast by closed-circuit telecast across the United States at local fund-raising events for the center. The President and First Lady as well as former President Eisenhower sat in the front row, with Janet at Jackie's side. Hugh sat one row behind them. Just as she had promised, the event raised a million dollars — equivalent to more than $8 million today — after which the funds really started to pour in, including $3 million more from the Ford Foundation.

There was one moment that night Janet would never forget. It was so simple yet, like some moments that seem simple on their face, one that would forever stand out. She was standing alone in a corner of the Armory, the success of the evening filling her with personal pride. Jackie caught her eye and walked over to her. Mother and daughter then stood side by side, taking it all in, the men in sharp tuxes, the women in flamboyant gowns, all enjoying themselves . . . the music . . . the celebrities . . . the reporters . . . coming together for a good cause. "Well done, Mummy," Jackie said, taking Janet's hand. "You had a very good night." It was clear from Janet's expression of gratitude that this praise meant the world to her.

At a subsequent tea at Merrywood, Janet, now emboldened by her success, intoned, "We cannot fail. We feel now that the whole country will pull together to make the cultural center possible. I see great possibilities for us. Let's keep this thing going!"

"For the next two years, Janet would continue to hold fund-raisers for business leaders and others at Merrywood and Hammersmith, all the way until November of '63," recalled Chauncey Parker III. "When the cultural center would finally open in 1971, it would be renamed the John F. Kennedy Center for the Performing Arts. At that time, one board member wrote in an editorial that 'it was during Janet Auchincloss' tenure of office that many people became very active in the Center and it is due to them that the Kennedy Center exists today.' Janet would remain involved in one way or the other for many more years."

As she found fulfillment in her philanthropic work, Janet Auchincloss certainly felt that 1962 had, thus far, been a good year for herself and her daughters, Jackie and Lee. Not only had both settled into marriages with impressive men (though these unions obviously had their troubles), they were also raising families, having given Janet four grandchildren so far. They had their challenges, of course, like most families, but things felt . . .

settled, the future looked good. All of that was about to change, though. Things were about to get turned completely upside down with the troubling emergence of a new character in the story of their lives — one who would change the course of their family's history forevermore.

GREEKS BEARING GIFTS

Because so much has been written and said about Aristotle Onassis, he's become a character of almost mythic proportions, like one of the Greek gods he so admired as a young man. Most of the seemingly overblown accounts of Onassis's extravagant life aren't even hyperbolic, though; he really was one of the wealthiest, most talked-about, and most scandalous men of his time.

By 1962, Onassis was fifty-six years old. Though certainly not tall in stature — he was only about five feet five inches — he was an outsized personality with an abundance of self-confidence and charisma. He wasn't an overtly intellectual or well-studied man; he'd had only a rudimentary education. Born in Smyrna (a town in present-day Turkey) in 1906, Aristotle Socrates Onassis immigrated to Greece as a teenager during the Greco-Turkish War. Moving to Argentina a year later, he became a successful tobacco trader and a millionaire by the age of twenty-five.

221

He invested in the cargo-shipping business during the Depression in the United States, when most people were trying to get out of that sort of enterprise. He had great instincts and was soon one of the most respected — and often despised — men in the business world, often tangling with major world governments with a take-no-prisoners attitude. His prized possession was the *Christina 0* — better known as just the *Christina* — his sleek 325-foot yacht, the largest and most well known of its time. It became a playground for the rich and famous, providing a luxurious getaway to everyone from celebrities to royalty to presidents and prime ministers.

With the passing of the years, his business interests continued to expand beyond his ownership of the world's largest privately owned shipping fleet with the addition of his own airline business, Olympic Airways. His business tactics remained suspect, though. For instance, during the Eisenhower years, Onassis was embroiled in a number of complex legal disputes after being indicted for fraud for not paying taxes on surplus American ships.

Onassis had an uncanny understanding of human nature and knew how to appeal to people, no matter their stations. He could engage in a lively and entertaining conversation with anyone and make that person feel as if he or she was the most important person in his life. "Onassis was a bit larger — no, *substantially* larger — than life, and he knew it," recalled his personal attorney of twenty years, Stelio Papadimitriou. "While he could sometimes appear empathetic, he was actually a narcissist, caring about only that which affected him directly. He tended to view people as pawns in a game meant only to enrich him, whether financially or, in the case of women, sexually. 'Think with the head, not the heart,' he liked to caution his two children, Christina [eighteen], and Alexander [fifteen]." Because both were in line to one day take over the family empire — Christina had more interest and business acumen than Alexander — Onassis didn't mind that both were just as coldhearted as their father. He taught them by example to be tough and competitive, just like "Poppa."

In 1946, Onassis had married Athina Mary Livinos — Tina — daughter of one the richest shipping moguls of the forties. He was forty. She was seventeen. Their relationship was explosive, always making headlines. By the fifties, he was famously involved in a highly publicized affair with the temperamental opera star Maria Callas. "He was the nicest man, the most successful man, but a man with the worst style," recalled Panagiotis Theodoracopulos, better known as "Taki." (His father, an industrialist, was an old friend of Onassis's; Taki and Onassis's son, Alexander, were also chums.) "He was a peasant in many ways, not a polished person. He could be a brute and, like a lot of Greeks, a complete chauvinist." In 1960, in the midst of Onassis's affair with Callas, his wife, Tina, divorced him.

Aristotle Onassis and Stas Radziwill were good friends, often seen socializing in the mid-1950s and early sixties at Claridge's Hotel, where high society VIPs often mixed with big-business moguls. Stas and Lee also hosted many parties at their home in London for Onassis and Maria Callas. They all became close. "Onassis was an outstanding man, not only as a financier but also as a person," Lee Radziwill would recall. "He was active, with great vitality, brilliant and up to date on everything. He was amusing to be with. And he had charm, a fascinating way with women. He surrounded them with attention. He made sure they felt admired and desired. He took note of their slightest whim. He interested himself in them — exclusively and profoundly."

In early spring of 1962, Lee and Ari began to meet for cocktails or dinner at Claridge's in London or Maxim's in Paris and share confidences with each other. Onassis was so flattering, viewing Lee as one of the most interesting people he'd ever met. He found her to be creative and admired her imagination. He loved hearing her stories of the times

she and Jackie spent in Europe and appreciated the fact that she seemed so close to her
mother and sister. Family had always been
important to him. Because he also thought
she was uncommonly beautiful, poised, and
collected, he was baffled by her lack of self-
esteem. Whereas Maria Callas was self-
confident to the point of being exhausting,
Onassis thought of Lee as a broken person
and wondered how that had happened to
someone so beautiful with so much to give.
He figured she'd probably experienced a lot
of pain in her past. "But pain is a part of
everyone's life," he told her. "We can't escape
it."

He fascinated her as much as she did him.
She loved his attitude about life and, especially, about money. "Money isn't just
luxury," he told her, "it is power," he said,
echoing a philosophy that had also been her
maternal grandfather's, Jim T. Lee. "That
power can be yours, too, if you'd like to be at
my side," he told her. He even said he wanted
to marry her, someday. Was he serious? Lee
wasn't sure, but she thought maybe so. "It
didn't take long before she was completely
swept off her feet by him," said Agnetta Castallanos, a vice president of Onassis's Olympic
Airways since 1960. "I was with Onassis as a
lover just before Lee came into the picture,"
she recalled. "We ended it because the business we shared complicated things. He talked

a lot about Lee. He was crazy about her. I told him I felt jealous, the way women do when they're being replaced. He wanted me to befriend her, telling me she was a sad and lonely little creature. 'Ari, I tend to shy away from charity work,' I told him. But I called her anyway and invited her to dinner."

"So, what's it like to have a sister who is the most famous woman in the world?" Agnetta asked Lee over their meal at Claridge's.

"I make it a policy to never talk about her," Lee snapped, as if by instinct.

"That's probably wise," Agnetta said.

"Indeed."

"So, what's it like being with one of the wealthiest men in the world?" Lee later asked.

"I make it a policy to never talk about him," Agnetta said with a wink.

"That's probably wise," Lee countered with a smile.

"Indeed."

"We became instant friends after that night," Agnetta said. "I thought she was fabulous. I saw what Ari saw. At first, she seemed like a winsome little thing, but once you got to know her, you saw the inner resolve. The stories she told about her mother! 'With a mother like mine, you have to be resilient,' she told me.

"Eventually, after a couple weeks, she opened up about Ari to me. She said they had a deep connection. 'It is not insignificant,' she told me. 'It's profound.' I said, 'Lee, I think you're falling in love with this man.' She said, 'I know. It was love at first sight, I admit it. But I also love my husband.' However, I believe Stas had come to represent sadness in her life — her postpartum depression, an affair he'd apparently had. I don't think she fully trusted him. Being with Ari was just better for her. She asked me if I thought a woman could love two men at the same time. I said I didn't know."

Stelio Papadimitriou added, "I saw Ari and Lee together many times in the spring of '62 and she would look at him with such adoration, I thought, 'My God, she worships this man, doesn't she?' To call it an affair I think might be reductive of it. Maybe for Ari it was simply that, but for Lee it was more."

After Ari and Lee became involved, Ari's sister, Artemis, opened her seaside estate in Glyfada to Lee whenever she was in Greece; the two women began to think of each other as family. Meanwhile, still standing in the wings was Maria Callas, watching and seething. Ari was not willing to let her go, and Lee knew it. She didn't mind, at least not yet. It gave her a little time to figure out what to do about Stas, who was back in London with their children, seemingly unaware, at this juncture anyway, of what was going on between his wife and the Greek tycoon. Maria, though, minded Lee's involvement with

Onassis. A lot. The writer Leo Lerman, who worked for Condé Nast for more than fifty years, wrote in his diary that Maria told him — and this was in the summer of '77, many years after that spring of '62 — "I never disliked Jackie, but I hate Lee. *I hate her.*"

"ENOUGH OF *Her*!"

On a Sunday night in the summer of 1962, Lee and Stas were watching television in their Buckingham Place home with four of their closest friends. As the small group of six watched a broadcast and drank expensive cognac, a special report commenced about Jackie. The commentator droned on and on for at least twenty minutes about Jackie's beauty and influence while everyone in the room fidgeted and tried not to look at Lee. Finally, Stas stood up, walked over to the television, and turned it off. A small smile flitted across his face as he said, "My God! Enough of *her*!" All eyes went to Lee for a reaction. Acting blasé, she swirled her cognac in her glass, took a sniff and a sip. "Yes, well, my sister is *quite* the spectacle these days," she remarked, staring off into the distance.

"We all understood," recalled Terrance Landow, who was present. "When you have spent your life in competition with your older sister for attention and you suddenly find yourself in a situation where there can *be* no competition, it's not easy. Lee would complain about it — though not often — and I would say to her, 'But, Lee, what have *you* done to deserve acclamation?' This question would upset her. 'What has Jackie done?' she would ask me."

Lee had a point. Jackie had just found herself in the right place at the right time and married someone who would become President. Lee believed that if it had been her in the same circumstance, she would have had as much impact on the world. She was just as chic, just as personable, and just as engaging as her sister, and some might argue even more so. But it *wasn't* Lee. It was Jackie, and this was difficult for her.

At this same time, Lee was still devastated by Stas's brief affair and, even though she was still seeing Onassis, decided to also find comfort in the arms of Taki Theodoracopulos, who by this time was a handsome Greek tennis pro and bon vivant. It was as if once she had broken the rules with Onassis, Lee felt emboldened to further experiment outside her marriage. She had met Taki back in the summer of '61 at Gianni Agnelli's palatial villa on the Riviera. (Agnelli, one of the richest men in all of Italy, was a successful industrialist and the head of Fiat.) "I was twenty-four and impressed with her," recalled Taki, "because, well, she was beautiful, she was the sister-in-law of the President of the

United States, *and* she was flirting with me, all of which was a lethal combination. When I saw that she had a rather loose marriage, I started pursuing her. Two years of on-again off-again romantic behavior then began.

"I had mixed emotions about Lee," Taki recalled. "On one hand, she was a magical creature who, when we were alone together, was romantic, charming, and lovely. However, when we were out in public, she would change. I never understood why. She would become bitchy, critical. She would say dreadful things about me, be very condescending. I would have to wonder, who in her life spoke to her like that, giving her license to then think she could speak to others the same way? Looking back, I think she just wasn't happy. She wanted love and acceptance so badly, it was crippling for her. The more time I spent with her, the more I knew she wasn't the one for me, nor was I the one for her. That said, for a little sliver of time there, I was crazy about her."

No doubt adding to Lee's discontentment during these years — which she sometimes called "the political years" — was that she wasn't really that fond of Jackie's other side of the family, the Kennedys. Though she loved the excitement of the White House — being in the presence of so much power and entitlement *was* intoxicating — paradoxically, she thought the Kennedys themselves were incredibly dull. It wouldn't be until many years later that she would look back on these years with wonder. "At the time, I didn't realize how special everything was," she would observe, "although [I was] aware certainly that there was magic in the air. We were presumptuous to assume this magic would continue. President Kennedy borrowed a credo from Sophocles, and inspired those around him to live their lives along the lines of excellence. Everyone wanted to give the most of themselves because that expectation was returned."

Lee was wise to Jack's indiscretions and she made sure he knew it. She didn't seem to mind them, though, maybe because she knew she had little room for judgment. "Jack used to play around and I knew *exactly* what he was up to and would tell him so," Lee recalled to Cecil Beaton years later, in June of 1968. "And he'd have absolutely no guilty conscience about it and would say, 'I love her [Jackie] deeply and have done everything for her. I've no feeling of letting her down because I've put her foremost in everything.' "

"Do you realize that I can reach anyone I want to from the White House?" Jack once asked Lee. "Do you understand the *power* of that?" The two laughed. It really was a heady thought. "Jackie doesn't get it," Jack told Lee with a wink. "She doesn't see how much *fun* this can be." Lee didn't comment, but she had to have smiled to herself. It's true that Jackie was solemn about her position. In her mind, Lee would have had more fun with it.

It wasn't as if Jackie didn't try to include Lee in the excitement of being First Lady, though. Earlier, in the summer of '61, Jackie had made plans to visit Greece on a vacation and thought it would cheer up Lee if she were able to tag along. The next year, in the spring of '62, the Bouvier sisters enjoyed another vacation abroad: their much-publicized and written-about trip to India and then Pakistan. If ever Lee could be thought of as a good sport, it was during this trip because, in the minds of most observers, especially in the press, she was an afterthought to the main attraction, the much-idolized First Lady. "Mrs. Kennedy was received as the wife of the President and Lee was kind of like her lady-in-waiting when we were overseas," recalled Secret Service agent Clint Hill, who was on the trip. Many thousands of people came forth to pay homage to Jackie, to give her gifts and to bear witness to what had become an international phenomenon. "We were always surrounded by too many people," Lee would later recall. "The banquet at the presidential mansion was absolute hell." Lee's memory aside, the popular pictures of the two sisters sitting atop an elephant (Lee wearing white leather gloves, of course!) and smiling as if they hadn't a care in the world seemed to suggest that a good and memorable time was had by both. Even that moment was a bit marred by what seemed to some to be a Freudian slip by Jackie. "Lee, let *me* take the reins," she famously said while the girls were on top of that elephant.

There would be yet another trip for the sisters in August of 1962, this one extended time off to enjoy Italy. Reams of press coverage were generated by this vacation as well, with hundreds of photographs published worldwide of Jackie and Lee in beautiful locations such as Amalfi and Ravello. While they were in Italy, though, the tension between the sisters was obvious to some observers. Nunziata Lisi, an Italian friend of Lee's, recalls, "Lee had been in Paris and planned to meet Jackie in Ravello. I made all of the arrangements for her. However, the planes were late and there were all sorts of travel problems. When she finally showed up at the resort, she was late, frustrated, and exhausted. Jackie was annoyed. 'We have *plans,*' she told her, petulantly. 'There are *people* I am supposed to meet for *dinner!*' Lee stared at her and said, 'I'm very sorry, Jackie, but your need to be loved, worshipped, and adored will have to wait until I shower and change my outfit!' "

At the time, some argued that Lee's sensitivity about Jackie was a shame because she most certainly had her own personal style and grace. Thanks to a number of photo layouts in fashion magazines after the Kennedy election — and more that she would do in the coming years — Lee would be viewed by some in the fashion industry as a tastemaker and trendsetter. Fashion designer Ralph Rucci noted to *Vanity Fair,* "Lee has always been an original. Mrs. [Diana] Vreeland said that Jacqueline Kennedy released style in this nation. Well, she had a great deal of assistance, and she had the best tutors. But Lee did it on her own! She understands clothes. Lee could put on a coat and will know how to turn her shoulder and her head and her arm and hold the coat so that it's perfection."

People paid attention to the fact that Lee understood fashion and knew what looked best on her model-thin five-foot-six frame, so much so that she would find herself on the "Best Dressed List" for many years in the sixties. She was once asked to judge new fall-winter fashion for *McCall's,* in Paris. She was even asked to model some of the clothing. She was also instrumental in introducing the world to André Courrèges, the designer many have credited for the "mod," pop look of the 1960s.

Not only did Lee receive accolades for her fashion choices and her modeling, she also demonstrated a real knack for writing when she temporarily worked for *McCall's* in Paris. It seemed that fashion journalism was a good fit. However, she wasn't satisfied, explaining that it was too "behind the scenes," not high-profile enough. Plus, Jackie had already made a huge impact on Paris when she was there as First Lady, speaking in French and handling herself in a way that made her country proud. (Everyone would always remember Jack's comment: "I am the man who accompanied Jacqueline Kennedy to Paris.") *That* was history, Lee felt, whereas what she was doing was far less significant. Therefore, when *McCall's* offered her a permanent position, she asked for so much money she sabotaged herself right out of the job.

"You must look inward, Lee," Taki told her one day over cocktails, "and find out what you want to do with your life." Lee seemed completely crestfallen on this particular day. She described herself to Taki as "just a woman trying to make a name for myself separate and apart from my sister's." Taki told her there was nothing wrong with wanting to do that for herself. "I say, 'Go for it, Lee,' " he told her. "Get what you want out of life. You are incredible! Make your own mark." Lee then lamented that every time she felt she was headed down the right path, it turned out to be the wrong one. "You will figure it out," Taki told her. "You will find your place. I promise you." At that, Lee reached out and took both his hands into her own. "Thank you for believing in me," she said, tears welling in her eyes. "I don't have a lot of support in my life. The one thing I know for sure is that I must keep daring," she concluded. "I *must* keep daring."

THE PRESIDENT AND HIS MOTHER-IN-LAW

It was August 24, 1962. Janet Auchincloss was lunching with Betty Tuckerman, mother of Jackie's secretary, Nancy Tuckerman, at the Colony Club in New York when a waiter approached the table to tell her that she was wanted on the telephone. "Who is it?" Janet wanted to know. The waiter leaned in to her ear and whispered urgently: "It's the White House calling. *It's the President.*" Janet got up and raced to the phone. "How in the world did you know I was here, Mr. President?" she asked her son-in-law. He said he actually had no idea where she was at that moment. He'd just told the White House switchboard to track her down. One of the many perks of being President was that he could find his mother-in-law at any given moment.

At this time, Jackie was in Ravello with Caroline and Lee on a vacation. It had been decided to leave baby John Jr. with his grandmother Janet; the baby's nanny, Maud Shaw, was also dispatched to Hammersmith. With Jackie and the children all gone, Jack told Janet he was lonely. It's fascinating to think of JFK as ever feeling lonesome considering all of the relatives usually available to him at the Kennedy compound in Hyannis Port. "Would it be convenient if I came up and stayed with Uncle Hugh and you?" Jack asked. Janet was delighted. "It would be perfectly wonderful," she exclaimed. "We'd be *thrilled* to have you." He then explained that the plan was for him and his friend Paul Fay to cruise aboard the *Marlin* around Hyannis Port early in the day. Jack would then arrive at Hammersmith in the afternoon of the 25th and stay until the 27th.

Janet later explained: "It wasn't as easy as all that to have the President of the United States spend the weekend with you because all sorts of furor ensued to which, I supposed, he was rather oblivious. The Secret Service appeared and ninety-nine telephones were pulled in and out, the Newport police went into a tailspin and put little [phone] booths here and there, and the Coast Guard whizzed around the dock."

Jamie elaborated: "When Jack became President, the government installed thirty phone lines, all connected to the White House switchboard. So when a person called the house to see whether I was going to play tennis with him at Bailey's Beach, an operator would answer by saying, 'White House Switchboard.' That call would be transferred to the Newport Naval Base. It would then again be transferred to the Secret Service command post in our basement. Then, it would be transferred to the pantry, where an agent was always on duty. That agent would then have to figure out where I was in the house, which was likely on the second floor in my bedroom. By the time the call came to me up there, the person on the other line was so frightened and confused, the last thing on his mind was the question of whether or not I wanted to play tennis with him at Bailey's Beach!"

"Jack always called me 'Mummy,'" Janet would recall. "For some reason, this always seemed funny to him, that anybody should be called 'Mummy.' I don't know why, but he thought it was very funny." They were getting along so well these days, Janet had all but forgotten how angry she'd been at her son-in-law for his absence when Jackie gave birth prematurely. It had been a number of years ago, after all, and it was hard for her to hold a grudge against him. He was so charming, she loved being in his company. Of course, he was also the nation's Commander in Chief and that carried weight with her, as it would with most people. She had great respect for the power of his office. "I remember one family dinner when Jackie contradicted Jack on something, Mummy was actually upset," recalled Jamie. " 'Jacqueline,' she said, scolding her, 'how dare you correct the President!' Jack loved that. For the rest of the day he kept ribbing Jackie, saying, 'How dare you correct me, Jackie. I'm the President!' Also, I think it bears noting that Mummy was only ten years older than Jack; she thought of him as a contemporary," said Jamie.

Maybe Janet herself summed up her evolving feelings about Jack when she said, "I suppose there's good in the worst of us. But bad in the best of us."

The night after Jack's arrival, Janet regaled him with stories about the raising of Jackie and Lee. It was just the three of them alone in the Deck Room — her, Hugh, and Jack — enjoying the view and the night air. The next day, Sunday, Jack spent the morning entertaining his young namesake while giving Maud Shaw time off to walk on the beach and collect her thoughts. Later, Janet did her exercises as Jack worked at Hugh's small desk in the study that adjoined Janet and Hugh's master bedroom. "He signed a good many bills there on the antique partners desk," Janet would later say. Among them were bills appropriating funds for the Peace Corps and the USS *Arizona* memorial at Pearl Harbor. (Later, Jackie would have a plaque made to commemorate the spot; a large, gold-framed

239

oil painting of Jack sitting in front of an American flag in 1961 would be hung on the wall next to the desk.) Afterward, Jack and Hugh played golf at the Newport Country Club. Then they cruised in the presidential yacht, the *Honey Fitz* — named after Jack's grandfather John Francis Fitzgerald, former mayor of Boston — on Narragansett Bay, with Janet, Jamie, and Janet Jr. They then all piled into a white convertible rented for the President, and headed to Bailey's Beach — with Jack driving — where they went swimming. That night, the family enjoyed another delicious meal prepared by the Hammersmith waitstaff. Jack then retired to the guest room on the top floor of the house, making his way up the steps slowly with the aid of the Irish blackthorn walking stick he kept at Hammersmith for those times when his back bothered him.

On Monday morning, it was time for the President to go back to work in Washington, scheduled to meet with his cabinet to discuss problems in the Middle East. He hated to leave. Before departing, he presented Hugh with a gift: the President's flag that had flown at Hammersmith down at the boathouse along with the American flag during his first stay there as Commander in Chief back in '61. Hugh had tears in his eyes as he accepted the gift. The flag would later be encased in glass with a plaque, the inscription of which would read: "The President's Flag Flown at Hammersmith Farm, Newport, Rhode Island, Presented to Hugh Dudley Auchincloss by John Fitzgerald Kennedy, President of the United States — 1961."

While the green-and-white presidential helicopter revved its engines on the gravelly beach in front of the estate, Janet and Hugh walked toward it with the President. Shouting because of all the noise, Jack asked Janet, "If it wouldn't be too much trouble, I might like to come back next weekend!" The following Friday, Jack returned to Hammersmith with Jackie and Caroline, who had just gotten back from Italy. This time, Janet and Hugh stayed in the Castle, giving Jack, Jackie, Caroline, and John (who had arrived earlier with Maud Shaw) as well as the Secret Service full run of the Big House. The President and Jackie spent that weekend in Janet and Hugh's master bedroom.

It's worth noting that when they got a little older, Caroline and John both always had their own rooms at Hammersmith, on the third floor, where the governesses also slept. There were five bedrooms on this floor, including those of the Kennedy offspring, across the hall from each other; these had formerly been used by Nini when she was at the farm, and also by Lee. Jackie's old room was up there, too, with its stunning view of Narragansett Bay and Jamestown on the island across the bay. Tommy's old room was on that floor as well, with its twin beds, as was Yusha's room with its magnificent ocean view. Once Yusha, Tommy, Nini, Jackie, and Lee were all permanently out of the house, their rooms were used by whichever children came to visit, but only Caroline and John had their own special rooms. One can't help but wonder what Lee might have thought about the fact that Tina and Anthony did not also have designated rooms for their occasional visits. "Mummy did play favorites," said Jamie. "You had to get used to it because that's the way it was, and Lee knew it."

The Kennedys would return in mid-September to watch the America's Cup races with the Auchinclosses from aboard the USS *Joseph P. Kennedy Jr.,* destroyer. At a dinner held for the yachtsmen at Hammersmith Farm on September 14, the night before the race, Jack made some comments that would long be remembered: "I really don't know why it is that all of us are so committed to the sea, except I think it's because in addition to the fact that the sea changes, and the light changes, and ships change, it's because we all came from the sea. And it is an interesting biological fact that all of us have, in our veins, the exact same percentage of salt in our blood that exists in the ocean, and, therefore, we have salt in our blood, in our sweat, in our tears. We are tied to the ocean.

And when we go back to the sea — whether it is to sail or to watch it — we are going back from whence we came."

During the time that Jackie and Jack spent at Hammersmith, they seemed happy, though, as was their custom, just a little frosty with each other. They were never really effusive with each other; it's just not who they were as people. Jack, as we now know, had other outlets for intimacy. Jackie didn't. However, that didn't mean she wasn't tempted. It didn't mean that at all.

A New Love for Jackie?

It was a warm night in October 1962. The location was the British embassy. They made a striking couple, she tall and svelte, he even taller with broad shoulders. While the orchestra played, couples all around them danced in perfect time, the women wearing elegant evening gowns, the men decked out in finely tailored tuxedos. However, no matter the glamour and sense of entitlement around her, all eyes were on them and she knew it. After all, there was only one First Lady, and it was she who happened to hold that distinction: Jacqueline Bouvier Kennedy. Anyone on her arm other than the President himself would only be basking in her reflected glow.

Tonight, Jackie would enjoy a dinner of London broil and red-cherry cheesecake and then dance the night away at the British embassy. Tomorrow she would present plans for one of her most valued pet projects, the saving and restoration of Lafayette Square in Washington, D.C. It was a center of town across the street from the White House where vintage nineteenth-century brownstones — such as the one that had been owned by Dolley Madison — had been targeted for demolition by the Eisenhower administration to make way for new, more modern white marble constructions. Jackie had made it her personal mission to see to it that no such destruction of this square would ever take place. She valued those homes and understood their importance to Washington culture and spoke of "lovely buildings being torn down so that cheesy skyscrapers could go up." "Perhaps saving old buildings isn't the most important thing in the world if you are waiting for the bomb," she said, "but I think we are always going to be waiting for the bomb and it won't ever come and so to save the old and to make the new beautiful is terribly important." To that end, Jackie would hire a world-class architect to help her find ways to restore those dwellings, build others in the same style that might complement what was already there, and then get governmental approval and funding to actually do the work. After all, she knew she had substantial influence as First Lady, so she figured why not use it to do something worthwhile? At first, she would be met with bitter resistance from the Fine Arts Commission as well as members of the elite architectural community. She would stay the course, though, determined to see it through. For tonight, though, she was happy and in a good mood, and in the arms of someone strong and exciting.

"Are you happy?" her dance partner asked her.

"Oh, Jack, now, what kind of question is that?" she asked as she looked up into his eyes. She was being coy and flirtatious. It was all in fun. Why not allow herself to be just a little swept away by Jack. Not Kennedy, either. Warnecke. Jack Warnecke — the architect she'd hired to work with her on Lafayette Park.

John Carl Warnecke — "Jack," as he was better known — was a man of great distinction, someone to whom she couldn't help but be attracted. A recent divorcé in his early forties, he was good-looking, with blue eyes and striking features. He was six foot three, about 215 pounds, and broad-shouldered, a ladies' man, too; he was dating the actress Joan Fontaine at the time. He was also accomplished, having quickly become one of the most famous architects of his generation, his recent design of the American embassy in Thailand garnering him international ac-

245

claim. The son of prominent architect Carl Ingomar Warnecke, Jack had homes in Georgetown, San Francisco, and Hawaii. He also owned an enormous, three-hundred-acre ranch on the Russian River, one on which he told Jackie she was welcome to ride horses anytime she liked.

It wasn't what he had acquired in life, though, that impressed her. What Jackie recognized on this night of their first meeting was his ability to make her laugh. She found herself opening up to him, which was unusual for a woman like her who liked to keep her own counsel. He told her that they could perhaps one day travel the world and find places that needed sprucing up. They would then do what he believed they were put on this earth to do, which was to leave it in better shape than they'd found it. He was so forward about forging at the very least a friendship with her that she was a little taken aback. After all, though they'd been communicating by telephone and letters for many weeks in discussions relating to Lafayette Square, they really didn't know each other. Yet, oddly, it felt to her as if they did.

Jack Warnecke had long been a friend of the Kennedy family or, as his personal assistant, Bertha Baldwin, put it, "The Kennedys were everything to him. He had known JFK since at least 1940 when he audited writing classes at Stanford University in California. At that time, Jack [Warnecke] was a star football player on the undefeated Stanford team that had made it all the way to the Rose Bowl. The team was so good, they were nicknamed the Wow Boys."

Though Kennedy had great admiration for Warnecke, as did most of his fellow students, it wouldn't be until '56 that Warnecke's Stanford fraternity brother Paul "Red" Fay (who would later be undersecretary and then secretary of the navy) would introduce Kennedy to him. "By that time, my dad was already a successful architect, having graduated from the Harvard Graduate School of Design," said Jack's daughter, Margo Warnecke Merck. "He'd become well known for his avant-garde way of conceptualizing design, his work at the University of California campus at Berkeley first distinguishing him."

He was having a good life. The question he posed to Jackie remained: Was she? Jackie may have suspected that the reason Jack asked the question was because he had some inside knowledge of the way her marriage was unfolding just based on previous experience as JFK's wingman: "I was a friend of Jack's. I knew him well. I knew all of the Kennedy men well. The first time I met JFK I was acting as a beard for him, back when he was a senator. Red Fay had set him up with a girl at a party. He asked me to tag along and act as if I was her date when, of course, she was actually Kennedy's girl. So, from the beginning you could say that I was sort of involved in some of JFK's private affairs. And I had my own monkey business, too." Or, as his daughter, Margo, would put it, "My handsome dad *loved* the ladies; and they loved him right back."

248

■ ■ ■ ■

PART FIVE:
TROUBLE BREWING

■ ■ ■ ■

LEE'S ANNULMENT

Back in 1958, Stas Radziwill had wanted a Catholic wedding to Lee Bouvier Canfield but wasn't able to have one because her divorce from Michael Canfield had not been recognized by the Church. Therefore, an annulment would be necessary. The couple had started the arduous process by filing the proper papers with the Church. But the procedure was suddenly interrupted when Lee became pregnant and felt forced to marry Stas, which she did before a judge in 1959. That civil marriage so piqued the Catholic tribunal charged with the decision about Lee's marriage — it dubbed it "an indignity" — that it threatened to never grant the annulment. Still, Lee and Stas remained hopeful. Then in '61, all hope was dashed when Church officials said they would definitely refuse it. The only person who could reverse the decision would be the Pope himself, John XXIII. Hopeless? Maybe for most people, but not if one's brother-in-law happens to be the President.

Now with Jack in office, more than ever Lee's attorneys began working with the Catholic Church to see what could be done to secure the annulment. Bobby took charge of the matter. "You supply the prayers, we'll provide the pressure, and God will deliver the miracle," he had told Lee. It was then arranged for Jackie to be interviewed by the ecclesiastical tribunal of New York about the sanctity of Lee's marriage to Stas. One can only imagine how she felt about being asked personal questions about her sister's personal life by a board of priests, but Jackie did what she was asked to do. Lee even then convinced Michael Canfield to swear that when he married Lee he never intended to have children with her. Was this true? If so, his lack of attraction to her started to make a little more sense to some observers. "I think the inference was obvious," Jamie Auchincloss would say. "Either Michael was gay, shy, or didn't want offspring. Whichever the case, it was grounds for annulment."

Lee then petitioned the Pope himself, writing a long, detailed, and quite passionate missive, dated July 18, 1961. "After my sister testified, I was fervently hoping that one day I would be admitted again into the Church, that my husband and my children would no longer be unhappy because I was the source of their pain and of the pain to my sister, Jacqueline Kennedy." Exaggerating the situation just a little, she continued, "I know that my sister is as desperate as I am. She tells me that, in a way, as the wife of President Kennedy, she feels responsibility for the apparent injustice of my trial. I would really like her to feel unloaded of all responsibility! If I could have a right of an appeal, then my suspicions and those of my sister [of a political motivation behind being declined] would be dissipated." Lee also alluded to her postpartum depression by writing, "Faith and hope in justice gave me unquenchable strength and saved me twice in my lifetime. I was *gravely* ill, *mortally* ill, in these last two years. Perhaps my faith was the miracle that saved me."

It was then arranged for Jackie to visit the Pope during the time of her and Lee's trip to India and Pakistan. She wasn't to say much to him and was not even to mention the annulment. All she was to do was stop off in Rome, visit the Vatican, kneel before the Pope, get his blessing, and exchange some kind words. This papal audience took place on March 11, 1962. The White House press office made certain that Lee was not in any of the photographs taken during that day, however. If, at any time in the future, Lee was able to secure an annulment, the White House didn't want it to appear as if the President or First Lady had had any influence over the process. Unfortunately, after meeting Jackie, the Pope *still* wouldn't grant the annulment.

Many more months of paperwork followed until, finally, the aging Pope got sick and, with his illness, came a bit more latitude. On November 24, 1962, Lee suddenly got her annulment. Could the timing have been any worse, though? Her marriage to Stas continued to be on shaky ground. She was still seeing Taki from time to time, though they both agreed it was not serious. However, she had also been dating Onassis for the last eight months, and this romance was definitely heating up by the end of '62. The two would rendezvous as often as possible in London, Paris, and Greece. Every second she spent with him she found blissful — and complicated. She had two small children, after all; making arrangements so that she could take off and be with Ari at a moment's notice was complex — but worth it to her.

Lee had also heard that Stas was now having an affair with Charlotte Ford, daughter of Henry Ford II, the grandson and namesake of the founder of Ford Motors. She told Taki she was sure about it but didn't want to ask too many questions of Stas, lest he start asking some of his own. Whatever the case, the prince still quickly made plans for a Church wedding in London to Lee. It would be small and private, he said. Lee knew that his father, Prince Janusz Franciszek Radziwiłł, a devout

Catholic, was insisting upon it. Unfortunately, Stas had the same relationship with him that Lee had with Janet, meaning that he was a domineering force in Stas's life and expected his son to do as he was told.

After everything everyone had gone through to secure the annulment so that the prince and princess could finally marry in the Catholic Church, Lee now felt pressured by time and circumstance to follow through with those plans. She had to wonder how she had gotten herself into such a mess

The wedding was set for July 3, 1963.

She had eight months to figure things out.

"YOU WILL ALWAYS COME FIRST"

The holidays of 1962 were stressful but somehow Lee got through them. She and Jackie and the kids spent them together, as usual. However, she and Stas were more distant than ever toward each other. She couldn't take her mind off her new obsession, Aristotle Onassis. The biggest problem with Ari, though, was that he was still involved with Maria Callas, and Lee wasn't sure how this relationship would affect her future with him. Ari and Maria continued to have a soulful, passionate, but also famously tortured romance. Everyone knew about it; all one had to do was check the gossip columns for weekly updates. He had told Lee several times that Maria had exhausted him. Every time he attempted to end it with her, he claimed, she would try to commit suicide. Lee didn't doubt it. She knew Maria fairly well and had always felt she was just a little unhinged. It would not surprise her that she would hasten her demise over a man, though Lee would never think to do such a thing. She thought Maria was weak. She also believed Ari needed strength in a woman, not weakness.

Six months passed.

By June, Lee was more in a panic than ever. The wedding was just a month away and she was no closer to an answer as to what she should do about it. When she suggested that it be postponed, Stas blew up at her, telling her that the plans were made, his father was looking forward to it, and that there would be no postponement. Though he knew the ceremony was imminent, Onassis seemed to not want to engage with Lee about it, maybe waiting for her to ask his opinion. Finally, she did. "What shall I do?" she asked him, this according to what she later recalled to Agnetta Castallanos. If she left Stas, would she have a future with Ari? "Do you want to be with me? Or not?"

Ari said he was not willing to commit to Lee at this time. "He cared about her, he said, loved her, even," recalled Agnetta Cast-allanos. "But, no, he was not ready to marry her. When she told him she was being pres-sured to marry Stas in the Catholic Church, he told her not to do it. Why was it so neces-sary? She was already legally married, he pointed out, and the Church wedding would just be a more significant tie to a husband about whom she was already ambivalent. 'Do not do it,' he told her, and he was emphatic about it. He warned her that if she renewed her vows to Stas, it would change things between them. She asked if it was because of Callas that he would not commit to her. He said no, absolutely not. 'I can make you no promises,' he told her, 'but I do care about you, Lee, and I do see a future for us,' he told her. 'But, as you must know by now, I am not a man you can pressure.' "

In mid-June, Ari invited Lee onto the *Christina* with a group of friends for a week. When she got aboard, she found Sir Winston Chur-chill and his son, Randolph, sitting on the deck with about a dozen others, all in casual wear baking under a hot sun, the men smok-ing cigars, the women with cigarettes, and everyone drinking daiquiris. A couple of months earlier, Churchill had been bestowed honorary citizenship of the United States by President Kennedy. He was in bad shape, though. At eighty-eight, he looked as if he was suffering from dementia, just staring

257

straight ahead as his son tended to him, laying a blanket on his lap, propping him up in his chair. His wife, Clementine, two years younger, also seemed frail and unwell. She sat in a chair, appearing almost comatose, her head tilted to the side as she gazed blankly out at the sea. As Lee debated whether or not to approach them, who should come sashaying onto the deck but Maria Callas. One can only imagine Lee's reaction.

Karina Brownley, whose father, Leon, had a number of business interests in common with Onassis relating to the shipping business, had sailed many times on Onassis's incredible voyager the *Christina,* sometimes with Lee on board. At the age of seventeen, she was on this trip in June of '63 along the coast of Italy. She recalled an evening when she and her father dined with Ari, Lee, Maria, the Churchills, and other friends on deck. There were probably fifty people at the table. It was formal, the men in sleek black suits and ties, the women in long evening gowns. Lee was wearing a pink-and-white lace dress and — perhaps because they were eating outdoors — a white organdy picture hat trimmed with a filament of delicate silk roses. Maria struck a strong contrast in a black chiffon shift and matching cocktail hat with draped veiling (which she pulled back from her face at dinner), and three-quarter-length silk gloves (which she did not take off while dining). The food — Greek, of course — was plentiful, as was the supply of costly wines and exotic liquors. A full moon coated everything on the deck with a patina of silver. "You must understand that mermaids are both good and bad luck," Onassis said, holding court, as always. "Good luck if you find one in the sea. But bad luck if you bring her aboard. Never ever bring a mermaid on board. Remember that." As always, every statement he made was with great authority. Maria hung on to his every word. Now and then, she glared at Lee, who then returned the favor.

After dinner, Lee and Aristotle excused themselves from the table, with Onassis saying, "Lee and I are going to be unavailable for the rest of the evening. Please," he added while grandly extending his arms, "enjoy the many pleasures of the *Christina*. Good evening." Lee gathered her things and got up without saying a word. "But will you be joining me later at the bar?" Maria asked Ari, her expression hopeful. Onassis swung his eyes to her and said, "I seriously doubt it, my dear. But let's gather in the morning for breakfast." Frowning, Maria muttered, "So be it." With that, Ari and Lee took their leave, but not before Lee turned to give Maria a small, wry smile.

Why had Onassis invited Maria? As he would later explain to Lee, he simply wanted to demonstrate to her that the two women could be in the same place at the same time, and he would choose *her* over Maria. "You will always come first," he promised Lee. On the one hand, Lee was flattered, but on the other, troubled. While she understood the gesture, it frightened her. She would later say she thought it was a sick game, a horrible thing to do to Maria. She certainly had no affection for the opera star, "but I am not a mean person," she said, "and that was cruel." She couldn't help but wonder if Onassis would humiliate Maria in that way, what might he one day do to her?

Brownley says that the contingent met the next morning for breakfast in the main dining room. A glowing Lee sat next to Onassis, her eyes sparkling, while Maria sat with some other gentlemen, looking dour. Later that day, Maria got off the *Christina* at its first dock.

The rest of the week was heavenly for Lee. Onassis treated her like a queen, telling her that every person working on the *Christina* was at her disposal, giving her expensive jewels every day, taking her shopping in small villages along the Italian coastline as they docked at this one and that one. He reminded her that she was young and beautiful and said that if she wanted to be truly happy, she needed to make some tough decisions about her life; otherwise, he said, she would end up like poor old Clementine Churchill — sick and sad at the side of someone sicker and sadder. As Lee would later tell Agnetta Castallanos, "Maybe for the first time, I thought, yes, this is what I want. Ari is what I want. Ari is what I deserve."

By the end of June, strong rumors about Ari and Lee had begun to make their way into gossip columns in the United States. These stories had built so quickly that people in Lee's life were beginning to believe they were true — and one of those people was her mother, Janet. After all, Lee was never in London with Stas when Janet tried to track her down. Where was she? Stas would always say he had no idea, but that he would pass a message on to her. "Well, who's taking care of the kids?" Janet would ask. Stas would explain that they had help, and then hang up quickly. Lee would never return the call.

While Lee was cruising with Onassis, Janet summoned Adora Rule into her large dressing room to make plans for a four-day visit from Jackie, Caroline, and John. On the wall was a large collage of family photos that she had designed herself, and then had framed in white. The overhead lighting in this rectangular space was purposely soft — fluorescent light emanating through latticework and rice paper. While practicing her isometrics in this quiet space, Janet gave a long list of instructions to Adora having to do with plans she

261

was making for family time. As she was wrapping up, she said, "Also, on an unrelated note, I want you to keep your eyes and ears open when it comes to Lee and this Onassis character."

Adora wondered if the two were friends. "Oh, don't be ridiculous," Janet said as she touched her toes without bending her knees. "Men and women cannot be friends." Adora then asked what it was that Janet was looking for. She said she didn't exactly know. "Is it true that Onassis has his own private island?" Janet asked. Adora said that, yes, it was true. She said she'd read in a newspaper that he'd just recently bought it and that its name was Skorpios. Trying to be helpful, Adora then added in a conspiratorial tone that she'd heard *many* stories about Onassis, that he was *quite* the subject of controversy. "Well, he's complicated, I'm sure," Janet said, her tone now suddenly sharp. Then, stopping her exercise, she regarded her assistant carefully and added, "Nobody is just one thing, Adora. We all have black marks somewhere in our past. Don't be so quick to judge. It's not very becoming."

STANDING IN FOR JACKIE

Lee Radziwill left the Onassis cruise after about a week's time at the port of Fiumicino, and headed for Germany, where she was to meet President Kennedy. Jackie, pregnant, had asked if Lee would stand in for her during the President's tour of Germany and Ireland. Of course, Lee was thrilled to do so, to see what it might be like to be in her sister's shoes. She met the Kennedy contingent in Bonn, where a dinner with the President of Germany was scheduled. She was also in West Berlin with Jack when he gave his historic *"Ich bin ein Berliner"* speech on June 26, 1963. Then it was off to Ireland. "What do I most remember about Lee on this trip?" asked Dave Powers, special assistant to JFK. "Her beauty. Her charisma. She was wearing a pure white coat when she got off the plane in Ireland and she looked marvelous. Everywhere she went, she just lit up the room. She was different from Jackie. Jackie was more, I suppose, *royal* would be the word. Lee was a little more accessible, easier to know. Everyone loved her. The press corps thought she was fantastic. She was funny. Very entertaining. I wouldn't say Jackie was entertaining, necessarily. But it was different for the First Lady. There was certain decorum necessary. Lee was free of that, and we all thought she was marvelous."

After Ireland, the contingent winged its way to England, where Jack would visit the grave of his deceased sister, Kathleen, in Chatsworth. There was also a stop at the estate of the Duke and Duchess of Devonshire before then returning to the States.

For Lee, this little tour was a bittersweet experience. It wasn't what she had hoped for in that she didn't really get to experience life as First Lady. Rather, she was viewed, even though respectfully, as just another noteworthy person with the Kennedy contingent. It was as if she had been so close to true glory, but not quite there, a First Lady also-ran, as it were. It made her feel depressed.

"You will always come first," Onassis had told her. That sentiment resonated with Lee. Now, more than ever, she wanted to come first.

A SACRIFICE FOR JACKIE

In Janet Auchincloss's mind, the problem was obvious: Her daughter Lee was the sister of her other daughter, Jackie, who happened to be First Lady of the United States. Lee was famously married to a royal; they had two children. Now she seemed to be involved with a high-profile crook. While Janet may have been able to give Onassis the benefit of the doubt in front of an employee like Adora Rule, she actually viewed Onassis as nothing less than a criminal. She needed to know exactly what was going on.

When Janet set her mind to finding out information, she usually did so. First, she called Jack Kennedy. However, he said he didn't want to discuss Lee's love life with her. In his position, it wasn't appropriate, he said. He suggested she call the attorney general, his brother Bobby, who had helped spearhead the annulment from Michael.

Janet and Bobby had an easy rapport these days; ever since Jack was inaugurated she had made an effort to get along with Bobby and his wife, Ethel. Bobby told her that he knew for certain that Lee was involved with Onassis, and that he didn't like it. If they were just dating, *maybe* he could live with it, he said, though he'd rather it not be the case. However, if it started looking as if she might divorce Stas and marry Onassis, no, that would not be something he or the Kennedys would ever be able to accept. They were all hoping for a second term for Jack, he told her, and any marriage between Lee and Onassis would scandalize not only the First Lady but the entire administration. More to the point, though, Bobby wanted to know what Lee was going to do about remarrying Stas, especially after everything that had been done to get her the annulment from Michael. Janet said she would take care of it.

In early July, Janet had what has been described by most people in their lives as a tense and upsetting conversation with Lee in New York after Lee got back from the Kennedy tour. The wedding ceremony to Stas was just days away, and Janet could see that

Lee was waffling about going through with it. Now Janet knew it was because of Onassis. True to form, though, Lee would not confirm that she and Ari were involved, but she would also not deny it. She simply felt it was not Janet's business. Of course, Janet disagreed.

During this conversation, Janet outlined Lee's duty as sister of the First Lady — which, at the very least, was to not bring scandal to Jackie's White House doorstep. She was quite clear with her daughter: Everyone had gone through a great deal of trouble to process an annulment specifically so that Lee could marry Stas in the Catholic Church. Jackie had put her reputation as First Lady on the line. The President had interceded. The attorney general had become involved. The Pope was enlisted. Even poor Michael Canfield had had to give a deposition and swear that he couldn't sire children and that Lee didn't know about it when she married him — further grounds for annulment. That there should be any question at all as to how Lee should now comport herself given these extreme circumstances was far beyond Janet's comprehension.

The clock was ticking. Janet said that Lee should end whatever she had with Onassis and reaffirm her vows with Stas, as planned. Period. If not just for the sake of propriety, then for Jackie's sake. "You must do this for your sister, the First Lady," Janet told Lee.

"But why?" Lee asked. Janet didn't want to hear it.

Apparently, Lee didn't have it in her to fight her mother, or Stas either, for that matter, who was pushing hard for the wedding, as were many members of his family — including his father. All evidence points to Lee not asking Jackie for an opinion. She probably felt it not wise considering what Jackie had gone through to help with the annulment. Also, Jackie's position on infidelity was quite clear. To think that she was making this big a sacrifice for such a disapproving sister must have been difficult for Lee, but she decided to do so anyway.

It wasn't as if Lee had any animus toward Stas. She didn't. He was a good man, father of her children, and she did have great affection for him. However, their marriage was long broken by both of their affairs. How ironic was it, then, that both were being pushed into a church marriage by their parents, he by his father, and she by her mother. One would have thought them old enough to make their own decisions — Lee was thirty, Stas forty-nine — but old habits die hard and their mutual impulse to subjugate themselves to their parents' will was deeply engrained.

When Lee telephoned Onassis to tell him of her plans, he was hurt and upset. This was their one chance to be together, he told her, and he feared she would live to regret her decision. However, he told her he understood her conundrum. He figured the Kennedys were behind it. In fact, he would later tell his biographer Peter Evans, "The Kennedys could accept me as Lee's lover: that was personal. What they couldn't accept was the idea that I might actually marry her: *that* was politics."

Ari wondered if they would still be able to see each other. Lee wasn't sure. She didn't know what the future would bring. He promised he would not abandon her, though. His magnanimity made her fall just a little deeper for him, but Lee knew Ari well. She knew that her decision would change things just by virtue of the fact that she was defying him. "She had a sense that she was making the biggest mistake of her life," said one person who knew her well at this time. "She just hoped that she would reaffirm her vows with Stas, wait an appropriate amount of time, and then, hopefully, continue with Ari and everything would be okay. She felt powerless to do anything else."

Therefore, on July 3, 1963, Prince and Princess Radziwill were once again wed, this time in a small, private religious ceremony at Westminster Roman Catholic Cathedral in London.

BABY PATRICK

On July 28, 1963, Jackie Kennedy celebrated her thirty-fourth birthday at the Kennedy compound with her husband's side of the family. By this time, the world knew she was pregnant again. She'd told Janet and Lee back in January, but the White House didn't make the official announcement until April. The news was met with great excitement by a country already swept away by the First Lady's signature style, taste, and personality. Even those who didn't agree with their politics couldn't help but be affected by the general wave of excitement; the last time a First Lady had been pregnant was back in 1893 when Mrs. Grover Cleveland gave birth to a daughter, Esther. With the baby due in September, plans were made for delivery by cesarean section at Walter Reed Hospital in Washington. A contingency plan, however, was put into place that, should the baby arrive early while the Kennedys were at the Cape, it would be delivered at Otis Air Force Base Hospital in Falmouth, Massachusetts.

On Wednesday, August 7, Janet and Janet Jr. were in New York making plans for the teenager's upcoming debutante party, scheduled to take place at Hammersmith on Saturday the 13th. However, while there, they got word that Jackie had gone into premature labor. Since she wasn't due for five more weeks, Janet was immediately worried. She and Janet Jr. quickly boarded a helicopter to be with Jackie at Otis Air Force Base Hospital.

By the time Jackie's mother and sister arrived at Otis, Jackie's personal obstetrician, Dr. John Walsh, had already performed an emergency cesarean section and delivered a baby boy who weighed less than five pounds. The baby's size — though small — was not the issue. It was what would later be diagnosed as the life-threatening hyaline membrane disease of the lungs — then the most common cause of death among premature infants in the United States — that generated the greatest concern. (Today the ailment is known as infant respiratory distress syndrome.) The situation was so dire, it was decided to have the child baptized by a Catholic priest in the operating room. Jackie, at this point, was sedated and not aware of the crisis.

Jack decided that, given the baby's condition, Jackie should see him immediately upon her awakening; he saw to it that the baby was wheeled into her room. With Dr. James Drorbaugh, the attending pediatrician, at her side, Jackie placed her hands into the portholes of the isolette — a rolling incubator — and lovingly adjusted the baby's warmed blankets and held his hand for a few minutes. She noticed his soft brown hair. He was fragile, his breathing labored. With oxygen escaping through the portal opening, the visit needed to be cut short. Downplaying the situation for Jackie, the doctor explained that the baby was having a little trouble breathing and, just as a precaution, would be transferred to Boston for more specialized care. Jack reminded his upset wife that John Jr. had also been delivered prematurely by Dr. Walsh and that he, too, had spent time in an incubator, "and look at him today." He did what he could to comfort Jackie, but, of course, he was anxious as well. Jackie then reaffirmed that she wanted to name the child Patrick, after Jack's grandfather, and Bouvier, in honor of her father.

When Jack and Dr. Drorbaugh left Jackie's room, they found her mother and stepsister rushing toward them. The baby was being wheeled down the hall. "No, no, let me see him," Janet said as she hurried to them. She leaned over the incubator and saw the struggling infant with a tangle of tubes attached to him. He appeared so fragile, the sight took Janet's breath away. She suddenly looked faint. Jack reached for her and held her tightly, telling her not to worry. Jack then also hugged Janet Jr. before rushing out of the hospital. Janet turned to go into Jackie's room, but hesitated for a moment. Finally, she steeled herself and with Janet Jr. at her side, walked into Jackie's room, closing the door behind them.

When mother and daughter emerged from Jackie's room about thirty minutes later, Janet looked shaken, so much so that she was seen steadying herself against a wall. Lt. Barbara Goodwin, who was Jackie's three-to-eleven night nurse, told Janet the next couple of days would be critical. She then said that the medical staff had done all they could over the last few months to prepare for any emergency, with precautions such as the selection of three healthy military men with the same blood type as Jackie (A1 Rh positive) in case any transfusions were necessary. "But Jackie and I have the same blood type," Janet said. "Why didn't anyone ask me?" Goodwin said that she was surprised that no one had thought to do so. If Jackie needed blood, Janet said, she wanted to be sure to be first on the list. She didn't want her daughter to have a transfusion from a stranger when her own mother was available. The nurse agreed to let Janet know if such a procedure became necessary.

Janet Sr. and Janet Jr. then went to the nursery to see Patrick in his incubator. There were eleven other babies in the nursery with him, all born in recent days and being cared for. Mother and daughter stood arm in arm for about fifteen minutes in silence, watching the baby as he struggled for breath. Suddenly, at a little before six that evening, there was a burst of activity, with doctors and nurses racing about and Secret Service agents barking commands at one another. It had been decided that Patrick would be taken by ambulance to Boston Children's Hospital. "I must call Lee," Janet told her daughter, her face grave. "You go, make sure Patrick is okay."

While Janet Jr. was seeing to the baby's ambulance departure, her mother asked Lt. Goodwin if she could use a telephone. She wanted to contact Lee, who she had heard was, again, on the *Christina,* docked in Athens with Aristotle Onassis. It was true. Just a month after renewing her vows to Stas, Lee and Onassis were together again. It wasn't easy making a long-distance telephone connection to the yacht, however, causing a stressed Janet to slam down the phone at the nurse's station several times in exasperation before finally reaching Lee. The specifics of their conversation are not known but, obviously, Janet told Lee about Patrick. Janet then called Adora Rule. "I was at Hammersmith waiting to hear from Mrs. A.," Adora recalled. "I was so nervous and upset because the television news was all about Jackie and Patrick and the fact that the infant was sick."

"How is the baby?" Adora asked Janet as soon as she heard her voice on the line.

"I need you to make Lee's travel arrangements," Janet said, ignoring the question.

"Well, where is she?" Adora asked.

"Where do you think she is?" Janet shot back.

"I knew what that meant," Adora recalled. "I didn't know how Mrs. A. knew the princess was with Onassis, and I didn't ask. I just told her that I would arrange for her trip back to the States. I then called Lee. She was crying when she picked up the phone, already having heard the news. She was frantic to be with Jackie. I felt that after what she'd been through with her baby, Christina, this situation was going to be particularly hard on her."

"CUT TO THE BONE"

The next morning, Thursday, August 8, Janet awakened and showered in the small quarters that had been given her at Otis. She then had a light breakfast before walking down the hallway to check on Jackie. Lt. Nancy Lumsden was taking Jackie's vitals when Janet walked into the room. "She's doing well," Lt. Lumsden observed. Jackie was certainly weak, but seemed better than she had the day before.

Shortly after, Jack was in Jackie's room giving her the encouraging news that Patrick seemed to be improving! She was relieved. The President then went back to Boston Children's Hospital, where he met up with his mother-in-law. She later recalled, "I remember him saying to me in the hospital in Boston that day, when Patrick was in the little incubator . . . I remember him saying to me — well, I'm going to misquote him because I can't remember the words now, but I remember him saying — 'Oh, nothing must happen to Patrick because I just can't bear to think of the effect it might have on Jackie.' I could see the effect it might have on him, too."

Things changed quickly. Later that same afternoon at Otis, after a brief telephone conversation with Dr. Drorbaugh, Jack pulled his mother-in-law aside and informed her that Patrick's condition had suddenly deteriorated. He told Janet that he was about to take a chopper back to Boston. Of course, Janet insisted that she accompany him. As soon as they got to the hospital and saw little Patrick, they both realized he was in even greater distress. Jack and Janet then had a meeting with the team of worried doctors about how to best proceed.

Janet said she wanted to call Dr. Samuel Levine, professor emeritus at Cornell University Medical Center and consultant pediatrician at New York Hospital, who three years before had treated Tina when Lee gave birth to her prematurely. The baby had made it. "He can do wonders," Janet said. "We should definitely bring him in." It was also decided, in the meanwhile, to place the infant in a hyperbaric chamber in the hope that its pressurized oxygen would assist in his breathing. This was a treatment not ordinarily done for infants in Patrick's condition, but it was a last resort. Jack agreed on both counts, contacting the doctor Janet had recommended and approving the chamber as a treatment. He personally called Dr. Levine and arranged for him to be flown immediately to Boston from New York. Then, as Janet later recalled, "We went down [to] the iron lung room, which they tried as a last resort to help his breathing."

While Patrick was being treated in the chamber, Dr. Levine arrived. Janet and Jack greeted him warmly, thanking him for coming. With the baby in the hyperbaric chamber, Dr. Levine wasn't able to do a physical examination of Patrick. Janet just wanted to make sure he agreed that the "iron lung" treatment was advisable. He said he agreed that it was the baby's only hope.

That night, Janet and Jack stayed at Boston Children's Hospital, not retiring until after midnight. At about two, the President was awakened with the news that Patrick was likely not going to make it. By this time, Bobby and Ted Kennedy had arrived at the hospital with Dave Powers, Jack's assistant. Powers suggested that they wake Janet, but the President felt there was no need to disturb her; there was really nothing she could do, he said, and she was already worn out.

At just a little after four, Janet bolted up from her bed, suddenly awake. She raced down to see the baby, and there she saw Bobby and Ted comforting Jack. "Oh my God," she said as she braced herself against the wall. Patrick had died. She watched as a sobbing Jack walked away from his brothers in order to be alone. "That was the one time I saw him where Jack was genuinely cut to the bone," Janet would later say. "When Patrick died, it almost killed him, too. This was such a dark time for our family, *such* a dark time. The doctors released Patrick from the lines and tubes, and President Kennedy was able to hold his son in his arms, for the first and last time."

On Saturday, August 10, a bereft Lee Radziwill arrived in Boston just in time for baby Patrick's funeral. Unfortunately, Jackie, still in the hospital, could not attend the Roman Catholic service, which was held in the chapel of the residence of Kennedy family friend Richard Cardinal Cushing. Bobby and Ted along with their wives, Ethel and Joan, stood next to Jack, who was also supported by a number of his other siblings. Janet Sr., Janet Jr., and Lee stood with Hugh and Jamie, both of whom had flown in for the service. "When the casket was closed, Jack was so overwhelmed, he just folded himself over it and wouldn't leave," Janet recalled years later. "My heart broke in that moment. I just will never forget it. We then buried the baby [at Brookline's Holyhood Cemetery]. All I could think about at that moment was Jackie. What was this going to do to Jackie?"

That night, Lee spent many hours with Jackie, just the two of them, alone in her room — Jacks and Pekes. Occasionally, when the door would open for a doctor or nurse to enter, Clint Hill would take a peek inside. He realized that Jackie was in much better spirits. "Her sister seemed to help her maybe more than anyone else could," he recalled. "Of course, I had been around the two of them quite often over the years, all over the world, actually, so I knew how close they were."

Lee would sleep in Jackie's room that evening, on a chair next to her bed. Lt. Goodwin — the three-to-eleven night nurse — had tried to encourage her into one of the guest rooms, but she wouldn't hear of it. "She's my sister and I'm not going anywhere," Lee insisted.

At about three in the morning, Janet — who had tried to get some rest in one of the bedroom suites — slipped down the hall into Jackie's room. By this time Lt. Nancy Lumsden had relieved Lt. Goodwin and was in Jackie's room, checking her vital signs. "I want to thank you for your care of my daughter," Janet said. She added that she was sorry she'd snapped at Lt. Goodwin out of frustration a day earlier while trying to telephone Lee. She asked Lt. Lumsden to apologize to her for her since she likely would not see her again. After chatting a while, Lt. Lumsden offered to take Janet back to her suite. However, Janet said she wanted to stay in the room with her two daughters.

A few hours later, as the sun rose, Lt. Goodwin entered Jackie's room to check on her. There, she found Lee curled up in Jackie's bed with her. Janet was sound asleep in a chair. Jackie was sitting up and gazing at them both with a sad but loving smile.

JFK'S "TWO JANETS"

Shortly after the death of Patrick, "the two Janets" — as Jack Kennedy sometimes called his mother-in-law, Janet Sr., and her daughter Janet Jr. — sat on the porch of President Kennedy's home at Hyannis Port enjoying a lunch of clam chowder and sourdough bread. The younger Janet was downcast. Of course, everyone was sad in these days after little Patrick's death.

Janet — who had turned eighteen back in June (and graduated from Miss Porter's at that time) — had always been a sensitive girl. Especially during the last year as she approached adulthood, she put herself through a lot with her own constant comparisons to

279

her glamorous half sisters, Jackie and Lee. "Janet was unhappy," her mother would recall about a year or so later. "She lacked self-confidence because she was a little overweight at the time and self-conscious about it. I'm not sure that she didn't have some complexes about having older sisters who were so good-looking and had exciting lives."

In truth, Janet was a lovely young woman. She wore her dirty blond hair in a short bob, parted smartly on the right side. She had delicate features, her hazel eyes soft and set wide, her nose slim. Actually, as she got older, she began to favor her father more than she did her mother. Always shy and retiring, she was timid. However, she was such an open-hearted girl, someone eager to lend a helping hand and be available to those she loved for whatever it was they might need from her. Jack, who always had a warm spot in his heart for Janet, had a clear understanding of her fragilities and insecurities. "Look at the women in her family," he told Yusha. "That can't be easy."

For the last few months, Janet and her mother had been planning her debutante party, a big coming-of-age celebration at Hammersmith just like the ones Janet had previously hosted for Jackie and Lee. Janet's good friend Effie Taylor — who was the daughter of Mrs. John Crawford III, another friend of Janet's and president of the Denver

Art Museum Volunteers — was also hosting a party the night before Janet Jr.'s ball. Therefore, many young women were coming from far and wide to attend both events, scheduled for Saturday, August 17.

After baby Patrick died, Janet Jr. couldn't imagine going through with the party. "She was frightfully upset about it all," Janet would recall, "and heartbroken for Jackie and the President." Janet Sr. wasn't so sure that the party should be canceled, though. She felt that maybe it was just what was needed to take all of their minds off the tragedy. The subject came up while the "two Janets" were having lunch with the President. As the wait-staff served them, Janet Sr. outlined the reasons she believed the ball should go on as planned. "There's so much sadness right now, we all need a lift," Janet said. She wanted to know if Jack agreed.

Besides the death of his son, on President Kennedy's mind this day would probably have been the fact that the situation in Vietnam looked more grim than ever as Communist guerrillas continued to make inroads in the Mekong Delta; atmospheric nuclear tests had been named as responsible for doubling the levels of strontium-90 in the nation's milk supply; and his approval rating had plummeted from 76 percent to 59 percent because of his strong position on civil rights. Still, Jack somehow managed to indulge his relatives by marriage and listen attentively. "Look, you have to have the party," he told Janet Jr. "This is the kind of thing that has to go on. You can't let all of those people down."

In the end, Janet's debutante ball would go on as scheduled. UPI issued a press release on August 13 saying that the plans for the party on the 17th would not be canceled, "because Mr. and Mrs. Kennedy want it that way." The ball was a big success despite a rainstorm that day; "Oh, my! The girls danced and danced and danced all night long," Janet Sr. later told the press. "It made me wish I was young again! *Such* a lovely, memorable evening, which I know my daughter will carry with her for the rest of her life."

LEE'S CONFLICT

On August 16, 1963, Lee Radziwill returned to Athens to be with Aristotle Onassis. Things had changed, though, as she feared they would when she made the decision to renew her vows to Stas. Ari wouldn't come out and say it, but she could feel she was no longer a priority in his life. True, he had told her she would always come first, but that was before she remarried Stas. It had just been a month and a half, and she had done everything she could think of to make Ari feel that he was still the man for her. However, he was distant and aloof. He had even taken to disappearing for days on end. She knew he was with Maria Callas. That hurt. But what else could she expect?

"By this time, I would say that Lee was who she would be for a long time to come, a deeply conflicted person," said Taki Theodoracopulos. "After she got back to Greece from seeing to Jackie in America, Onassis installed her at his sister's house in Glyfada for a week, where she often stayed. He promised to join her at his sister's by the end of the week. After about six days alone, she called me and told me that she was going nuts. She wanted to have dinner to take her mind off things. We did just that, right by the sea next to my house."

"So where's your boyfriend?" Taki asked her, speaking sarcastically of Onassis.

"I don't have the vaguest fucking idea," Lee said as she picked at the strawberries on her ice-cream dessert.

"What in the world are you doing, Lee?" he asked, concerned about her.

"Please. Can we not discuss this, Taki?" Lee asked, pain and confusion evident on her face. "I love you as a friend," she said, "but I can't bear to talk about this right now."

"I don't think she knew what she wanted or where she was going," Taki would say. "My heart went out to her. You couldn't be with Onassis if you were a confused, broken

283

person. You needed all your strength and resolve to be with him because he could put a woman through a lot. So I was worried about her."

On August 22, Lee and Ari attended the opening of the Athens Hilton in Greece. Nicky Hilton was responsible for the grand event. (Nicky, whose father, Conrad, was founder of the wildly successful Hilton Hotel chain, had previously been Elizabeth Taylor's first husband.) He and his beautiful wife, Trish, stood at the head of a long receiving line of executives, greeting all of the guests as they arrived, including Lee and Ari. Nicky's friend Bob Wentworth, who was along on this junket as public relations representative for the Hilton organization, said, "What I remember most about that night was what a striking couple Lee and Ari made. When they walked in, he in his tux and she in her long, shimmering gown, there was something magical about them. Everyone oohed and aahed and cleared the way for them as if in the presence of true royalty. Trish, who was wide-eyed, said, 'My God, she's absolutely gorgeous. Isn't she a princess or something?' I answered yes, and told her that she was married to Prince Stanislaw Radziwill. She wondered where the prince was, and why the princess was with Onassis. We then noticed that every time he put his arm around her, Lee pulled away a little and seemed uncomfortable. It was as if she wanted to be with him in public, but then again, she didn't. Nicky and I walked over to talk to them."

"Fine hotel you have here," Onassis told Nicky and Bob. "This place had to have cost a fortune," he said, looking around and seeming impressed.

"Well, yeah, but my dad *has* a fortune," Nicky said. It was as if he was suddenly in competition with Onassis over who was wealthier.

"Really," Lee remarked, "talking about money is *so* gauche, don't you agree?"

"Not if you have it," Ari said with a smile. He went to kiss her on the cheek, and she pulled away. He then grabbed her roughly and kissed her on the lips. She seemed dazed.

"Why in the world are all these *photographers* here?" Lee later asked Nicky. He looked at her like she was daft. "Because this is a *Hilton hotel opening,*" he exclaimed. "This is big news, and we are all at the center of it. You gotta love it, right?"

"Not really," Lee said, looking around with a bewildered expression. It appeared that she really didn't wish to be the center of so much attention while with Ari, and that, somehow, she had misconstrued the high-profile nature of the event to which she and Onassis had been invited. Later, Bob Wentworth overheard a strange conversation between Nicky Hilton and Onassis. Wentworth recalled, "Nicky told him, 'She's a real looker that one,' referring to Lee, 'you're a lucky man.' Onassis said, 'I am lucky. She's magnificent, isn't she? You know she's Jackie Kennedy's sister, don't you?' The way Onassis said it was as if *this* was what distinguished Lee most, her relationship to Jackie. Nicky looked at Onassis with a puzzled expression. 'Well, I think she's even lovelier than the First Lady,' he said. Onassis smiled and said, 'She is, isn't she? Jackie seems empty-headed. But not Lee. Lee is smart.' Later, I saw Ari and Lee in a corner, deep in conversation, completely captivated by one another as if no one else was in the room. Even from a distance, you could feel the heat between them."

A couple of days later, the *Washington Post* columnist Drew Pearson wrote about the couple's appearance at the hotel opening and posed the question: "Does the ambitious Greek tycoon hope to become the brother-in-law of the American President?" That same day, Jackie called Lee in Greece to ask her what was going on with Onassis, saying that their picture was in all of the newspapers in America. She said she was concerned about how Stas would react. From all accounts, Lee told her that she would worry about Stas, that Jackie should not concern herself with it. Besides, she said, she and Onassis were just friends.

Lee then went back to Onassis and told him

she was angry that their picture had been published everywhere, along with Pearson's tantalizing commentary. In front of his attorney, Stelio Papadimitriou, Lee angrily accused Onassis of having planted the item. "First of all, you do not raise your voice to me," he told her, putting her in her place. "I can all but guarantee you that your present tone will never serve you well," he added. Then he blew up at her. After choosing Stas over him, how dare she be the least bit confrontational with him about anything? She was lucky, he said, that he would even be seen with her at all! He berated her and brought tears to her eyes, telling her that she was obviously naïve about the way it works when one is seeing Aristotle Onassis. "I make news," he said, "and whoever is with me makes news. This is something you'll have to learn to live with," he told her, "that is, if you want to be with me." Did she still want to be with him? She said yes, she did. "And do you want to make news, Lee?" he asked her, looking deeply into her eyes. "Do you want people to notice you?" he asked her. It was like a crazy mind game. First, furious. Then, loving. "Because you deserve to be noticed, Lee," he said, "if that is what you want. *Is that what you want, Lee?*"

She didn't even have to think about it for half a second: of course, that's what she wanted.

ANNIVERSARY AT HAMMERSMITH

It was September 12, 1963, Jack and Jackie's ten-year wedding anniversary. The Kennedys would celebrate it at Hammersmith Farm, lately referred to by the media as "the Summer White House." (The Secret Service's moniker for the estate was "Hamlet.") Jackie arrived early in the afternoon. Physically, she was better. However, emotionally she was in bad shape, depressed and sad. She was expected to stay at Hammersmith for several weeks; Jack would visit on weekends.

As the household staff awaited the President's arrival, Janet's assistant, Adora Rule, dutifully typed out correspondence on a small desk set up in the corner of the large, red-carpeted, and beautifully appointed formal living room. This was her makeshift office while the one she usually used off of the kitchen was being recarpeted. Earlier in the day, she'd placed two framed photographs of family members on her desk. However, Janet asked her to put them away. She didn't want pictures of people she didn't know displayed in her home. This living room was practically never used except as a reception room where guests were greeted. It was big and roomy, though, and Janet liked to stretch out in the middle of it to do her exercises.

As Adora typed, she witnessed an enlightening conversation between mother and daughter. She hadn't heard the beginning of their talk, but quickly gathered that it was about Patrick's death.

At the time, Janet was reclining on a slant board propped up on the cushion of an antique French director's chair with wooden gilded-swan arms. She had covered the gold-and-brown upholstery with a large white towel. She had a pad over each eyelid soaked in her special concoction of witch hazel and boric acid, a part of her beauty regimen. Meanwhile, Jackie was sitting "Indian-style" in the middle of a large cabbage-rose-patterned overstuffed sofa in front of the bay window with its burgundy-and-gold drapery and white sheer curtains.

Jackie's brown eyes were sunken; she looked drained. She said that she thought the new baby would change things between her and Jack, and with him now gone she wasn't sure what to think.

As much as Janet liked Jack, she would never approve of his unfaithful behavior. By this time, she had almost an expectation that elite men would cheat on their wives, but that still didn't mean she liked it. She did her best to look the other way and not to dwell on it. "So many women, so little sense" is how she put it at the time. (Others weren't so forgiving; Jackie's protective stepbrother Yusha, for instance, would be conflicted about it his entire life.) Janet felt strongly that Jackie loved Jack more than he loved her, "but," she asked Sherry Geyelin — the daughter of Hugh's partner, Chauncey Parker — "when is it ever equal between partners?" She knew that Jack's cheating was ripping Jackie apart, but she also knew he was her whole world. What could she, as the mother, do about it? It was bigger than just a private dysfunction between a married couple, anyway. Any decision Jackie made about it would likely end up involving the whole country.

Earlier in the year, Janet had sat next to Jackie and Lee as JFK gave his State of the Union address. That was a proud moment, the kind upon which she preferred to dwell. She now noted that if Jack was to run again in '64, Jackie would probably have to be at his side, no matter how she felt about him. The party would expect it of her. Jackie shook her head. "I know," she said, "but I don't know that I trust him, Mummy."

"Trust is for the weak," Janet said brusquely, still on her slant board with her eyes covered. She seemed a little leery of where the conversation was headed; she wasn't good with these sorts of emotional moments, and she must have felt one in the offing.

Changing course, Jackie wondered if maybe Patrick's death had been the result of her smoking habit. At this, Janet took the pads off of her eyes, sat up, and looked at her daughter. She reminded her that dreadful things had happened to all of them in the past, and she said that she was afraid that more of the same would occur in the future, "because that's just how things work." For now, though, she wanted Jackie to swallow her sadness and pull herself together before Jack arrived from Washington. She said she was certain Jackie wouldn't want him to see her upset. She wanted Jackie to try her best to make the anniversary weekend a good one, for everyone's sake. She then reclined once again and placed the pads over her eyes.

Jack was scheduled to join Jackie at Hammersmith Farm on the afternoon of September 12. To that end, Newport police were put on high alert, with six officers assigned to guard the two entrances to Hammersmith on Harrison Avenue. Phone booths were installed along the route for their use. Meanwhile, the Secret Service would stay in accommodations in the main house. Early in the day, Jack's duties included the signing of an order that would amend the draft to prevent the conscription of married men. Other than that, it was a light day, and he was, therefore, eager to join Jackie in Newport.

On his way, Jack would take Air Force One from Washington to Quonset Naval Air Station in Rhode Island. Along with him would be the famous reporter (and Jack's fellow

Harvard alumnus) Ben Bradlee and his wife, Toni. From Quonset, the Kennedy contingent took a helicopter to Hammersmith. As usual, the chopper landed on the beach between the main house and the shoreline, with everyone — Janet Jr., Jamie, and Yusha as well as his children, Maya and Cecil, along with Janet and Hugh — noisily running out to meet the President with hugs and good cheer.

Also already present was Sylvia Blake, the wife of the American diplomat Robert Blake, who was stationed in the Congo at the time. (Sylvia's mother, Mary, was a good friend of the Auchinclosses.) Ben Bradlee would later describe the moment Jack arrived at Hammersmith as "a scene that was half space-age pomp and half *Wuthering Heights.*" He would recall that Jackie greeted Jack "with by far the most affectionate embrace we had ever seen them give each other. They [were] not normally demonstrative people, period."

"We loved the helicopter," Cecil, who was four at the time, recalled. "As kids, we were like, 'Wow! It's a big bird coming down!' All the children would run out to greet him. The other thing [Jack and Jackie] had when they were staying here was this great big white convertible — a Lincoln or a Cadillac. It was huge and it was all white with red leather interior. All of us children would sit on the backseat and just ride around Hammersmith Farm, because we had all these roads. We would all play football out where the teahouse is. Everything that the President did with us was very active. He would be tossing a football around, throwing the Wiffle ball, or whatever. And there would be big family dinners and cocktails. Grampa and Aunt Janet — my father's father and stepmother — always loved to have their cocktails out on the terrace of the big house overlooking Narragansett Bay. All of the kids would be sort of gathered for that and running around."

The first night of the Kennedys' visit, a lavish dinner was served by uniformed waitstaff in the dining room at a table that could open to seat sixteen people. The chandelier above the table was lovely and ornate, made of bronze and crystal and from the English Regency period, an heirloom from Janet's side of the family. A floor-to-ceiling window looked out at the bay. Controlled by buttons on the wall, the window could be lowered all the way into a casing in the basement.

"After dinner, drinks and deserts were served in the Deck Room," recalled Sylvia Whitehouse Blake. The Deck Room was quite large, with highly polished teak floors and a cathedral ceiling of matching redwood beams. It was said that it had been built to resemble an upside-down ship, the beams of the ceiling like the ribs of a sea vessel. In this room, there were also four large overstuffed purple sofas situated atop large gold area rugs. Even given the Victorian and eighteenth-century pieces carefully placed about the space, it had a casual atmosphere, comfortable in its airiness. A grand piano sat in one corner — the same one that was played at Jackie's wedding — a large chess table for Hugh in another and, in another, a small television with period antennae. The green tiled fireplace — with iridescent tiles chosen by Emma Auchincloss decades earlier in Italy — was roaring, especially this late in the season. Four sets of doors led out to the adjoining covered terrace.

Most prominent in the Deck Room was a large stuffed pelican hanging from the ceiling, which Hugh had caught accidentally in a fishing net off the coast of Florida several years earlier. Because it had drowned in his net, Hugh felt so bad about it he had it mounted and hung facing the water. There was also a large mounted pheasant on a bookshelf; the poor bird had accidentally flown into a window and broken its neck. Hugh maintained that if any living thing wanted to come into the house that badly, it should be not only be allowed in, it should be allowed to stay. However, Janet, at least according to Sylvia Whitehouse Blake, "found the dead pelican and pheasant ghastly, just ghastly."

"Jack loved daiquiris and my father loved daiquiris, too," Yusha recalled. "So I made a special daiquiri for the President: lemon juice, lime juice, a little bit of sugar. I said, instead of two different kinds of rum why don't we have a medium rum, a light rum, and a dark rum? Jack called it a 'New Frontier.' "

Holding court, as always, Janet stood in the middle of the room and offered a toast. "To all of us," she said, raising her daiquiri. "We are family," she said. "We are friends. And we love you, Jack and Jackie. Happy Anniversary." Everyone clinked glasses. Jackie, sitting next to Jack on one of the large purple couches, kissed him on the cheek. About thirty minutes later, the telephone rang. When the butler said it was "the princess," Jackie jumped up to talk to her sister. She was gone for about a half hour, catching up with her sister by long distance.

"At one point, little John, who was about to turn three [in November], ran down the stairs in his pajamas to say good night to us," recalled Jamie Auchincloss, "and he stood at the entrance to the dining room and he yelled into the room, 'Poo-poo head!' And Jack showed his shock and said, 'I don't think I have ever heard anybody call the President of the United States a poo-poo head before!' We all laughed. And then John turned around and raced back up the stairs so nobody could catch him. Jack and Jackie looked at one another and you could just see the pure joy on their faces."

"It was a lovely evening," Sylvia Whitehouse Blake recalled. "Everyone was so charming, they all had such beautiful manners, were so happy to be in each other's company, full of jokes. I just thought it was a wonderful celebration for Jack and Jackie, personal and homey."

"I felt that they were closer," Janet would later recall of this evening in her oral history for the Kennedy Library. "I can't think of two people who had packed more into ten years of marriage than they had. And I felt that all their strains and stresses, which any sensitive people have in a marriage, had eased to a point where they were terribly close to each other. I almost can't think of any married couple I've ever known that had greater understanding of each other, in spite of Jackie's introvertness [*sic*], stiffness — I mean that it's difficult for her to show her feelings. I think one felt in those rare moments when one could be alone with them on a quiet evening when there weren't a million pressures pending — that they were very, very, very close to each other and understood each other wonderfully."

LEE'S OFFER TO JACKIE

By the end of September, more than a month had passed since baby Patrick's death. Jackie was no better. If anything, her psychological state had only deteriorated. There were a few happy moments, such as the one at Hammersmith in celebration of the Kennedys' anniversary, but when she returned to the White House from Hammersmith on September 23, Jackie was still in a dark place. Lee wanted to help her in some way and made the extremely bold suggestion that Jackie cruise with her and Aristotle Onassis on the *Christina*. While it seemed like the perfect getaway, most people in Lee's life were astounded that she would even make the suggestion to her sister, given what was going on between her and Onassis. It made no sense. It was as if Lee wasn't thinking straight. She knew Jackie wouldn't approve of anything she saw between her sister and Ari. Was she just really trying to find a way to help Jackie? Only Lee would know the answer to that question. All we know for sure is that she extended the invitation.

Because of Onassis's notorious reputation, Jackie realized that any vacation involving him would lead to problems between her and Jack. Onassis had recently been sued by the government for removing oil tankers from United States territories, which he had purchased with the promise of keeping them there. It ended up costing him about $10 million in fines. Like most people, the Kennedys viewed him as a criminal. Jackie didn't have the energy to deal with any contention about him, though. "Lee told me that Jackie was adamant that she wanted to stay with her children," said Lee's Swiss friend, Mari Kumlin. "But Lee felt it was really about her not wanting to upset Jack. 'He has lived his life his own way for as long as you've been married,' Lee told her. 'Trust me, Jacks,' she said. 'You don't know the half of it. He should let you have this one goddamn thing. And if he doesn't, you should take it for yourself and screw him! He doesn't run your life. *You* run your life!' "

Finally, Jackie agreed that she would at least ask Jack. The last time she went to Greece, which was back in 1961, her husband had been clear with Clint Hill where Onassis was concerned. "Whatever you do in Greece," he'd told Clint, "do not let Mrs. Kennedy cross paths with Aristotle Onassis." (The two never did see each other during that trip.) However, Jack was now so worried about Jackie's emotional state, he was willing to reconsider his position on Onassis. Clint Hill recalled, "I felt it was a testament to his love for Mrs. Kennedy that he was willing to put aside any reservations and allow her to take part in what we all couldn't help but think was a strange idea for a vacation. When the President agreed to let her go, she was grateful."

Jackie decided to tell Janet about her plans

rather than have her hear about them from someone else. Because she suspected her mother wouldn't approve, she wanted to give her the respect of at least allowing her to weigh in, though her mind was made up about it. As expected, Janet was unhappy. "Remember who you are," she told her daughter. *"You are the First Lady,"* she reminded Jackie. She said that consorting with a known criminal like Onassis was likely to be viewed in a negative light by the American public. "But I am also a woman," Jackie told her mother, and she said she desperately needed the vacation.

To Janet, the position of First Lady was so vital a role in the administration, she couldn't imagine why Jackie would want to take a chance of staining it. Surely, Mamie Eisenhower wouldn't have considered time away with someone like Onassis. However, she also realized that the Kennedys were a much younger administration — Jackie was thirty-four, Mamie had been sixty-seven! — and not as wedded to conventional wisdom about protocol. Still, this business with Onassis was getting out of hand. It hadn't even been three months since Janet fought with Lee about him, and now Jackie? As far as she knew, she'd already convinced Lee to end whatever she had with Onassis and marry Stas in the Catholic Church. Now Jackie wanted to go on a cruise with the Greek? None of it made any sense to Janet. She told Jackie not to go. However, Jackie refused to acquiesce to Janet's will. She said she was going, and that was that. Therefore, Janet decided to take the matter up with the President.

One of JFK's Secret Service agents recalled, "I was standing in the Oval when Evelyn [Lincoln, JFK's secretary] announced that Mrs. A. was on the line. The President looked at me, grimaced, and said, 'I expected this call.' By this time, Mrs. A. and the President had a pretty good rapport. During the call, he told her that, obviously, Jackie should not go. However, because she had suffered so much lately he said, 'Let's just give her this little break and hope for the best.' He said he felt the country had such empathy for the First Lady that there was little she could do to jeopardize all of the goodwill. He also said he would appreciate it if Mrs. A. let it go, and he added that he didn't want to hear another word about it. He was fairly firm with her, while also polite and respectful. She was very obsequious and said, 'Yes, Mr. President,'" and that this was the end of it for her."

Not quite. Apparently, Janet then called Lee, upset. After all, it was all Lee's idea. What was she thinking? "She told Lee that bringing the First Lady of the United States into whatever was going on with Onassis was going too far," recalled someone with knowledge of the conversation. "However, Lee had

300

had it with her mother by this time. 'You must stop telling me what to do, Mummy,' she told her, according to what I heard. 'I am a grown woman. I know what I am doing. Jackie needs this vacation and I am going to give it to her. One would think you would be proud of me, not cross with me.' In the end, Janet lost this particular battle. She got nowhere with Lee, just as she'd gotten nowhere with both Jackie and Jack. 'Has everyone just lost his mind?' she asked, frustrated. 'Am I the only one who sees this as a problem?'"

Sisters in Greece

On October 1, Jackie, her Secret Service agents Clint Hill and Paul Landis, and her loyal personal assistant, Providencia (Provi) Paredes, left for their two-week trip, first taking a TWA flight from New York to Rome and then on to Athens. When they arrived in Athens, Lee and Stas greeted them, along with the United States ambassador Henry Labouisse. Jackie, Lee, and Stas were then taken to the villa of Greek shipping businessman Markos Nomikos, at Cavouri Bay, a seaside resort about twenty miles or so outside of Athens. Here, they and a few friends would spend a couple of days in seclusion with other guests of Nomikos, including Stelina Mavros, who, for the last three years, had been employed as his special assistant.

After spending a few days in Athens, the coterie finally made it onto the *Christina*, which was docked in Glyfada. "There was a big welcoming team of people," Clint Hill recalled, "and, sure enough, there was Onassis, standing on the deck, all smiles. He wasn't the best-looking guy in the world. Short. Big nose. Bushy eyebrows. Though he was weathered, he did have a certain presence. Lee offered her right cheek to him. He kissed it, then the other cheek. He did the same to Mrs. Kennedy. Something about it made me cringe. I didn't like it, probably because I knew the President would have had a fit had he witnessed it."

Also present on the yacht were Franklin D. Roosevelt Jr., JFK's undersecretary of commerce, and his wife, Suzanne Perrin; Silvio Medici de Menezes and his wife, Princess Irene Galitzine, the founder of a glamorous fashion house in Italy (which popularized the wearing of ornate pants as formal wear in the 1960s); Alexis Minotis, the handsome actor who had also directed Maria Callas in Greek productions of *Medea* and *Norma;* Onassis's older sister, Artemis Garoufalidis, and half sister Kalliroi Patronicola; and Lee's friend Accardi Gurney.

On their first morning at sea, Onassis had the entire ship decorated with decks of colorful roses and gladioli. The ship had been abundantly stocked with twenty-six different vintage wines, eight different varieties of caviar, as well as a variety of exotic fruits he'd had flown in from Paris. Two chefs — one Greek, one French — were on call to prepare meals, which included caviar-filled eggs, foie gras, steamed lobsters, and jumbo shrimp. Jackie seemed taken aback as she took in her surroundings. She was used to luxury, as was Lee, but Onassis's love boat really was impressive. "So *this* is how kings live," Jackie reportedly whispered to Onassis as he took her by the hand that first day. He threw back his head and roared with laughter. "Mrs. Kennedy is in charge here," the mogul then announced to the throng of media who'd gathered to watch the First Lady board. "She's the captain," he said with a roguish glint in his eyes.

The first stop was Istanbul, Turkey, where Jackie, Lee, and their friends would visit the Topkapi Palace, the Blue Mosque, and Hagia Sofia, the Greek Orthodox basilica. Then it was off to Crete, where they toured the Palace of Knossos. After that, they would dock in Levkas and then visit Onassis's private island of Skorpios. He'd bought it about a year earlier and was in the process of spending more than $10 million on improvements, so it wasn't much to look at yet. Still, it was lush and isolated and the Bouvier sisters loved it.

Thus far, the vacation had been all fun and games for Jackie and Lee. Things took a serious turn, though, once they got to Smyrna, Ari's hometown (now known as Izmir). Both sisters wanted Ari to take them on a tour. He agreed. As the small group slowly strolled down a street in town, Jackie and Ari chatted while he pointed out sights and waxed nostalgic about his childhood. Lee trailed miserably behind them with the rest of the group. As he reminisced, according to most accounts, Ari confided in Jackie about his difficult relationship with his father and admitted that the primary reason for his drive and ambition was to prove himself to his dad. Obviously well pleased with himself, he said he had made his first million by the age of twenty-five by purchasing ocean freighters at a bargain price and then charging huge fees to governments to use them to ship supplies during the war. Jackie, with an arched eyebrow, asked, "Isn't that illegal?" He responded by saying, "That depends on how you look at it, my dear." Turning personal again, he also discussed his grief over his mother's death when he was just a boy. As he opened up to Jackie, she listened attentively. It was as if they had reached a surprising level of intimacy.

"I remember we were all sitting on a curb watching people go by on one side of the street, and she and Ari were sitting together on the other side," recalled Stelina Mavros. "I looked at Lee and she appeared to be confused and unhappy. She and Stas had, apparently, had a fight and he fled the cruise, headed back to England. So she was alone. At one point, she got up and sort of meandered across the street and sat with Ari and Jackie. Finally, she got up and crossed the street and joined the rest of us. It was as if she didn't know her place, where she was supposed to be."

Imagine it: just four months earlier, Onassis had invited Maria Callas to cruise on the *Christina* simply to demonstrate to Lee that he would always choose her. Now it had to feel as if he was choosing *Jackie*. This is how quickly things could change in the Onassis world. "I think when Lee looks back on this trip she believes it was the second biggest mistake she ever made," said one person who knew her at that time, "the first one being renewing her vows to Stas."

Any tension didn't last long, though. Before returning home, the sisters stopped off to see Morocco. At one point, they found themselves at the king's palace waiting for his late arrival. They had a terrible time making small talk with about a hundred women — his harem, his father's harem, *and* his grandfather's. Dressed in golden caftans, all of the women sat in rapt adoration of Jackie as she and Lee tried to figure out what to say to them. Finally, Jackie stood up in the middle of the room and announced, "My sister would now like to perform our mother's favorite song for you, 'In an Old Dutch Garden Where the Tulips Grow.' " Lee was horrified but, ever the trouper, she stood right up and began to sing — while Jackie burst into gales of laughter.

On October 17, the Bouvier sisters and their entourage finally boarded a Pan Am flight headed back to New York City. "It will be so wonderful to get home," Jackie told Clint Hill and Paul Landis. "I've missed the President so much." It was apparently true because, from Greece, Jackie wrote JFK a letter that would later be widely quoted in biographies about her: "I think how lucky I am to miss you . . . I realize here so much that I am having something you can never have — the absence of tension. I wish so much I could give you that. But I can't. So I give you every day while I think of you. [It is] the only thing I have to give and I hope it matters to you."

Jackie and Lee would spend most of their flight home talking about their fun time, sitting directly behind the Secret Service agents. They were both lighthearted and eager to chat, not whispering conspiratorially but talking openly while sipping sparkling wine. Bringing her tapered fingers together in an arc, Jackie said, "He's a bit of a pirate. Or maybe he's like Odysseus," she added, painting Onassis's earthy and dominating masculinity in a romantic light by comparing him to the hero of Homer's epic poem *The Odyssey.* In the end, the sisters had to agree that Onassis was also a lot like "Daddy" in terms of sex appeal and persuasive charm, and that wasn't necessarily a good thing. "You two are just friends, right?" Jackie asked Lee. "You know how I feel about these things."

"It's complicated, Jacks," Lee told her.

"I'm a smart woman, Pekes," Jackie countered. "Explain it to me."

"No," Lee said. "Not here!" she exclaimed, lowering her voice. Obviously, not there — *people were listening,* and she knew it! She then added with mock solemnity, "I would never do anything to bring embarrassment to the First Lady." Jackie winced. "That sounds so dreary," she said, rolling her eyes. "*The First Lady!* Why, it should be the name of a *horse,* not the title of a woman." It was an old joke of Jackie's, but every time she made it, she and her sister laughed.

According to an agent sitting with them, Jackie thanked Lee for allowing her to have what she called "this wonderful time away." It was exactly what she needed, she said. She then reached into her purse, pulled from it an antique crystal rosary, and gently placed it around her sister's neck. She explained that it was from the Vatican, and that it had been blessed by the Pope. She then kissed Lee on the forehead and told her that she loved her.

····

PART SIX:
THE ASSASSINATION

····

11/22/63

It was like a knife to Janet's heart. "Mummy, he's dead," Jamie told her. "I just heard it on the news. *Jack is dead.*" The phone dropped from her hand. She steadied herself against a wall and then crumpled into a chair. She picked up the receiver and tried to speak, but her throat tightened with a rush of emotion. "Are you sure?" Janet managed to ask. He said he was certain. There was no doubt about it. The President was dead. "I need you to come home right now, son," she said. "Take the next plane. Get here as soon as you can." Then she hung up and began to shake.

One of the reasons most people who were alive remember where they were when President John Fitzgerald Kennedy was assassinated on Friday, November 22, 1963, is because, of course, it started out just like any other day. By early afternoon, however, it had become a day defined by shock, despair, grief, and anger. For the family, though, those directly impacted by the tragedy, it was a day from which they would never truly recover.

About an hour before she received that fateful call from her son, Janet Auchincloss had returned to her new home at 3044 O Street, centrally located in Georgetown's East Village — on the corner of O and 31st — after a pleasant outing. Always full of drive and energy, she'd just played a lively round of golf with her British-titled friend, Lady Margaret Walker, wife of John Walker, director of the National Gallery of Art. Though Janet had taken the morning off for fun and exercise, she knew that the rest of the day would be busy. At this time, her work on the board of the Hearing and Speech Center of Washington Children's Hospital was taking up a lot of her time; she was in the midst of planning its annual picnic and pony ride for the kids at Hammersmith in the spring. Opening the estate for the young ones was always a joy for her. She was also active at this time on the committees of the American Field Service, the Red Cross, and the World Affairs Council.

Janet and Hugh had bought the enormous house on O Street about a year earlier after selling the Merrywood estate. As much as the Auchinclosses hated to admit it, it had become impractical to afford both Merrywood and Hammersmith. Therefore, they put Merrywood on the market in 1959 for

312

$850,000 (about $7 million today). Anticipating the sale, in January of '60, Janet compiled a scrapbook of black-and-white photos taken of Merrywood and gave it to Hugh with the inscription: "For Hugh D. — A souvenir of 18 years together at 'Merrywood.' With all my love, Janet." It took two more years for the house to sell, though, and for $650,000. Janet hated to see it go. However, at least they still had Hammersmith, and she was determined that that property would never be sold. After the Merrywood sale the Auchinclosses bought the O Street house, a monolithic four-story, nine-bedroom, Queen Anne–style structure with all of its impressive towering peaks and gables.

Upon her return from her golf outing, Janet was on her way up the stairs to her bedroom when the telephone rang. It was Nancy Tuckerman. Janet had known Nancy for years, going all the way back to when she and Jackie attended school in Farmington together. Nancy had recently taken over as Jackie's social secretary from Letitia Baldrige, who had left the White House exhausted from Jackie's schedule. "I'm afraid I have some bad news," Nancy told Janet. Then, perhaps realizing that there was no good way to say it, she just blurted it out: "The President has been shot."

Janet would recall suddenly feeling lightheaded and bracing herself against a wall.

"Jacqueline," she managed to say. "What about my Jacqueline?"

Jackie had not been injured, Nancy told her, though she was with Jack when it happened. Nancy then explained that there had been a motorcade in Dallas, that the President and First Lady were in an open car, and that Jack had been struck by a sniper's bullet. Nancy told her that Jackie was still in Dallas and would soon be en route to Washington. "I promise to let you know as soon as Air Force One leaves Texas," she told her. Janet said she needed to call Lee in London. It wasn't necessary, she was told. Bobby had already been in touch with her and Stas, and the Radziwills were on their way to the States.

"Is he . . . ?" Janet couldn't even finish the sentence.

Nancy said she wasn't sure of the President's condition, but it didn't look good.

After hanging up with Nancy, Janet had to sit down to collect herself. The first order of business was to contact her other family members. First, she called her daughter Janet Jr. at Sarah Lawrence and told her to make plans to come to Washington as soon as possible. Yusha, who was also in New York, was Janet's next call. She was about to call sixteen-year-old Jamie at Brooks, her hand on the phone and ready to dial when it rang.

"I had a terrible time reaching Mummy," Jamie Auchincloss would recall. "Trying to call Washington from outside of Boston was impossible. I dialed the number accurately three times and each time was connected to a wrong number in three different states. In those days, telephone companies had lines that would only accommodate a normal amount of traffic. But the number of people calling Washington after the assassination was so much greater than usual, it fouled up the system. So, before finally reaching Mummy, I found myself calling perfect strangers and telling them that the President had just been murdered. They would then break down in tears and hang up. To think that these people found out about the tragedy from me, the President's brother-in-law, by way of my dialing a wrong number is difficult to fathom even today, so many years later."

After hanging up with her son, Janet's hand was still on the phone when it rang. It was Hugh calling from the Metropolitan Club, where he'd been having lunch. He wanted to make sure his wife had heard the terrible news. She asked him to please come home as soon as possible. Then Janet summoned her butler and told him to please gather the household staff in the drawing room for an important announcement. "By this time, it was about one-thirty in the afternoon," recalled Adora Rule, "and I had just gotten to work, having been with Mrs. Auchincloss late the night before at a charity event. I walked into the house to find the entire staff of eight sitting in the drawing room, crying. Then Mrs. A. came into the parlor. She asked me to take a seat. 'I have terrible news,' she said, standing before us all. 'The President is dead.' There was a collective gasp. I noticed her knees buckle. I leapt from my chair to steady her. 'No, no, I'm okay,' she told me. 'I'm fine.' She glanced at her watch. 'I must go upstairs and change,' she said. 'I'm going to church and then to the White House. My daughter needs me.' She then walked out of the room on unsteady footing."

No sooner had Janet gone upstairs than there was a knock on the front door. Adora, in tears, opened it to find Katherine del Valle Jones, wife of John Wesley Jones, ambassador to Peru, and the second-highest-ranking member of the diplomatic corps. Already, people were coming to the house to extend their sympathies. "I told her that Mrs. Auchincloss was indisposed at the moment," recalled Adora Rule, "but she insisted that she see her. So I took her card. Following strict Auchincloss household protocol, I went to the desk and found a small white envelope. I slipped the card in the envelope and handed it to the butler. He put the envelope on a round, silver tray. He then went upstairs with the tray. Five minutes later, Mrs. Auchincloss appeared wearing a knee-length black dress, which I had seen her wear at the function the night before, but which now seemed perfectly appropriate given the circumstances of the day. 'Thank you for coming,' she told the visitor. They spoke for a few moments and I couldn't help but notice how composed Mrs. Auchincloss appeared, how she continued to push aside her tremendous emotion in order to receive the ambassador's wife."

After saying good-bye to her guest, Janet knew that there would be more condolence calls and, though able to compose herself for Mrs. del Valle Jones, she felt she needed time to be alone. "Before I go to the White House, I think I have to go to church," she said, as four different phone lines rang throughout the house. "It's a madhouse here. I can't think."

"No, Mrs. Auchincloss, wait, *wait!*" exclaimed Adora Rule. "What shall we tell people?"

"The truth," Janet said. "I don't think we have any choice. The President is dead." Then she paused as if she couldn't believe the statement she'd just made. She repeated it, trying to convince herself of its truth: *"The President is dead."* The two locked eyes. Janet quickly turned away and went upstairs. A few moments later, she returned wearing her hat and coat, and she left the house without saying anything more to anyone. Janet then walked down the street to Christ Church, the historic Episcopal church she and her family still attended every Sunday. She expected to be alone with her thoughts and prayers. However, much to her surprise, the church was filled with parishioners already praying at a special service. Janet took a seat in the last row, bowed her head, and joined in their prayers.

After the service, Janet walked alone back to her home along the quaint brick-lined street. She found the stillness and quiet on her block to be peculiar; it was as if the whole world had suddenly come to a standstill. It was unseasonably warm, too — maybe sixty-five degrees — almost too warm for her heavy wool coat. The sky was a piercing blue, unblemished by even one cloud. Not a leaf seemed to move on any tree, the air was just that still. She was baffled. "Such a strange day for winter," she would later remember thinking.

Janet had feared that her short walk home would be interrupted by strangers recognizing her and offering sympathies. However, there was not one person in sight. As she approached her home, she began to hear an awful racket, the sound of grinding machinery. She wasn't sure what it was until she got closer and saw tow trucks in front of her house hoisting automobiles from the ground. She stood and watched for about twenty minutes as four cars were towed away, each quickly replaced in its spot by either a sleek black Mercury Monterey or a similarly dark Country Squire station wagon, vehicles customarily used by high-level government employees. All around her, she suddenly noticed men in black suits with automatic weapons, speaking urgently into walkie-talkies. It was as if they'd come from out of nowhere. Two such men stood in front of a home across the street from her own, crushing their cigarette butts out on the sidewalk. Janet watched as her neighbor, an elderly woman, came trundling down the steps of her house and began wagging her finger at the agents while pointing to the ground. All of it just seemed so surreal.

SECRET SERVICE — HIGH ALERT

As soon as Janet returned to her O Street home, she was told that Maud Shaw, her grandchildren's nanny, was on the telephone. She raced to speak to her. The two women then began to commiserate over the tragedy, "our conversation interrupted from time to time because neither us was able to stop crying," Maud would recall.

Maud said that a Secret Service agent had told her that Jackie didn't want Caroline and John-John to be at the White House when she returned to it. The First Lady wanted time to compose herself before she saw the children, or so Maud said she was told. Because Maud now knew she needed to get the young Kennedys out of the White House, she wondered if it would be all right to bring them to the Auchincloss home. Janet was a little surprised. She thought the best place for them was probably at the White House, their own home, but she agreed anyway. She was happy to have a purpose, something to do. "Of course," she exclaimed. "Bring them over to me." She said that anyone who wanted to seek sanctuary could find it at her home. "This is the place for you all," she told Maud. "Come, stay here." Maud said she was going to pack a suitcase for the children and have them at O Street as soon as possible. When she hung up, Janet realized that she'd forgotten to ask if the children knew of their father's murder. Should she be the one to tell them? What would Jackie want? If only she could talk to her daughter to find out.

As Janet sat and wondered about how to handle the children, Maud Shaw was at the White House packing them up. She told Caroline and John that they would be staying with Grandmère and Granddad — which is what they called Janet and Hugh — and quickly managed to get them into a Country Squire with their Secret Service agent, Tom Wells. Then, with another vehicle of agents following, they drove to Janet's home.

Suddenly, two cars screeched to the curb in front of the house. All four doors of the second car opened at the same time and out of it came four men in black suits, each with a rifle. They ran up the steps and began pounding on the door. The butler let them in and they raced past the staff and began scrambling throughout the house to secure it, hollering at one another into their walkie-talkies and telling each other that it was "all clear." As they tore about the house, they began closing all of the heavy brocade drapes so harshly they almost pulled them from their rods. The agents went into the kitchen and scared poor Nellie Curtin, the longtime family cook, half to death with their rifles, which they just stacked on the kitchen table as if it was nothing unusual. "Why are you acting this way?" the butler, James Owen, asked them, upset. "Because we don't know what's happening," an agent told him. "All of you could be in danger. We are on *high alert*. Just be glad we are here to protect you!"

Then two other agents hustled Miss Shaw and the children, both of whom were wide-eyed and confused, into the house. It was all so hectic and upsetting, what with the phones also ringing off the hook and staff members scurrying around trying to manage things. Maud took one look at Adora and said, "God help us all. It's the end of the world."

At about four in the afternoon, Jamie

landed at the airport in Washington. Walking through the terminal on his way to the car that Janet had sent to retrieve him, he noticed the dailies being delivered to newsstands. Seeing the headlines for the first time — such as "President Kennedy Assassinated" — in the *Washington Times* and *Washington Post* was more than he could bear. He broke down and began to cry. He and his brother-in-law had a personal relationship born not only of great respect, but also no small measure of fascination. For instance, Jamie was always astonished by the fact that Jack would change clothes five times a day, never satisfied with anything he was wearing. Jamie also couldn't help but laugh whenever he would recall how impressed Jack was by the way he took care of the menagerie of animals at Merrywood and Hammersmith. "Great kid, that Jamie," Jack would say. "Great kid with ducks." Jamie liked to muse that this presidential quote would likely be the epitaph on his tombstone: "Great kid with ducks."

The last time the brothers-in-law saw each other was at a cocktail party for "The New England Salute to President Kennedy" dinner at Boston's Copley Hotel back on October 19. "Would you like me to introduce you to some of my friends?" JFK asked Jamie. "With your permission, may I take a liberty and introduce *you*?" Jamie asked him. Jack smiled and agreed. Then, Jamie, with the

President standing directly behind him, walked up to a distinguished-looking gentleman and said, "Sir, I'm James Auchincloss. And you are?" The man said, "I'm Philip Hoff, governor of Vermont," to which Jamie responded, "Nice to meet you." Then, stepping grandly aside to reveal the President, he announced, "And *this* is my friend Jack Kennedy. He *also* works for the government." It was a funny moment, one that Jamie would never forget. Driving back to Brooks School in North Andover that night, he had a weird premonition: "I think that will be the last time I ever see Jack alive." And it was.

Jamie's driver finally found him and helped him to the car. When he got to the house, Jamie raced up the front steps and tried to open the front door but, of course, it was safely locked. He rang the doorbell; Janet answered. Mother and son then embraced in the doorway before Janet let him into the house.

By early evening, Janet knew she needed to get to the White House to be with Jackie. She decided to leave the children in the care of her capable staff and her son. "Make sure that they are bathed when I return," she told the help. She gathered both children in her arms. "Uncle Jamie is here now," she said just as he walked into the room and tried to force a smile. "Bad Boy James?" Caroline asked, using a favorite nickname for her uncle. (It was given to him because he used to sneak into her bedroom and steal her Zwieback teething cookies as a running joke between them.) "Yes, Bad Boy James," Janet said, holding her tightly. "He'll play with you now. Grandmère loves you both." Then, turning to her son, Janet said, "Make sure all of the radios and televisions remain unplugged." He told her not to worry. "We'll play cards," he said. "It'll be fun, right, kids? You want to play War? Or Go Fish?"

"As I was saying good-bye to Mummy, we lost track of Caroline for just a second," Jamie Auchincloss recalled. "I ran to find her and saw that she'd stumbled into the kitchen to ask for a glass of milk. Just as I got there, the Secret Service agents scrambled to block her view of their rifles, which had been placed openly on the kitchen table. Marie got Caroline some milk and we got her out of there fast."

"A SILLY LITTLE COMMUNIST"

Slowly cutting through the densest of traffic in their chauffeur-driven vehicle, Janet and Hugh made their way to the White House. It was such a laborious drive because the streets were so crowded with automobiles that, maybe not so surprisingly, all seemed to be headed in the same direction — to the White House. Once at their destination, Janet and

324

Hugh found their friends Ben Bradlee and his wife, Toni. With nothing to do but wait for Jackie, the four of them, along with Nancy Tuckerman, tried their best to make small talk and force down ham-and-cheese sandwiches. They soon learned that Jackie would be landing in Air Force One at Andrews Air Force Base, and that she would then be accompanying the President's body to the Naval Hospital in Bethesda. At that point, it was a mad rush by all — the Auchinclosses, the Bradlees, Nancy Tuckerman, and Jack's sister Jean Kennedy Smith — to a waiting automobile, and then a ninety-mile-per-hour race through the streets of Washington to Bethesda. One there, they were all quickly ushered into a suite at the hospital.

Janet's eyes swept the room and, as she turned her head to the left, she finally saw her daughter. That's when she had a shock like none she'd ever experienced. It hit her hard, the details still fresh in her mind a year later when she recounted them for her oral history with the JFK Library. There was Jackie, standing alone, in her pink wool suit covered with ugly splotches of dried blood. She had a haunted look in her eyes. Her hair was mussed; there was blood streaked on her cheek. A stunned Ben Bradlee was the first to reach out to her. They embraced. "Here's your mother," he said as Janet took a hesitant step forward. "Mummy," Jackie managed to say. She then fell into her mother's arms and began to cry softly. Or was she crying? Janet would later say she wasn't sure.

Janet held her daughter in her arms. As she tried to comfort her, Janet then made the strangest of statements to her daughter. "Oh, Jacqueline," she said through her own tears, "if this had to happen, thank *God* he wasn't *maimed*!" Jackie recoiled and stared at her mother. Everyone else in the room also seemed stunned by Janet's odd remark. Later Janet would confess that it was a comment made out of sheer shock and disbelief. She truly was not conscious of the words coming from her mouth, unable to even begin to comprehend the moments as they unfolded before her. A few minutes later, she said, "I hope you will never live anyplace but in this country because Jack would want that." It was as if she was already thinking ahead that Jackie might hold Jack's murder against the United States and maybe want to leave it for Europe. Jackie just looked at her with a strange expression, as if to say, "What in the world . . . ?" Why, she must have been wondering, were they discussing these sorts of plans in this horrible moment? Finally, after a beat, Jackie just said, "But of course I am going to live in Georgetown, where Jack and I were."

After a while, Bobby Kennedy walked over to Jackie and, in a voice barely audible, told her that Jack's murderer had been arrested. He gave her a few more details. Jackie, still dazed, then reached out to Janet again. In a faltering voice, she said, "He didn't even have the satisfaction of being killed for civil rights — it had to be some silly little Communist." Janet embraced her tightly as Jackie stood stiffly in her arms. Jackie seemed to be crying but, again, Janet would later say she just couldn't be sure. As Janet held her daughter, she tried to recover from the sight of so much blood on Jackie's clothing, but it was difficult. Trying to compose herself, she began to do what she did best, which was to outline a plan to at least try to control the uncontrollable. "Will you stay with me tonight?" she asked Jackie. "You know, the children are at O Street now," she added. Jackie suddenly pulled away from her mother. "What are they doing there?" she asked, alarmed.

"Jackie, I had a message that you had sent from the plane that you wanted them to come there and sleep there," Janet said. Why, one wonders, didn't she just tell her that Maud Shaw had asked her what to do about the children, and that she had suggested bringing them to O Street? Again, she would explain that she was just in shock, that she didn't even know what she was saying, or why she was saying it.

Jackie was perplexed. "But I *never* sent such a message," she said, trying to figure out what was going on.

"You don't want them there, then?" Janet asked.

"No," Jackie said, emphatically. Now she was on the verge of becoming upset. "The best thing for them to do would be to stay in their own rooms with their own things so their lives can be as normal as possible," she concluded. Janet promised that she would see to it that the children were returned to the White House immediately; she then told a Secret Service agent to go back to O Street and get Maud and the children and bring them to the White House. "But how shall we tell the children what happened?" Janet then wanted to know. Jackie considered the question. "Miss Shaw should do exactly what she feels she should do," she said. "She will have to judge how much the children have seen or heard. She will just have to use her best judgment." Janet then reached out and took Jackie in her arms once again and said that she would talk to Maud Shaw.

"Will you stay at the White House, Mummy?" Jackie wanted to know. In Janet's eyes, Jackie now seemed like a vulnerable little girl. "Will you sleep in Jack's room?" she asked in a tiny, fragile voice. "Anywhere you like," Janet answered. She was "touched," she would later recall of the moment, and realized that her eldest child didn't want to be alone. "Would Uncle Hughdie stay, too?"

Jackie asked. "Of course," Janet answered. "We love you, Jacqueline."

"LET THIS CUP PASS . . ."

Once she got back to the White House, Janet Auchincloss raced up to the second-floor residence and found Maud Shaw alone in one of the bedrooms, crying. Seeing her, Janet just blurted out the words: "Mrs. Kennedy wants you to tell Caroline and John that their father is dead." The stout, gray-haired, and bespectacled Maud looked stricken. She immediately said no, she didn't want to do it — "Let this cup pass from me," she exclaimed, quoting Jesus Christ before the crucifixion. However, Janet insisted. Maud was just as adamant; she really didn't want to do it.

Janet would later say she wondered if maybe she shouldn't have been the one to tell the children of their father's death. It actually made more sense to her that she be the one to do it, not Maud. Or, better yet, what about Jackie? However, Jackie had already given her instructions. Janet told Maud that she had no choice, that *she* was to tell the children the news and to please stop debating with her about it. At that, Maud began to beg. "Please, *please,* can't someone else do it?" she asked. "No," Janet said abruptly. "Mrs. Kennedy is too upset," she added. With that, she turned around and stormed off, leaving the crying nanny alone with her misgivings. She'd always thought Maud was a little odd, anyway. This tense conversation had been upsetting, though. She couldn't understand why the nanny, who had been reliable for so many years, would make such a fuss about such a specific instruction, especially during an evening that was already so difficult. She was disappointed in her.

As Janet tried to collect herself, she wandered about the White House, her mind racing, as she would recall it, with painful thoughts about Jack's murder and how such a thing could ever have occurred. She tried to distract herself by going from ornate room to ornate room, examining the décor and admiring Jackie's work at having restored the old dwelling. Janet may have also done so with an eye toward saying good-bye to the place because she knew she'd never freely walk these hallowed halls again. She was proud to have been so close to the seat of power, and prouder still of Jackie. It had taken Jackie a year or so to warm up to her role, but by the time she gave her much-talked-about tour of the remodeled White House to a national television audience in February of '62, Janet knew that Jackie had found her rightful place in the Kennedy administration. "She didn't fight her destiny," Janet would say of her daughter, "she *em-*

braced it."

As Janet slowly roamed the White House alone, she probably couldn't help but acknowledge that she would miss this place. She likely remembered the night cellist Pablo Casals played here; she and Hugh were present and it was a wonderful evening, as was the sensational dinner Jackie gave for André Malraux, France's first minister of cultural affairs. She'd certainly miss those kinds of special events. She'd also miss all of the dedicated people who worked here at the White House. She would say that during her first weeks as mother of the First Lady, she wondered if she would ever get used to the idea of being in the White House. It never failed to take her breath away, though. She would always find herself just a little light-headed and starstruck by the trappings of so much history.

When she wandered into the East Room, Janet's eyes lingered on the black decorations being set up by employees. This was where Jack would lie in repose. "So, what do you think, Mrs. Auchincloss?" The voice came from above. Janet looked up and saw the White House curator, James Ketchum, on a ladder draping a chandelier in black. She was so well known at the White House by now, it seemed as if everyone knew her name. Certainly, she'd miss that, too. She gave the room a slow look of appraisal. "Shouldn't there be a flag somewhere, Mr. Ketchum?" she asked. "Yes, of course," Ketchum said as he climbed down from the ladder. He then instructed one of his helpers to go off in search of one. Janet stood in place in the East Room and took it in, her eyes trained on its awesome enormity, its stately design. "Horrible day, Mrs. Auchincloss," Ketchum said as he extended his hand. "I'm so sorry." She shook his hand and nodded. "Mrs. Kennedy is a big admirer of yours," she told him, according to his memory of the conversation. "Thank you so much for all you did for her in the restoration of this place. It's quite magnificent."

As the two spoke, Ketchum explained Jackie's instructions to him relating to the upcoming ceremonial process in the East Room. "When the President's body lies in repose here, Mrs. Kennedy wants the room decorated just as it had been for Abraham Lincoln ninety-eight years ago when he was assassinated," he said. He added that he and his team had been examining books and photographs in search of any clues as to exactly how the East Room looked during that mourning period. He pointed to a wooden framework against one of the walls. "That's the Lincoln catafalque," he said. "The real one?" Janet asked, incredulously. He said it was authentic, that it had been found at the Capitol. There were also two candelabra beside two enormous urns filled with magnolia leaves. He explained that the cuttings came from a magnolia tree President Andrew Jackson had planted on the South Lawn. "The history here," Janet exclaimed, "never ceases to amaze me. Has Mrs. Kennedy seen any of this yet?" James said she hadn't. "I understand that she will be back here at the White House at around two in the morning," he said. "We're to have it ready for her by then."

"Well, I'm sure she will love it," Janet said. She noticed tears in Ketchum's eyes. He took such pride in his work; all he wanted was to do the President proud and please his First Lady. She asked if he would be staying on with the next administration. He said he didn't know, but he certainly hoped so, adding, "This is my *life,* Mrs. Auchincloss. I love this place." She put her hand on his shoulder. "Duty and honor," she said, the admiration she had for him ringing in her tone. (In fact, Ketchum would remain with the White House for another six years.)

Janet said good-bye to James Ketchum and watched as he climbed back up his ladder with an American flag that had just been handed to him. She then turned and walked out of the East Room into the hallway and then to the living quarters. Now, after having had a chance to calm down, she felt bad about the scene she'd had with Maud. When it came to "duty and honor," certainly Maud had demonstrated as much in her loving care of Janet's grandchildren. She wasn't about to apologize to the nanny, though. Janet apologizing to the help would be a rare occurrence. Besides, she was sure she was not in the wrong. However, she decided to knock on Maud's door anyway, to see if she and the children were all right.

When Maud answered the door, it was clear that she had been crying. However, she seemed more relaxed and composed. "Miss Shaw told Caroline [the news] that night, before she went to bed," Janet would later recall. "John, of course, wouldn't understand what death meant, and Caroline not very much more. But Miss Shaw told [Caroline] . . . that her father had gone to heaven and talked a bit with her, and [she told me] that Caroline had cried a good deal." As the two women spoke in hushed tones, it was clear that any hard feelings between them had been settled even without apologies. Maud told her that, in the end, she believed it was good for Caroline to hear the news before going to bed. Janet remembered, "Miss Shaw said, 'You know, when children are Caroline's age, it's better for them to get a sadness and a shock before they go to sleep so that it won't hit them very hard when they wake up in the morning. I think this was wise.' " After the two women embraced, Janet asked Maud to be sure to tell the children that she and Hugh would be staying in their father's room that night. "I don't want them running in expecting to see Jack in the morning," she said. Maud agreed.

"Jackie had earlier said to Daddy, 'Can you please sleep in Jack's four-poster bed?' " Jamie Auchincloss recalled, " 'because I don't want it empty.' It had a hard board under the mattress because of Jack's bad back. So Daddy didn't get any sleep that night at all. Mummy did, though. They either rolled in another bed for her, or there was another bed already in the room. I'm sure they didn't sleep in the same bed."

Janet woke up at about eight, and much to her astonishment, she found Jackie sleeping next to Hugh. As she later learned, about two hours earlier Jackie had come to the door and told Hugh that she couldn't bear to sleep alone. Hugh suggested that she crawl into bed with him. Janet now watched as Jackie tried to get comfortable by slipping just a little farther under the warm covers. She wondered how her daughter would ever again sleep soundly. She feared that she would probably never be the same, not after the horror of Dallas. How could she recover from such an ordeal? Though she was just thirty-four, Janet knew that the days, months, indeed the years ahead would pose all manner of challenges for Jackie, the likes of which, in that moment while watching her try to sleep, she probably couldn't even fathom.

"GOOD NIGHT, MY DARLING JACKS"

Early Saturday morning, November 23, Lee Radziwill arrived from London just in time for a ten o'clock Mass in the East Room for Jack. Lee, Janet, and Jackie were able to have a tearful reunion before the service.

Later that morning, Lee and Janet decided to take a stroll through the West Wing. They wanted to have one more look at the Oval Office. They'd never forgotten — nor would they ever — the night Jackie surprised them by taking them there for the first time two and a half years earlier. They walked down the colonnade, past the press quarters and the Cabinet Room before finally getting to the Oval Office. They stood in place in the doorway, astonished. It was already being dismantled, workers taking framed artwork off the walls, moving furniture out. Jackie's remodel of the room had just been completed, the red carpet just installed. She hadn't even had a chance to see it! Nor had Jack. They were going to celebrate the redesign as soon as they returned from Texas. Now most of it was being quickly remodeled to Lyndon Johnson's specifications. Even the Resolute desk would be moved out, since Lyndon felt it was too small for his lanky frame. "But it hasn't even been twenty-four hours," Janet said, upset. "You mean to tell me that Johnson can't wait even a day?"

Actually, as is now well known, Secretary of State Dean Rusk and Secretary of Defense Robert McNamara had urged Johnson to move in as quickly as he could to make for a fast and painless transition. He would try to do just that in a few hours' time, after this visit by Janet and Lee, but he'd find Jack's loyal secretary, Evelyn Lincoln, at her desk. He'd ask when she might be able to move on so "my girls can come in." Lincoln would be so upset by what she viewed as a callous question, she'd report it to Bobby. In turn, Bobby would pretty much order Johnson to not even try to set foot in the Oval Office until after Jack's funeral. Therefore, Johnson would wait.

Lee took a book off a cart as it was being hauled out of the room. It was a copy of Kennedy's *Profiles in Courage.* She opened it to the first page to see if it was signed. It was. Saying that she didn't want it to end up in a stack of books somewhere in the basement, she said she was going to hold on to it and give it to one of Jackie's children later, as a gift. The worker pushing the cart of books just shrugged as if he couldn't have cared less what she did with it. As mother and daughter stood on the scarlet carpet in the middle of the historic room, they looked around, sadly. "It's the end of an era," Janet told her daughter. She said she was angry — very angry. The two then walked out of the Oval Office knowing full well that they'd never step foot in it again.

Jackie, Lee, Janet, and Hugh then went to O Street to check on Jamie and Janet Jr., leaving Stas behind at the White House nursing a vodka and tonic. He, like everyone, was shaken, having been so close to Jack.

Janet and Hugh decided to spend the night at O Street while Jackie and Lee went back to the White House. In fact, Jackie said she wanted Stas to sleep in Jack's bed, just as Hugh had done the evening before. Lee couldn't understand Jackie's determination that her family members spend these awful nights in Jack's bed, but if that was her wish, she was determined to see it through.

Stas wasn't so sure he approved of the sleeping arrangements. Disoriented, he took a look around the room at his old friend's beloved books and his many prescription medicine bottles on the two nightstands next to the four-poster bed. There was no way he could sleep in that bed, Stas decided. He said he wished he could just spend the night in the Lincoln Bedroom instead. That's where he usually slept when he was at the White

House, whereas Lee took the bed in the Queen's Room. However, Lee told him that Bobby Kennedy would be spending the night in the Lincoln Bedroom. There are dozens of other rooms in this massive house, he argued. Why must he stay in Jack's? "Because it's what Jackie wants," Lee said. She didn't like it, either, she said, but if Hugh had managed to deal with it the night before, Stas would just have to bear it tonight. "Well, I'm sorry my dear, but that is not going to happen," he told her. He then made a few calls and arranged for a cot to be rolled into the room. He set it up at the foot of Jack's bed, and that's where he slept. "With his old-fashioned European dignity . . . he even refused to use the bathroom," William Manchester would later write in his book *Death of a President.* "No one knew where Stas shaved; razor and toothbrush in hand, he wandered through the mansion for ablutions elsewhere."

Jackie had also asked Lee to sleep with her in her bedroom so that she wouldn't have to be alone. Lee did as Jackie asked, and would rise before Jackie. When Jackie woke up, she found a note from Lee under her pillow: "Good night, my darling Jacks — the bravest and noblest of all. L."

ONASSIS IN WASHINGTON

It was Sunday morning, November 25, when the phone rang in the White House's private quarters. A maid picked it up. "It's a Mr. Onassis," she told Jackie. Jackie was surprised. She took the phone. "Ari? Is that really you?"

Aristotle Onassis was in Washington?

On the night of the assassination, Lee had received a telephone call from Onassis. He was in Germany at the time, where he had launched a 50,000-ton tanker called *Olympic Chivalry,* when he heard about Kennedy. He was concerned about Lee, he said. He knew how close she was to Jack, and he wanted to make sure she was all right. She said, according to one account, that she was deeply grieving, but that it was nothing compared to what she knew Jackie was going through. Onassis then said he wanted to express his sympathy to Jackie. Apparently, she had given him her private phone number while they were on the *Christina* together. However, he told Lee he couldn't get through to her because of the congestion of telephone communication to Washington. Lee said she would pass along his condolences. He then surprised her by saying he wanted to go to Washington to attend Jack's funeral. Was this appropriate? He wasn't a friend of Jack's and he barely knew Jackie. It would seem from all available evidence that Lee definitely didn't want Onassis in Washington, not at this difficult time anyway. Her family was anguished; Stas was going to be in town . . . it just wasn't a good time. However, as was well known about him, Onassis wasn't the kind of man to take no for an answer. He said he would fly into Washington and promised to sit tight and wait for Lee to contact him at the Willard Hotel for further instructions.

Alone, with no secretary or other assistant, Onassis quietly checked into the Willard. He didn't stick to the plan, though. Instead, he picked up the phone and called Jackie. From all accounts, she was surprised to hear from him. The details of their conversation would remain known to only the two of them, but at some point Jackie, apparently, insisted that he check out of the Willard and stay at the White House. She apologetically explained that all of the formally named rooms were occupied and that, much to her embarrassment — especially considering the extravagance he had shown her on the *Christina* — she would have to put him in one of the more simple guest rooms. Onassis was so pleased to be invited to the White House for the first time, it didn't matter to him where he stayed. By midafternoon he was on his way. "In a cab," Taki said with a chuckle, considering the tycoon's great wealth. "He took a *cab* from his hotel to the White House."

341

"Years later, Lee told me that she had an uneasy conversation with Jackie about Onassis's arrangements," said one friend of Lee's. " 'Ari called. I arranged for him to stay here at the White House,' Jackie told her. Lee said that Jackie shouldn't have troubled herself, that Onassis was *her* guest and that *she* would have seen to it that he was taken care of. 'Well, what am I to do, Lee, when this man calls me and puts me on the spot during such a difficult time?' Jackie asked. And that's how Lee found out that Onassis had telephoned Jackie directly. That's also when she realized that once he was loose in Washington, she wouldn't be able to control him. Knowing the terrain at the time, I would have to say that this worried Lee. After all, she knew Ari. She knew him well."

"Well, look, Onassis was a fast mover," said Taki. "He had been with Lee, the sister-in-law of the President. Now that the President was gone, knowing him as I did, he'd already decided to go for the real prize, the sister — the former First Lady. That was very Onassis, always planning ahead to the next acquisition. This decision would have had nothing to do with Lee. There was no reason that he shouldn't have *both* sisters if he wanted them — and I'm pretty sure that this is what he wanted."

That evening, Rose Kennedy dined with Stas Radziwill upstairs at the White House, while Jackie and Lee ate with Bobby Kennedy in the sitting room. Onassis, with a few other guests — including Kennedy acolytes Robert McNamara, Dave Powers, and Phyllis Dillon (wife of C. Douglas Dillon, JFK's secretary of the treasury) — ate in the family dining room. At about ten, Bobby joined McNamara, Powers, Dillon, and Onassis for dessert and coffee. It wasn't a maudlin scene. Despite the fact that Bobby could not have been too thrilled to see Ari there — and was probably quite surprised — the levity of that time they spent together was described later by McNamara as "rather like an Irish wake."

That same night, Ari visited Jackie in her private quarters. Their time together was brief. Since neither ever spoke of it in detail, no one can know for certain what was said between them. All we know is that the idea of Onassis seeing Jackie without Lee's permission was more than a little unnerving to Lee. It all seemed strange but, given that everyone was in shock, the events seemed to just unfold quickly without anyone having much time to analyze them.

The next morning as everyone slept, Aristotle Onassis slipped out of Washington. He didn't even attend the funeral, nor did he tell Jackie or Lee he was leaving.

It would be about a month before Janet would find out that Ari had even been in Washington. Over dinner at O Street, Lee slipped and said something to Jackie about "when Ari was at the White House after Jack died." According to one of Janet's household employees, Janet smacked both hands to the table, bolted up from her chair, and exclaimed to Lee, "Please do not tell me you invited that man to the White House, Lee! Please do not even tell me that!" Jackie, according to the source, took one look at Lee's bewildered expression and decided to cover for her. "No, it was *my* idea, Mummy," she quickly said. "Mr. Onassis was so nice to me after Patrick died. When he called to offer his condolences about Jack, *I* suggested he come to the White House." Lee offered no information at all. When Janet wanted to know why she'd not seen him at the funeral, her daughters said he left before the services. "The disrespect that shows boggles the mind," Janet decided. She was glad he left, though, she said. This dark time was awful enough, she said, without having to think about where Aristotle Onassis was, and what he was doing.

Though she didn't give it voice yet, now Janet had another fear about Onassis — something that hadn't previously occurred to her: Was he also interested in Jackie? "This was something she didn't see coming," said someone who knew her well at the time. "I think she hoped she was being overreactive — 'fear does stoke the imagination,' is how she put it to me — but her mother's intuition was telling her otherwise. She said she had a bad feeling about the future where Onassis was concerned. She didn't know what to do about it. Not yet, anyway."

"NOTHING BUT BLACK"

What can be written that hasn't already been reported about the historic funeral services for America's fallen 35th President, John Fitzgerald Kennedy? After lying in state in the East Room for twenty-four hours, JFK's flag-draped coffin was carried on a horse-drawn caisson to the Capitol, where it would be viewed by hundreds of thousands of people. There would be a Requiem Mass at St. Matthew's Cathedral, then the burial at Arlington National Cemetery. "The day before the funeral, we heard that Oswald had been shot by Jack Ruby," recalled Jamie Auchincloss. "It was all so shocking that, looking back on it now, I think we were all just numb. So much was going on, such a dramatic chain of events, it was as if nothing was actually registering." Throughout it all, of course, Jackie remained a symbol of strength and courage for the country. "It was her sense of duty that got her through it," recalled Jamie, who marched behind his sister during the caisson procession to the Capitol. All of Jackie's family was present, of course, "and we just tried to be there for her — me, Mummy, Daddy, Lee, Janet Jr., Yusha, Tommy, Nini . . . all of us . . . but, really, what could one do? Yes, it was a huge tragedy for the country, the magnitude of which we couldn't even grasp at the time, but for us — for the Auchinclosses — it was . . . *Jack.* The grief we felt cannot be described."

Though Janet wanted to be of assistance to Jackie in planning the state funeral, there really was nothing she could do. The deeply grieving former First Lady had so much assistance from the White House, the military authorities, as well as Jack's immediate family, Janet had to abandon her maternal urge to be of help. She also had to push aside any hurt feelings of being completely excluded from the process. She would just do whatever she could for Jackie, even if that only meant — as it did — standing at her side.

"It's a blur," Janet Auchincloss would tell Janine Rule — daughter of her loyal assistant, Adora — many decades later when speaking of those awful November days of '63. She said that she sometimes sat down and purposely tried to remember it, but she couldn't. It was as if she'd blocked it all. She said, "I have fleeting glimpses of Jackie with the black veil . . . John-John saluting the casket . . . Hughdie trying to force back tears in the East Room . . . Jamie walking to the Capitol beside Sargent Shriver and behind Bobby, Jackie,

346

and Ted . . . but mostly," she concluded, "it's just black. Nothing but black."

"The day after the funeral we celebrated John Jr.'s third birthday," Jamie Auchincloss recalls. "Jackie had planned a small gathering in the private quarters of the White House. A table was set up and Jackie brought out ice cream and a cake with three candles on it. Bob and Ethel Kennedy, with a few of their children and my sisters, Lee and Janet, were there. My mother was there as well. We all sang 'That Old Gang of Mine' and 'Heart of My Heart.' Everyone's emotions were strained to the limit."

It all felt hopeless, the future grim. Janet recalled being in the White House residence after the burial helping Jackie pack her things when Mary Barelli Gallagher came over to her and whispered, "It will be difficult for all of us to go back to our lives after this." Jackie looked at Mary, shook her head in dismay, and said, "Go back to *what*? There's nothing for us to go back to, Mary." Janet shook her head. It wasn't true, she said. "You have your *children,* your *family,*" Janet reminded her daughter. She was still young, she told her, and she had everything to live for. However, Jackie just stared at her mother with a blank expression.

■ ■ ■ ■

PART SEVEN:
RECOVERY

■ ■ ■ ■

DEAD HEADS

"You have no respect!" Bobby Kennedy shouted at Jack Warnecke. "What the hell is wrong with you?"

"It's all right, Bobby," Jackie said, patting him on the arm. "He didn't mean anything by it. Calm down. It's fine."

It was November 30, 1963, and Jackie and her brother-in-law Bobby were in a meeting with Jack Warnecke and his associate Harold Adams. They were at the Kennedy compound discussing the construction of a permanent memorial for President Kennedy. The grave in which he was now buried was precarious at best. "The whole thing was threatening to slip down the hill because of foot traffic," explained Harold Adams many years later. "The Kennedys had no choice. It had to be moved to a safer, more stable location."

"I need your help," Jackie had told Jack Warnecke in a telephone call on November 27. "When can I see you?" Jack told her he was getting his hair cut in Georgetown the next day and suggested that, afterward, he could stop by the White House to see her. When she said she would just meet him at the barbershop, Warnecke recalled, "that told me that there was an urgency to it. The next day, I'm getting my hair cut and in walk Jackie and Bobby, which caused quite a scene, as one can imagine. We then drove over to Arlington [Cemetery]. There must have been a hundred press people there. I thought, 'Oh God, this isn't good.' Both crying, Jackie and Bobby walked right past them to the grave, knelt in front of it, crossed themselves, and started to pray. The three of us then talked about possible ideas for a new memorial. Jackie said she wanted it to be simple and dignified. Nothing ostentatious. No statutes or large buildings. We agreed that the Eternal Flame should be its centerpiece."

"The first step to designing this new memorial was to educate the family on the history of grave sites for presidents," added Harold Adams. Adams, a key associate in Jack Warnecke's firm, was quickly appointed project coordinator for the new grave site. He would also be responsible for compiling the minutes of each meeting relating to it. "We quickly put together a history book on presidential grave sites, especially McKinley and Lincoln since both were assassinated, and gave it to the family to digest. It was clear from the outset, though, that this project was going to be complicated. There would be *a lot* of Kennedys weighing in. At the end of November, we were all at the famous Kennedy compound, trying to figure it out."

As well as Jackie, Bobby, Jack Warnecke, and Harold Adams, present were Bobby's sister Eunice and her husband, Sargent Shriver. As soon as Jack and Harold spread the plans they had drawn up out on the dining room table, Jackie burst into tears and Bobby, who was already emotional, had to comfort her. "It was the first of many meetings where they would become so emotional we would wonder if we could actually work," recalled Harold Adams. "After they composed themselves, we finally began to talk things over."

"There's not enough religious symbolism," Eunice Kennedy Shriver said, pointing at the blueprint. "There should be angels crying over the grave site, don't you think?"

"And it should be more modern and ornate," Sargent added, "and, yes, I agree with my wife. Angels. Definitely, angels."

Jackie looked at Jack and shook her head. She went over to him and, under her breath, said, "The last thing I need right now is a feud with these people over angels. I need you to bring in all of the experts you can find to help resolve the symbolism issue. I want it simple, Jack. It should not look like something out of a Dracula horror movie."

Jack said it would be no problem, that there were any number of liturgical consultants he could contact. As they talked it over, the severity of Bobby's expression did not change. It had become clear during the early stages of the Lafayette Square redesign that he didn't like Jack. He'd even told his wife, Ethel, that he felt Jack had been a little too familiar with Jackie. Now, with his brother gone, Bobby definitely had his eye on him.

After the discussion of symbolism was temporarily put to rest, Jack held court, outlining other concerns. "As we all know, this hillside is going to slip with the passing of not much time," he said, pointing to the technical drawing. "There are a lot of dead heads here," he added, waving his hand over the mechanical of the cemetery. "So we really need to move the grave site away from all these dead heads."

Bobby bolted to his feet. "What do you mean, dead heads?" he asked, approaching Jack menacingly. Within seconds, the five-foot-nine Kennedy was inches away from the six-foot-three Warnecke, looking up at him and poking him in the chest with his finger. "There are a lot of dead heads here?" Bobby said, exploding. "What is *wrong* with you? How dare you say that!"

"It's just an engineering term, Bobby," Jack said, mortified. "Dead heads are mechanical devices put into the hill to hold it up. I'm sorry, I didn't realize. . . ."

Bobby told Jack he needed to be more sensitive, at which point Jackie got between the two men and tried to defuse the situation. "It's all right, Bobby," she repeatedly said while patting her brother-in-law on the arm. "Jack didn't mean anything by it. It's just a construction term."

"Well, it's not right, Jackie," Bobby said, unwilling to let it go. "In fact, nothing about this Warnecke guy is right," he concluded as he stormed from the room.

ALL HER COURAGE

Sunday, December 1, 1963.

The shrill ringing of a telephone in the middle of the night roused Janet Auchincloss from a deep, predawn sleep. She reached groggily for it. It was Jackie. Janet was so alarmed to hear her voice, she caught her breath in surprise. Given what they had all just been through, it was understandable that she would be on edge. Jackie, her voice flat and devoid of expression, said without preamble that she needed a favor. She had just spoken to Richard Cardinal Cushing about a plan in which she wanted to enlist her mother.

"I want to bury my babies next to Jack," Jackie said. "I need you to get my baby girl and bring her to Arlington." She also said

355

that she'd asked Cushing — of the Archdiocese of Boston and a close friend of the Kennedys — to "go and get Patrick."

Janet wasn't sure she understood. Jackie had never before mentioned anything about disinterring her deceased infant children. Her immediate reaction was that the timing couldn't have been much worse. Hadn't they all been through enough? She wanted to ask Jackie if she was certain, but before she could finish the question, Jackie cut her off. She explained that in planning Jack's state funeral, she'd learned that the body of Abraham Lincoln's son Eddie, almost four years old when he died, had been exhumed from his grave and moved to a new resting place next to his father's in the Lincoln Tomb at Oak Ridge Cemetery. She now wanted her late children — the daughter stillborn at seven months back in 1956 and Patrick, who'd passed away just a few months before — to be laid next to Jack.

Janet could tell from Jackie's resolute tone that there was nothing more to say other than the words that finally came forth: "Yes, Jacqueline. Don't worry. I'll take care of it." They spoke for a few more minutes with Jackie giving specific instructions and telling her mother of the arrangements she would make for her trip. After hanging up — as she would later recall it — Janet rolled over and tried to rest. But after such a troubling phone call, she found herself constantly awakening from a fitful sleep. With the passing of hours, another day was about to dawn. The worst ever, she suspected, and considering recent events, that was saying a lot. She rose, showered, and dressed slowly in a cream-colored skirt and long-sleeved white cashmere sweater. She then wrapped a matching scarf around her head. After examining herself in the mirror, she put on a heavy wool pinch-waist beige coat with broad, square padded shoulders and a half belt in back. It had been designed for Jackie by Oleg Cassini, and Jackie had given to it Janet as a birthday present the year before last.

"Come, Jamie," Janet called out as she slipped on kid leather gloves. "It's time to go." She'd earlier decided that since sixteen-year-old Jamie had to return to Brooks boarding school in North Andover, Massachusetts, she would drop him off on the way. Once again in front of the mirror, she donned a bold pair of oversized sunglasses just as Jamie came bounding from his bedroom, suitcase in hand.

Mother and son got into a car waiting for them at the front entrance of the O Street house. "Washington National," said Janet tersely to the uniformed driver. On the way to the airport, she was quiet, not wanting to talk. Instead, she stared straight ahead, avoiding the steady gaze of her son. Jamie studied her with concern. He knew a little about what was going on — just what his mother could explain without going into great detail. "Mummy knew what she had to do and she was determined to see it through," Jamie Auchincloss would recall many years later. "The sun was barely rising as we drove along. It was cold outside, so the windows were up. It was dark. Silent. Just the hum of the motor. As I watched the scenery slip by, my mind was racing. I knew enough about what was happening to know that Mummy probably would have been upset if Jackie had sent a secretary to take care of it. It was something Mummy would have felt was the specific responsibility of the mother of the widow, or the mother-in-law of the martyred President. This was a personal mission, a mother's duty — and she would have to call on all of her courage to get through it."

Finally at Washington National Airport, Janet and Jamie were greeted by Edwin J. Zimny, the stocky and bespectacled forty-seven-year-old commercial flight instructor and owner of Zimny's Flying Service of Lawrence, Massachusetts. A pilot with World War II experience, he customarily flew members of the Kennedy family on trips up and down the East Coast. Zimny was to take Janet and Jamie in his Aero Commander 680, a light, twin-engined, propeller aircraft, from Washington to Newport, Rhode Island, with one stopover in North Andover. Once at the airport in Andover, Janet got out of the plane with Jamie. On the runway, she embraced him, holding him tightly, kissing him on the cheek. After one more embrace, Janet walked back toward the plane. The pilot then helped her on board.

The rest of the flight to Newport would take less than an hour. Once they landed, Janet shook the pilot's hand and thanked him, having no idea that she would never again lay eyes on him. In six months, Edwin Zimny would be dead, tragically killed while piloting JFK's brother Ted to a campaign speech in the exact same plane in which he'd just transported Janet. Ted would be critically injured in the crash.

Once in Newport, Janet rendezvoused with John F. Hayes Jr., director of the family-owned and -operated O'Neill-Hayes Funeral Home. The two then were driven by hearse to St. Columba's Catholic Cemetery in Middletown. Soon they found Section 40, and not much later, a small slate grave marker on which was etched the words: "Daughter — August 23, 1956."

Janet stood before the grave, tightening her wool coat around her slim shoulders and bracing herself against the chilly wind blowing in from the bay. As she did so, memories of the past played vividly in her mind, jolting flashbacks of an awful time seven years earlier when Jackie, seven months pregnant, lost the child that was buried in this plot, little "Arabella." Janet watched as John Hayes carried a small coffin from his hearse and laid it on the ground right next to where she was standing. Then two gravediggers began shoveling away the dirt in search of a small wooden coffin they knew had to be about six feet below the surface. When they reached it, the two men attempted to lift it from the yawning hole.

Janet lurched forward, gaping into the opening in the ground. Then, much to her horror, the bottom of the coffin gave out, having rotted away over so many years. Gasping, Janet turned her head. Somehow, though, she would see it through; she was just that determined. Continuing to steel herself, she watched as the gravediggers shoveled the remains into the new coffin. As this occurred, Janet would later confess, her heart clenched achingly in a way that she'd never before experienced. Finally, the work done, John Hayes nodded his approval and the new casket was closed. Janet drew a deep breath and bowed her head. Then she and Hayes were driven back to his funeral home, where the coffin was deposited.

Janet spent the night at Hammersmith Farm in Newport. Before retiring, she telephoned Jackie to tell her that the deed had been done. She said she would be arriving in

Washington in the morning with the baby's remains.

"MAKE STRAIGHT PATHS FOR YOUR FEET"

At twilight on the morning of December 3, Janet walked up the steps of the Episcopalian Trinity Church in Newport. Built in 1725, this large, white wood-and-brick structure with its soaring five-story spire and tower had been one of her places of worship ever since marrying Hugh. She tried to open the front door; it was locked. She then looked around the corner and up at the enormous clock below the steeple and realized that it was only six in the morning. She stood in place, wondering what to do. Waiting for just a few moments, she then walked around to the side of the building to a small cemetery. After opening a small gate in the nineteenth-century cast-iron fence, she let herself into a burial ground dotted with gravestones dating back as far as the eighteenth century. She sat on a cement bench to collect her thoughts.

The night before, she'd not been able to sleep, finding it impossible to get over what had happened at St. Columba's Catholic Cemetery. She felt she needed guidance. Therefore, as a brilliant sun began to rise in a Newport sky, she started to pray. A priest who was walking from the rectory to the church to open its doors took notice of her and went to sit by her side. "I told him what had happened, the terrible thing I witnessed with my grandchild," Janet would later remember to one relative, "and that I didn't know if I would be able to get through the rest of what was to come. He understood. We then prayed together." Janet said that the priest placed both his palms on her head. "Lift your drooping hands and strengthen your weak knees," he intoned, "and make straight paths for your feet." She remembered, "In that moment, I was filled with such a sense of peace. I knew then that I would find the power to continue. I knew what I had to do."

That evening at close to midnight, Janet — by now her face pale, drawn, and etched with fatigue — found herself on the tarmac of Newport's Quonset Naval Air Station. After walking slowly across the landing strip, she was greeted by Jack's youngest brother, Ted Kennedy. Also present was Richard Cardinal Cushing. At Jackie's earlier request, Cushing had watched as the small casket of the infant Patrick was exhumed from his burial spot at Holyhood Cemetery near Brookline. Now Janet watched as the baby's coffin was carried onto the *Caroline* aircraft, followed by his sister's casket. She, Ted, and Father Cushing then boarded the plane. Ted sat alone in the front of the cabin while Janet and the priest sat in the back. Between them, in the narrow aisle, were the two coffins lined up in a row. No one spoke on the flight to Washington; "Not one word was uttered," Cushing would later recall.

On Thursday night, December 5, at about eight-thirty, Janet and Lee — who had arrived earlier in the day — stood next to Jackie at a grave site at Arlington National Cemetery, along with Bobby and Ted Kennedy. Also present were Father Cushing and the Most Reverend Philip Matthew Hannan, the auxiliary bishop of Washington who had long been a close friend of the Kennedy family. Jackie had called him earlier to ask him to be present, telling him that an army staff car would pick him up at the rectory and bring him to the cemetery. She'd stressed the importance of secrecy.

"The sight of two such tiny white caskets was truly heart-wrenching," Father Hannan would recall many years later. "Before starting the ceremony, Jackie and I placed each coffin on the ground near her husband's fresh grave. The graves had already been dug. As a crane lowered the first casket, I began to recite the words of the Lord's Prayer."

"Our father, who art in heaven, hallowed be thy name," the priest said as the workman lowered the coffin into the ground. Then, the second coffin. He continued to pray — *"Hail*

Mary, full of grace, the Lord is with thee" — as the workman covered both coffins with soil. "Conscious of Jackie's fragile, emotional condition, I decided to offer only the prescribed short prayers of the ceremony," the priest recalled.

After the brief service, Jackie stood alone at the graves of her husband and children while the rest of the small, sad coterie stepped away to give her a moment of privacy. With a somber expression, she genuflected, made the sign of the cross, rose, and stood in place for a long time, her head bowed. She wasn't crying. Rather, she appeared to be numb, frozen in place.

Later, as the small group made its way back to the car, Jackie began peppering Father Hannan with questions. He would later recall, "She asked if she could have the ritual book and stole that I'd used for the service. As I gladly handed them over, they seemed to unleash a torrent of spiritual concerns that only a priest could possibly help her work through: Why had God let this happen? What could possibly be the reason? Jack had so much more to give, was just hitting his stride. What was our destiny in heaven? Did I think he was there? How would the children ever understand? What should she tell them?

"The more she talked, the more that Jackie's real feelings surfaced, her comments frank and to the point," he remembered.

"Particularly galling, she confided, was the public's surprise at her stoicism while preparing — and during — the funeral. Why had so many columnists marveled at her composure? It was the least she could do for Jack. He would have expected nothing less.

"Given the presence of her mother and sister, I thought it might be more appropriate if she and I, privately, continued our conversation at my rectory or the White House," he remembered of that night. "But Jackie was undeterred. 'I don't like to hear people say that I am poised and maintaining a good appearance,' she said, resentfully. 'I am not a movie actress.' "

Finally, Janet and Lee couldn't take it another second. They approached their loved one. "Come now, dear," Janet said as she took Jackie by the hand. She seemed determined not to allow her resolve to crumble in front of her daughter, no matter her personal anguish. Lee tried to mirror her mother's stoic demeanor. "It's over, Jackie," Lee told her sister. "Your babies are with Jack now. Let's go. Please."

Janet took Jackie by one arm. Steadying her gently, Lee took her sister by the other. The three Bouvier women then walked slowly and uncertainly to a waiting limousine.

JACKIE'S TORMENT

By early February of 1964, Jackie and her children had vacated the White House and, after a brief time at a temporary residence, were living at 3017 N Street in Georgetown. Lee had found the place for her, a good-sized, twelve-room, eighteenth-century Colonial house. Billy Baldwin, the Kennedys' designer and good friend, recalled being concerned when he first saw the place. "It had been chosen for Jackie with the greatest possible bad decision by her sister. I think the home was designed by someone for purposes of publicity. There was no hope for privacy, it was out in the open, high atop a mountain of steps. When I saw it, it looked like a monument. I thought, Why, Lee, why? *Why?*"

Lee's idea was that she would momentarily move into the second floor with Jackie to help out and keep an eye on her. Because Stas had business in New York, the couple was thinking of relocating there. Meanwhile, Lee would be able to spend more time with her sister; her children, Anthony and Tina, would sleep on the third floor with Caroline and John.

It was also at this time that the Bouvier women's Mother-Daughter Tea came back into their lives. Janet insisted upon it, especially with all three living in Washington; Janet liked the high tea service at the Mayflower Hotel, a few blocks from the White House. It was at that first tea, though, that Janet and Lee saw plainly that Jackie wasn't the same woman she'd been before the assassination. The trauma she'd endured in Dallas had, not surprisingly, changed her, especially coming just three months after the death of baby Patrick. She was, understandably, upset, constantly crying and, she admitted, never sleeping. She confessed that she was drinking too much, taking pills, and, basically, doing whatever she could do to get through the day.

Shortly after the sisters moved into the N Street house, they invited Janet to dinner with a group of other friends, including the Bradlees; Arthur Schlesinger Jr. and his wife, Marian; and Franklin D. Roosevelt Jr. and his wife, Suzanne. They were to be joined by Tom Braden, president of the state board of education and former CIA official, and his wife, Joan, one of the Kennedys' most loyal confidantes. Once everyone was settled in the parlor, Janet could immediately tell that Jackie was in no shape for company. Her hair wasn't properly combed, her clothes disheveled. She even seemed wobbly, as if she'd been drinking again.

Prior to February of 1964, Janet had heard only a few details of Jackie's version of the events surrounding the assassination. Lee knew more since her sister had confided in her while they were living under the same roof. With Jackie's remembrances this evening, though, Janet would be privy to much more. Her face wiped clean of all emotion, Jackie recited the story with eerie stoicism, as if it had happened to someone else, not her. Tom Braden remembers, "She poured it all out in detail, in shocking detail. Things you wouldn't expect to hear, she told, such as, 'I realized suddenly I had his brains in my hand.'"

Because Jackie was nursing a Scotch and soda as she told her story, Janet had to wonder if what she was saying was even true. She thought the morbid scenario might possibly be drawn from one of Jackie's nightmares. Certainly there seemed no end to the grisly events of late. It made sense that Jackie's imagination had run wild. "Jackie, you know that none of that really happened, don't you?" Janet said, squeezing her daughter's hand. Smiling faintly, she suggested that Jackie had imagined it, or maybe dreamed it. With anger flaring in her dark eyes, Jackie said, "Of course I didn't make it up, Mummy! Why would I make up such a thing?" Everyone was at a loss for words.

Finally, Lee spoke. "You're not going to get through this without the love of your family," she told Jackie, according to what Joan Braden would later recall. Lee then reminded her sister that they were all there for her. Since they were already together, Lee suggested, "Let's just sit and share stories about Jack that will make us remember him. Would that make you feel better, Jacks?" Jackie nodded. For the next two hours, her friends and family surrounded Jackie with warmth as they sat around the fireplace and remembered their beloved Jack.

JANET'S ADVICE

By July, Jackie was really no better. Today we understand all too well that she was suffering from PTSD — post-traumatic stress disorder. Back then, however, it really wasn't recognized as such. In fact, the American Psychiatric Association wouldn't add PTSD to its *Diagnostic and Statistical Manual of Mental Disorders* until 1980, and mostly in response to those suffering from it after serving in the Vietnam War. However, in retrospect, the symptoms Jackie exhibited could not be clearer in pointing to a diagnosis of PTSD. A car's backfiring would send her into a tailspin, reminding her of a gunshot. Any sudden noise, in fact, would startle her to the point of practically immobilizing her. She kept insisting she had no reason to live and often threatened suicide. She couldn't sleep; she had recurring nightmares. She blamed herself for Jack's death, wishing it had been her instead — "If I had just been a little more to one side, it could have been me." She was sad and morose all of the time, and there was really nothing anyone could do to help. Everyone felt powerless.

The latest development was that Jackie couldn't bear being around her own children. For the most part, she was leaving the kids in the care of their nanny. Janet certainly didn't like the way that sounded when Lee told her about it. It was unlike Jackie. She and Lee were the ones who left the raising of their children to nannies, not Jackie. Jackie was the maternal one!

Feeling the need to step in, Janet telephoned Jackie and suggested a visit to Hammersmith. "Therefore, Jackie came to Hammersmith for a week," recalled Jamie, who was at the farm just prior to returning to boarding school. "She arrived on the nineteenth and brought Caroline, but not John. This was when Mummy saw how bad off Jackie still was. She never laughed. She never cried. Mummy noticed bottles of prescription pills on her bedroom dresser and wondered what was going on."

Because she couldn't sleep, Jackie would drag herself down to the Deck Room in the middle of the night and set up her easel in a corner. She would then open the French windows along the wide terrace on that side of the house, the west side, and allow the cold bay air to flood the room, all the while wrapping herself in a robe for warmth. She would

370

then begin to paint, using her watercolors until about four in the morning. Exhausted, she would then go back up to her room at four-thirty. Maybe she would sleep with the help of tranquilizers. Maybe she wouldn't.

Janet's schedule at Hammersmith had always been precise. Breakfast was served to her in her bedroom at eight in the morning and then to everyone else in residence at exactly eight-thirty, and not in their rooms either, but in the kitchen. That's the way it had been for years, and it would never change. By nine-thirty, the servants were supposed to be making the beds and cleaning the guest rooms. Then it would be time for them to prepare for lunch. After lunch, they usually had a few hours off, during which time they would be free to go to their own accommodations on the north side of the Big House. At about four, they were to be back at the main house to begin preparation for the cocktail hour and then dinner. "Because Jackie had been up all night, she would rise at about noon and call down for breakfast," Jamie recalled. "Then she would want it served in her room, not in the kitchen. Well, by that time, the serving of breakfast was long over and lunch was supposed to be up next. This rearranging of the household schedule quickly became an issue for my mother. Maybe it was for the best, though, because it would be the catalyst for a serious talk

Mummy would have with Jackie."

One afternoon, after Jackie finished with her late breakfast, she dragged herself down to the beach to join Janet and Jamie under an umbrella. She looked dreadful, maybe medicated or hungover. Janet was as annoyed as she was worried. "Jacqueline," she began — and this is according to Jamie's memory of the conversation — "we've all lost Jack, but it's been eight months! You have to snap out of it."

Jackie looked at her mother with a perplexed expression. Janet continued by telling Jackie that she would no longer be permitted to awaken at noon and then expect the servants to prepare breakfast for her and bring it to her room. Instead, Janet continued, she would be expected to rise in the morning with everyone else, and eat breakfast at eight-thirty in the kitchen. "You cannot keep treating my servants like this," Janet said. Jackie nodded her agreement. Janet then reached for her daughter's hand and said, "The only way you'll ever get through this thing is to start living your life again in a normal fashion. Do we have an understanding?"

Jamie recalled, "Jackie was a little startled. She blinked a few times and then she said, 'Thank you, Mummy. Somebody had to tell me that. Because nobody has said no to me in a long time. I guess it takes a mother to say "snap out of it," doesn't it?' Mummy nodded. Then Jackie said, 'I really needed to hear that today.'"

WHAT TO DO ABOUT JACKIE?

Jackie Kennedy realized that in order for her to hope to recover from what had happened to her, from what she had witnessed in Dallas, she needed to leave Georgetown. She couldn't bear her residence there another day. It was too much like a fishbowl, with people camping outside her front door, watching for her, waiting for her, wondering about her. The scrutiny it invited from the public just added another level of stress to her life. Therefore, in July of '64, she followed Lee to New York, purchasing a fourteen-room apartment at towering 1040 Fifth Avenue, on the fifteenth floor. It was just seven blocks away from Lee and Stas's cooperative. However, even after moving in, Jackie still found herself feeling alone and depressed. She sent the children to Hammersmith to spend the summer with Janet, who was happy to take them but worried about her daughter.

"I don't know what to do about her," Lee told Sherry Geyelin, the daughter of Hugh's late partner, Chauncey, over lunch one afternoon at Sardi's. Oatsie Charles, Janet's socialite friend, was also present, as was Adora Rule's daughter, Janine, who had just started working for Oatsie as a secretary. "I haven't slept in a month," Lee said. "I am up all night with Jackie, either in person or on the phone. She's in dreadful shape. I'm scared to death for her." The stress was evident on Lee's face. She seemed drawn and exhausted.

Lee said that, a week earlier, Jackie had called her in the middle of the night to say she was experiencing a strong impulse to take as many pills as she could and wash them down with vodka, all in the hope that she wouldn't awaken the next morning. Frantic, Lee raced to Jackie's apartment and stayed up all night with her, talking to her, trying to reason with her, drying her tears. The next day, she decided not to leave Jackie's side; she spent the next three days caring for her sister. "But I am not a psychiatrist," she said. "I don't know what I'm doing! I'm just a sister trying to come up with answers!" Lee said that while Jackie slept she went rummaging about the apartment, finding drugs prescribed by doctors and then flushing them down the toilet. She was amazed at how many doctors Jackie had, and how many different kinds of drugs she was taking. She said there should be "some sort of law" to prevent doctors from overprescribing serious drugs to patients who were clearly in danger of hurting themselves.

Lee also said Jackie wasn't open to the idea of seeking professional help and that, instead, she'd been talking to a Jesuit priest named Father Richard McSorley. The two would sit and talk for hours. Jackie said she had told him she was considering suicide; she wondered whether she did such a thing would she see Jack on the other side, in heaven? Because of her global celebrity, she even said she figured her suicide would set off a rash of suicides among Americans. Maybe this fad would not be such a bad turn of events, she reasoned. At least those people who made the decision would be set free from their pain.

"Do you know what she said to me just yesterday?" Lee asked. "She said, 'I should have just married John Husted and then none of this would have happened to me.'"

"Who in the world is *that*?" asked Sherry Geyelin.

"Exactly!" Lee exclaimed. (Of course, Husted was the man to whom Jackie had been engaged in 1951, the one from whom Janet instigated a breakup.)

Janine Rule recalled, "Lee said that she'd asked Aristotle Onassis to keep an eye on Jackie that week because he happened to be in Manhattan on business. Mrs. Charles said, 'Do you trust him?' Lee said, 'With my life.' Mrs. Charles and I looked at one another with raised eyebrows as if to say, *'Really?'* But we didn't say it. Lee was under enough pressure. I had never seen her so upset. I didn't want to add to it."

In fact, Ari stopped by to see Jackie quite often. He'd call first and then visit with gifts for her and the children. He said he didn't believe she should be locked away. She was young and vital and full of life, he told her. "You have to mourn, Jackie. But, soon, you must live," he concluded.

Meanwhile, Lee's affair with Onassis continued unabated. It was strained, though, and definitely not the same. They argued constantly. He wasn't kind to her. In fact, he was a brute most of the time. However, she still cherished their rare good moments together and held on to each one tightly, hoping against hope that he would soon return to the dashing, loving man he'd been in her life before she renewed her vows to Stas. It also worried her that Onassis seemed just a tad too invested in her sister's happiness, but what could she do about it? She just had to wait, hope for the best, and see what developed.

Maybe Lee didn't have anything to worry about where Jackie was concerned. Though Ari was certainly solicitous to her, it was really Jack Warnecke who held Jackie's interest. Whenever he came to town, her spirits were lifted. The two had been growing closer ever since she had hired him to design JFK's new tomb. She was impressed with him. He'd consulted at least fifty different architects, painters, stonemasons, and calligraphers to put together what he thought she'd most appreciate for her late husband. With work set to begin in the fall of '65, it was as if Jackie had one foot in the past with the old Jack and another in the future with the new one. Dogged by indecision, she didn't know what to do.

Bobby Kennedy didn't make things any easier. He still strongly disliked Jack, so much so that Warnecke's associate Harold Adams was now forced to act as a liaison between the two men. It was better if they weren't in the same room together. Though there were rumors that Bobby and Jackie had somehow become involved, these stories simply were not true. However, Bobby definitely didn't want Jackie to be with Warnecke, and he didn't want to be around him, either. Jack felt the same way about Bobby

JACKIE'S LITTLE CEMETERY

November 1964.

Two lone figures were walking through a lush oasis behind Hammersmith Farm called the Sunken Garden. They were holding hands. "What do you think of this one?" the man asked. They stopped at a small gray block of marble protruding from the ground. It was about two feet long and just as high. He bent over and pushed aside a cluster of red and gold leaves obstructing the engraving of a small cross and the words "President John Fitzgerald Kennedy — 1917–1963." The woman stood before it and scrutinized it. "Too shiny," she decided as she studied the marble. He agreed. They walked another couple of feet. "How about this one?" he asked as they stopped before another stone. This one was slate, its hue slightly darker than the marble. Inscribed on it were the same words: "President John Fitzgerald Kennedy — 1917–1963." She crouched down to get a closer look. "I actually like this one," she said. "Put this one on the top of the list," she added, saying she appreciated the way the light shimmered off it. She noted that the slate came from Vermont, whereas the marble had originated in New Hampshire. As the two talked, the heavy cloud cover began to clear to reveal the sun. With the new flickering light, shadows of at least fifty similar stones began to take shape around them, each emblazoned with the name of her deceased husband, his date of birth and of death. It was like being in a miniature cemetery, but with all of the gravestones paying respect to the same person: "President John Fitzgerald Kennedy — 1917–1963."

Jamie Auchincloss recalled: "I loved taking unsuspecting visitors there, preferably on a foggy night. As we walked along carefully, they would inevitably stumble over a gravestone and scream out, 'My God, what is this?'

And I would shine a flashlight on it, and the stone would say, 'President John Fitzgerald Kennedy — 1917–1963.' It would completely freak people out that my sister actually had a faux graveyard at Hammersmith."

Jack Warnecke had come to Hammersmith Farm to help Jackie make the final selection of stone for the JFK memorial at Arlington, upon which would be engraved words from Jack's inaugural address. The actual tombstone itself would have etched on it just a simple cross — nothing like what Eunice and Sargent Shriver had earlier suggested in terms of grandiose religious symbolism. Janet had recommended a stone carver in Newport, which was why the two were at Hammersmith walking through a plot of ground Jackie called "my little cemetery." Hopefully, their final selection would be made this weekend.

This project had consumed Jack for the last few months, so much so that he had opened another office in Georgetown, just a block away from where Jackie had lived on N Street. He also had his children come east with him, giving his ex-wife a nice summer break. It had been a fun few months, the Warnecke brood getting along well with Jackie's children, Caroline and John, all of them taking road trips together, such as one to Williamsburg, where the adults had a chance to teach the young ones about the Civil War. Though Jack's kids returned to California in

September for school, he stayed on and continued to work on the JFK site. Throughout this time, he and Jackie grew even closer.

Jack, who was now forty, realized that Jackie was in no shape to jump into another relationship. She wasn't herself, and he knew it. Once, they were in her kitchen when someone in the house slammed a door. She began to shake and have trouble breathing. He took her into his arms to calm her.

That night, Jack and Jackie had dinner with Janet and Hugh. They had a lot of laughs; Hugh could really get on a roll with his corny jokes once he had a few drinks in him. After the foursome put Chubby Checker's new album on the stereo in the Deck Room, Jackie tried to teach her stepfather how to do the twist while Jack and Janet watched and good-naturedly criticized poor Hugh. Finally, Janet decided to call it a night and took her husband up to their room, leaving Jack and Jackie curled up in front of the roaring fireplace. "Jack, if you'd like your shoes polished," Janet said before she took her leave, "just leave them outside your bedroom door and they shall be polished by morning." After Janet and Hugh were gone, Jackie mentioned that she needed to go back to Hyannis Port in the morning. Jack suggested that she let him drive her there. She then dozed off at about eleven; he placed a wool blanket over her to keep her warm and then went up to his room — the same one President Kennedy used to sleep in when he would visit Hammersmith.

"MONEY IS POWER"

The next morning, the two rose before Janet and Hugh. Jackie noted that it was good that they'd gotten up on time, that if they missed breakfast, they could forget about eating anything until lunchtime. With a laugh, she observed that her mother ran Hammersmith Farm like a hotel, "a very *strict,* very *mean* hotel in a Communist country." After they ate, Jackie wrote a note saying she would call Janet later that day. At the bottom of the note, Jack scrawled: "My dearest Janet — The room was not too hot. Nor was it too cold. It was just right. Love, JW." The couple then left the manor and jumped into Jack's black Mercury convertible. It was a beautiful fall day, and the drive to Hyannis Port was invigorating.

When they got to the compound, Jackie took Jack into the home she had once shared with her late husband, walking him up the stairs and onto the porch. They stood there for a while, admiring the view before going inside. They were alone; the kids were in Georgetown with the housekeeper. Therefore, the two spent the day walking along the shore, taking about their lives. "What matters

381

to you?" Jack asked her. It was such a broad question, Jackie hardly knew how to answer it. "Freedom," she said, after a moment's thought. "I want to be able to live a good life and not have any restrictions put on me by the public." She talked about how much she loathed the public's and the media's desire to keep her as, what she called, "The Widow Kennedy." She said that she didn't want to be locked in time. "I had a life before I was a Kennedy and I hope to still have one now that my husband is gone," she said. She also said she wanted her children to be able to live "as normally as possible" and spoke a little about how much she hated the Secret Service protection of them, even though she knew it was necessary. She said she longed, more than anything, to be able to just remember details of what happened in Dallas in 1963 without also reliving those terrible events.

Then, as Jack would later recall it, Jackie said something apropos of nothing that took him by complete surprise. "Power is important," she said, succinctly. From the expression on his face, she must have known she had to elaborate. "Power matters, Jack," she added. "I don't necessarily have to wield it but, definitely, any man I am with has to have it at his disposal."

"Are you talking about money?" he asked.

"Sure," she said. "Money is power," she

continued, repeating the family's long-standing mantra. "I'm a practical woman, just like my mother, like all of my relatives, really."

This conversation, which he would always remember, left Jack Warnecke feeling uneasy. He wasn't sure what Jackie intended by sharing this information with him, he only knew that he felt a little bothered by it. He was also under the impression that she was a wealthy woman. She was getting $175,000 a year from Jack's estate — more than a million dollars a year in today's money — so she wasn't exactly broke. However, Jack would later say he felt Jackie was worth a whole lot more. Maybe he felt she would be entitled to the Auchincloss fortune but, of course, this was not the case. She had big spending habits, though, and he knew that about her, too. While he had his own money, would it be enough for her?

"Don't get it wrong, my dad was all about power, too," said his son Fred Warnecke. "Being with Jackie Kennedy, part of that was about power for him. As much as he liked her and maybe even loved her by this point, he understood that associating with her helped his business. Being with the Kennedys, those relationships gave him a certain power. He wasn't some naïve guy who didn't understand the importance of power. He liked his position in life as a powerful man. But I'm not sure he understood, at least until she cleared it up for him, that Jackie had the same kind of interest, except that hers was tied more to money in the bank."

That night, Jack and Jackie ate clam chowder from Millie's, one of her favorite little diners, closed for the season. Jackie had some of the soup frozen in containers in the refrigerator. She heated the soup on the stove for dinner. It tasted awful. "Just goes to show you that you can *not* freeze clam chowder," she said, slightly embarrassed.

After dinner, they spent a couple of hours in the living room, chatting. They began to kiss. "I love you, Jackie, you know that, don't you?" he said to her, according to his later memory. "I love you too, Jack," she said. "I'm not sure, though . . ." she added, her voice trailing. "I fell in love with you the first time I ever saw you, at the British embassy," he then told her. "Do you remember?" She laughed. "We danced and danced that night," she recalled with a smile. "It was wonderful."

From there, it all just seemed to unfold naturally between them. Eventually, Jackie took Jack by the hand and walked him up the stairs to the room she once shared with the other Jack, the first one in her life. She kissed him fully on the lips. They reaffirmed their affection for each other. She then led him to the bed, the one in which, tonight, they would first make love.

After Jack left her home, Jackie spent a

couple of days alone there, trying to put into perspective what had happened. Now she was filled with regret. What in the world had she been thinking? It wasn't that she didn't have feelings for Jack, but making love to him in the bed she had once shared with her late husband? One year to the month since Jack's murder? That was definitely going too far. It was as if her judgment had been severely crippled. Jackie felt she had moved too fast with Jack, and now she wanted nothing more than to slow things down. "It all happened with my dad so quickly after the President's death, she had questions," said Jack's son Fred. " 'Is this really right? Is this what's best for my kids?' " She spent the next week drinking, taking pills, and trying to come to terms with her rash decision, all the while still suffering from nightmares.

Of course, Jack was disappointed that Jackie wanted to put the brakes on their romance, but he understood. "We'll take things at your pace," he told her. Was her reluctance because she was interested in other men? In fact, there would always be rumors of other affairs — Roswell Gilpatric and William David Ormsby-Gore (better known as Lord Harlech) would be seen with Jackie at times.

However, there was still another man on the periphery, and he seemed to show up when Jackie least expected it. It had happened more than a few times in the last six months: a call from the front desk with someone announcing that "Mr. Onassis is here to see you." Surprised, Jackie would tell the guard to let him into the building. Moments later, the elevator into her apartment would open and there would stand Aristotle Onassis, again a Greek bearing gifts for her and the children. They would talk. He would make her laugh. "Are you trying to live your life?" he would ask her. "Are you recovering from what happened?" She would tell him that it was difficult but she was trying her best. Then, as suddenly as he appeared, he would vanish. She would then think to herself, "What a nice man" and just go about her day like any other.

PART EIGHT: TRANSITION

WHEN WAS LEE
AT HER HAPPIEST?

"I'm sick of all of it," Lee Radziwill said at the beginning of 1965. She told friends that she was "sick of money, power, politics, and family. *I want out!*" She was also tired of Stas, Taki, and, now, especially Ari. What had happened to change her view of him? Put it this way: in the last two years, they had gotten no closer. In fact, recently, Ari seemed to not even mind that she was still with Stas. He liked Stas so much he even gave him a position on the board of his Olympic Airways. Stas took the chair and actually enjoyed working for Onassis, which Lee found very disconcerting. Onassis, famously known for his jealous temperament, would ordinarily insist that the woman he was with not be with anyone else. He certainly wouldn't allow Maria Callas to have other paramours, let alone a husband! He also wouldn't have befriended that husband. What was wrong with this picture? Onassis *should* be jealous!

This inner conflict about Onassis seemed

to make Lee painfully conscious of the emptiness of her life. She would often quote an early mentor, the art historian Bernard Berenson, who believed that people in a person's life were either "life enhancing" or "life diminishing." In fact, as Lee explained it, "The life-diminishing people are passive — they don't care about anything, have little curiosity, and always want and expect to be amused or entertained. The life-enhancers aren't always creative, but they always have an appreciation, a caring that make everyone around them feel *bigger.* They're the givers." She said she had grown very weary of the "life-diminishing" variety.

Time seemed to be of the essence, too. Lee's bout with postpartum depression had profoundly changed her. She was more keenly aware than ever of the finite nature of life and determined to now make the best of it. Certainly, what Jackie was going through also served to underscore that fact for Lee.

At this time, at a cocktail party at Lee's home in Manhattan, a good friend who had a successful career as a television producer suggested to her that she stop looking outward for satisfaction and validation. She would be better served by looking within — pretty much what Taki had once told her. This time, the suggestion resonated with Lee. "I'm full of shit, aren't I?" she asked that friend, as if struck by the revelation. His answer? "Yes, Lee, I'm afraid you are."

As a result of that one simple conversation, 1965 would turn out to be quite the watershed year for Lee Radziwill. She would spend much of it trying to come to terms with her life. "What people often mistake as her cold, insensitive nature hides, in fact, a deeply pragmatic and sensible outlook," said her friend the writer Nicky Haslam. "She certainly recognizes her own faults, which are sometimes dusted with a longing for fairy-tale glitter, and flattery, but when anyone is as ravishingly beautiful as she was and even now is, that's understandable."

In 1965 Lee started exploring books about feminism and New Age thinking, grappling with life-affirming ideas and notions she'd never before considered. As sometimes happens, once Lee opened the doorway to self-discovery, people began to walk through who might assist her in her new quest. Through connections made in high-society London, she'd recently become friendly with the talented dancers Rudolf Nureyev and Margot Fonteyn. Both talked to her about the freedom of self-expression and how valuable it was to the purpose of living a good and fulfilling life. Her new friend Truman Capote — who really did idolize her, and the feeling was mutual — talked to her about his great work as a writer, how it gave him a reason to live, and how, without it, he would truly be lost. His book *In Cold Blood* was about to be published; his star was sure to be ascendant. The photographer and designer Cecil Beaton also encouraged her, assuring her that if she committed herself to something of artistic value, she would most certainly not regret it. These friendships and others like them seemed to blossom for Lee at a time when she was trying to come to terms with the age-old question of what makes a person happy and, specifically, what would make *her* happy.

Certainly, whatever Lee had been doing of late hadn't been working for her. Therefore the question before her was: When was she at her happiest? The answer was easy. It was back when she was working for *Harper's* for that brief sliver of time before she married Michael. Or when she was working for *Vogue* in Europe. "I hate floating," she would say. "I'm never happy unless I am deeply involved."

Lee realized she was happiest when she was doing something creative for herself or others, something that had nothing to do with Michael or Stas or Ari or just staying at home and raising children. She was happiest when she was *engaged* with people, with art, with culture. "What I am seeking is self-expression by exploration and by opening up my mind to different ways of life," she told her friends. She said that a quote from Jean Cocteau kept coming to mind: "To be gifted is to be defeated if you do not see clearly enough in time to build up the slopes and not go down them." She said she felt she had many talents and that she just needed to explore them to then find her passion or, at the very least, some degree of personal satisfaction.

"I was brought up to be the fat, delicious one that everyone liked to squeeze," Lee would later recall, "the fat, happy child who would marry someone in the Racquet Club and drive around in a station wagon all the time to pick up the twelve children and bring them home to the rose-covered cottage."

That was never going to be Lee Bouvier Radziwill. She had other ideas.

ACTRESS

In the summer of 1965, at a cocktail party, Lee Radziwill asked the actress, singer, and popular game-show panelist Kitty Carlisle Hart, a good friend, what she felt she might do with her life in terms of a new career. "My God," Kitty exclaimed without a second's hesitation. "You're a natural for the stage, Lee!" Maybe Kitty had a point. Certainly few people were as dramatic as Lee Radziwill in the way they led their lives, or in their telling of their outrageous adventures to others. Possessing such flair, though, didn't necessarily mean Lee could act. However, it was an intriguing proposition. Lee asked Kitty to make a few inquiries as to how she might proceed.

At the time, Kitty was in rehearsals for a play called *The Marriage-Go-Round,* with the famous theatrical producer Lee Guber. Kitty asked Guber if he would be willing to have Lee do a reading for him, not exactly an audition in that she wouldn't have to memorize anything, just a reading to see what she sounded like onstage, and how she looked in a spotlight. He agreed to have Lee read a scene from a comedy called *Catch Me If You Can,* which Guber was then mounting (not to be confused with the 2002 Leonardo DiCaprio film of the same name). It was set for an afternoon from the stage of the Morosco Theatre, near Times Square. Extremely nervous about it, Lee brought Jackie along for moral support.

As Lee read for Lee Guber, Jackie sat in the back of the theater, watching in the dark. She was impressed. She probably didn't know if Lee was good or if she was bad, but it didn't matter to her. She was going to support her sister, and that was the end of it for her. "Fantastic," Jackie exclaimed in front of the others as she embraced Lee, who seemed a little embarrassed. "Was I really good?" Lee asked. "Yes," Jackie answered. "Absolutely."

"I thought the princess terribly attractive in that well-bred Dina Merrill style," Guber later said, referencing a popular blond actress of the 1950s and '60s who, at the time, was touted as "Hollywood's New Grace Kelly."

"Do you have any magazine articles about yourself that I might be able to read?" Guber asked after the audition.

"I do, but they're all lies," Lee answered. "Each and every one of them. Lies!"

"Except, of course, for the one written by your wife," Jackie said quickly. Guber was married to Barbara Walters, who happened to have written an in-depth article about Lee for *Good Housekeeping.*

"Oh, yes, except for that one," Lee said. She glanced at her sister with appreciation.

Lee would have two more readings in front of Lee Guber. In the end, he decided she wasn't ready to be onstage. She had potential, though. She just needed training. *Of course* she needed training. This wasn't news to her, and Lee welcomed the challenge. If she was going to act, she decided, it had to be a legitimate endeavor, not just a vanity project.

Finally, Lee felt she had a real purpose, something to which she could and would commit herself fully. She began taking classes in London with a drama coach who believed from the start that Lee had great potential. She did express concern that Lee was starting out in such a competitive field so late in life — she was about thirty-two at the time. However, Lee was already famous and that was currency that would make a big difference to anyone interested in casting her in a movie, television program, or play.

It was good that she was encouraged by her coach because others in Lee's life were not so forthcoming with support. Back in the States, Janet and Hugh and some other members of her family viewed acting as just another passing fancy for Lee. They were also worried that endeavoring to be an actress would expose her flaws to the world and set her up to be judged. Stas agreed with the naysayers. "Why are you doing this to yourself?" he asked his wife. Her answer was simple: "Because I must."

"I tried to tell her she wasn't cut out for the stage," Stas told the writer George Carpozi at the time, "but she just wouldn't listen to me. I believe she is overcome with the mania to be an actress." He added that he would "set her free to pursue that desire. I shall not stand in her way." Today his son, John Radziwill, concurs, that "my dad wasn't really that supportive, but he was a man of a certain era."

Making things all the more complex — and troubling — for Lee was the fact that Aristotle Onassis didn't seem to have any problem at all with her career aspiration. When Lee told him about it, he was actually encouraging! Contrary to what one might imagine, she did *not* take this as a good sign. After all, this was a man who had spent years discouraging Maria Callas in her opera career, wanting her all to himself. He would do anything to make her quit, and she did so many times, just for him.

On the one hand, Lee didn't want Ari to feel about her acting aspirations the way Stas felt about them, but on the other hand . . . she did. The fact that Ari was as complacent about her career as he was about her marriage to Stas made Lee question, now more than ever, whether or not there was a future with him. Recently, he'd also been given to kissing her on the forehead instead of on the lips. This, too, did not bode well. In fact, it was a gesture that reminded her of Michael Canfield. She definitely needed a little more time to figure out what was going on with Onassis. Meanwhile, she started outlining what she wanted to do with her new career as an actress.

"I'd like to do new plays or films," Lee told a reporter at this time. "Tennessee Williams, Capote, interesting older women, alcoholics. I have the greatest sympathy for those who end in despair."

Certainly Lee had experienced enough despair in her life — especially given her postpartum depression, the effects of which still lingered — to be able to empathize with those who were struggling. The press didn't know this about her, though. No one other than her immediate family knew of her postpartum difficulty; it was a closely guarded secret. Therefore, most writers took her to task, observing that she had enjoyed an entitled existence and hadn't a clue as to how the other half lived. When Lee read criticism of herself before she'd even so much as acted in one scene, she realized then that she would have an uphill battle with the media, that every word she ever uttered would be scrutinized, analyzed, and then somehow used against her. It wasn't going to be easy, this new endeavor upon which Princess Lee Radziwill had settled. She was definitely willing to put in the work, though.

JACKIE'S HAWAII LOVE

On June 5, 1966, Jackie Kennedy arrived in Hawaii with her children, Caroline and John Jr. She and Jack Warnecke had decided on a vacation together, time away to take her mind off her problems. Jack was in the middle of a major design project, the mid-century modern Hawaii State Capitol building. He wanted her to be at his side for as much of the summer as possible. He would recall, "I would ask how she was doing and she would say she was well, but I knew better." He suspected that she was struggling, that it took real effort for her to appear happy and upbeat and to look to the future. He loved her all the more for her courage to try so hard not only for herself, but also for her children.

A good friend of Jack's, Cecily Freitas Johnston, an accomplished real-estate developer from Hawaii, arranged for Jackie to lease the Honolulu home of Colorado Senator Peter Dominick and his wife, Nancy. A team of security guards stood at the ready when Jackie arrived at the very private estate. "I was already there when she walked in the front door," Jack Warnecke recalled. "I had three of my four children with me — Roger, Fred, and Margo. We were staying at a house I'd just bought at Diamond Head whereas Jackie was staying in the rented house two properties away from Cecily Johnston's. She'd said she wanted her privacy, and I wanted to respect that."

"I certainly had no clue that Jackie Kennedy would be visiting," recalled Cecily Johnston's son Don. He would meet the former First Lady at a dinner party at his mom's. "I bent down to kiss my mother hello and out of the corner of my eye, who did I see? The most famous woman in the world," he recalled, laughing. "I didn't even know my mother knew her! Mom said, 'I'd like to introduce you to .. ,' and I said, 'Please, Mom. I know who this is!' It was a pretty heady experience."

The next morning, as Jackie and Cecily enjoyed their coffee, Cecily said she wanted to play a joke on her son. She got a tray from the kitchen and arranged on it an elegant breakfast. She then gave it to Jackie, who took it and knocked on Don's door. "Who is it?" he asked from his bed. The door opened and there standing before him was Jackie, wearing a brightly colored muumuu and a matching head scarf, breakfast tray in hand. " 'Oh, man!' I exclaimed, 'My mother has the best help ever these days, doesn't she?' We had a laugh; she was a good sport. She sat down and I gave her some pointers, some touristy ideas. It was fun. *She* was fun."

In Jack Warnecke's mind, he and Jackie had an understanding: they were eventually headed to the altar. Maybe it was wishful thinking, though, because he also knew she had reservations. "As much as he loved her, she was a total mystery to him," said Thomas McLaren, an architect who was working with Jack at the time on the Hawaii project. "She was not forthcoming. She seemed sad. They had fun, but when it came to in-depth conversations about her life, there was little of that. He hoped that would change when they married, that she would open up to him. I told him, 'No, that kind of thing doesn't change, Jack. It just gets worse.' Still, he wanted to marry her."

Apparently, the idea of marriage came up when Jack took Jackie on a tour of his new five-bedroom house on Diamond Head Road on Black Point. One night, the couple went out on the upstairs veranda of the master bedroom to enjoy the colorful sunset. Standing behind her, his arms wrapped around her, Jack asked what she was thinking. Jackie said she was thinking about the little den off the living room. He nodded knowingly. "You want to redo it, don't you?" She turned around and smiled at him. "You know me so well," she said. "The answer is yes!" He looked at her and, according to what he would later remember, he had a feeling that she was agreeing to more than just a remodel of a den. "Do you want to?" he asked, eagerly. "I do," she said with a big smile. "And that was it," he would recall many years later. "I knew we were getting married. I thought she was sure. In that moment, anyway, I thought she was sure."

In the coming days, the two would become more specific about the future. Jack said that the capitol wouldn't be finished for another three years — "Who knows," he said, "but we may buy another house here before then." Jackie said she wanted a Catholic Church wedding. However, because Jack had been raised a Presbyterian, he agreed that he would take catechism classes as soon as they returned to the mainland and then convert. "What are we going to do about Bobby Kennedy?" he asked. "I'll take care of him," Jackie said, reassuring him. Meanwhile, she went to work redesigning the den. (Jack's son Fred

401

still has one of the prized sketches she made of her remodeling ideas, signed "JBK.")

The month flew by. When Jackie called Lee in England to tell her about her plans, Lee was worried. She'd heard that Bobby didn't approve of Jack and was sure he would make life difficult for Jackie if she married him. Also, she had met Jack a number of times and thought he was nice enough, but she didn't see any spark between him and Jackie. However, she would say she never saw anything much between Jackie and JFK, either, "and that's just the way my sister is." Lee didn't want to be discouraging, just cautious. She knew that Jackie was not yet over Dallas, and she wondered how the effects of such trauma might impact a new relationship. She wanted a chance to talk to her about it again. "Don't elope, that's all I ask," she told her.

When the month was over, Jackie wanted to stay in Hawaii longer. Since her lease was up, Jack assumed they would now stay together, but she said she needed time alone. This was strange. Why, if she loved him and was preparing to marry him, would she need to be on her own? "It's like she gets close, then pulls away, then gets close and pulls away again," Jack told Thomas McLaren.

Jack arranged for Jackie and the children to move into the enormous cliffside guesthouse of the sprawling Koko Head estate of wealthy industrialist Henry J. Kaiser. Almost every day after that, and at great expense, Jack chartered a helicopter to pick up Jackie, Caroline, and John on the front lawn of Kaiser's estate and then take off for exciting destinations. "This is when things started to go bad with the business," said Harold Adams, by this time Jack's firm-wide administrative assistant and also manager of his Washington, D.C., office. "Jack was not out drumming up new accounts as usual. He was spending not only all of his efforts on Jackie, but all of his money, too. He was having a hard time keeping up with the financing of her lifestyle.

"At this same time, Jack jumped into opening up a New York office," continued Harold Adams. "I felt sure that the reason for this office was solely for him to be close to Jackie. The business was falling apart pretty quickly. A lot of money was owed by Jackie and the Kennedys, too, for different services. Most of it was to be paid for by the Army Corps of Engineers but there was some dispute about even that. It was such an emotional time, however, we never felt right about bringing up the subject of money."

Jack tried to ignore what was happening on the mainland with his business and focus on what mattered to him most at this time: Jackie.

Of course, as often happens, there were a few scrapes with the children while the families were on vacation in Hawaii. In particular, Caroline cut her foot on coral and John burned himself on a charcoal fire. There was a strange moment, too, one that anyone who witnessed it would likely never forget. Coincidentally, the house next to the one Jackie leased was owned by Hugh's nephew John Nash (Hugh's sister Esther's son from her first marriage, Esther being the one who had suggested that Janet Bouvier meet Hugh Auchincloss many years earlier). Nash had six children, all of whom became playmates of John and Caroline. One afternoon, one of Caroline's little friends found a lipstick in someone's purse, and the girls proceeded to use it draw on each other's faces. When Jackie saw what Caroline had done, she completely lost it. She slapped Caroline hard, first with the palm on one cheek, and then with the back of her hand on the other — just like Janet! Caroline screamed out in pain; the other children were terrified. "I thought, wow," recalled John Nash. "I was only a little older than Caroline, but I had never seen anything like *that* before. All the kids stood there stunned."

One night soon after that little fracas, Jack recruited his son Fred to babysit Caroline and John. It was then that Fred realized how difficult this transition in their mother's life was to her children. "They both started crying and telling me how much they missed their father," he remembered. "They were nervous that their mom was with this new guy, my dad. I went through the same thing when my dad divorced my mom, so I tried to talk to them, comfort them a little. I couldn't do much, though. I was only twelve and even I wasn't a hundred percent sure of my father's intentions."

If there was any ambiguity in little Fred's mind about what was going on between his father and Jackie, it was soon cleared up for him. One evening, Jackie spent the night at the Diamond Head house with Jack. Early the next morning, there was a telephone call. "Freddie, go up and get your dad and tell him he has an important telephone call," said the family's cook, Hazel. Fred dutifully ran over to his father's bedroom in the private suite of the estate. He knocked on the door. No answer. Since he was told that the call was "important," the youngster felt that he'd better rouse his dad. He opened the door, and much to his dismay, he found his father in bed having sex with Jackie. "Jackie jumped up in shock and started screaming," Fred Warnecke recalled many years later, "and my poor dad was saying, 'No, no, no, Freddie! Get out! *Get out!*' So I slammed the door and ran away as quickly as I could. It was pretty mortifying," he recalls. "My dad never mentioned it to me, and neither did Jackie. Of course, I stayed clear of her for a few days."

Jackie and the children finally returned to the mainland on July 26, two days short of her thirty-sixth birthday, which she would spend with Janet at Hammersmith. Jack stayed behind with the intention of meeting her in Manhattan in about a week.

JANET JR.'S WEDDING

It was July 30, 1966. "Thank goodness you aren't marrying a politician, that's all I can say," Jackie was telling her half sister, Janet Jr. Jackie, Janet Sr., and Janet Jr. were seated on an outdoor patio at Hammersmith Farm, admiring the sweeping lawns and pastureland, the rock gardens with Egyptian tiling and Italian vases amid charming lily ponds encircling the Big House "There's nothing wrong with politicians," Janet Sr. said. "You did well with one, didn't you, Jacqueline?" Ignoring her mother, Jackie continued her conversation with her sister. According to a witness to it, Jackie told Janet that the life of a politician was nothing but "dreary." She said that the only thing that made it worthwhile for her was that Jack Kennedy had been such a charismatic, powerful person. Janet Jr. asked if such was not the case with most men in politics. "Not the ones I've met," Jackie said, laughing.

As it would happen, Janet Jr., who was twenty-one in 1966, almost did end up with someone in politics; she had been dating John Forbes Kerry, twenty-two, for the last couple of years. Kerry, of course, would go on to become a United States senator, Democratic nominee for president (in 2004), and secretary of state in the Obama administration. Back in '66, though, he'd just graduated from Yale and was beginning his political career first as the chairman of the Liberal Party of the Yale Political Union, and then as president of that union. "I introduced John Kerry to President Kennedy," recalled Jamie Auchincloss. "I had this aspiration that Kerry would make a good president, and I hoped that introducing him to JFK would maybe inspire him in some way. I also thought that the fact that Kerry's initials were JFK was a coincidence maybe too good to pass up. My sister Janet would have made an excellent First Lady, by the way. She was bubbly and personable and, to be honest, maybe even a little more than Jackie."

For a brief time, Janet thought she was in love with John Kerry — even though her stepbrother Yusha wasn't too crazy about him — that is, until she took another look at Lewis Polk Rutherfurd, a Princeton senior and later Harvard graduate. The two had been introduced by Virginia Guest Valentine, Lewis's first cousin, during a spring break in Hobe Sound, Florida. Lewis was the tall and good-looking son of Winthrop Rutherfurd II, whose father, Winthrop I, was best known for his marriage to Lucy Mercer, mistress to President Franklin D. Roosevelt. (Lewis is not Mercer's son, though; his mother was Winthrop's first wife, Alice Morton.) "He was just dazzling," recalled Sylvia Whitehouse Blake of Lewis. "He looked like a movie star. We all thought, my gosh, what a great catch for Janet!"

"Lewis was so bright," recalled his cousin Virginia, "with a great sense of humor. He decided he wanted to be in Oriental studies. After he graduated from Princeton with his bachelor's degree in East Asia Studies, he won a fellowship at Chung Chi College of the Chinese University of Hong Kong."

In the few years since she was fretting to Jack Kennedy about her debutante party back in '63, Janet had grown into a lovely and smart young woman. She was also remarkably unspoiled, considering her entitled background, and full of upbeat energy. By the age of twenty-one, she was ready to take on the world. Majoring in music, she'd attended Sarah Lawrence College and had just landed a job as a secretary at Parke-Bernet Galleries, the nation's largest auction house. However, she decided against taking it when Lewis asked her to marry him. She said yes, and then agreed to move to Hong Kong with him. It was not easy for Janet Sr. to accept, but she wanted her daughter to be happy.

The wedding of Janet Jennings Auchincloss to Lewis Rutherfurd was held at St. Mary's Church in Newport, which, of course, was where Jackie had married Jack back in 1953. (Though Janet had been raised Episcopalian, Lewis was Catholic, thus the Catholic Church wedding.) Janet, just eight then, had been Jackie's flower girl. Now she was a bride, looking gorgeous in a short-sleeved, sheer organza dress with gossamer silk petals, designed by the Italian fashion house Sorelle Fontana of Rome. Janet's hair was swept into a classic chignon to reveal the shadowless brow and patrician mold of her chiseled features. A single strand of pearls was at her neck, a gift from Jackie.

The wedding day was as chaotic as one might expect, given that Janet was the half sister of Jacqueline Kennedy. More than eight thousand people showed up just to get a quick peek at Jackie in her two-piece, short-sleeved canary-yellow dress ensemble. Her appearance caused such bedlam, it was everything police could do to keep the crowds in control in front of the church. For a moment, Jackie and Janet Sr. were blocked by a team of photographers at the top of the steps. Jackie looked stricken as flashbulbs went off in her face, the popping sounds seeming to unnerve her. Finally, her mother, looking deceptively dainty in a pink dress with a large white picture hat and matching gloves, shoved one of the paparazzi. He tumbled into another until, finally, the whole lineup of them fell over themselves like circus clowns.

By the time the bride arrived on the arm of her father, Hugh, the scene was out of control. People were shouting Jackie's name and demanding that she come out of the church and make another appearance. *"No! No!"* Janet Jr. exclaimed. "Tell them to go away," she said from inside the car. "They're ruining everything!" Hugh opened the door slowly and, sheltering his now-sobbing daughter from the onslaught, rushed her up the stairs and into the church as quickly as possible.

Winthrop Rutherfurd III, Lewis's brother, who was his best man, recalled, "What a mob scene! We had a hell of a time getting into that church, and the entire time I was fighting my way in I was wondering how we were going to get out. There was such a craze to see Jackie. Janet was terrified. We were all caught off guard by it."

After the service, Janet and Lewis and everyone else couldn't leave the church. "Tell them to back up!" the bride shrieked to police. "We can't even get to our car!" Lewis held on to his new wife tightly as they made their way through the throng. Janet recoiled as clawing hands tore at her dress. As soon as everyone was out of the church and on their way back to Hammersmith, the crowd rushed inside and tore everything apart looking for souvenirs, bits of flowers, program booklets, whatever they could find. They even hauled down the canopy outside the church's doors.

"There were almost another two thousand people outside the front gate at Hammersmith wanting to just get a look at Jackie," recalled Jamie Auchincloss. "Mummy was pretty upset."

"Animals!" Janet Sr. exclaimed when everyone finally got back to Hammersmith for the reception. Though she was on edge, she pulled herself together quickly. "In the end, it was a great party," Jamie recalled. "If there was one thing Mummy knew well, it was how to entertain, and she made it very special for Janet, having planned every last detail many months in advance. There was a lot of gourmet food and liquor with dancing — a very good time for friends and family to celebrate this big day in my sister's life."

While guests mingled under an enormous green-and-white-striped canopy on the backyard of the estate, Jackie pulled her sister aside and apologized to her for the mêlée her presence had caused at the church. Janet said she was just glad Jackie was there, that she couldn't have had the wedding without her. "Jack would be so proud of you today," Jackie said, holding her sister's hands and smiling at her. She then presented Janet with two blue leather-bound books by JFK, *Profiles in Cour-*

age and *Why England Slept.* Both were inscribed to Janet; Jackie had Jack sign them back in 1963, she explained, anticipating that one day they, as a couple, would present them to Janet on her wedding day. "And now, here we are," Jackie said, "without him. But somehow I feel that he is here with us."

No one could sum up better what happened next than Stephen Birmingham, one of the best of Jackie's biographers: "Suddenly, at the foot of the great cascade of lawn, the New York Club's sailing cruise swept into the bay — hundreds of sails billowing like a host of butterflies composing a backdrop for the party. One guest gasped and said, 'I don't believe it! It's not real! It's being produced by Walt Disney!' But it was just another example of the Auchincloss style. Janet Auchincloss Sr. knew that the cruise was scheduled. She had guessed it would arrive in time to help decorate her daughter's wedding. It did, and in her chosen colors: white on blue."

OBSERVATION DECK

November 1966.

Jack Warnecke and Jacqueline Kennedy stood on the observation deck of the new fifty-foot-high windmill on Hammersmith Farm. His four kids — Roger, Fred, Margo, and John — and her two — Caroline and

412

John — stood with them, their eyes as wide as saucers. "Man, you can see *the whole world* from up here," John Jr. exclaimed. Jack and Jackie, their arms around each other, gazed out at the vista of ocean and sky and the arcing Jamestown cantilever truss bridge spanning the west side of Narragansett Bay. "Look what we did," Jack told Jackie as he kissed her on the forehead. He took a lit cigarette from his mouth and placed it between her lips. She inhaled deeply, tilted her head back, and exhaled the smoke into the sky.

A year or so earlier, the old windmill at Hammersmith Farm, which was about a hundred years old and was once used to pump and store water for the estate, burned to the ground. But what was Hammersmith without a windmill? Of course, a new one needed to be built and straightaway.

Janet and Hugh had never been happy with the location of the old windmill. They had the perfect spot in mind for the new one, about a quarter of a mile from its original site and closer to the shoreline. One day, Janet rented a forklift that could raise her and Jackie high up into the air so that they could inspect the view from that vantage point. It was spectacular. How would the new site look from the main house, though? With Janet at the potential site perched high up on the forklift's platform, her skirt blowing in the wind, she communicated by walkie-talkie with Jackie in the main house half a mile away. "To the left," Jackie said as Janet then shouted down that instruction to the forklift operator. "Okay, a little bit to the right now," Jackie decided. "No, no! To the left, Mummy! The right! There, that's it. *That's it, Mummy!*" Once mother and daughter finally figured out where the windmill should be built — Janet would later call it "a great example of Bouvier women teamwork" — they knew there was only one architect who could design it for them, and that was Jack Warnecke. (Hugh had actually originally hired designer Anna M. Tillinghast, but then sued her after blaming her for the fire to the original structure, which occurred while she was dismantling it.)

When Jack thought it would be more fun if he and Jackie designed the new structure together, it soon became their pet project. The new windmill would end up being much bigger than the original. Now it was fifty feet high with four floors — one room to a floor — and an elevator between them. There was a large entertaining room on the ground floor; a dining room on the second; an enormous bedroom on the next; and, on top, a circular observation deck from which one could see far out into the Atlantic Ocean. It wasn't quite finished by Thanksgiving, but enough was done that Jack and Jackie could take the kids up to the deck for a thrill. The price tag for this renovation was well over $30,000 — about $220,000 today. (It should be noted that while this structure was called the Windmill, it did not have blades. It was, basically, just a well-appointed tower.)

The trip to Hammersmith had been a surprise for Jack's children. "They didn't know where they were all going," recalled his personal assistant, Bertha Baldwin. "And they told me that when they got there, they were all excited. 'Where the heck are we? What is this great place?' And then Jackie walked out and surprised them. 'You live *here*?' they asked."

This was actually the first time Jack's sixteen-year-old daughter, Margo, would spend time with Jackie, since she'd been away at boarding school in Manhattan for most of her father's relationship with her. "All of us kids knew that Dad was head-over-heels in love with Jackie by this time," recalled Jack's son Fred. "Not that I want to get too private, but, many years later, I was driving my dad to the airport and he told me a story. He said that he and Jackie had once been at a party. On the way home, he pulled over to the side of the road. They couldn't keep their hands off one another, so the two of them had sex, right there in his car. I said, 'Really, Dad? Is that true? Or, are you making that up? Because the idea of you and Jackie Kennedy doing it on the side of the road is sort of

415

crazy.' He said, 'Of course I'm not making it up. You think I didn't have any fun in my life? That I was only about business? No. I *lived* my life.' So, yeah," Fred Warnecke concluded, laughing, "he had his fair share of fun, put it that way. And so did Jackie."

LEE'S BIG BREAK?

After about a year of training, Lee Radziwill still didn't feel she was ready to go forward with her acting career and take on any significant roles, and she was probably right. Many novices train much longer than just a year with stakes not nearly as high as they were to be for Lee, someone for whom the press and much of the public would be gunning as soon as she went before a camera or walked out onto a stage. One of the greatest influencers in her life at this time, Truman Capote, encouraged her to abandon her preliminary training, though, and just jump headfirst into a role. He convinced Lee that too much training might erode her natural ability and charisma. A true and loyal friend — at least at this juncture — Truman really did believe that her greatest asset as an actress was her own innate personality and character, organic and real. "He thought there was nothing I couldn't do, and that I must go in the theater and I would be perfect," Lee recalled in 2016. "He would arrange it with such taste. He was convinced that I could do this."

Prodded on by Truman, Lee accepted the role of Tracy Lord in a play called *The Philadelphia Story*. *The Philadelphia Story* had been a movie success in 1940 as produced by George Cukor and starring Cary Grant, James Stewart, and Katharine Hepburn. It was a romantic comedy based on the Broadway play of the same name — which had also starred Hepburn. Hepburn played Tracy Lord, a rich, Main Line Philadelphia socialite who is torn between three men: her ex-husband, a wealthy suitor, and a tabloid reporter. (The movie was later remade into a musical called *High Society*, starring Bing Crosby, Grace Kelly, and Frank Sinatra.)

The Philadelphia Story was scheduled to run for four weeks at the Ivanhoe Theater in Chicago, starting on June 20, 1967. When the show's producer, Charles Booth, told Lee that he wanted to bill her as "Princess Lee Radziwill," she balked. She said she wanted to be known as "Caroline Bouvier" in order to distinguish her new career from her public persona. This acting venture was about her, not her husband or her marriage, she said. Producer and star debated the issue until, finally, they settled on "Lee Bouvier" for the marquee. However, Booth wasn't happy about it, feeling strongly that no one would recognize the name. Lee also said there should be no mention of Jackie in her Playbill biography. This also made no sense to the producer. Why were people coming to see her if not for the fact that she was Jackie's sister?

Much of The Philadelphia Story had to do with class, status, and the concerns of the entitled. Immediately, the press felt that Lee had been stereotyped. Of course, noted many a reporter, Lee knew all there was to know about life as a wealthy, superficial woman. Lee bristled at the suggestion. She said she felt that The Philadelphia Story was just "frivolous, charming nonsense fluff." She explained that Tracy Lord was a woman unlike herself. "Tracy is a charming, pleasant, attractive, amusing girl, but I don't think I have much in common with her," she said. "Not many ideas have crossed her mind." She added that Tracy "has none of the feelings I understand of sadness or despair or of knowing loss. I am so much smarter and have so much more going for me than Tracy Lord," she said. "I try not to be insulted when people claim to know me so well and have such a low opinion of me, but it's difficult."

When Lee called Jackie to tell her the exciting news about The Philadelphia Story, Jackie was elated. She was also worried. This diversion of Lee's had just gotten real; she was going to be onstage and in front of people! Jackie said that just because she herself could never do it wasn't reason to project her fears onto her sister. However, she told relatives that she was worried. She and Lee were hypersensitive, she said, to criticism "just because of the way we were raised." She couldn't help but wonder how her sister would deal with what she feared was in store for her.

JANET'S SURPRISE ENCOUNTER WITH ONASSIS

In the fall of 1966, Jamie Auchincloss was studying at Cambridge in London. His mother, Janet, went to visit him at that time and, while she was in London, thought it might be fun to pop in on Lee. She called Lee and Stas's home at Buckingham Place and learned from one of the Radziwills' functionaries that Lee wasn't there. Lee had taken a suite at Claridge's Hotel. Janet wondered why Lee would have a suite at a London hotel when she had a perfectly beautiful home nearby? She knew that Lee and Stas continued to have trouble in their marriage, though. In fact, according to Jamie, Stas had recently complained to Janet about Lee. "He told Mummy that Lee was plowing through his money," Jamie remembered. " 'I'm almost wiped out!' he told her. Mummy said that perhaps she would talk to

Lee about her spending, but that she couldn't guarantee results."

It just so happened Claridge's was exactly where Janet and Hugh were staying while in London — a happy coincidence, Janet thought. Janet decided to surprise her daughter by just going ahead to her suite without trying to make further contact. "She found out where the suite was," Jamie recalled, "and went right up and rang the bell. No answer. She banged on the door. No answer. She tried the doorknob. It was open! So she walked in and she saw an older, gray-haired man on a sort of a raised platform sitting behind a Napoleonic desk. He had wet hair and was wearing a dressing gown. He had his feet up on the desk while talking on the telephone."

It took a moment for Janet to realize who she was looking at, but not long. She'd never even met him before, but she knew the one and only Aristotle Onassis when she saw him. "Where is my daughter?" she demanded to know.

Onassis was startled by the intrusion. He hung up the telephone. "Well, that depends," he said. "Who is your daughter?" he asked, looking at her quizzically. "In fact, while we are at it, who are you?"

"My daughter is *Princess Lee Radziwill*," Janet said, "and *I* am *Mrs. Janet Auchincloss*."

"Oh," Aristotle said. "Then your daughter

just left."

The two strangers stood staring at each other for a moment before Janet, by now upset, turned around and stormed from the suite.

"Understandably, my mother was left speechless," Jamie Auchincloss would recall. "She saw Onassis in a dressing gown with wet hair, his feet on the desk. And Lee had just left? It wasn't difficult for her to draw her own conclusions."

Later that day, she saw Lee and confronted her about Onassis. What was going on? In a heated discussion about it, Lee told Janet it was none of her business. She made it clear that she wasn't going to discuss Onassis with her. She also didn't deny or confirm anything.

Janet was still upset when she left England a few days later. As soon as she got back to the States, she called Jackie and told her about it. Jackie, too, was surprised. This was the first confirmation she'd had that while he was calling her, stopping by and giving her and her children presents, Onassis was also probably in some way involved with her sister. She was also concerned about Stas and hated to see him get hurt. "Jackie and my father were still close after the President was killed," said his son John Radziwill. "She would come to him for advice all the time. She still liked my father a lot." Lee knew how Jackie would feel about her relationship with

Onassis, which, Janet figured, was probably why she hadn't discussed it with her. Jackie was upset. She said she would talk to Lee about it, "after I have a chance to cool off."

Taking time to cool off was Jackie's choice, but not Janet's. About a month later, when Janet heard that Onassis was going to be in New York, she decided to see him.

"I was with Margaret one day when a very upset Janet came in to talk to Hugh," recalled Delores Goodwin, best friend of Margaret Kearney, who worked for Hugh Auchincloss in the Washington bureau of his brokerage firm. "She walked into his office and slammed the door. Thirty minutes later she came out and told Margaret, 'Hughdie has an assignment for you. Please make sure you complete it.' Hughdie then came to us and said that Aristotle Onassis was in New York and that Janet wanted to meet with him. He wanted Margaret to set it up. 'But I don't even know him, and I don't know anyone who does,' she said, protesting. He said, 'Figure it out,' and went back into his office and slammed the door. Margaret said, 'What in the world is going on around here?' She and I then went to lunch. I told her I'd once read in a newspaper that when Onassis was in New York he stayed at the Pierre Hotel. I said, 'Why not just call the hotel, ask for him and see what happens?' We agreed that it was a long shot, but why not? So, when we got back to the office, that's what she did, and sure enough, she was connected to someone who said he was Onassis's assistant. Margaret said she wanted to make an appointment for Mrs. Auchincloss, and it was made on the spot. We were astonished. Margaret then went into Hugh's office and told him, and he was delighted. 'I don't know what my wife has planned,' he told her, 'but thank you for making it possible. Now maybe she will give me a moment's peace about it.' Two weeks later, Mrs. Auchincloss was on her way to New York to meet with Aristotle Onassis."

JANET'S ENTREATY TO ONASSIS

There are many different accounts of Janet's meeting with Onassis in New York at the Pierre Hotel, from relatives to whom she gave details to members of her staff with whom she discussed it to members of Hugh's staff who heard about it secondhand from him. What we know is that the meeting was at least cordial. Janet — like most people — found Ari to be exceedingly charming. On a superficial level, she could probably understand what Lee saw in him. He reminded her — as he had Jackie and Lee — of that dark figure from her long-gone past, Black Jack Bouvier.

Now that Jackie was no longer First Lady, the biggest problem Janet had with Lee and Onassis was that Lee was still married to

423

Stas. Janet remained committed to the sanctity of marriage, and that would not change. Other than that conundrum — and it was a big one — Janet took no issue with Onassis. At least he had money, and a lot of it. If Lee was going to leave Stas, it may as well be for someone as wealthy as Onassis. Janet wanted her daughter to be set for life, and Onassis could certainly do that for her. "As always," she told one of her relatives, "Lee thinks I'm the enemy," she said, echoing her words to Lee back when Michael Canfield was the subject of contention between them. "I am not," Janet said. "If she would confide in me about Onassis, I just might have some good advice for her."

In talking to Aristotle Onassis in his suite at the Pierre, the biggest problem Janet saw was that he was as uncommitted as Lee when it came to defining his relationship with her. "She may risk her *marriage* for you," Janet reportedly told him, "and I need to know that it will be worth it to her. Stas is a good man!" Onassis said he understood that Janet was concerned about her daughter's future. He said that his son, Alexander, was in a romantic relationship with someone he didn't approve of — this would have been Fiona Thyssen, sixteen years Alexander's senior, divorced from a baron and with two children — and that what he'd learned from the experience was that his meddling in it only caused dissension between them. "We have to let our children live their own lives, as difficult as that may be," Onassis said.

Janet had never heard a more ridiculous statement. According to what she later recalled, she told Onassis that she'd been protecting her children since the day they were born, that she would continue doing so until she was dead and buried, and that if they thought she was meddlesome, that was just too bad for them. She was doing her job as their mother. At that, Onassis chuckled. "I like you, my dear," he told her. "I think I understand your daughter Lee better now. You two are exactly alike."

"Janet left the meeting feeling she had an ally in Onassis," said Delores Goodwin. "From what I understand, Janet asked Onassis to keep the fact that they'd met between the two of them because she knew how Lee would feel about it. She didn't want trouble with Lee. She just wanted to meet him face-to-face so that the two could know one another and have an understanding." The fact that Onassis agreed to a secret pact with Janet probably made her feel that they had a relationship of sorts. It also likely gave Janet the feeling that *maybe* she had a little more agency in how things might work out between him and her daughter.

While she was in Manhattan, Janet tried to set up one of her Mother-Daughter Teas with

425

Jackie and Lee, but it was impossible. It was as if they both knew what the topic might be and went out of their ways to make themselves unavailable. Instead, Janet had tea with her other daughter, Janet Jr. However, for some reason, the idea of the Mother-Daughter Tea only felt right when it was with Jackie and Lee. Some people believed that Janet favored her older daughters. They were a link to her first husband, after all, who was probably the love of her life. There was a history there that the three of them shared. Of course, Janet always got along well with Janet Jr. — the two rarely fell out with each other. However, it seemed to most family members that she had something deeper, something maybe more profound, with Jackie and Lee. She was definitely more protective of them.

After her trip to New York, Janet felt reassured that she could keep an eye on what was going on with Onassis. Apparently, though, she wanted to exert a little more control over the situation. One afternoon, back at O Street, she told Adora Rule that she was being reassigned to New York, working out of Hugh's office. She explained that Hugh needed a new assistant. Adora protested. She'd just moved to Georgetown with the Auchinclosses and didn't want to now pick up again and move to Manhattan with her young daughter, Janine, "and I'm not doing it," she said, putting her foot down. Janet

426

glared at her. "I have a temper, too, Adora," she said, "but I know when to use it and when to just be quiet." She told her not to be so shortsighted; she was presenting her with a wonderful opportunity. However, Adora soon suspected that Janet had an ulterior motive when she said: "You can also keep an eye on my Lee for me there."

Since Adora needed the job, she packed up her things and moved to New York. Janet set her up in a spectacular apartment overlooking Central Park. It took about two weeks, but sure enough Adora had something substantial to report. "Mrs. Kennedy and the princess had a meeting at Mr. A.'s office about some financial holdings," she remembered, "and from the moment they arrived, it was tense between them. Mr. A. was delayed. The sisters were in his office arguing while I was in an adjoining office. I couldn't hear the details. I just heard Mrs. Kennedy angrily ask, 'How dare you say that?' Then, I heard her say, 'Don't you *dare* lecture me!' Then . . . a loud crack. It sounded to me like a slap. Then another. I thought to myself, is it possible? *Two* slaps? Can it be? So, I went to the doorway and just as I got there I saw Mrs. Radziwill bolt from the office. Mrs. Kennedy then ran after her. They never returned."

This was unusual; the sisters ordinarily didn't have these kinds of dramatic scenes. Some thought they would have been better served if they had, that it would have helped clear the air between them. However, it was rare. Usually, they just let things fester until it was too late to do anything about them.

Did Adora report the scene to Janet? "No," she said. She explained that she didn't because "I didn't know for sure what had happened, if those were slaps or not — even who slapped who? — and Mrs. A. would have wanted me to be sure of every detail. Otherwise, in her mind, it would have just been idle gossip. I could just hear her saying, 'Now, Adora, don't be so quick to judge. It's not becoming.' So I decided to just stay out of it."

A SURPRISING CONFESSION

By March 1967, Jackie Kennedy and Jack Warnecke had been together for two and a half years, if one considers their lovemaking in November of 1965 to be the true commencement of their romance. They hadn't set a wedding date, but Jackie seemed to be in no hurry. Bobby Kennedy still posed a big problem. He didn't believe Jack was the man for Jackie, telling her that he didn't have the financial stability he knew she would require. Jackie thought that was hogwash. After all, since the day she met him, Jack had been lavishing her with expensive gifts. He owned a couple of estates, and they'd even been talking about buying another one when they married. He'd just opened an office in New York. Obviously, Jack had money . . . or so she thought. One day in March, he called her in New York from his home in California. "There's something I have to tell you," he said, this according to his memory.

"What is it, Jack?"

"The thing is . . ." He paused and stammered a bit, clearing his throat. "Well, Jackie, I'm in a little trouble. I think I'm . . . I'm . . . $650,000 in debt."

"Oh?"

"But the bank is telling me it's more like a million," he said, "and I don't have it." Later he would explain that because he knew how much Jackie equated money with power, this was a difficult conversation to have with her. However, he felt strongly that if they were to be married, he should be completely transparent.

"What are you going to do, Jack?" Jackie asked, alarmed. Was he asking her for a loan? She probably *hoped* not.

"I have to focus on my business," he said. He told her that this decision would mean fewer extravagant trips for them. Whatever they could do to cut back was what they now needed to do, he explained. She told Jack she was confident he would "figure things out," sounding — as Jack would later recall it — "rather distant." He wondered if his surprising admission would change things between them. No, she said, of course it wouldn't. He closed by saying, "I love you, Jackie." He then waited for a similar response. Instead, she simply whispered, "Good-bye for now, Jack."

"The truth was that Jack was stretched to the limit," recalled his personal assistant, Bertha Baldwin. "He had about two hundred employees in five offices — San Francisco, Los Angeles, Washington, Boston, and the new one in New York. There were people depending on him. He had no partners. It was all him. The time he spent away with Jackie was unusual for him and showed how much he loved her because, really, Jack was usually all about business. 'Everything I do is business,' he once told me."

"At the end of the year [1966], our employees didn't get their bonuses," Harold Adams remembered. "That's when I knew we were in trouble. Turned out, Jack had spent their bonuses on Jackie. Our employees began to say, 'We think our careers are more important than Jack Warnecke's pursuit of Jackie Kennedy.' Therefore, we started to lose some key people. I could see the pressure weighing on Jack. He was at a crossroads. I asked him, 'Are you prepared to throw away your life's work, self-respect, pride, integrity, and everything else for Jackie? Or has the time finally come for you to focus on business, take control of your firm, and live up to your responsibilities?' I'm proud to say he decided on the latter."

When Jackie discussed Jack's revelation with her mother, Janet was astonished. She liked Jack very much but, given these new circumstances, was now completely unwilling to endorse marriage to him. Still, even given that Jackie was raised to place a premium on a man's bank account, she couldn't completely dismiss Jack. He was a good man, had been kind and generous to her and also wonderful to her children. She loved him even if perhaps she wasn't in love with him. She was torn. He must have had good reasons to have been so withholding about his finances, she told Janet. Janet wouldn't hear of it, though. "*Every*one who lies has a reason," she countered. She added that Jackie "better wake up and smell the coffee" because Jack's indebtedness would end up being hers, too, if she married him.

The timing couldn't have been worse for Jack's confession. JFK's body was about to be reinterred at Arlington National Cemetery. This was, of course, the new memorial Jack and Jackie had been working on for the last few years. It was beautiful in its simplicity, exactly what Jackie wanted. However, she didn't count on how difficult it would be having another service not only for her late husband, but also for Patrick and Arabella, who would remain buried close by their

431

father. It took place in a secret ceremony the night of March 14, 1967, attended by Jackie, Teddy and Bobby Kennedy, as well as President Lyndon Johnson. Afterward, without Jack Warnecke to lean on, Jackie just sank deeper into despair, taking prescribed amphetamines to get through the days and sleeping pills to get through the nights.

Making matters even more complex, at about this same time, Janet confided in Jackie that she and Hugh were having problems with the upkeep of Hammersmith Farm. She said that they were up late at nights trying to figure out what they could do to cut back, afraid for the future of the family homestead. The point she was really making was that the Auchincloss fortune was presently being challenged, so Jackie definitely shouldn't expect to be bailed out by it. Instead, she needed to find a man who could support her and her children in the manner to which they'd long been accustomed, and if that man wasn't Jack Warnecke, so be it.

JACKIE CHOOSES

The next major event in Jacqueline Kennedy's life happened so suddenly, it was probably difficult for her to imagine that it was even true. Certainly others in her life would spend the next few years trying to figure it all out. It started with a simple phone call in the summer of '67, Aristotle Onassis calling Jackie to ask how she was doing, as he often did. Though she said she was fine, he seemed to know better and invited her to spend time with him on Skorpios. She decided to go. She also opted not to tell Lee about it. She also didn't tell Jack Warnecke; after his confession about his finances, she had seemed to pull away from him. Now she just wanted to go off and have a good time with an exciting man, and not have to explain it to anyone.

Jackie had a wonderful time with Ari in Skorpios. Of course, as expected, he was smart, funny, and spent the entire week doing anything he could think of to make her happy. When they went to dinner, she would unfold her napkin on her lap and an expensive jewel would fall from it. He was unfailingly romantic and wanted nothing more than for her to forget her horrible past and live for the good moment. Simply put, he completely swept her off her feet, just as he had done to Lee years earlier. If Lee crossed their minds, from all accounts anyway, Jackie and Ari didn't discuss her. By the time Jackie returned from Skorpios, she was as clear as she could be that she wanted to end it with Jack Warnecke and explore at least the possibility of a future with Aristotle Onassis. Her choice was made. "I hope you understand," she told Jack. "I have to do what's best for me and my children," she said. "I want to see what might be there for me with Aristotle Onassis."

Jack was stunned. *Aristotle Onassis?* He wasn't even aware that he was in competition with one of the richest men in the world. Had he known as much, maybe he wouldn't have confided in Jackie about his financial setback. "Is it the money?" Jack asked.

"Of course not," Jackie answered.

"Jack immediately realized that he would not be able to provide for her like Onassis could," said Bertha Baldwin. "He was still in love with her. He felt that, okay, maybe later we can make this work. I'll let her go now and do what she has to do with Onassis, but when the time is right and she sees what she has with me, maybe things will change. He didn't stop loving her just because she had chosen Onassis."

Jack's son Fred recalled, "What I heard was that Bobby said, 'Look, Warnecke is not right for you. What you want is someone who can support you and take care of you in the life-style you're used to.' Bobby certainly didn't mean for her to run to Onassis, though. This was tough on my dad. He obviously had money; this was just a temporary problem. In fact, he would have it sorted out within two years. But by then it was too late."

June 20, 1967.

"I am so nervous, I can't stand it," Lee was saying. She was in her makeup chair backstage at the Ivanhoe Theater in Chicago. It was opening night of *The Philadelphia Story*. She'd put everything she had into preparing for this moment — months of rehearsal along with intense acting lessons. "Who am I fooling?" she kept telling her friends. "I'm not an actress!" However, she still believed she had to try.

"I knew how lucky I was to have such an opportunity," Lee said at the time, "but there was a price to be paid. I was walking into an incredible barrage of criticism — much more than most actresses onstage for the first time. I knew everybody would be out for blood. People were waiting to laugh. But it would have taken more than that to stop me."

Lee fully expected Jackie to be present for this momentous occasion. "Talk to her," she had said, handing her costar Jack DeMave the telephone a couple of days earlier. Jack was a little starstruck and reluctant. "Just talk to her," Lee insisted, smiling. "She can be nice." He got on the phone with Jackie. He said how much he was looking forward to seeing her at the show. "Oh, but I'm not coming," Jackie said. She explained that she didn't want to steal Lee's spotlight, that it was her sister's time to shine and that wherever she (Jackie) went, a circus was sure to follow. She asked him, as one of Lee's leading men, to please take care of her. "I want her to be okay," Jackie said. "Do you promise?" Jack told her he would do as she asked, and then handed the phone back to Lee. She took it to a corner and quietly finished her conversation with her sister.

At that time, Jackie was on her way to Ireland with her children. On the day of Lee's opening, she planned to be greeted by Eamon de Valera, President of the Republic of Ireland, and his wife, Sinéad, at the house of Arus An Vactaria. That night, she was scheduled to attend a state banquet at Dublin Castle. She said she probably wouldn't be able to fly back at all, not for *any* performance during Lee's entire four-week run! This was strange. After all, Jackie had months of advance notice. For jet-setting women like the Bouvier sisters, Lee knew that jumping on a plane to the States for a day or so and then returning to Europe wasn't that big a deal. So what was really going on?

Lee was not naïve. She and Jackie had the same friends; they ran in the same circles. She knew that Jackie had gone to Skorpios at Aristotle Onassis's invitation. This was upsetting, especially since Jackie hadn't told her about it. She heard it through the grapevine and then confirmed it with Onassis's secretary. To make things a little more disconcerting, Ari was suddenly unavailable to her when she called him. He was always in a business meeting or in some other way indisposed. What was going on? Beyond her concern about her relationship with Ari, one thing was certain: Lee needed Jackie in Chicago more than she needed anyone else there. Instead, Jackie sent a mauve jewelry box as an opening night gift, along with a telegram: "Dearest Pekes, As many good wishes for your last night as for your first and all love. Will call when you are in New York. Jackie."

Lee would have to go forth without her sister. She had no choice.

The problem with *The Philadelphia Story* "starring Lee Bouvier," as evidenced on opening night, was that — as feared — she simply wasn't ready for such an undertaking. Mounting a show with an actress at its center who had no prior professional experience was a big mistake, and everyone knew it after that first show. "I did my best to give her a quick course in theater conduct," recalled her costar Jack DeMave. "It should be second nature but it does come from years of working. How to sit. How to stand. How to pivot. How to use your hands. We were performing in the round with audience on all sides, challenging even for old pros. When I held Lee in a scene, I could feel her trembling."

After that first performance, Lee looked

drawn, her face gaunt. She hadn't had a good night's sleep for months; she'd felt nauseous every day. Truman Capote had spent a great deal of time in Chicago trying to bolster her confidence. He would sit in the balcony during rehearsals and, under his breath but loud enough for others to hear, utter one-word pronouncements such as "Fabulous!" or "Amazing!" or "Perfection!" However, all the support in the world from him couldn't make up for what Lee most needed: time and training.

In the days to follow, the notices would be scathing. There were a couple of good ones, but even those Lee wasn't able to take seriously. "It's funny, isn't it?" she later remarked, "all the compliments and nice things in the world can be said to you but if you didn't hear them as a child — or even thought you didn't hear them — then you just never believe them."

Lee thought it best that Janet and Jamie wait a couple of weeks before seeing her in the show. She wanted time to polish her work. "Unfortunately, it was still pretty bad," recalled Jamie of the performance he and his mother saw on July 7. "Lee looked nervous and very arch. She's such an appealing person, but that didn't come through in her acting. The disconnect made sense, though. After all, we're from a family used to concealing deep emotions. As an actress, though, Lee needed to be open and transparent. Maybe if she'd had more time."

"So, what did you think, Mummy?" Lee asked Janet backstage after the show. "Was I just awful? Tell me the truth." Wearing a simple white miniskirt and a matching silk blouse, Lee still had her heavy stage makeup on, with her hair teased out theatrically.

Even Janet didn't have the heart to be critical. "Lee, my God! How did you ever remember all of those *lines*?" she asked. "I could never do that! *Never!*" Then, with her arm around Lee's waist, Janet turned to Jamie and said, "Your sister didn't make one mistake, did she, Jamie? Not a single one. Wasn't it just great?"

Lee smiled as she hugged her mother. At least Janet was there for her, trying to be supportive. It meant a lot, especially given Jackie's absence. "I was surprised at how much Lee became unglued every time Jackie's name was mentioned during the run of the show," said another of her costars, John Ericson. "We all wondered what their relationship was like. We began to glean that it wasn't good. The fact that Jackie never showed up seemed to confirm it."

The night of her third performance, Lee could be found — as usual — sitting at her vanity in her dressing room before a mirror upon which she had taped a dozen or so good-luck telegrams. Vases of red roses were carefully placed around her, framing her image, sent by friends from around the world. One friend — a relative of Hugh's late business partner, Chauncey Parker — flew in to see the show. "No Jackie?" she asked. "That's so odd, isn't it?" Though Lee said that she didn't want to discuss it, this friend began apologizing for Jackie, saying that she knew for a fact that Jackie was in Ireland — as if Lee didn't already know it herself! Running a brush through her hair, Lee stared at her reflection in the mirror. "She couldn't even be here one night out of four weeks?" Lee asked. "No," she decided. "She would be here unless she had a very, very good reason." She then held up her hand; she didn't want to hear another word about it. "I am telling you, I know my sister better than anyone," she concluded, "and something is very wrong!"

No Money from Grampy Lee

On January 3, 1968, Janet's father, James T. Lee — "Grampy Lee" — died at the age of ninety. His estate came to $11.6 million, about $80 million in today's money.

The family had never really gotten over the fact that James Lee didn't attend JFK's inauguration because, he had supposedly explained, that same day he was giving up his job as president and taking over as chairman of the board of Central Savings Bank. Was this true? Jackie always suspected that Janet had talked him out of attending lest he be under scrutiny that might have invited inquiries into his background, which then would have exposed her own fictional history. Others say that she held a grudge against him for the way he treated her back when she was married to Black Jack. Others blamed it on Lee's long-standing animosity toward Democrats, especially the Kennedys. Jackie wouldn't forgive her grandfather for his absence from the inauguration. In fact, the entire time she was First Lady, he was never once invited to the White House.

Much to Janet's chagrin, when Adora finally was able to track Jackie down so that Janet could tell her about Grampy Lee, she learned that her daughter was with Onassis in Greece. Janet and Jackie had a tense conversation about Janet's father, during which Jackie told her mother that she wouldn't be returning for the funeral. (Lee wouldn't go, either.)

In the end, because of poor planning, much of Jim T. Lee's money went to Uncle Sam. Luckily, Lee had also set up the James T. Lee Foundation Inc., with about $1.5 million; that charitable foundation is still in existence today. His heirs received $3.2 million, most going to Janet and her surviving younger sister, Winifred, and Winifred's children, as well as the offspring of their late older sister,

Marion. In fact, pretty much everyone in the family got money from Grampy Lee — Janet Jr. and Jamie included — with two notable exceptions: Jackie and Lee. He didn't leave either sister one dime. "Figures," Janet said, and there wasn't much more she could say about it.

Apparently, Jackie and Lee were counting on *some* money when the old man died. It was understandable, at least from their vantage points. After all, from the time they were very young, they understood that they would not inherit anything from the Auchincloss estate. Janet had constantly reinforced in them the thinking that they'd have to marry well, that this was likely the only way they'd be able to continue with the lives to which they'd become accustomed. In the back of their minds, though, the Bouvier sisters had always hoped for a windfall from Grampy Lee.

Lee actually didn't need the money as much as Jackie. Stas was doing fairly well in his British real-estate investments, and even though he, too, had certain financial challenges, Lee wasn't affected by them and really didn't know much about them. He kept any problems from her. They owned the London town house, the Windsor country estate, and the Fifth Avenue apartment and always seemed to have plenty of money with which to finance rich, full, and contented lives.

Jackie, however, was always living beyond her means. Though JFK had left her about $70,000, she went through it quickly. There were also two Kennedy family trusts, valued at about $10 million, but because of numerous restrictions placed upon them, Jackie wasn't able to access the money. As earlier stated, she was living on an allowance of about $175,000 from the Kennedys, and they were loath to give her any more; as a personal favor, Bobby had already raised it for her from $150,000. "Tell her mother to cash in some of that Auchincloss fortune," Rose Kennedy had said. "Jackie just doesn't know how to cut corners."

While Jackie was happy dating the successful Jack Warnecke, she really wasn't content with the status quo of not having her own wealth. She constantly complained to her business manager, Andre Meyer, that she was tired of worrying about money. (Meyer was a senior partner at Lazard, Frères & Co., the preeminent investment company in New York. He had long managed the Kennedy fortune, having been brought into the fold by Stephen Smith, Jean Kennedy Smith's husband, who handled the family's business affairs.) At a recent meeting with Meyer, Jackie had to acknowledge that "the Kennedys can't support me forever." She also confessed that she spent money on clothes and jewelry as if she were a very wealthy woman. "And *that's* where all my money is going, I admit it," she told him, "but I am expected to have nice things, André, and so, yes, I buy nice things. What can I tell you? I like nice things!"

"And you should have nice things," Andre told her, according to his memory of the conversation. "You deserve nice things."

"Thank you," Jackie said. "I agree with you."

In Jackie's mind, a girl could never have enough "nice things"; she had really been counting on some inheritance from Grampy Lee. It wasn't forthcoming, though. Therefore, by the beginning of '68 she was beginning to realize that she'd have to find some other way to secure her future.

Laura

At the beginning of 1968, the letdown Lee Radziwill experienced after *The Philadelphia Story* was crushing. After having worked so diligently and obsessively on something that was now over and maybe best forgotten, she didn't know what to do with herself. She also couldn't shake the feeling that something was going on with her sister, and she was pretty sure it had to do with Ari, which was disconcerting. Worried about her, Truman Capote felt that Lee needed another big project. Therefore, he and David Susskind, the accomplished talk show host and television producer, cooked up an idea that Susskind then sold to ABC. It was a two-hour TV special starring Lee in a new version of the Vera Caspary story *Laura;* Capote planned to write the script.

Originally dramatized in a 1944 film with Gene Tierney in the starring role (directed by Otto Preminger), *Laura* was a mystery-thriller about a beautiful socialite who is ultimately murdered, and also about the unsavory characters she allows into her life. "Just imagine the ratings," Susskind said. "The whole country will tune in to see Jackie Kennedy's sister and, for God's sake, she's a princess too!"

The idea took off quickly. Argentinian director John Llewellyn Moxey was hired. Hollywood casting director Alan Shayne then assembled a cast that included George Sanders, Robert Stack, and Arlene Francis.

John Moxey met with Lee at her and Stas's home to go over the script line by line. Lee observed, "When the detective asks me if I know who would have wanted to murder me, I am supposed to say, 'I can't conceive.' But this is wrong because everyone knows that I *can* conceive. Why, Stas and I have two children, Tina and Anthony! So, obviously, that line must be changed to: 'I can't *imagine.*' " He thought she was joking. She wasn't. She also objected to a scene with Farley Granger that was to be played as if the two had just made love. "I just don't want to do that kind of thing," she said. "And besides, I'd be too embarrassed to act it!"

Years later, John Moxey recalled, "I refused to believe she was that empty-headed. I thought there must be something else going on. Her quibbles were so pedestrian, it was as if she had no idea how to act or how to even *feel.* She, therefore, found moments in the script to take issue with so that it would appear that she was at least somewhat engaged in the process."

Another problem for Lee was that as much as she wanted to be taken seriously as an actress, she was still an entitled person who expected to be treated a certain way. It's not as if she — who still had her maid follow her into the bathroom to drop gardenias into the toilet — had ever tried to act like just any fledgling actress. When her London agent, Dick Blodget, met her for the first time during the negotiations for *Laura,* he recalled of the meeting, "I was greeted by a butler in a white coat who said to me, 'The princess will see you in the greenroom.' I was received with a great deal of hauteur and condescension. I come from a theater background. My feeling was that there were princesses, and I presume they belong in palaces, and then there are actresses and they are either on a stage or on a set, and they behave in quite a different way."

Alan Shayne recalled the day he was dispatched to Lee's home to run lines with her. They were working with a prop telephone in a scene in which "Laura" receives a phone call. "Ring," Shayne said, cuing Lee. She walked over to the prop telephone, picked up the receiver, and, as she was raising it to her ear, she said, *"Hel-lo-o."* He stopped the rehearsal. "Lee, you have to wait until the phone is to your ear before you say hello." She sighed. "I know that," she told him. They tried it again. He said, "Ring!" She walked over, picked up the phone, and, before it was even halfway to her ear, she said, *"Hel-lo-o."* He stopped again. "Lee, as I just *told* you, you have to wait until you get the phone up to your face before you say hello!" She seemed insulted. "I know that!" she said. "Don't you think I know that? My God! Obviously, I know that!" He said fine, they would do it again. "Ring!" She grabbed the phone and, as she was raising it to her face, she said out into the air, *"Hel-lo-o."* Shayne shook his head in dismay. "Okay, I give up," he muttered. "Fine. Can we just proceed with the scene," Lee said, irritated. "I think we have established that, yes, I *shall* answer the telephone!"

Laura aired on January 24, 1968. Lee and Stas hosted a viewing party at their home in New York, which Jackie attended. Babysitting John and Caroline back at Jackie's home was her and Lee's brother, Jamie. "The kids loved *Laura,*" he recalled. "Just seeing their auntie on television kissing another man made them both 'oooh' and 'aaah.' But I knew it was bad. I had a sick feeling in the pit of my stomach, thinking, oh, no! My poor sister."

Meanwhile, at the Radziwills', everyone watched the program while paying compliments to its beleaguered star. Jackie sat transfixed in front of the color television. Other than the readings she'd witnessed Lee give for Lee Guber, she'd never seen her sister act before and, from her expression, was surprised. However, Lee felt something was still off with Jackie. For the last six months, she'd been so distant. She hadn't been returning Lee's telephone calls, and, in fact, Lee wasn't even sure she would show up for the screening.

"That was great, Lee," Jackie exclaimed when the program was over. "I could never have done anything like that, ever." After she embraced her sister, she took her leave as quickly as possible, as if she couldn't wait to go. "Well, *that* was certainly strange," Stas said with an arched eyebrow. "Clearly, my sister-in-law has a bus to catch!" It was a funny line and broke the tension. Then the other guests stayed for hours, showering Lee with praise as only friends and relatives can.

Lee definitely needed the boost from supportive friends because, again, her reviews would be negative. *TV Guide* called the show "a shoddy effort to cash in on America's fondness and sympathy for Jackie Kennedy."

448

The critic for the *Chicago Tribune* called Lee "taut and brittle-looking," and dubbed her performance "emotionless." He recognized, though, that the ratings would likely be through the roof because of Lee's notoriety. He was right: 38 million people watched the program, which provided a huge rating for the network.

The stellar ratings didn't matter much to Lee, though. Of two major acting appearances, she could now count the good notices on one hand. She cared what critics said about her. She didn't want to, but she did; she cared *deeply*. It's just the way she was wired. Many years later, in 2000, she had enough distance from it to be able to admit to *The New York Times* that *Laura* was a "perfectly terrible TV show."

Lee had wanted to make a difference in her life by doing something worthwhile that wasn't attached to her sister, to the Kennedys, to Stas, or to anyone else. In years to come, though, she would never truly reconcile the disappointment of her foray into acting. Despite her admirable work ethic, she wasn't able to survive that with which even the most seasoned professional has to contend — criticism. In her defense, though, what was said about Lee by the media wasn't always just professional, it was often personal. "Perhaps the most depressing part was that whatever I did or tried to do got disproportionate coverage purely because of Jackie being my sister," she would recall in 2013.

Discouraged, Lee would never act again. She didn't actually say, "I quit." Rather, she just slowly lost interest, stopped talking about it, and, eventually, moved on.

Jackie understood. She knew criticism was hard for Lee. It was hard for her, too — and it also wasn't easy for her to hear it about Lee from others. In fact, she would not tolerate it, at least as evidenced by her vociferous defense of Lee at a cocktail party shortly after the broadcast of *Laura*.

The scene was at her home in New York with close friends and a few members of the Kennedy family. Janet and Lee were not present. However, Hugh was there, along with the new, young office assistant who'd just been hired at Auchincloss, Parker & Redpath, Garrett Johnston, just twenty-one at the time.

"One guest, David Burke, Ted Kennedy's administrative assistant, was chatting with me and a group of people," recalled Garrett Johnston, "when he said, 'Lee's quite nice. However, the poor dear has never had a genuine moment in her entire life. One wonders then what makes her think she can act.' Jackie, who I had only met for the first time just moments earlier when Mr. Auchincloss introduced us, overheard the comment. 'How dare you?' she demanded of Burke. 'You don't even know my sister! Have you even met her?' Though Burke was immediately apologetic, Jackie wouldn't accept it.

She gave him a real dressing-down. Burke just kept apologizing. Finally, Jackie said, 'It's one thing to critique my sister's acting, which, by the way, I think is very good, but it's quite another to critique her as a person. I'm disappointed in you, David. To think that there is a *war* going on in Vietnam right now, and that *this* is what you're gossiping about is quite astonishing to me!' With that, she walked away from David Burke, who just stood there with his mouth wide open."

THE FARIAS

In the spring of 1968, Winfred Burgess, the caretaker who had worked at Hammersmith for many years, retired. To replace him, Janet and Hugh Auchincloss hired a man who would become a close friend of theirs for years to come, Manuel — Mannie — Faria. He and his wife, Louise, and their one-year-old daughter, Linda, moved into what was called the Caretaker's House. This was a two-story, three-bedroom structure on the top of a hill to the right of the Green House and the Carriage House and abutting the Potato House and the massive vegetable and flower gardens. In a year, the Farias would welcome another child, Joyce.

From the beginning, Janet felt a close kinship with the Farias. Of Portuguese descent, both Mannie and Louise were born in the United States, in Middletown and Newport

451

respectively. While Mannie was invaluable as the property's caretaker, Louise was an integral part of the household staff, too. She was responsible for making sure accommodations were always in order for guests.

"The Caretaker's House was a wonderful place to grow up," Joyce Faria Brennan recalled. The Faria daughters would live at Hammersmith until they were in their twenties, "our entire childhoods and early adult lives," she says. "It was my home. I still feel as if it's my home."

A normal day for Janet often included spending time at the boathouse and dock, where she would feed the pigeons before then walking five minutes down to the new Windmill. There, she would usually have lunch. Then she would continue to walk up a steep hill and through the barnyard (where a half dozen horses were maintained in pens on either side) along a gravelly road before reaching the Caretaker's House. Once there, she would sit and chat with Mannie, Louise, and their girls. "We were always treated as if we were a part of the Auchincloss family," recalls Joyce Faria Brennan. "There was a genuine respect for what my father did. My dad was on call for Mr. and Mrs. A. twenty-four/seven. He could do anything — handyman, farmer . . . whatever Mrs. A. needed. He would walk around with this enormous wad of keys, for every door in every room of every house of Hammersmith, so you can imagine how many keys that was! You could hear him coming from a mile away with all of the jangling noises." (Verification of Janet's affection for Mannie Faria is found in an inscription she wrote on a birthday card for him: "I send you every wish for every happiness. We could never live without you and Louise — and we love you very much. Janet Lee Auchincloss.")

It's worth noting that Jackie was also not conscious of class when it came to her employees. For instance, Providencia Paredes remained close to Jackie after their time together in the White House. Her son Gustavo practically grew up with Jackie's and Lee's sons, John Jr. and Anthony, and would remain one of their best friends for the rest of their lives. "My mother and I considered ourselves family," Gustavo recalled. "I can't think of anyone closer to us than the Kennedys — and John and Anthony and I spent *decades* getting into trouble together. The Auchinclosses, the Kennedys, the Radziwills, they always found value in people of all walks of life."

"Why do you spend so much time with the Farias?" Oatsie Charles once asked Janet. "Don't get me wrong. I think they're lovely, too. I just have to wonder. They are the help, after all."

Janet smiled. "Because they are real hardworking people who have taught their children *respect*," she said. "That's why."

Janet remained somewhat chagrined that Jackie and Lee didn't show her the reverence she felt she deserved. She felt she gave up a lot for them when they were young and that they never appreciated it. When she was with the Faria girls, she basked in the reverence they had for one another as a family and the respect they had for her. "If you couldn't find my mother around Hammersmith, you'd know that she and her Jack Russells were probably up at the Caretaker's House," recalled Jamie Auchincloss.

ONE DOLLAR FOR EACH YEAR

In March of 1968, Jamie visited Jackie at her home in Manhattan and then spent a few nights there with her. Janet stayed two floors below with her friend Mary Whitehouse.

March 4 was Jamie's twenty-first birthday. To celebrate, Jackie hosted dinner at her home and presented him with a birthday cake. Then she took him to see Neil Simon's *Plaza Suite* at the Plymouth Theatre on Broadway, along with Caroline and John Jr. "We got to the theater late," Jamie recalled. "New York audiences are notoriously annoyed when people show up late for a Broadway show. So, the lights are out and the show is on, and we're trying to find our seats, stumbling over people in the dark, when someone recognized Jackie. Then, the whispers started, and they grew and grew, going from one row to the next until, finally, there was so much excitement that the management really should have just stopped the show, turned up the house lights, and had Jackie take a bow.

"During intermission, Jackie asked me to stand outside the restroom and try to prevent women from going in while she was in there," Jamie recalled. "Earlier, I had told her that maybe we should have the Secret Service with us, but she said she didn't want them that night. As traumatized as she was, she was also stubborn. She needed protection, but she also abhorred it. So, of course, I tried my best for her, but forget it. Try telling a mob of pushy New Yorkers they can't go into the bathroom because Jackie Kennedy is in there! Finally, by the time Jackie came out, she was really frazzled and looked like a deer in the headlights. She seemed stricken by the whole ordeal. I felt terrible for her. 'I'm so sorry,' I told her, 'I really tried.' "

Every birthday, Jackie would give Jamie a check, a dollar for each year and an extra dollar on top of that. (This year, of course, it would be for $22, which is actually about $150 in today's money.) Jamie always took the check to the National Camera store on 17th and Pennsylvania in Washington and used it to buy film. The store would never cash the check, though. Instead, the owner would frame it on a wall with all of the other checks Jackie had written Jamie over the

455

years. "Each check was worth more to them as a historical memento than it was for its amount," Jamie would recall, laughing. "No one wanted to let go of a signed 'Jacqueline Bouvier Kennedy' check, certainly not in the 1960s. She told me once that she could never properly balance her bank account because the checks she wrote to people were never cashed!"

Imagine it. Your half sister is one of the most famous women in the world, America's former First Lady, Jacqueline Kennedy, and she has given you a check for your birthday — $22. It certainly doesn't seem like much, but as they say, maybe it really is the thought that counts. Perhaps Jackie felt this gesture was the best she could do at the time? If so, things were about to change for her in a big way.

■ ■ ■ ■

PART NINE:
ONASSIS

■ ■ ■ ■

* * * *

* * * *

to see them off. Then I came back about an
hour later. I looked out my window and there

MOVING FORWARD WITH ARI

In May of 1968, Jackie Kennedy joined
Aristotle Onassis on a cruise of the Virgin
Islands on the *Christina*. Joan Thring, who
was Rudolf Nureyev's assistant and a friend
of Ari's, was on board prior to Jackie's arrival. The ship left the dock on May 21 with
Cary Grant, billionaire investor Kirk Kerko-
rian and his wife, dancer Jean Maree Hardy,
and Onassis's friend and attorney Johnny
Meyer, among others. On the 25th, most of
the guests were getting ready to depart at St.
John, except for Joan Thring and a few other
trusted Onassis allies. Suddenly, she recalled,
Onassis's staff began preparing the yacht by
positioning photographs of JFK and Jackie
all about the premises, "and we all laughed
with each other," she said, "because Ari never
told you anything, it was very secretive. He
never said, 'Well, Jackie's arriving tonight,' or
anything like that. So I said to them, 'Guess
who's coming to dinner — it must be Jackie.'
They were all getting off that day, so I went

459

to see them off. Then I came back about an hour later. I looked out my window and there was Jackie, arriving."

Apparently, it was on this excursion that Jackie and Ari began serious discussions about a possible future together. However, Joan Thring reports that the two still slept in separate rooms. "There were no endearments or touching or anything like that," she recalled. "I was absolutely convinced that nothing had gone on while we were there. I think in the afternoons they spent an hour or two together and they were sort of working out some sort of agreement."

Apparently, it was on this cruise that Ari asked Jackie to marry him, assuring her that if she agreed she would still have her freedom. Perhaps more important, though, she would also have protection by his army of security men, seventy-five strong, some with machine guns. For a woman still suffering from PTSD from the murder of her husband, this was vital information. He loved her, he said, at least in his own way — which meant that he, too, would have his freedom, ostensibly to see other women, like Maria Callas. What Jackie didn't know was that just six months earlier, he and Maria had set a wedding date of November 4. After a ferocious argument that had to do with Maria's decision to have someone other than Ari manage her two-thirds interest in a merchant ship, the wedding was called off on the eve of the ceremony. It's possible that if Jackie had really understood just how mercurial Ari could be in matters of the heart, she might have had second thoughts about becoming involved with him. However, as it was, she felt she finally deserved some happiness and security in her life, and she was going to get it one way or the other; if it was with Ari, so be it. She left that cruise on May 28 when the yacht returned to St. Thomas.

Some may have argued that, as a matter of loyalty to Lee, Jackie should have stayed clear of any man with whom her sister had ever been involved. In Jackie's defense, though, never once did Lee confirm to her that she was even involved with Onassis! He didn't, either. Jackie had to have suspected it, though. *Everyone* suspected it. After all, it had been going on for about six years! Apparently, Jackie was also unaware that Lee had defied Onassis and married Stas in the Catholic Church rather than risk tainting her sister's reputation as First Lady. True to form in a family where transparency was almost never the case, Janet never told Jackie about it. Making things even more complex, Jackie decided not to discuss Onassis's proposal with either Janet or Lee. In other words, the secrets and lies of omission just kept stacking up among the three Bouvier women.

Jackie did talk to Bobby Kennedy about

Onassis, though. He wasn't happy, no surprise there. He hadn't been pleased about Jack Warnecke, either, but, in his mind, Onassis was far worse. He had thought Lee's assignation with him was bad, but this was catastrophic.

Bobby asked Jackie to put things off until after the November election; he'd decided back in March that he was going to run for the presidency. She said yes, she would do that for him. She didn't want to hurt his chances. "There was a lot going on in the country, what with Martin Luther King's terrible murder and unrest in the streets over the war in Vietnam," recalled Jamie Auchincloss. "We all felt that maybe Bobby was the answer for the country. Jackie decided to wait."

"THE NEW HORROR"

It was the night of June 5, 1968. Bobby Kennedy had just won the California primary for the Democratic nomination for president. Jackie was in bed in her New York apartment when the telephone rang. It was Stas calling from London. "Isn't it wonderful?" Jackie asked her brother-in-law. "Bobby has won! He's got California."

"But how is he, Jackie?" Stas asked, sounding concerned.

"He's fine," Jackie exclaimed. "I just told

you, Stas! He won California!"

"No, I mean, is he okay? What have you heard?"

"What in the world are you talking about?" Jackie asked. "He's doing great! I just spoke to Ethel."

"Jackie," Stas told her. "He's been shot. Lee and I just heard it on the news. You didn't know? *Bobby has been shot!*"

It was true. Bobby had taken a bullet to the head in Los Angeles and was now in critical condition. For Jackie, the nightmare of Dallas seemed to be repeating itself. Stunned, she immediately made plans to go to Los Angeles to be at Bobby's side.

"The next morning at about 1:30 A.M., Jackie came into the hospital very shaken but, as always, trying to be strong," said Richard Goodwin, who was an adviser and speech-writer for RFK. "She took in the situation — Ethel crying, Ted despondent . . . people coming and going in a panic, Secret Service agents . . . doctors and nurses. She saw Bobby, just lying there, obviously not going to make it. She asked the doctor if there was hope. He said no. She conferred with Ethel and Teddy. Both said they couldn't give the doctor word to turn off the equipment. They didn't have it in them. Ethel asked Jackie to do it. She went and talked to the doctor, and he then came into the room and turned off the life support. Jackie and Ethel were in there with him as Bobby took his last breath."

Bobby Kennedy was only forty-two. He had ten children and Ethel was pregnant with another.

Meanwhile, in London, Lee was so distraught about Bobby that she couldn't stop crying long enough to even drive safely; she had a car accident. Though no one was hurt, she was later charged with reckless driving. However, she had to admit that she didn't even remember what happened, she'd been so upset. She would plead guilty and later be fined.

It would seem that Lee was not only sad about Bobby but also distraught about what his death would likely mean for her where Jackie was concerned. Obviously, Jackie was still not over what had happened to Jack Kennedy. Lee feared for everyone's future now that Bobby had been taken from them the same way.

Lee was drained, practically immobile. Therefore, Stas went ahead to Los Angeles to see to Jackie while Lee stayed behind an extra day to fortify herself. That night, she had dinner with the award-winning designer Cecil Beaton, Charles Wrightman — the oil millionaire — and his wife, Jayne Larkin. After the couple departed, Lee couldn't contain her frustration about her sister.

"You don't know what it's like being with Jackie," Lee said to Cecil, who was a close friend of hers, someone she greatly admired and trusted. "She's really more than half round the bend! She can't sleep at night, she can't stop thinking about herself and never feeling anything but sorry for herself. 'I'm so unprotected,' she says. But she is surrounded by friends, helpers, the FBI. She certainly has no financial problems, but she is bored. She takes no interest in anything for more than two minutes. She rushes around paying visits but won't settle down anywhere or do anything. She can't love anyone!"

Lee added that she feared Bobby's death would probably trigger a whole new series of catastrophic events for Jackie. "The new horror will bring the old one alive again," she promised — all of this according to Beaton — "and I'm going to have to go through *hell* trying to calm her. She gets so that she hits me across the face, and apropos of nothing!

"She's so *jealous* of me," Lee went on, "but I don't know if it's because I have Stas and two children and I have gone my own way and become independent. But she *goads* me to the extent that I yell back at her and say, thank heavens, *at last* I've broken away from my parents and *you* and everything of that former life."

Once Lee got started on Jackie, it was difficult for her to stop, her crippling grief, her abject anger and despair all spilling out, unfiltered. "But how can we help her?" she asked Cecil Beaton. "Could you find a strong man to bully her, to make her listen to him? Could we find someone to influence her into taking her painting more seriously? No," Lee said, answering her own questions, "she is not really interested. The cultural center bores her. Everything bores her and as the years pass, the situation only becomes more difficult."

ONASSIS AT HAMMERSMITH

Lee was right. The "new horror" most assuredly did "bring the old one alive again." Bobby's Kennedy's murder triggered more nightmares for Jackie, along with more bouts of depression and prolonged crying jags. Her dependency on prescription medication also increased, these medications driving every mood, every decision, just as much as the PTSD they were being used to treat. Again, she was talking about suicide. She was so tortured, Jackie told intimates, that she didn't even want to wake up in the morning. Making matters all the more troubling, she was receiving death and kidnapping threats against her children. These had started after Jack's death, had subsided in recent years, but now, according to the FBI, had become more frequent. In fact, the situation all around was worse than it had been in the past, so bad that Jackie seemed, more than ever, to be gravitating toward Onassis. She'd known she needed him for financial security ever since her grandfather died, but now she was sure she also needed him for the protection of her children. "If they're killing Kennedys," she famously said, "then my children are targets." She was truly desperate. In years to come, some would feel her great concern for her children would cloud her judgment relating to Onassis, but if that was the case, so be it. Nothing mattered to her more than protecting Caroline and John. Therefore, it was time to see if she could work Onassis into her life, starting with an introduction of him to her mother.

Of course, Janet had met Ari once before — twice actually, the first time in Lee's suite at Claridge's in London when it appeared that he'd just gotten out of the shower and then, a few months later, at the Pierre in Manhattan. Apparently, Onassis kept his end of the bargain he'd made with Janet about that second meeting; he kept it mum. Surely, if he had told either Jackie or Lee about it, it would have caused friction between them all, and no such friction existed at this time, at least not that anyone recalled.

On June 22, Jackie and the kids stayed at Hammersmith for a few days so that Jackie could get her bearings after what had happened to Bobby. During her visit, she announced to Janet that she was thinking of bringing Onassis to Hammersmith at the end of the summer, "just for a day or two," she said. She also confided in her mother that she was considering a relationship with him. This was the worst-case scenario Janet had feared ever since she'd heard that Onassis had visited Jackie in the White House after Jack's murder. Caught off guard, she needed time to process it. "She said, 'Oh no, Jackie, you can't mean it,' " recalled Jamie. " 'You must be joking.' " He elaborated, "Mummy asked, 'For what reason? I'm not sure I approve. None of this bodes well for our family!' Jackie made it clear she didn't want anyone's approval," Jamie added. " 'Then why bring him to our home?' Mummy wanted to know. 'Why put us through it?' "

Janet's head must have been spinning. "Crippling her thinking at this time was the fact that Mummy was still in shock over what had just happened to Bobby a couple weeks earlier," Jamie continued, "as was I."

As a twenty-one-year-old Columbia sophomore, Jamie had great admiration for his sister's brother-in-law and often saw him and corresponded with him. Because he'd been hired to take photographs of RFK's California stops, he had been with Bobby right before he was killed. He and his parents attended the funeral together, "and we really hadn't recovered yet," he said. "We believed in Bobby. Mummy thought he would end the

468

war in Vietnam, the escalation of which she blamed on Johnson. She was *so* hopeful about Bobby. We all were. When he was killed, it almost sent Mummy into a nervous breakdown. It was as if her brain just shut down, and she couldn't cope. She just couldn't function, she was so much in shock. Therefore, she was in no position to have a big debate with Jackie over Onassis."

On August 29, Lee showed up at Hammersmith to spend the week with Janet; she brought along Anthony and Tina, of course. While they all had a wonderful time, Janet felt conflicted the entire week. Should she tell Lee that Jackie was bringing Onassis to Hammersmith in a month? How would Lee react to this news? Janet suspected it would not go well, and she just didn't have the energy to deal with it. At the end of the week, Jackie called to tell her that she and Ari had finalized their plans; they would be arriving on September 23 — *for five days.* Lee still had two days left at the farm. Now Janet had to wake up on those days and face Lee knowing all the while that she had a big secret. She reasoned that maybe Jackie would change her mind. Why get Lee all worked up without cause?

The weeks passed quickly, too quickly for Janet's taste, especially with the promise of five glorious days with Aristotle Onassis. The day before his and Jackie's arrival, Janet went to Trinity Church to ask a priest for guidance. The details of her consultation with the priest are unknown. However, afterward, Janet tried to contact Onassis at the Pierre in New York, but was told he was in Greece. She then asked Adora Rule to find him in Greece, but Adora had no luck. Time was running out. Soon he would be at her front door. Janet definitely wanted to talk to him in advance of that visit, if only to find out what his intentions were with Jackie. It wasn't possible, though.

By the middle of September, again the family secrets mounted. Following Janet's lead, Jackie didn't tell Lee she had invited Onassis to Hammersmith. Of course, neither sister knew that Janet had already previously met him. If it seems like Janet had quite a few plates in the air, one of her friends put it this way: "If you think about it, Mrs. A. was actually the only one who had all of the information, certainly more than each of her daughters, so in a sense, knowing her, she probably felt she was still somewhat in control. But also knowing how high-strung she was ordinarily, I would imagine she was probably filled with a lot of anxiety, too."

JANET AND ARI
REACH AN IMPASSE

Monday, September 23, 1968.

To truly grasp its peculiar nuances, a person would have had to have been present the moment Jackie Kennedy introduced her mother to Aristotle Onassis for what she *thought* was the first time. Jamie Auchincloss was standing right there, though, and says that Janet and Ari gave no indication whatsoever that they'd ever before met. Apparently, they were each other's equal when it came to remaining calm during awkward social situations. In other words, they pulled it off. Other than his knowledge of the time Janet walked in on Onassis in London, Jamie actually wasn't sure there'd even been a previous meeting. He also wasn't sure that there *hadn't* been one. "In my family, we kept a lot close to the vest," he would say. "Everyone was polite and welcoming when Aristotle Onassis showed up at our front door at Hammersmith Farm, as was our custom."

Jackie came not only with Aristotle, but also with his sister, Artemis Garoufalidis, who was two years older. Lee used to stay with her in Glyfada when Onassis was off with Maria Callas. Though Artemis and Jackie had met in 1963 aboard the *Christina,* now they had reason to be close. "Unfortunately, his daugh-

471

ter, Christina, was also present," Jamie recalled. "She had already developed a strong dislike for Jackie, which made things a little uncomfortable. I was put in charge of keeping her occupied. She was seventeen, spoiled, and a real handful. Basically, she just wanted to lie around, complain about her life, and drink plenty of Coca-Cola."

As soon as she arrived at Hammersmith, Jackie realized that John Jr. had come down with the measles and would have to be quarantined. Janet Jr. and her husband, Lewis, were also supposed to come to Hammersmith for an extended visit. They had made it as far as New York from Hong Kong when Janet Sr. called to tell them to stay put for a few days. Since Janet Jr. was pregnant, her mother didn't want her exposed to the measles. In all of the confusion, the guests forgot to sign the guest book. It was really required; Janet enjoyed going back over it to remember who had come to visit and when. She decided to sign the guests in herself, which she did; the guest book, in her own handwriting, has Jackie, Ari, and Christina signed in for their visit, but Janet forgot to sign in Artemis.

"When she wasn't seeing to her son, Jackie was trying to encourage conversation between Mummy and Aristotle," Jamie recalled. " 'He's so fascinating, Mummy,' she kept saying. 'You really should try to get to know him.

After all, he won over the Kennedys when I took him to meet them. Rose loved him!' she said. [Jackie had taken Onassis to the Kennedy compound on July 28 to introduce him to that side of her family on the occasion of her thirty-ninth birthday.] Mummy was surprised to hear this and, given what she knew about the Kennedys' view of Onassis, didn't quite believe it. True or not, *she* would not be so easily swayed."

Janet had two issues with Onassis. First of all, he had coaxed one daughter into an extramarital affair. Now he was, apparently, trading her in for the other daughter. No matter how wealthy he was, Janet would never approve of any arrangement that would pit Lee against Jackie. After meeting with Onassis in New York, she actually thought they'd reached some sort of understanding, at least where Lee was concerned. Apparently, this was not the case. More than anything, she now needed another private meeting with him to clarify things. She would get it on Wednesday afternoon, after Ari and Jackie returned from a day at Bailey's Beach.

That morning, Onassis cut quite a figure in his tight little swim trunks. Eileen Slocum, sitting in her own cabana, was captivated — and not in a good way. "He was the strangest sight," she recalled. "He had long, long arms, with short legs and a chest covered with dark hair." She says she thought to herself, "He

473

resembles a frog."

Apparently, according to accounts of Janet's talk with Ari from numerous sources, Ari told Janet that things had taken a dramatic and unexpected turn since their previous meeting at the Pierre Hotel. Because of RFK's murder, he said, he now felt a responsibility to Jackie. She needed him more than Lee, he explained. She was worried about her children, he said, and he could take care of them all. His heart had gone out to Jackie, he told Janet, and he wanted to protect her and the kids. In fact, he now felt it was his "duty" to do just that.

"Just as you took care of my Lee?" Janet asked. "Has Lee ever complained to you about me?" Ari wondered. No, Janet had to admit that Lee had never found fault with him. Then again, Lee hardly ever mentioned him to her. "Then I would say that I have taken care of your Lee," he concluded.

Janet said she was certain Lee would never be able to accept Onassis being with Jackie, and that this surprising new relationship was sure to cause problems in the family. Janet was worried about her grandchildren, too, but she just felt there had to be some other way to protect them. She was as clear and as direct about it as possible: "Here's what's going to happen, Mr. Onassis," she finally told him, according to all accounts. "You will stay away from *both* of my daughters. We all have to heal after what's happened to Jack and Bobby, and we can't do that with your interference."

The meeting ended with Ari telling Janet that her daughters were grown women and that "they would make their own decisions," said one source. "It wasn't just up to him, anyway, he said. Jackie had a mind of her own and, apparently, she wanted to be with him. It would be up to *her* to work it out with Lee, he said, not him. None of this sat well with Janet. But what could she do? She stated her case. He stated his case. In the end, they reached a sort of impasse. It wasn't as if they had weeks to work things out. He was leaving in a couple of days! Before the meeting ended, she asked him point-blank, 'Do you love Jackie?' He said, 'Yes. Very much.' So what could she say?"

The week just dragged on. Janet noticed that every night after everyone had gone to bed, Onassis spent the evening in the Deck Room listening to cassette tapes of Chopin, Tchaikovsky, Beethoven, and Mozart. At the time, cassette tapes and their players with built-in microphones were just beginning to come into style. Though the technology had been introduced a few years earlier, Janet had never actually seen one. When she walked in on Onassis in the Deck Room on Wednesday morning, he was playing his music on the strange contraption. Onassis explained that the cassettes were quickly taking the place of cumbersome reel-to-reel tapes. He then unplugged the machine from the wall and handed it to her. "Here, for you," he told her with a smile. "You may have the tapes, too." Janet reluctantly accepted the gifts.

"Of course, we later learned that when Onassis visited Rose Kennedy earlier in the summer, he gave her a very expensive brooch," recalled Jamie Auchincloss. "My mother got a tape recorder that cost about a hundred dollars, if that. She didn't know how cheap it was, though. It was so revolutionary a device; she actually believed he had given her something quite unique and expensive."

On the final day, Saturday, September 28, Janet hosted a buffet luncheon in Jackie and Ari's honor. During that meal, she couldn't help but notice that every time Jackie would light a cigarette and start smoking it, Onassis would quickly pluck it from her hand and put it out. Jackie would then just keep talking, as if she hadn't noticed. Ten minutes later, the same thing would happen. When Janet asked Ari about it, a smile crossed his craggy face and he said, "Women should not be seen smoking, don't you agree?" Of course she did! She used to do the exact same thing with Jackie's cigarettes when she was in the White House. So there were moments when she and Onassis seemed somewhat simpatico. They'd also had a reasonable discussion about religion during which she learned that he, too, had a deep and abiding belief in God, went to church every Sunday, and encouraged his children to do the same. However, despite these brief moments of shared views with him, by the time the luncheon was over, she was eager for him — and for Jackie — to just leave.

"Thank you for giving Ari a chance," Jackie told her mother after pulling her aside, "even though he told me that you don't really approve," she said, with a raised eyebrow. She didn't seem angry. Of course, she couldn't have expected five days to be the catalyst for great change in Janet's opinion. "No matter how hard I try," she then told her mother, "my thoughts keep going back to him. I hope you can understand that, Mummy." Janet looked as if she wanted to say something, but since there were other people in the entrance hall getting their things together to leave, she probably didn't want to cause a scene. She elected not to say anything. Instead, she just embraced her daughter and told her that she loved her.

Ari then walked over and kissed Janet's hand. "It's an honor to meet you," he told her, still acting as if it was the first time.

"Yes," she said with icy reserve. "I imagine it would be."

When Ari tried to kiss her hand, Janet pulled it back and recoiled, almost as if bitten by a snake. In the battle for balance of power with her, though, it would certainly seem that Aristotle Onassis had won by simply being vague, reasonable, and noncommittal. An astute businessman, he seemed to understand that, sometimes, the best way to comport oneself in an adversarial situation is with simple complacency. If anything, it does give one's rival less to oppose, as was the case with Janet Auchincloss. He was surprised, though, that he hadn't been able to fully win her over, the way he had Rose Kennedy earlier in the summer. There was no victory for Onassis at Hammersmith, just no real casualties.

After Ari bid Jamie good-bye, his sister, Artemis, kissed everyone on both cheeks. Christina just walked outside without saying anything to anyone. The contingent made its way toward two vehicles that had driven down the long graveled drive and appeared under the house's wide porte cochere, one for them and one just for their luggage. Hugh pulled up in his shiny blue Bentley, beeped the horn, and waved good-bye to all as he drove off, his destination unknown. As the houseman loaded all of the bags into the one car, Janet bid farewell to her guests. Relieved that the week was over, she then closed the front door very quickly before they had even gotten into their car.

JANET'S FICTION

"English Catholic," Janet Auchincloss stated. "My entire background is English Catholic." She made the statement in September 1965 while being interviewed for *Good Housekeeping.* The writer probably couldn't help but be suspicious of the claim, though. After all, for the last couple of years there'd been a few inconsistencies when it came to pinning down Janet's heritage. Another rumor was that Janet's family was full-blooded French. This one actually was started by Janet. Using the French last name of her first husband, Jack Bouvier, helped make it easy for the uninitiated to believe it was true. Of course, it wasn't. Another story was that the Lees were actually Jewish by some twist of biology. Apparently, this rumor was started by Hugh Auchincloss's first wife, Maya, for no reason other than that she was jealous of Janet. There was also the more persistent story that Janet's family, the Lees, were related to the Lees of Maryland, an aristocratic offshoot of the Lees of Virginia — the Robert E. Lees. This was Janet's favorite fib and one she would go to her grave insisting was true. It wasn't.

Actually, it was Irish blood that ran through Janet Lee Bouvier Auchincloss's veins. However, she believed the Irish were looked down upon, since most had come to America (back in the mid-1840s) to escape a devastating potato blight during which more than a million had perished from starvation. She — like a lot of others of her time — believed that the claiming of Ireland as her homeland would be counterproductive to her goal of moving about high society. There really was no ethnic taint for her to eradicate, no reason for her to be so ashamed of her forebears. In fact, most were smart and industrious people, great successes in the New World.

Jim Lee's grandfather — Janet's great-grandfather — Thomas Lee was born in County Cork, Ireland, in 1810. His wife, Frances, was also of hardy Irish stock. They raised their family in Ireland until 1852, when they moved to the United States in time for the birth of James Lee, Janet's paternal grandfather. (Another fiction spun by Janet was that James Lee had been born in Maryland and had fought in the Civil War. Actually, he was born in New Jersey in 1852, nine years before the start of the Civil War.) James Lee was well spoken — fluent in German and Italian — college-educated, and interested in the arts. He became not only a fine teacher who went on to hold the position of associate superintendent of schools in New York City, but also a medical doctor with a thriving private practice. James married Mary Theresa Norton in 1875, also the child of Irish immigrants. Two years later, they had their only son, James Thomas Aloysius Lee, who would be Janet's father, James T. Lee.

It wasn't that unusual for people of Janet's time and place in a class-conscious America to create fictitious lineages. Certainly, the Bouvier side of the family had its own share.

In 1940, John Bouvier II, Black Jack Bouvier's father, self-published a book he called *Our Forebears.* In it, he invented a brand-new biography from whole cloth. He falsely maintained that the Bouviers were "of an ancient house of Fontaine near Grenoble," and therefore related to a prestigious list of French patriots and other royal aristocrats of noble stock. The truth was that John Bouvier II's great-grandfather Michel Bouvier was a Catholic French immigrant who settled in Philadelphia and made a name for himself as a carpenter and cabinetmaker. He also became wildly successful in the real-estate game, making millions in that venue. He had two sons, Michel and the first John Vernou Bouvier. Both were also successful in real estate, and the Bouvier family's holdings were valued at more than $40 million by 1914, almost a billion dollars by today's standards. Once in Manhattan, the Bouviers and their relatives all intermarried into wealthy high society, their names found in the New York Social Register by the early 1900s.

Despite his family's amazing success in the New World, John Bouvier II was not content with the truth, which is why he made up his own fantastic history. His inaccurate account of the Bouviers' story — one in which hardworking shopkeepers became proud nobles — was taken as not only the family's truth but that of all of those who married into it, and remained so for years. As young girls, Jackie and Lee loved these stories that John Bouvier II read to them right out of his own book. They were romantic, impressive . . . and untrue. But the girls believed every word, as did most people. In 1961, Mary Van Rensselaer's authorized biography of Jackie Kennedy quoted liberally from *Our Forebears,* and — with Jackie's endorsement — repeated all of the untruths about the Bouviers' history.

In the fall of '68, Janet, now sixty, continued to insist that her family was related to the Lees of Virginia. As a result, she'd become an expert on the life and times of Robert E. Lee, general in chief of the Confederate armies. Because she was able to talk about him in such great detail, she was convincing when it came to her fictional biological relationship to him.

Sometime back in '66, Janet had made contact with Stratford Hall Plantation, the house museum in Westmoreland County, Virginia, that had been the plantation home of four generations of the Lee family of Virginia. After donating a significant amount of money to the museum while using the name "Janet Lee," she received news that she'd been approved as a committee board member. Because she'd worked so well with the museum by sponsoring benefits for it at Hammersmith, everyone on the board took it for granted that she was related to the Lees. After all, she was Jackie Kennedy's mother! Why would she lie? In fact, it didn't really matter. One didn't have to actually be related to the Lees to be on the board. Janet was an asset to Stratford just by virtue of her connections and her ability to raise money. Plus, she was a capable researcher and she cared a great deal about the Lees' place in history; she really didn't need to fib her way into the ranks of Stratford. By 1968, though, she wanted to take things one step farther: she wanted to become Rhode Island director for Stratford Hall.

"After Jack and Bobby were killed and we were out of politics, there was such a void to be filled," Jamie Auchincloss recalled. "Suddenly, there was nothing but our own little petty lives and fights and disturbances. There was nothing to look at in terms of a bigger picture. When you are a part of history and, suddenly, you are on the other side of it, that's a big adjustment for a family to make. Mummy was such a patriot, she loved — loved — the Kennedy years. Now that they were gone, she needed something else in her life that mattered — and Stratford Hall mattered."

In doing its investigation, the directorship of the Robert E. Lee Memorial Association board didn't have much paperwork to prove Janet's claims one way or the other. They even called Jamie to see if he could help. Jamie was, and still is today, a dedicated history buff. He often visits presidential libraries across the country to learn more about his famous family's relationship with other administrations. While he was in the midst of working with the directorship to try to authenticate his mother's claims, Jackie happened to call Hammersmith to talk to Yusha. Jamie answered. "Jackie, I have to ask you something," he told his half sister. "This business about our family being descended from Robert E. Lee. That's true, right?"

Jackie's answer was quick: "Oh, no, Jamie, that's not true," she said. "Please!"

Jamie was stunned. "Well, what about the story that Mummy is English Catholic, is that true?"

Jackie laughed. "No, *of course* not," she said. "She's *Irish* Catholic. You mean you didn't know that?"

Jamie said he had just believed what their mother had told him over the years. "No one ever told *me* this information wasn't accurate," he said. Jackie didn't know what to tell him; all she knew was that he shouldn't continue to operate under false pretenses. Publicly, people weren't always entitled to the truth and certainly Jackie had often suggested, especially at the beginning of her time in the White House, that she was more French than Irish. Privately, though, she saw no use in family members fooling themselves. After that call with his half sister, Jamie decided to keep what she had told him to himself rather than take a chance on jeopardizing his mother's goals at Stratford Hall.

RUSHING INTO MARRIAGE?

On Monday, October 14, 1968, Janet took the two-hour drive along the Potomac River to Chesapeake Bay. Once she got to Stratford Hall, she found her assigned, nicely appointed bungalow. She made herself comfortable and spent the rest of the day and into the early evening chatting with the other women about what had been planned for the seminar. That night, she spent hours studying her two favorite books, *Tidewater Dynasty: A Biographical Novel of the Lees of Stratford Hall* and *Stratford Hall: The Great House of the Lees.* She knew she would be formally elected to the board on Tuesday and couldn't help but be a little nervous about it.

Of course, Janet had nothing to worry about. When she presented herself at her first board meeting on Tuesday — wearing a smart, businesswoman's ensemble, a long-sleeved silk blouse and burgundy scarf with a chocolate-brown skirt and sensible, soft leather pumps — she walked in as a noted public figure. She was a true celebrity in the midst of the other society women who comprised the board, most of whom were Republicans, her image of strength and resolve all the more burnished by the recent tragedy of Bobby's death. After all, she'd been photographed at the funeral, seen with Jackie and the rest of the Kennedys while in mourning, and also quoted in the press about the ordeal. Still, she wanted to impress. Therefore, she came prepared.

A couple of weeks earlier, Janet had gone to Fort Adams in Newport to do some research after hearing that Robert E. Lee had once been stationed there. She wanted to not only confirm it but see what else she might uncover. Janet soon learned that Lee really hadn't been stationed at Fort Adams at all. However, to her delight, she uncovered a number of interesting letters from him to the Fort Adams commanding officer, Lt. Joseph Gilbert Totten. Since she couldn't take possession of the documents, Janet took copious notes, which she intended to bring with her to the retreat. When she finally had the opportunity to show everyone at the board meeting what she had uncovered, they couldn't have been more impressed with her work. After a quick recount of votes to make certain there were no objectors, Janet Auchincloss was officially named to the board.

The next morning, Wednesday, Janet enjoyed a celebrative breakfast in the dining hall with her colleagues. Midway through, she was told that she had an important telephone call. She raced to the front desk, understandably alarmed. When she heard Jackie's voice, she steeled herself for the worst. What now? In a sense, it actually *was* bad news — though, thankfully, not of a life-threatening nature. Jackie, who was calling from her Manhattan apartment, told Janet that she had decided to marry Aristotle Onassis, immediately. Janet was stunned.

By this time, rumors of a possible wedding between America's former First Lady and the Greek shipping mogul to whom she seemed so ill suited had spread like wildfire. Official denials from Jackie's spokespeople, as well as those of the Kennedys, did little to stop the media frenzy. In fact, Jackie explained to Janet that she'd just been informed that the *Boston Herald Traveler* was going to confirm the story. She said that, as a result, she now feared her life would become completely unmanageable, with the media hounding her and her children everywhere they went.

Janet didn't want to hear it. She suggested that Jackie take the kids and go into hiding, saying it wouldn't be the first time she took such measures. No, Jackie insisted that she had to marry Ari as soon as possible, on Sunday, in fact. She told Janet to get her travel documents in order because the wedding was going to take place in Greece. She explained that Kennedy acolyte Pierre Salinger had suggested that it would be better if she married Onassis there rather than in the States, so that not all of the Kennedys would be expected to show up, just the ones who could bear it. Janet wondered if Jackie had talked to Lee about her decision. Jackie said she hadn't had time to do so. "You need to stop and think about this," Janet told her daughter, according to her later recollection to family members. "You're not thinking straight. It's Jack! It's Bobby. It's the children. *It's all of it!*"

Though extremely upset, Janet tried her best to go back to the business at hand at Stratford. However, less than two hours later, while Janet and the other board members were studying a documentary about Robert E. Lee in the Council House, Jackie called again. Mother and daughter then had another upsetting conversation.

Janet decided to telephone Hugh in Washington to ask for his assistance. Hugh's colleague at Auchincloss, Parker & Redpath, Garrett Johnston, recalled, "Mr. Auchincloss later told me that his wife suggested that he call Jackie and offer some sort of allowance to her so that finances might not figure so heavily into any decision she would make about marriage. Mrs. A. said she suspected Jackie had struck a deal, and that maybe Hugh could offer something as a replacement."

Now Hugh was torn. He wasn't sure he agreed with Janet that a marriage between Jackie and Ari was such a bad idea. Business wasn't what it used to be; he'd been stretched to the financial limits for some time, ever since selling off Merrywood. "He said that Lee was taken care of, as were his biological children from his other marriages — Nini, Tommy, and Yusha," recalled Garrett Johnston. "However, Jackie was still at her wit's end when it came to managing her extravagant lifestyle." Hugh also had to view Jackie's decision in the context of what was going on in her life at the time, though. She was deeply troubled and hadn't been herself for years. Was she even capable of making such an important decision?"

When Hugh called Jackie on Wednesday night, he asked her a number of questions, all of a practical nature. What about the age difference? What about the children's schooling? Where would they all live? By the time they finished their ninety-minute conversation, though, Hugh was reasonably certain Jackie knew what she was doing. *She* had

489

convinced *him.* Importantly, though, he did not offer her any sort of financial incentive to dissuade her from marrying Onassis. When he reported back to Janet that he believed Jackie was being rational, she asked him if he had brought up the idea of an allowance. Hugh apparently lied and said he'd done so, rather than have to face his wife's wrath. He then compounded the lie by saying that Jackie had turned it down. "Poor Daddy, he probably couldn't help it," said his son Jamie. "He was so intimidated by Mummy."

There was a third phone call from Jackie. During this one, Jackie said she was worried about how it would look to others if Janet wasn't present for the wedding. The two went back and forth, arguing about it. Finally, Janet relented and agreed to go to Greece for the ceremony. By the time she hung up, though, she'd pretty much had it with her daughter. Now Janet would have to cut her important retreat short by two days, drive back to Washington, and then pack for a last-minute trip to Greece. "My goodness, Janet, what's the problem?" asked trustee Mary Tyler Freeman Cheek McClenahan. "I would not say it's critical," Janet told her, "but it is an emergency, something I need to tend to." McClenahan, one of Richmond's most prominent civic leaders, asked if there was anything she could do. No, Janet told her. "I have a sense you will be reading about it in the papers, though, soon enough," she said.

When Janet got back to her home on O Street, she found the telephone ringing in the parlor. She raced to it and picked it up herself rather than wait for one of the maids. It was Nancy Tuckerman, who was now Jackie's secretary in New York. "Mrs. A., we're releasing a statement about Jackie's marriage to Aristotle Onassis," Nancy told Janet, "and I need your help." The two women then spoke and agreed that a prepared statement would simply announce that "Mrs. Hugh D. Auchincloss" had informed Nancy that "her daughter, Mrs. John F. Kennedy," would marry Aristotle Onassis, "sometime next week. No place or date has been set for the moment."

Her emotions still running high, Janet then telephoned Jamie at Columbia. "Can you believe what your sister is doing?" she asked. She told him she was beginning to believe that Jackie's marrying Onassis was really just her way of punishing her mother for divorcing her father so long ago. To Jamie, Janet's theory seemed unlikely. "No, Mummy," he said, "that can't be it." Janet said she didn't know how else to explain it. Jamie suggested that maybe Jackie really *was* worried about the children. Certainly, she had good reason to be. "Look what's been going on in our lives," he exclaimed. Janet wasn't so sure. Her gut told her it was not about the children at all, that it was really about money. "Well, if so, why is that such a problem?" Jamie asked, well aware of the premium both his mother and sister had always placed on marrying well. Janet didn't want to discuss it any further, though.

Actually, there *was* a money deal in place.

A significant amount of haggling had recently concluded with Ted Kennedy getting Jackie about $1.5 million from Onassis in an immediate lump sum. André Meyer then managed to double that amount for a lump sum of $3 million (which, in today's money, would be more than $20 million). Jackie would also receive $30,000 a month for expenses, after taxes, for the duration of the marriage (again, about $200,000 in today's money). Each of her children would receive $1 million, the annual interest on which would revert back to Jackie. Mona Latham, who was André Meyer's assistant, recalled, "After it was all over, Jackie told André that she'd had a 'crisis of conscience' over it. On one hand, she was raised to consider a man's finances before marriage. On the other, I think she viewed this deal as being unsavory. I believe she wanted to forget it had ever happened."

During their telephone conversation, Jamie asked if Janet was going to the wedding. "Of course I am," she said without hesitation. "She's my daughter! But do I approve? No, I do not." She then told him that he should be careful not speak to any reporters. Too late. He'd already talked to *The National Enquirer* and *The Washington Post*! "They got to me so fast," Jamie said, worried. "But I didn't know anything yet. So I couldn't say much." A loud sigh escaped Janet's lips. "Oh my God, Jamie," she said. "Don't even answer the phone, then! I have enough problems with your sister."

After she hung up, Janet tore through her bedroom looking for her passport. Where was it? Her maid and butler searched the house to no avail. Adora Rule suggested that perhaps it was at Hammersmith in Janet's dresser drawer. However, when Janet contacted the superintendent there, Mannie Faria, and had him search her bedroom, he couldn't find it. She was frantic. Nancy Tuckerman suggested Janet pull a few strings by calling Frances Knight, director of the United States Passport Office. Knight — a staunch Republican — was controversial at the time because of her seemingly dictatorial decisions about whom she would allow access to the country. When Janet reached her, Knight told her how much she loved Jackie (from afar, they'd never met) and eagerly agreed to have a replacement passport sent by messenger to O Sreet within the hour.*

* Nine years later, in 1977, Jamie Auchincloss would be applying for a passport in Washington when a

Meanwhile, Hugh, at his office in Washington, asked his secretary, Margaret Kearney, "Do you have my passport?" When she wondered why he needed it, he explained to her that it looked like he and Janet were headed to Greece. "Jackie is marrying Onassis," he told her, seeming weary about the whole thing. "Is that a good idea?" Margaret asked. "I spoke to her for an hour and a half last night," he answered, "and she's got a mind of her own, that one. Pretty much like you-know-who," he said with a chuckle.

In a few hours' time, Janet and Hugh flew from Washington to New York. There, they were joined by Jackie and her children, as well as her former sisters-in-law Jean Kennedy Smith and Pat Lawford, and Pat's young daughter, Sydney. All told, with Secret Service agents and other functionaries, it would be a party of eleven boarding a chartered Olympic Airways jet headed to Greece.

---

government employee would approach and tell him, "The director would like to see you." A shiver went down his spine. "Why in the world would the head of the U.S. passport agency want to see *me*?" he asked. When he was ushered into her office, there was Frances Knight. "You know, I gave your mother her passport so that she could go to Greece to see your sister marry Onassis," she said with a smile and a handshake.

The plane landed at a military airport on the Peloponnesian peninsula, where it was met by Ari. The small contingent then took another flight to Preveza. From there, they boarded helicopters, their destination Skorpios.

"I NEED THIS, LEE"

"How could she do this to me?" Lee Radziwill asked Truman Capote, at least according to the later memory of the writer Eleanor Perry. Perry was collaborating with Capote on writing a screenplay for television when the call came in from Lee. She says that Lee was screaming so loudly, she (Perry) could hear her words through the receiver: "How could she? How could this happen?" Truman didn't know what to tell her. "She's crying and weeping and *sobbing,*" he later told friends of Lee. "I can't tell you what she said, but it's going to be in the news. It's the biggest piece of gossip *there is,* and she's crying her *eyes* out because of it."

After Truman had a falling-out with Lee (in 1977), he made more than a few telling statements about the famous siblings. Since he had been Lee's best friend, his commentary can't be ignored, though it should probably be put into context by noting that the ending of their friendship was particularly bitter. "Once, Lee called me in a rage," he

495

recalled. "She said Jackie had just told her that everything Lee had in the world she owed to Jackie. I didn't say it to her at the time, but there's a lot of truth to that. I don't think Jackie had the vaguest idea the extent of Lee's obsession with her. Lee used to say that *she* was the one who was good-looking, who had taste, who was chic, who could run a home, who was clever, who read books, but it was always Jackie who got all the publicity. And, of course, there was some truth to that, too."

Where the shipping mogul was concerned, Truman said, "Lee really thought she had Onassis nailed down. She pretended to have great contempt for Onassis and the marriage. She wasn't in love with him. But she liked all those tankers."

Obviously, Truman Capote couldn't have known for certain whether or not Lee was in love with Onassis, since she herself seemed to have so little clarity about it. However, she knew for sure she'd missed out on her golden opportunity with the shipping tycoon, that small sliver of time when she could have had him to herself back in the summer of 1962. Ari had specifically asked her not to renew her vows to Stas in the Catholic Church, but she'd decided to do so, anyway. Things had never really been the same for them since.

"It was actually a simple equation," reasons Jamie Auchincloss. "Jackie's husband and brother-in-law were now both dead. Onassis was, in effect, saying to Lee, 'I'm going to be the person whose shoulder Jackie can cry on now. I can provide her with the protection, the security, the love, and the money nobody else can.' It wasn't exactly him saying, 'Lee, I'm choosing your sister over you.' It was more the equivalent of: 'Though I know this is hard on you, I feel it's my duty to help a widow in distress. I also can likely get a lot of mileage out of doing so just in terms of status in the world. Given that you know me better than anyone else, I'm sure you understand. It's nothing personal.' That's the nicest light I can put on it, anyway."

Lee learned about the pending nuptials from Aristotle Onassis, who called her while she was on a vacation in Tunisia to extend a personal invitation. "He begged me to come," is how she later put it. The details of their conversation are unknown, but one might imagine it was tense, considering their painful history. The fact that Jackie wasn't the one to call Lee had to have stung.

Of course, Lee was angry and upset when she arrived in Greece on Saturday, and she would be the first to admit it. However, when she eventually laid eyes on her sister standing on board the deck of the *Christina* with Onassis, both bathed in moonlight, Jackie was laughing. Lee had to stop and try to remember the last time she'd seen her sister truly happy; most certainly, it had not been in years. This was a defining moment for Lee, as she would later recall it to intimates. Was it possible that this man, Aristotle Onassis — someone who had vexed and confounded her for many years, a man with whom she'd had such a tortured relationship — could be a worthwhile, valuable person in her sister's life? From a safe distance, she stood and watched the two speak to each other for about half an hour. There was nothing romantic about their interaction, just something easy and relaxed. Lee hadn't spent much time with Onassis lately, but whenever she did, there was nothing but tension and angst between them. There was no doubt about it; Lee had to acknowledge that Jackie seemed happy.

The most searing images of Jackie in Lee's mind of late were of her taking copious amounts of prescription pills just to get through the days and nights. There was her talk of suicide, her musings about joining Jack in the afterlife, her great despair, which had only gotten worse after Bobby's death. In fact, after his funeral, Jackie sometimes even seemed delusional, talking about Jack and Bobby as if they were still alive, fretting about some imagined White House duty as if she was still First Lady. She seemed to be losing her grip on reality. Moreover, the recent spate of death and kidnapping threats against Caroline and John had made it so that she was afraid to even leave the house with them. She was frantic. "If anything happens to either one, I will never forgive myself," she had told Lee in front of other family members, "and I would also never survive it. I simply would not survive it." There was no arguing that she had good reason to be worried. Therefore, to see her now, smiling, laughing, and appearing so lighthearted, was stunning for Lee. To hear her tell it, it brought real tears to her eyes.

After a while, Lee approached. Onassis, apparently, didn't have the heart to even face her. When he saw her come close, he turned and walked away from Jackie after giving her a small peck on the cheek. The two sisters then stood on the massive deck of the *Christina,* alone in the shadows. Jackie embraced Lee and thanked her for coming. Then, according to what Lee would remember, Jackie firmly grabbed her forearm with her two hands and, with great urgency, said just four words: "I need this, Lee." That was all she said — "I need this, Lee." Lee looked at her closely, studied her anguished face . . . and she knew it was true. "I know you do," she said. "And you should have it." That was the full extent of the Bouvier sisters' discussion about Aristotle Onassis.

Jackie then asked Lee to be her matron of honor. Lee agreed.

"IT's NOT TOO LATE!"

Sunday, October 20, 1968.

"Jacqueline, you don't have to *do* this," Janet whispered in her daughter's ear as they took measured steps in the group procession up the middle aisle of the small chapel in Skorpios. *"Mummy, please!"* Jackie hissed out of the corner of her mouth. This heated back-and-forth between mother and daughter would, in years to come, become a big part of the family's history of Jackie's wedding to Ari. Janet was still trying to prevent Jackie's marrying Onassis from coming between the sisters. Eventually, Jackie's stubborn defiance and her insubordination began to vex Janet almost as much as her concern about how the marriage might affect her daughters.

It was five P.M. in Greece and raining outside the little chapel known as Panayitas — the Little Virgin — as the ceremony to join Jacqueline Lee Bouvier Kennedy and Aristotle Socrates Onassis in holy matrimony commenced. As she walked down the aisle on Hugh's arm, Jackie was a beautiful bride in a cream-colored chiffon-and-lace knee-length pleated dress with long bishop sleeves and a mock turtleneck. It had been designed by Valentino of Rome. A small procession of family members followed, with Janet on Jackie's heels, her neck craned upward as she spoke in her daughter' ear. "Janet told me she did everything she could think of to talk Jackie out of it," recalled Eileen Slocum. " 'Don't do it,' she kept whispering in her ear. 'It's not too late to back out!' She said that Jackie kept whispering angrily back at her, 'Stop it or I will never speak to you again!' "

Meanwhile, a beaming Aristotle Onassis, jaunty and as debonair as ever in a smart dark suit, stood at the altar with a priest as he watched Jackie and the procession approach him and Father Polykarpos, a close friend of Onassis's from Athens. A trio of Byzantine choristers harmonized as Caroline and John took their seats in the front of the church. Onassis's children, Alexander and Christina, watched warily from a corner, neither appearing to be happy about their father's decision to take Jackie as his wife.

Marie-Hélène de Rothschild, a French socialite from the prominent Rothschild banking family, was a close friend of Ari's who attended the wedding. She once recalled, "It was so crowded, you couldn't see a thing, really. I could barely see Jackie and Janet as they walked down the aisle. It seemed to me that Mrs. Auchincloss and her daughter were having a disagreement about something. They were whispering to one another through clenched smiles."

Finally, and mercifully, Jackie made it to the front of the chapel, where she took her place next to Ari. Hugh then accompanied Janet to her seat. Sitting in the front row with Stas, matron of honor Lee probably couldn't help but be bemused. As a Bouvier woman, she certainly knew a whispered argument when she saw one.

Forty-five minutes later, Jackie and Ari walked together around the altar three times and then kissed as man and wife. "Servant of God Aristotle Onassis is wedlocked to the servant of God, Jacqueline," intoned the priest, first in Greek and then in English, "in the name of the Father, Son, and the Holy Ghost. Amen."

LIKE MOTHER, LIKE DAUGHTER?

While Jackie and Ari continued on to their honeymoon aboard the *Christina,* Janet and Hugh took John and Caroline back with them to O Street for a few weeks. Janet so appreciated Hugh's support. Even though he had not been able to talk Jackie out of marriage, he was there for Janet, always with a shoulder for her to cry on. "Isn't it wonderful to be married to a man you love?" Janet remarked to her niece Joan Gaylord at this time.

When finally Jackie returned to retrieve her children, Janet calmly asked her to join her in the master bedroom. Then, according to what

Janet would later recall to family members, she and Jackie became embroiled in another passionate exchange about Onassis. During their argument, Janet apparently told Jackie that she hoped she had a good financial deal in place with the Greek magnate since she was now sure this was the only reason for the marriage. Of course, it was about more than just money for Jackie. It was also out of concern for her children that she married Onassis. However, if Janet wanted to make it only about money, fine. Jackie must have decided she could also play that game. "You mean for the exact same reason you married Uncle Hughdie?" she shot back at her mother.

For Jackie to bring up the fact that Janet had long ago married Hugh Auchincloss for money was a low blow, at least in Janet's view. After all, she'd done so to provide a better life for her two daughters. It came with a steep price, too. It meant giving up true passion, accepting that she would never have it with Hugh, and then making the best of it. Happily, Janet felt she had married someone with more strength of character than her first husband's, not less. Now Jackie was drawing a parallel between her choice to marry Ari and Janet's decision to marry Hugh? This was going too far, even for the most famous, most celebrated woman in the world. Without saying another word, Janet just hauled off and slapped her daughter across the face, twice — first on her right cheek with the palm of her hand, then on her left with the back of it — just as she had done so often when her girls were younger. Janet then angrily told her that she should have taken similar action in Greece, and that if she had done so, maybe *then* Jackie would have listened to her admonitions about Onassis.

"A Matter of Life or Death"

Three months after the wedding, Lee's friend Agnetta Castallanos had dinner with her at the Manhattan restaurant La Caravelle, during which the two discussed Jackie's marriage to Ari. Lee said she regretted that she and Jackie had not been able to more fully discuss Jackie's desire to marry Onassis. She said she was afraid it spoke volumes about the lack of candor in their relationship. Agnetta couldn't help but wonder, though, if Lee would have understood. "Not at first," Lee admitted with a sigh. She was more self-aware than to think she would have said, "Oh, great, Jackie! That's marvelous! Take Ari. I'm fine with it." No, she said she would have been hurt and angry. In fact, she probably would have experienced a wide spectrum of emotions, all of which she felt would have been justified.

However, after she first saw Jackie on the deck of the *Christina* with Ari the night before their wedding, there was no way she could have kept them apart. "It had become a matter of life or death for my sister," she said, "and I knew it." She finally realized that Onassis was Jackie's "lifeblood." She concluded, "In the end, she needed him more than I did. It was as simple and as complicated as that."

Agnetta questioned why Lee never told Jackie what she'd done for her back in '63 — the sacrifice she'd made of giving up Onassis rather than scandalize the First Lady. Many people in Lee's family who would later learn of this selfless act would wonder the same thing. "What would have been the point?" Lee asked. What if, as a result of that revelation, Jackie had decided not to marry Onassis? How would Lee ever live with herself if something were to then happen to her sister, her niece, or her nephew as a result of Onassis's absence in their lives? Considering what they'd all gone through in the last five years with Jack and Bobby — "loss upon loss" is how Lee put it — it wasn't as if Lee's fear for her sister was irrational.

Many years later, in 2000, Lee Radziwill published a coffee-table book of photographs, *Happy Times,* which included extended captions about both the good and bad times of her life. In the introduction, she wrote of

JFK's assassination and hinted at the inner turmoil it caused everyone: "Then the President was killed and things became flat. Many people couldn't handle his loss; their true colors began to show. The carefree and exciting times vanished. People had to struggle with themselves."

"Over the intervening years, I don't think anyone in her family — including Jackie — ever fully acknowledged the sacrifices Lee made for her where Onassis was concerned," Agnetta Castallanos would observe years later. "It has always bothered me when people questioned Lee's love for her sister. The depth of love one has to feel for someone else to sacrifice so much cannot be measured, it is just that great. As I see it, the facts speak for themselves."

"SECRETS. THAT'S WHAT WE DO BEST."

With the passing of time, Jackie continually tried to smooth things over with Janet by inviting her and Hugh to cruise on the *Christina*. They always begged off, however; after the wedding, never once did they step foot on Onassis's yacht again, nor did they ever return to Skorpios while Onassis was alive. Jackie and Ari would visit Hammersmith several times in the years to come, but it would be an overstatement to say that things were copacetic. Janet had a lot on her mind, anyway. The rest of '68, '69, and the beginning of the 1970s found her dealing with Hugh's declining health, his emphysema having taken a turn for the worse.

Also, Hugh would soon have to close the Washington branch of Auchincloss, Parker & Redpath. "Because the war in Vietnam continued to rage on, a sense of unpredictability caused most of our clientele to forgo big investments," said Garrett Johnston. "As a result, their portfolios shrunk dramatically, meaning less income for Auchincloss, Parker & Redpath. We ended up with an SEC citation because our record-keeping was a little shoddy. In the end, we had no choice but to merge with Thomson & McKinnon, Inc. The new firm name would then be Thomson & McKinnon, Auchincloss. None of this was good for Mr. Auchincloss, his ego taking a real beating."

Keeping their money troubles from scrutiny by friends in high society was becoming next to impossible. "You don't say you have money problems when you are an Auchincloss," Letitia Baldrige, who had been Jackie's social secretary, once said. "Mrs. Auchincloss would never admit it to others, and her husband could barely admit it to her! Everyone knew, though, that they were in trouble by the end of the 1960s."

As the decade came to a close, life continued to unfold for Janet and Hugh with unpredictable twists and turns. Janet remained committed to her work with Stratford Hall. And her many grandchildren — both natural from Jackie, Lee, and Janet, and step from Hugh's offspring — continued to give her great pleasure.

With the wearing of the years, Jackie's life with Ari unraveled. In the end, many of Onassis's associates would come to believe that Jackie was as much an acquisition for him as she was his wife. His personal assistant at that time, Kiki Feroudi Moutsatsos, says, "At first, Ari swept Jackie away from her troubles. When he was with her, he gave her all of his attention and made her feel like the most important person in his world. He also got along with the children; John, in particular, admired him greatly. And, yes, he did protect them. To Jackie's great relief, no one could even come *near* the kids. Between their own Secret Service detail and Ari's hard-core security force trailing them, she knew Caroline and John were finally safe."

After about two years, though, things began to sour. Onassis's relationship with Maria Callas continued, and likely there were other women, too. Jackie once again found herself in a marriage with a cheater.

By the beginning of the 1970s, Jackie seemed to have a better understanding of the

PTSD symptoms that had motivated her marriage to Ari. After a couple of years, she began to realize that Onassis was a choice she probably wouldn't have made at any other time in her life. It had been driven by despair, fear, and pain, and not just over Jack and Bobby. She told one confidante at this time, "There's not a day that goes by that I don't think about the children I lost."

Going back to the White House in February of '71 helped a lot; the Nixons invited Jackie and the children so that they could see the official portraits of her and Jack before their unveiling. For years, Jackie had refused to go back. She decided, though, that it was time to face her fears and return to the place where she and Jack had once been so happy. "Never have I seen such magnanimity and such tenderness," she wrote to President Richard Nixon and First Lady Pat after the visit. "Can you imagine the gift you gave me to return to the White House privately with my little ones while they are still young enough to rediscover their childhood, with you both as guides?" Jackie closed saying, "Thank you with all my heart. A day I always dreaded turned out to be one of the most precious ones I have spent with my children."

By the summer of '71, Lee had managed to reconcile herself to and even accept Jackie's marriage to Ari. From a strictly practical standpoint, there was a certain lifestyle attached to remaining a part of Onassis's world. After all, even as just his sister-in-law, she traveled in the highest strata of society. There were exotic vacations; leisurely shopping expeditions; the enjoyment of fabulous restaurants and nightclubs all over the world. There would always be the spark and excitement of adventure in the air — and money perks, too. "[Lee] owned a valuable piece of land in Greece," Truman Capote once observed. "She got it from Onassis."

"Lee was a smart woman," said Kiki Feroudi Moutsatsos. "*Of course* there was an upside to her continuing to have Ari in her life. Ari was generous, put it that way."

While it was not easy, Lee tried not to look back with regret at any of her decisions relating to Onassis. Janet, for one, had great admiration for the way her daughter had handled things. "She put family first," Janet told one relative. "I will always respect that about Lee."

In the years to come, there would be countless family moments — holidays, birthdays, and other special occasions that would bring the Onassis, Radziwill, and Auchincloss families together. Once they got on with their lives with their respective spouses and children, the sisters made the best of it. It's doubtful that Caroline, John, Tina, or Anthony had anything but happy memories of growing up together as cousins. "Jackie and Lee took a joint approach in raising their children," said Gustavo Paredes, the son of Jackie's White House assistant, Provi, who was close to all of them. "There was a lot of flow between the households. Jackie thought of Anthony and Tina as her own, and Lee thought of John and Caroline as hers. The kids never knew anything about their mothers' private lives, just as it should have been. They were raised in a safe world without adult concerns, which their mothers created for them."

Though Janet respected Lee's devotion to family, she knew both of her daughters well. She would go to her grave believing that they would never get past the Onassis complication, a man she felt had seriously damaged the trust between them. She noticed a marked difference in their relationship. For instance, in the spring of '71, she watched the sisters interact at a party at Hammersmith. It appeared friendly between them. However, after Jackie walked away from Lee, Janet could detect a flicker of hurt in Lee's eyes. In that moment, said Janet, she could discern that Lee harbored something, maybe resentment, maybe pain, she didn't know for certain what it was, but, as she put at the time, "there was definitely *something* there, something that kept me up that night."

Janet decided to schedule a Mother-Daughter Tea to clear the air between Jackie and Lee. She arranged for her daughters to meet her at the Plaza in New York, their favorite place for such conferences. During the tea, as Janet later recalled it, she very plainly told them, "Whatever is going on with you two, we need to settle it right now. We are not leaving here until it is settled." However, Jackie and Lee remained resolute that there was no problem. Maybe there wasn't. After all, it did seem as if, with few words but an abundance of emotion, they had settled things somewhat on the deck of the *Christina* the night before the wedding. Obviously, both were grown women with complex lives and children of their own. There was only so much their mother could do to try to repair any damage she feared existed between them. For Janet, it was maddening. "No one ever *talks* in this family," she complained. "Secrets. That's what we do best."

Janet and Jackie greet guests at the White House for their joint tea for National Cultural Center campaign officials on June 22, 1962. Left to right: the previous first lady, Mamie Eisenhower; Jackie; advisory committee members Joan Braden and Grace Hendrick Phillips; and chairman of the Washington Area Campaign Committee, Janet. (ABBIE ROWE/WHITE HOUSE PHOTOGRAPHS/JOHN F. KENNEDY PRESIDENTIAL LIBRARY AND MUSEUM, BOSTON)

Jack Kennedy arrives at Hammersmith Farm; he loved spending time there with Jackie's side of the family, the Auchinclosses. Left to right: Yusha, JFK, Janet, and Janet Jr. (ROBERT KNUDSEN/ WHITE HOUSE PHOTOGRAPHS/JOHN F. KENNEDY PRESIDENTIAL LIBRARY AND MUSEUM, BOSTON)

Jackie with John Carl ("Jack") Warnecke, September 25, 1962, viewing Jack's plans for the preservation of Lafayette Square, Washington, D.C. It's worth noting that Jackie is wearing the same dress she would wear in Dallas in 1963 when JFK would be killed. After his assassination, Jackie and Jack Warnecke would have a three-year romance. (ROBERT KNUDSEN/WHITE HOUSE PHOTOGRAPHS/JOHN F. KENNEDY PRESIDENTIAL LIBRARY AND MUSEUM, BOSTON)

The Kennedys and Radziwills celebrate Christmas in December 1962 in Palm Beach, Florida. Left to right: Caroline Kennedy, Gustavo Paredes (son of Jackie's assistant, Provi), Jackie (holding Lee's son, Tony), John Kennedy Jr., JFK, Prince Stanislaw Radziwill, and Lee (holding daughter Tina). Also included are two of the Kennedys' family dogs, Clipper and Charlie. (CECIL STOUGHTON/WHITE HOUSE PHOTOGRAPHS/JOHN F. KENNEDY PRESIDENTIAL LIBRARY AND MUSEUM, BOSTON)

Janet helps her granddaughter Caroline (Jackie's daughter) open presents at a joint birthday party for her and her brother, John, on November 27, 1962, at the White House; Jackie stands at right in the background. (ROBERT KNUDSEN/WHITE HOUSE PHOTOGRAPHS/JOHN F. KENNEDY PRESIDENTIAL LIBRARY AND MUSEUM, BOSTON)

The days of Camelot ended with the assassination of President Kennedy. JFK lies in repose in the East Room of the White House; the flag-draped casket of President Kennedy sits out of frame at left, prior to a funeral procession to the Capitol Building. Left to right: Jackie and her children, Caroline and John Jr., Bobby Kennedy, Jean Kennedy Smith, Lady Bird Johnson, President Lyndon Johnson, Lee, Steve Smith, Jamie, Janet, with Hugh behind her, and Janet Jr. (CECIL STOUGHTON/WHITE HOUSE PHOTOGRAPHS/JOHN F. KENNEDY PRESIDENTIAL LIBRARY AND MUSEUM, BOSTON)

Funeral procession to St. Matthew's Cathedral. Left to right: Jamie Auchincloss, Bobby Kennedy, Sargent Shriver, Jackie, and Ted Kennedy (ROBERT KNUDSEN/WHITE HOUSE PHOTOGRAPHS/ JOHN F. KENNEDY PRESIDENTIAL LIBRARY AND MUSEUM, BOSTON)

Janet at Bobby Kennedy's gravesite. Bobby's death would impact the lives of just about everyone in Janet's family, most notably her daughters, Jackie and Lee. (JAMIE AUCHINCLOSS COLLECTION)

Jackie (left) and a deeply grieving Lee at Bobby's funeral at St. Patrick's Cathedral in New York City, June 8, 1968. (BETTMANN/GETTY IMAGES)

Jackie with her son, John, and half-brother, Jamie, at an Arlington Cemetery memorial for Bobby Kennedy. (JAMIE AUCHINCLOSS COLLECTION)

Jackie's marriage to Aristotle Onassis on October 20, 1968, changed everything for her and her sister, Lee. The sisters would have to work hard to rebuild their relationship. (PHOTOFEST)

Though she would choose Aristotle Onassis over Jack Warnecke, Jackie would remain friends with Jack for the rest of her life. Here they are during the 7th Annual RFK Pro-Celebrity Tennis Tournament at Forest Hills in New York City, August 26, 1978. (RON GALELLA COLLECTION/WIREIMAGE)

By the 1980s, Mannie Faria had been a trusted employee at Hammersmith Farm for decades. Here he is with Jackie in 1987. . . (JOYCE FARIA BRENNAN/FARIA FAMILY COLLECTION)

. . . and with Lee. (JOYCE FARIA BRENNAN/FARIA FAMILY COLLECTION)

Jamie sees his parents, Janet and Hugh, off on a cruise that will take them from New York City to Capetown. (JAMIE AUCHINCLOSS COLLECTION)

Linda and Joyce Faria grew up at Hammersmith Farm and became very close to Janet Auchincloss. (JOYCE FARIA BRENNAN/FARIA FAMILY COLLECTION)

Jamie and Janet in the spring of 1983 on their cruise to Hong Kong to visit Janet Jr. (JAMIE AUCHINCLOSS COLLECTION)

Though Lee seemed to distance herself as Janet became older and more frail, here they are in a happy moment in 1986. (ROBIN PLATZER/TWIN IMAGES/THE LIFE IMAGES COLLECTION/GETTY IMAGES)

When Jackie feared that her mother, Janet, had become the victim of elder abuse, she became extremely protective of her. (JAMIE AUCHINCLOSS COLLECTION)

A deeply grieving Jackie is escorted by her stepbrother, Yusha Auchincloss, as she leaves Trinity Church in Newport, Rhode Island, after attending the funeral of her mother, Janet, on July 27, 1989. (JIM GER-BERICH/AP/REX/SHUTTERSTOCK)

Left to cope with the deaths of Janet and Jackie, Lee went on with her life, happy for a while in her marriage to the noted film producer Herbert Ross. (RICHARD YOUNG/REX/SHUTTERSTOCK)

Still just as stunning as ever, today Lee Radziwill is eighty-four. (NEIL RASMUS/BFA/REX/SHUTTERSTOCK)

■ ■ ■ ■

PART TEN:
SHIFTING TIDES

■ ■ ■ ■

Part Ten:
Shifting Tides

PETER BEARD

"What a strange, quirky man," Jacqueline Onassis said of Peter Beard when she first met him in the spring of '71 at a party in New York. She was fascinated by the blond and beautiful thirty-three-year-old bon vivant as he told his story of growing up in New York and becoming so strangely obsessed by African culture that he would feature it as the centerpiece of his photographic work. He'd been to Africa twice before graduating from Yale. After graduation, he returned and got a job working at Tsavo National Park in Kenya. He'd also begun to photograph wildlife threatened with extinction, the pictures eventually being compiled for his first book, *The End of the Game.*

Peter was a real eccentric, known for composing collages of noteworthy moments from his life by incorporating photographs, newspaper clippings, and poetic musings about pop culture and the world around him. A fixture of nightlife in Manhattan, he also

515

loved to party with A-listers like Andy Warhol, Mick and Bianca Jagger, Dick Cavett, and anyone else who made the New York social scene so much fun at that time. He hailed from a family that had made great wealth in the railway business. However, as in the cases of Jackie and Lee, not much of the family's money ever really trickled down to him.

In the summer of '71, Jackie invited Peter to spend time with her and Ari on Skorpios. It's been repeatedly published in many biographies over the years that the only reason Peter was on Skorpios was to "amuse" Jackie with his painting and sculpting. He was also babysitter to Jackie's children and any other kids who happened to be on the island. Since Jackie found marriage to Onassis increasingly challenging, having a young sexy guy around made her situation a little less bleak. However, her stance on fidelity remained unchanged; she would never sleep with Peter.

Jackie had also invited Lee to Skorpios to lift her spirits since she'd been recovering from a hysterectomy for the last several months. While there, Lee, who brought Stas with her, became as "amused" by Peter Beard as Jackie, which would lead to a conclusion many in their lives found inevitable.

Peter and Stas were complete opposites in almost every way. Peter was fun and creative whereas Stas was, at least in Lee's view, dour and uninspired. About twenty-five years younger than Stas, Peter was also passionate in a way Lee's husband hadn't been in years. She had a hard time resisting Peter when he came on to her. For his part, he found her more beautiful than Jackie and more interesting. He told Jackie's biographer Sarah Bradford that Jackie was a "person hiding from in-depth experiences in life. She was on the surface of life, trying to remain there." Lee, though, had a "sense of adventure and devil-may-care attitude I could not resist." When asked about the Jackie/Lee sisterhood, Peter described it this way: "All the older sister, younger sister cliché . . . . Jackie the classic responsible older sister, Lee the rebellious younger one. Lots of loyalty, lots of bad things."

"Peter was the *anti*-Ari," is how one of Lee's friends at that time put it. "Onassis was rich. Peter was poor. Onassis demanded the best hotels and living accommodations everywhere he went. Peter was happy sleeping in a tent. Onassis bought expensive art. Peter made collages. Everything Onassis was, Peter was not, and everything Peter was, Onassis was not, and Lee knew it. She told me, 'I had a chance to be with a man who had all the money in the world, and I decided against it. That was *my* decision. Now I have decided on Peter.' "

When Ari saw Peter sneaking out of Lee's bungalow, he knew something was going on between them. When he mentioned it to Jackie, she said she didn't want to know anything about it. Lee was obviously having an affair with Peter; she admitted it openly. Jackie decided to stay out of Lee's business; she had her hands full with Ari, anyway.

Typical of the way Lee and Stas had begun to conduct their marriage, Peter soon became a third player in it, going on safari with the Radziwills, visiting them at their home in London, and staying with them for extended periods of time. Ironically, Stas had a prior intersection with Peter back in May of 1969 when Stas was hunting in Africa (much to Lee's horror, Stas loved big-game shooting, especially in Kenya). Beard had been arrested for beating up an antelope poacher. He had stuffed a glove in the poacher's mouth and tied his hands and feet to two separate trees. Six months after Peter's arrest, it was Stas — along with the successful Kenyan entrepreneur Jack Block — who paid Beard's bail to get him released from a dank Nairobi prison. Eventually, Peter would be found guilty and sentenced to eighteen months — which he served — and a dozen lashes with a rhinoceros-hide whip.

At the end of '71, Audrey Cheaver and her husband, Thomas, visited Lee and Stas at Buckingham Place. They were surprised to see the Radziwills acting so chummy with Peter Beard. "Stas had made up his mind to accept what was going on with Peter," recalled Audrey Cheaver. "He and Lee had an understanding, an arrangement. That was the way it was back then, you were exceedingly polite in awkward situations. However, Stas later told me it annoyed him that he'd helped Peter out of a tight spot and now Peter was showing his gratitude by doing a walkout with his wife. However, Peter's position was that he'd ended up doing prison time anyway, so how much help had Stas really been?"

Stas hadn't been faithful to Lee for some time. After his first affair years earlier, he had tried to devote himself to his marriage. However, his rapport with Lee was never the same after the children were born. "If I am with other women, it makes her feel less guilty about wanting to be with other men," he told Thomas Cheaver. "By this time, our infidelities cancel each other out," he added.

"Stas still loved Lee, though, and said he didn't want to let her go," recalled Thomas Cheaver. However, with Peter now in the picture, it would seem that Lee was already gone. " 'He just gave me so many more interests and so much more curiosity about possibilities,' Lee would later explain."

"I have to re-create myself," Lee said at this time. "I still have a chance to change things. What I most fear is one day coming to the realization that it's too late. But that moment hasn't arrived yet. I still have a chance to start anew."

With hope continuing to spring eternal for Lee Radziwill, she now wanted a chance to right her life with Peter Beard. She wasn't thinking of marriage yet — after all, she was still married to Stas — but she was thinking of some sort of long-term future with him that might one day include taking him as a husband. Apparently, her mother didn't share her enthusiasm.

A story handed down from one generation of Auchinclosses to the next has it that Janet and Lee had harsh words about Peter while Janet was visiting Lee in London. The two were in a limousine being driven to a theater in Piccadilly Circus when Janet said she didn't approve of Peter. Not only would she never approve of Lee's affair with him because of how she still felt about the responsibility of marriage, but she'd also heard that Peter had no money. Therefore, the situation made no sense to her. Lee tried to explain. Hadn't they learned anything at all from the Onassis imbroglio? Hadn't they seen what resulted from placing a premium on a man's bank account rather than on his personal integrity? Were they just destined to repeat the same mistakes with the men in their lives? Peter didn't have money but, unlike Onassis, he was a decent man, Lee argued, and he treated her with respect. That had to count for something!

Janet didn't want to hear it. "Stop the car," she demanded of the chauffeur. He slammed on the brakes and pulled over to the side of the street. "Out," Janet told Lee. Lee looked at her mother with a confused expression. Then, at the top of her lungs, Janet shouted, "Get out of the car, Lee! Now! Get out! Get out!" Lee gathered her things as quickly as she possibly could and did as she was told. The car then pulled away, leaving the princess stranded in the middle of a busy Piccadilly Circus mob scene.

JANET ASKS JACKIE TO APPEAL TO ARI

In late November of 1971, Janet and Jackie had what would turn out to be a fateful lunch at the Colony Club in New York. During their meal, Janet gave her daughter the upsetting news that it looked like the family's storied homestead, Hammersmith Farm, would have to be sold. According to a later recollection, she said that she and Hugh felt dreadful about it. It was a shame, she said, especially given how hard Hugh had worked to keep the place going.

For many years, Hugh Auchincloss had managed to support a large family — Janet

521

and her daughters Jackie and Lee, as well as his offspring from his two previous marriages, Yusha, Nini, and Tommy and their own broods, along with his and Janet's children, Janet Jr. and Jamie — in a lifestyle they'd all enjoyed. However, by the end of '71, with his brokerage business in New York in serious trouble, it had become clear that serious cutbacks were needed across the board. Hugh's reversal of fortune was not particular to his own entitled family as much as a response to the country's economic recession. The Auchinclosses had been cutting back for years, going all the way back to when they were forced to sell Merrywood, and would have no choice but to continue to do so, like many others in the country, no matter their economic situations. "We just have to continue to adjust down" is how Hugh put it.

"Adjusting down" was not a concept Janet relished, but she was used to doing so these last few years. At sixty-two, though, she said she was "heartsick about what cutting back would do to Hammersmith," recalled her son, Jamie, "but, yet, letting it go was not something she and Daddy would ever have wanted." There seemed no way to keep the farm, though, especially given that they couldn't afford the property tax on it, which was almost $32,000 a year (about $190,000 today).

Of course, Jackie knew that Janet and Hugh had been struggling for years to keep Hammersmith going; the first time Janet had confided in her about it was back in '67 when Jackie told Janet about Jack Warnecke's surprising financial problems. Jackie had long felt that Hammersmith was just too much for her mother and stepfather to afford, but she knew how much they loved it and just hoped they'd be able to find ways to keep it. Janet did have an idea, though, as to how to solve the long-standing problem of Hammersmith Farm. What about Ari? Could he possibly help? After all, he was one of the wealthiest men in the world. Maybe he would like to purchase Hammersmith so that they could keep it in the family?

Though Janet and Ari didn't have much of a relationship, they did have what could at least be described as a cautious rapport. Earlier in the year, when Jackie had brought Ari to Hammersmith with the children for a week, Janet did her best to keep the peace. Ari joined her for her walks along the beach every morning, the two reminiscing about their fascinating lives. He was her son-in-law now, and just as she had accepted Michael Canfield, Stas Radziwill, John Kennedy, and Lewis Rutherfurd, she would try to do the same with Onassis. He was family, and Janet was all about family. Three months after that visit, Jackie and Ari returned for more quality time with Janet and Hugh, with whom Ari enjoyed playing chess and even sailing. So, it's not as if Janet had no foundation to ask Jackie if it was possible for Onassis to help save Hammersmith.

When Jackie said she would have to think about whether or not to ask Ari for help, Janet was surprised. She just assumed Jackie would immediately say yes, and couldn't understand her reluctance. After all, she and Lee were raised at Hammersmith. Moreover, Hugh had been born there. Even Jack Kennedy had loved the place. Did Jackie feel no sentimental connection to the property at all? In Jackie's mind, though, it was a *business* decision. She said she wasn't going to ask Ari for help until she had André Meyer look into the feasibility of purchasing the farm. Having reached a stalemate, mother and daughter left their luncheon displeased with each other.

Janet felt that the clock was ticking on Hammersmith and she was desperate to do something about it. At a Kennedy Center party for the Fivers, an exclusive dancing club in Washington, the first week of December, Janet — on Hugh's arm — may have looked gorgeous in a black velvet gown with pearl earrings, but she wasn't feeling well. While at the event, she told her good friend Oatsie Charles that her "blood pressure is sky high." Oatsie recalled, "She also said she was desolate about Hammersmith. She confided in me that the bills were mounting, as was the pressure."

It was more than just finances, though. Janet had a real emotional attachment to Hammersmith. Not only had it been her home for thirty years, it remained a strong connection to a time in her life that had meant a lot to her, the White House years. She would say that she could still sense Jack's presence in many of the rooms. "I can't let it go," she told Jamie. "It's a part of me. A part of us. We *must* find a way to keep it in the family."

Back when Jackie married Ari and Janet would rail against it to anyone who would listen, their mutual friend Bunny Mellon had told her, "Oh, dear Janet. No worries. You haven't lost a daughter. You've gained a gold mine!" Now, when Janet relayed that anecdote, she would end it with, "Apparently not!"

After Janet told Hugh about her difficult conversation with Jackie, he knew what he and Janet had to do. Jackie had been their last resort, and he had to admit that even if she'd agreed to do so, he wasn't sure he would take her or Ari's money. It's not known if Jackie talked to Andre Meyer or even Onassis about the possible investment at this time. All we know is that the Auchinclosses felt they had no choice but to put Hammersmith Farm on the market, listing it with Sotheby Parke-Bernet for $985,000 (which would be about $5.5 million in today's money).

ANDY WARHOL AND MONTAUK

One evening in the spring of 1972, Peter Beard introduced Lee to Andy Warhol by bringing the iconic artist to her apartment in Manhattan. Warhol was a real character. With his pale face, haunted look, and surprising silver wig, the filmmaker and commercial illustrator was known back in the 1960s as much for his hard-partying ways as for his artistic output. By the 1970s, though, he was living a more relaxed and sedate life, seriously intent on fine-tuning his work as a filmmaker, photographer, and pop art illustrator.

At the same time she met Andy, Lee also became acquainted with his business manager and close friend, Paul Morrissey. The two owned an expansive property in Montauk outside of East Hampton on Long Island, an enclave that had once been a fishing camp back in the 1920s. The twenty-acre estate's primary, five-bedroom home was perched high atop a cliff, among a cluster of smaller clapboard structures. When Lee first saw it, she fell in love with it. She then made the swift decision to officially leave Stas in London and move to the States with Peter and her children, both of whom were about to start their summer vacations from school. Stas was unhappy about all of it. Though he still wanted to work on the marriage, Lee was done with it. Because she'd not had her needs met by Stas for a long time, she was simply unable to resist the possibility of a life with the much more exciting Peter.

Within about a week's time, Lee and Peter were living together in Montauk, and there they would remain for the rest of the summer of '72, "one of my best summers of my entire life," she would recall. Every day was fun and energizing, with no arguments or high-stakes drama, which, for Lee, was a big relief after her recent years of tumult.

These days, Jackie could see a real change in Lee for the better. One night over steaks and wine, Lee, Peter, Andy, and Jackie started brainstorming ideas for Lee, who, as usual, was trying to find a new proposition for herself. What they came up with was the idea of Lee writing a book and producing a companion documentary about her and Jackie's summer days as little girls in East Hampton with Black Jack. Those had been wonderful times for the Bouvier sisters, even though Lee would have to admit they meant more to her than they did to Jackie. "Jackie was absolutely ready to marry and move on to a bigger screen and more scope, and excited about it and curious," Lee would recall of those early days she and her sister spent in East Hampton. "I was, I'd say, fearful, sorry to leave East Hampton because I loved my life there, and I suppose it was the happiest time and certainly the time I felt the safest."

As she considered her documentary and book idea, Lee thought she might utilize certain childhood memories to illustrate important life lessons, such as what she picked up from her father while struggling with horseback riding. Jackie excelled at riding, of course. Lee didn't. However, she had still been forced by Jack to ride an unruly pony called Dancestep. While trying to jump her first fence, she was thrown off the horse no fewer than three times. She remembered Jack forcing her to remount each time, telling her he would not let her quit until she got that stubborn horse over a fence. He warned that if the pony sensed her fear, it would always have its way with her. In the end, Lee never did get Dancestep to jump successfully. In fact, she would finish the day with a broken front tooth and the indentation of a hoof print on her stomach! However, as a grown woman, her father's words resonated with her. In looking back, she saw that hostile critics had sensed her fear of acting and making a fool of herself during her beleaguered time onstage in *The Philadelphia Story*. This, she now believed, was why the reviews had been so scathing. She knew that her acting could have used improvement, but she now felt that if she had presented herself with more self-confidence and assurance, it might have influenced the way people viewed her.

In both the book and the accompanying documentary, Lee thought she would interview Bouvier relatives about their own happy summers in East Hampton. She would also include archival photographs and film footage. Jackie thought all of this was a great idea and said that as soon as she got back to her apartment in Manhattan, she would start rummaging for pictures to help out.

In weeks to come, Lee and Peter put together a comprehensive proposal for the book and documentary, which they wanted to release simultaneously. They hoped the documentary might even air on network television. They soon hired filmmakers Albert and David Maysles. Unfortunately, it would be the introduction of the Maysleses into this vanity project that would, ultimately, end up completely ruining it for Lee.

GREY GARDENS

As Lee Radziwill and Peter Beard walked up to the enormous monstrosity of a mansion before them, Lee couldn't quite believe her eyes. The three-story aging structure was all but hidden by a wild tangle of vines, overgrown bushes, and hanging tree limbs. Its many windows were cracked and broken. Its front door seemed to be barely hanging from its hinges. There were obvious gaping holes in the roofing. In fact, the structure was so dilapidated it looked as if it should have been demolished years earlier. It was difficult to believe that, once upon a time, she and Jackie had spent many happy moments here at the East Hampton Grey Gardens estate of their Aunt Edie and their cousin Edie.

The senior Edith Bouvier Beale was Black Jack Bouvier's sister, making her Lee and Jackie's aunt. In 1917, "Big Edie," as she was known, married lawyer and stockbroker Phelan Beale. They had three children, a girl, Edith — "Little Edie" — and two sons, Phelan Jr. and Bouvier. In 1923, Phelan Sr. bought the enormous twenty-eight-room Grey Gardens mansion with its ocean view, in East Hampton. After a series of financial setbacks, Big Edie's life went into a downward spiral. Worried about her mother's state of mind, Little Edie, who had attended Miss Porter's School like Jackie and Lee, moved in with her in 1952. As the years passed, the two women became hermits, rarely venturing from the security of their home, hoarding their possessions and other junk. By 1972, the elder Edie, seventy-six, had resigned herself to a life that had never quite worked out. However, the younger Edie, fifty-four, harbored concerns that she could have had it better — she could have had it like Jackie and Lee, in fact — if only time had been kinder to her.

In the spring of 1972, the Beales' plight became the subject of great attention when the Suffolk County Board of Health raided their estate and reported its deplorable conditions. "My God, you should have seen the place!" Lee would say in 2013. "And *them*!" she exclaimed of her peculiar relatives. When she told Jackie about it, Jackie was certain she was exaggerating. So she went to see for herself. She was just as shocked as her sister. She then telephoned Ari in Greece to tell him about her relatives' plight. Ari agreed that something should be done about it. He volunteered to have new heating and plumbing systems installed at Grey Gardens as well as a new roof, and, later, to also have around a thousand bags of trash carted away from the home. It cost him about $32,000, a little less than $200,000 in today's money.

Because of her immersion in the documentary and book she was endeavoring to create, Lee was already in quite the sentimental mood. Now, after coming face-to-face with the Beales, she couldn't help but think that only chance and circumstance had separated her from the fate of her destitute relatives. "Our stupid little problems and silly disagreements make me feel so ashamed," she told Jackie that night at Hammersmith, which still

531

had not been sold. "How could we let such nonsense bother us? *Look at our lives,*" she exclaimed. As she motioned to their gorgeous surroundings, it was as if a strong feeling of bittersweet nostalgia had swept over her. "I love you, Jacks," she exclaimed. Jackie wasn't as moved by the Beales' dilemma as she was by Lee's emotional reaction to it. "I have to agree," she said. "We *are* fortunate, aren't we? And I love you, too, Lee."

Janet thought her girls were just being sentimental but, if it made them closer, so be it. She personally felt that the Beales had exactly the kind of life they wanted. She hadn't seen them in quite some time but actually had made the trek out to Grey Gardens before Lee and Jackie had thought to do so. She had realized that Jamie hadn't ever been to East Hampton and, as he recalled, "she wanted me to see it, to get to know it, and maybe understand a little more about the Bouvier history. So we went all about East Hampton and eventually ended up on the doorstep of Grey Gardens. It was quite an education. My mother told me that, many years earlier, Big Edie would show up at family functions and sing 'I Love You Truly' to her, completely embarrassing her but also touching her deeply. My mother didn't feel sorry for them, though. She knew that relatives had tried to help them and that they'd turned them down. They were happy in their world, Mummy felt. She certainly didn't feel that Big Edie should have to end up in an old folks' home." In fact, according to one account, Janet told Jackie, "When I get to be that age, please do not try to put me in a home, Jacqueline. Please promise me." Jackie made that promise.

Lee couldn't get the idea of helping the Beales out of her mind. In talking to Peter Beard about them, an idea came to her. What if they featured them in her documentary? Certainly, the Beales' plight was the flip side of the pristine and romantic story of the Bouvier sisters' entitled youth in East Hampton. The extreme contrast could make for interesting viewing. She thought that maybe Big Edie might even narrate it. The idea seemed viable enough for Lee to bring to her new producers. Of course, they wanted to meet the women right away. Lee made it possible.

Upon meeting them, the Maysleses found the Edies fascinating — more fascinating, in fact, than Jackie and Lee! Suddenly, they wanted to focus Lee's documentary exclusively on the Beales, to the total exclusion of the Bouvier sisters. Lee was ambivalent about this unexpected development. She'd been cultivating her own concept for months. Still, she was smart enough to at least give the Maysleses a chance. After all, they had a history of filmmaking — they were just coming off of the Rolling Stones' *Gimme Shelter.* Therefore, she allowed them to get the Beales on film.

"Absolutely not," said Lee after viewing the filmmakers' preliminary work. She found the new take on the Beales' story too cruel and "on the nose" and even suspected that the Maysleses had encouraged the women to exaggerate their behavior. Lee had a completely different vision. It had to do not only with her and her sister's time in East Hampton but with her relatives' places in society and how the public's response to their living conditions reflected the mores of upper-crust society. She wanted to produce something deeper and more meaningful than what might result by just taking a camera into the run-down home of two eccentric people in hopes that they might act in an outrageous manner. Therefore, she wanted to go back to her original idea; she refused to give the Maysleses permission to use the film, which she and Peter Beard had paid for.

Not surprisingly, the Maysleses just quit Lee's documentary and decided to make their own. After Onassis's renovations on Grey Gardens were complete, the brothers went back to the Edies and gave them $5,000 each, along with a promise of a percentage of potential profits. The Beales hoped that this opportunity might ensure not only that mother got to stay in her beloved home, but that daughter got to leave it for a possible career as a singer in New York. They agreed to the deal. The brothers then reshot the interviews with the Beales for their own program. When Albert Maysles was asked by the writer Dan Rattiner how Lee felt about the Maysles brothers stealing her idea, he answered, "There wasn't much she could do about it. The Beales willingly allowed us to make this film."

Suddenly, Lee found herself without her filmmakers and without her documentary. This was truly exasperating. How did *her* documentary about herself and her sister end up being *their* documentary about Big Edie and Little Edie? Of course, such creative and financial hurdles are par for the course in filmmaking. However, for Lee, this surprising occurrence was just more of the same: self-involved, uninspired people standing in her way, making it impossible for her to achieve her dreams. She could have continued with her own documentary, but now she had lost her enthusiasm. She'd work on her book instead.

JANET'S DISMAY OVER JACKIE

Janet Auchincloss was pacing back and forth in her living room at Hammersmith while talking on the telephone to Sherry Geyelin. She was upset. "How could she do this?" she

535

asked angrily, her eyes flashing. "I just do not understand that girl." She said that Jackie had somehow gotten Aristotle Onassis to take care of the Beales, relatives Jackie hadn't seen in years. Yet when Janet had asked her to appeal to Onassis to help save Hammersmith, she refused to do so, saying she wanted to first speak to Andre Meyer about it.

By late 1972, at the age of sixty-three, Janet was at her wits' end over what to do about Hammersmith Farm. Though the estate had been on the market for a year, it had still not sold. The bills continued to mount; the property was draining Hugh's coffers. Garrett Johnston, now of Thomson & McKinnon, Auchincloss, recalled meeting with Hugh about the problem. "It was hopeless," he said, "there was no way to save it. Since it hadn't sold, they were vacillating between lowering the price and taking it off the market. I told Hugh to just let it go. He said he would but Mrs. A. was still pushing to find a way to save it. If it were up to him, he said, he would have sold it two years earlier. He couldn't take the stress, he told me. However, his wife still didn't really want to sell it. 'It means more to her than it does to me,' he said. He said Mrs. A. felt that the historic relevancy of Hammersmith was such that it should be kept in the family. He was worried about her, that it was all too much for her — for both of them. 'Keeping all of those people at work is going to kill us both,' he told me. He said that Janet was not well, that she was having some health challenges, or emotional problems . . . he wasn't clear about it, only that she was not right."

These days, Janet did seem less focused. She had always been a detailed-oriented person with her notebooks and calendars, every moment of every day structured. By '72, she was more undisciplined. She was also more temperamental. Jamie recalled that she had a drawer in her bathroom "that was filled with prescription bottles. I stumbled upon it one day and was startled by it. I wondered why Mummy was taking all of these medications. She was a fairly high-strung person already, so I really had to wonder what these drugs were doing to her." The question was never answered. "To this day, I don't know if it was drug induced or not," he said, "but the thing with the Beales really did set her off."

For Janet, the question was a simple one: Why had Jackie asked Onassis to help save Grey Gardens when she would not ask him to help save Hammersmith? Of course, the truth was that Jackie hadn't asked Onassis for assistance at all, he'd volunteered it. "I'll bet she didn't do property research on Grey Gardens," Janet said, dismayed, "yet she wants to know all of Hugh's private business in relation to Hammersmith." In Janet's mind, Jackie had used her sacred relationship with Onassis to the advantage of the Beales, no questions asked. Why not do the same for the betterment of her own more immediate family? She said to one relative that she and Hugh had "poured our life's blood" into Hammersmith and that Jackie's lack of caring about it was impossible for her to reconcile. "This is what family is all about," she added, "helping one another. If that's not what we do, then what good are we to one another?"

After reconnecting with the Beales, Jackie actually began to forge a relationship with her aunt and cousin, the two Edies. She began to have late night telephone calls with them and wrote them long letters saying how glad she was to have them back in her life. It took her a little longer to appreciate what the Beales represented than it did Lee, but once she realized that her relatives were a link to an important past, she was not willing to let them go. She would maintain a relationship with both women, by telephone and correspondence, as well as the occasional visit. None of these developments made Janet feel any better about the situation, though. How Jackie could help the Beales and not "our own family" would remain a point of contention between mother and daughter for many years to come.

When Jackie brought the children to Hammersmith for Thanksgiving in November of

1972, Janet barely said two words to her. Jackie kept to herself, horseback riding with the kids, talking to Yusha, Tommy, Nini, their children who were also present, as well as to Hugh and Jamie, but not very much to her mother.

One night a few weeks later, shortly after the Beales made their deal with the Maysleses, Jackie was again visiting Janet at Hammersmith when she had a car take her into Manhattan, ostensibly so that she could spend the night at her own home. The next morning she returned to Hammersmith after a nearly four-hour drive. Of course, Jackie had a chauffeur, but, still, it was exhausting. She walked into the wood-paneled kitchen and found Janet having coffee. She greeted her cheerily. With an icy expression, Janet said, "Hello, dear. Did you spend the night with the Edies, your new favorite relatives?" A flicker of annoyance crossed Jackie's face.

On the warming shelf above the stove, Janet had arranged her expensive Minton china, which she'd had since before she married Hugh. Jackie grabbed one of the antique cups. She then sat down at the table and poured herself a cup of coffee. Reaching into her purse for her cigarette case, she took one out and lit it. She slipped it between her lips. However — according to one of the ever-present maids — before she could even inhale, Janet reached over, snatched the cigarette out of Jackie's mouth, and plopped it into her cup of coffee. Glaring at her mother, Jackie rose and calmly walked out of the kitchen.

Janet would never see the Grey Gardens documentary; she just wasn't interested in it. However, Jackie, Lee, and most of the immediate family shared the same feelings about it when they finally saw *Grey Gardens:* they found it completely unwatchable. It was difficult for them to accept that the lovely and sentimental documentary Lee had envisioned about her and Jackie's summers in East Hampton had somehow been transformed into such a tragic story about destitute relatives. Even with Onassis's generous renovations, the dilapidated Grey Gardens manse reeked of squalor on the screen. The entire project was a disappointment and embarrassment to Janet and her daughters, and they just hoped it would soon disappear without a trace. Instead, of course, it went on to become nothing short of iconic. In fact, it would ultimately be transformed into a Broadway musical (earning Christine Ebersol a Tony for her portrayal of Big Edie) and then an HBO movie (starring Jessica Lange and Drew Barrymore as Big and Little Edie).

"EVERY WAVE IS THE SAME. EVERY WAVE IS DIFFERENT."

Lee Radziwill was gravely disappointed by the failure of her documentary idea. To give her time to regroup, Truman Capote suggested she accompany him on the Rolling Stones' *Exile on Main Street* concert tour that summer of 1972. He was covering it for *Rolling Stone*. "And so he said, *'Honey,* you gotta' *come!'* " Lee explained to Sofia Coppola in an interview, imitating Truman. "I said, 'I would *adore* to!' " Once Lee decided to go, Peter Beard was hired to take photographs. Off they then went to join Mick Jagger and company on the road in June. It was a fun and exciting couple of weeks, a far cry from anything Lee had ever experienced; she slept on a tour bus in bunk beds. Always open to new experiences, she had the time of her life and was completely fascinated by the groupies that followed the Stones to every stop. Lee would say that she could see how people would find Mick Jagger sexy, "but I found him a little repulsive."

While Lee was on the road with the Stones, some noticed that she seemed to be drinking too much. Perhaps one of the reasons was because her relationship with Stas was more tense than ever before, especially now that she was openly with Peter Beard.

541

Once back from the Stones tour, Lee sent for her children in August and anticipated five good weeks with them at Montauk. Both seemed to have grown overnight. She really didn't want to send them back to England, where they were being schooled. She had no choice, though, come September. That's when she decided to "collect her life," as she put it, and finally tell Stas that she wanted to end her marriage. She was thirty-nine and determined to close the Princess Radziwill chapter of her life by the time she hit forty.

Stas made it easy on Lee by being the one to file. "She's been gallivanting around the world," he told the writer George Carpozi for an article in *Photoplay* called "Nobody Wants a Part-Time Marriage," adding, "I barely saw her last summer. My decision was the only solution to this irreconcilable situation. It makes me very sad but she left me with no alternatives."

In a sworn declaration to the court, Stas added of Lee, "There was no way I could talk sense into her. She was prepared to continue her abandonment of wifely obligations in the furtherance of whatever it was that she was pursuing."

"He still loved her and was upset," said Stas's son John Radziwill. "Lee wasn't the wicked stepmother, though. While she could never replace my mother, she was in our lives for a long time and we grew to love her. In

542

the end, my father was generous to her. He gave her everything she wanted and more. He said, 'I'm giving Lee *a lot*. I want her to be okay, and the kids, too.' " (It's worth noting that Janet and Stas remained friendly after his divorce from Lee; he often visited her at Hammersmith. One year, he even attended the annual "Coaching Day" at Stratford Hall in honor of Robert E. Lee, dressed in eighteenth-century garb and riding atop a coach with Janet in the parade!)

Now emotionally free of Stas, Lee continued to look forward to a future with Peter, even if some thought they were mismatched. He was bohemian, always disheveled and sloppily attired with his moccasins and fringe vests and casual wear, whereas she was, well, she was Lee — impeccably dressed, done up to the nines. They got along well, though, rarely argued, and had a strong bond between them. Lee felt they just needed time to clarify their relationship. She and Peter went back to the apartment Lee still had on Fifth Avenue, and began their future lives together.

As her divorce made its way through the courts — it wouldn't be finalized until 1974 — Lee felt, more than ever, an urgent need to stay busy, especially since the children were still being schooled in England. (While the Radziwills tried to work out custody, both Anthony and Tina would stay with their father rather than be uprooted from their schools.) Though the documentary was now out of the question, she still wanted to write the book about her and Jackie's summers in East Hampton. "I feel the way I have always felt," she told a reporter, "and that is that I am deserving of every opportunity to achieve my goals." To that end, Andy Warhol convinced her to pen about a thousand words on the subject for *Ladies' Home Journal.* The idea was to sell the story to the women's magazine as an "extract" from the book, which the editors would tout on its cover. Meanwhile, it was Truman's idea to throw a book launch party and invite the crème de la crème of the publishing world to it — publishers, editors, advertising people, publicists. Hopefully, these executives would meet Lee and be impressed with her. The next day, if all went as planned, her agent's phone wouldn't stop ringing with offers to publish her memoir. This was unconventional; these sorts of parties were usually held *after* a book was published, not before. However, for Lee, maybe an exception could be made.

The *Ladies' Home Journal* piece hit the stands at the end of December '72 with Lee's "book extract." Its headline touted Lee's new book *Opening Chapters,* promising "enchanting memories and photos of her early life with Jackie." (Jackie's name did not appear anywhere in the magazine article, only in some of the photo captions.) The feature's text was fairly oblique and would likely concern any editor hoping for complete candor. "Everything was so simple then," Lee wrote. "Complication, confusion, wounds, suffering hadn't entered our lives. That's why I like to recall those days. . . . . I still feel total freedom . . . in tune with the ocean and this part of the world [East Hampton], which is rapidly changing. Every wave is the same, every wave is different, it's a kind of infinity."

The party for Lee was held at the elegant Four Seasons hotel in New York. Excitement was in the air as she mingled with the publishing elite and Manhattan glitterati. Looking fetching in a black turtleneck sweater and matching slacks with a chain necklace and gold beaded belt, she talked about how much her book meant to her and said she was serious about writing it.

At one point, a huge commotion in a corner of the room caused everyone to dart over. It was Jackie. Unfortunately, as often happened in these kinds of situations, she captivated everyone to the point where, suddenly, Lee was no longer the focus of attention. Jackie seemed excited to be present and surrounded by influential people from the publishing world. At one point, she had so many executives around her, she couldn't even be seen in the pressing mob. She spent a great deal of time talking to Tom Guinzburg, publisher at Viking Press, as Lee watched with great curiosity. She had to wonder: How did Jackie do it? How was it that no matter where she was, Jackie was always able to bask in the glow of acclamation without ever feeling awkward or out of place? Lee had too many insecurities to be so completely comfortable all of the time. She usually pulled it off, but she had to actually *work* at it. However, Jackie never had to exert any energy at all; she was just . . . *Jackie.*

As hoped, in the weeks to follow the offers did come rolling in for Lee's memoir. Eventually, she signed a book deal with Delacorte Press for *Opening Chapters,* giving her an advance of $250,000, quite a hefty amount for a memoir in 1973 (about a million and a half in today's money). She wasn't the only one who would benefit from that party at the Four Seasons, though. Jackie had something up her sleeve, too — though Lee didn't know it yet.

"BRED FOR IT"

In January of 1973, death would once again instigate great change in Jacqueline Onassis's life when Aristotle's only son, his beloved Alexander, was killed in a crash while flying his own twin-engined Piaggo. Grief-stricken and angry at the world, Ari turned on Jackie, accusing her of having first cursed the Kennedy family with death and now his own.

However, much to the surprise of most people, Jackie seemed to love Onassis *more,* not less, after the tragedy. He had given her and her children a good life; she remained grateful. She wasn't going to hold against him horrible statements he'd made while deeply grieving his only son. She understood such despair firsthand and how it could twist a person's logic and emotions. She still wanted to be with him and made plans for the two of them to take a summer trip to America together and stay at Hammersmith.

Six months later, during a gala at the Newport home of Candy and Jimmy Van Alen on July 10, Janet told her society friends Eileen Slocum and Oatsie Charles that Jackie and Ari were coming to visit at Hammersmith at the end of the month. "We muddle through," Janet said, when speaking of her daughter and Onassis, "that's what families do." She said she was "getting along" with Onassis and that when he and her daughter were in residence at the farm, "I put them in the Castle, where I used sometimes to put Jackie and the President. Yes, I admit, it's strange," she told her friends, "but we have no choice but to just go on, don't we?" She also said that after Alexander's death, Jackie put a stop to the flying lessons that Caroline had been taking at Hanscom Field in Middlesex County, Massachusetts. Caroline had been learning to fly a Cessna two-seater.

"Jackie said, 'That's the end of that. Caroline is upset about it, but she'll get over it.' "

Jackie and Ari had a history at least five years in the making; special, private moments that were romantic and fun. "I'm just not giving up on him," she said after Alexander died. Maybe Janet said it best in July of '73 when Janet Jr., Lewis, and their kids came to visit Hammersmith for five weeks, a trip that would overlap with the Onassises'. In front of Janet and Lewis, Oatsie Charles asked Janet how Jackie was able to put up with Onassis. Janet thought it over and answered simply, "She's been bred for it, I guess." Janet Jr. seemed a little surprised by her mother's answer. She said she wouldn't put up with the kind of marriage her half sister had "for even one second." Janet Sr. smiled at her daughter and, patting her on the knee, said, "Well, good for you, dear." Then, giving Lewis a hard look, she added, "And well you shouldn't."

CHANGING WINDS AND SHIFTING TIDES

A year and a half flew by; it was now July 1974 and once again Jackie and Lee were aboard the *Christina,* this time sailing with Ari from Palm Beach to the Bahamas. Along for the ride were their friends Jay Mellon and

Karen Gunderson Lerner. They were also with their children, John and Caroline and Tina and Anthony. Of course, in addition there were many other friends and at least fifty ship employees, many of them servants at the beck and call of Onassis's guests.

Unfortunately, Lee's personal life was in a bit of a shambles as the *Christina* pulled away from its dock in Palm Beach. Just when she had felt herself completely committing to him, Lee found Peter Beard in bed with another woman. She had hoped he had more personal integrity, and she had certainly argued his merits to her mother. As it happened, Peter left her for a model named Barbara Allen Kwiatkowska. "[Lee] was crazy about him and felt that I had taken him away from her," Barbara would say. "To be fair, she was right. I did. But their personalities were just so different. It was as if they were from two different worlds, and I think they had even less in common with the passing of time."

"It was her breakup with Peter Beard that really shook her to the rafters," Truman Capote once observed of Lee. "That was the beginning of this period of hers of feeling totally undone . . . she was really devastated by it."

A proud woman, Lee didn't want others to know the details of why the relationship ended, especially Janet. After she told one family member about it, she said, "This secret dies here. I do not want my mother to know a thing about it." On this cruise, though, Lee managed to maintain her sense of humor about things. When Jay Mellon asked how she was doing, she was overheard saying: "Well, let's see now. My sister married my rich ex-lover. My marriage to a prince just ended in divorce. I had an affair with a man who sleeps in a tent and doesn't have a pot to piss in. And I learned recently that *he's* been cheating on me with a pinup model. But all things considered, I'm doing quite well, thank you for asking."*

While Lee was going through her breakup with Peter, she was still dealing with one of the most upsetting consequences of her divorce from Stas: Anthony and Tina were separated from each other. The divorcing couple simply could not come to terms about custody of their children. Therefore, they decided that Stas would keep Anthony, fifteen, who was attending the prestigious Milford Academy boarding school in England, while Tina, fourteen, would move to America to be with Lee. It was a terrible idea and everyone in the Radziwills' circle knew

* Peter Beard would continue his work as a renowned wildlife photographer. In years to come, he and Lee would mend their relationship. Today they remain the best of friends.

it, but it seemed the best solution at the time; one child for each parent. Of course, the siblings would be miserable without each other, each subsequently blaming their parents for breaking up their home.

As the Bouvier sisters sailed, they seemed to have more in common than they'd had in some time, especially given that Jackie's marriage to Ari continued to unravel. Jackie confided in Lee that Ari had recently told her he wanted a divorce. She refused to grant it, she said, because she felt he now needed her more than ever. He had recently been diagnosed with myasthenia gravis, a debilitating nerve disease. Lee had to admire Jackie's loyalty to Ari. Many years later, in 1999, Karen Lerner — who would soon divorce Alan Jay Lerner, the lyricist of the Broadway show *Camelot* — would say of this particular time, "I felt the sisters were close, that they were bound by tradition, family, and blood. It's never easy to understand the complexities of sisterhood . . . the changing winds and shifting tides."

Lee's intended memoir greatly contributed to the sisters' renewed closeness. Jackie was genuinely excited to see her sister so heavily invested in a project in which they both believed. Their summers in East Hampton together *had* been a special time for them, and they now spent hours remembering those moments while Lee jotted frantically on a yellow notepad. They even made plans to raid Janet's attic once they got back to the States to see what they might discover there in terms of photographs or letters that would assist Lee in her project.

"Each random memory was special to the Bouvier sisters. For instance, they recalled the time they, as little girls, won a school costume party dressed as farmers with floppy hats and matching striped shirts," recalled Karen Lerner. "Lee was missing her front tooth, she recalled. They'd won a silver cup that day, which they would treasure for years, that is until Jackie lost it. They reminisced about Central Park in the winter, and how much they loved to sled down what, as kids, seemed like slopes as steep as any at Mammoth. However, it was always the summers they loved most, those months away from the city with Black Jack. No matter how angry Janet was at Jack, she always allowed the girls to have their time with him."

Now, with Jackie about to turn forty-five and Lee forty-one, the sisters had to wonder how they'd ever let anything come between them. After a long night of drinking margaritas and reminiscing, Jackie seemed to recognize as much when she became surprisingly candid in front of witnesses. "I haven't been a good sister to you, have I?" she asked Lee as she put her head on her shoulder.

In some ways, Lee probably would have

agreed with Jackie's assessment of their relationship. However, she also saw the great value Jackie had in her life. For instance, Jackie was a wonderful aunt to her children, always taking care of them whenever Lee was out of sorts or distracted with one of her projects. Jackie was known in the family as being a great and protective mother, whereas Lee would have to admit to always being challenged in that respect. Of course, there would be areas Jackie could improve upon when it came to her relationship with Lee — she could certainly be more open and more trusting, for instance — but to say that she was not a good sister? Lee would never go that far. Despite their differences and disagreements, they had too much shared history, too much affection, a special, magical kind of intimacy that only they, as sisters, could fathom. "I know we can *both* do better," she told Jackie. It was a magnanimous answer, and one Jackie obviously appreciated because it brought tears to her eyes.

It had been a memorable time on the *Christina* for Jackie and Lee. At its conclusion, when the yacht docked back in Palm Beach, Lee embraced Jackie good-bye, saying she was looking forward to seeing her at Hammersmith Farm for their "treasure hunt" — and she meant it, too. Just before they parted company, though, Jackie looked at her sister with an impish expression. She tapped her on the shoulder. *"You're it, Lee,"* she said as she raced off. *"Oh, no, I'm not!"* Lee exclaimed as she ran after her sister. Then, as everyone on board watched and laughed, the two raced all over the deck of the *Christina,* kids once more.

RAIDING JANET'S ATTIC

In September of 1974, Janet was delighted to find that both Jackie and Lee were available to attend a special dinner she was planning to host at Hammersmith Farm for the World Affairs Council, a nonprofit organization to which she belonged. Janet had recruited an international relations expert to speak about foreign policies after the meal. She and Hugh would be at opposite ends of the table while Jackie, Lee, Jamie, Yusha, Nini, and Tommy and a host of others would be seated in the middle on both sides, including Jackie's children, Caroline and John, and Lee's daughter, Tina. (Anthony had just left for the UK a day earlier.) One of the other guests was Linda Murray and her mother, Jane, who worked with Janet on the World Affairs Council. She recalled, "My mother met Mrs. A. in 1972 at an Affairs Council summit; I was about eighteen. Mom adored her, said she was smart, funny, and blunt." Also present were Sherry Geyelin and her husband, Philip, who was the editorial page editor of

The Washington Post.

The Bouvier sisters actually had an ulterior motive for visiting Hammersmith at this time. They wanted to explore Janet's attic for mementos — the "treasure hunt" they had planned while on the *Christina*. To that end, as soon as they arrived at the farm, they ran up to the cramped space above the third floor of the Big House. There they found dozens of cobweb-covered boxes. When they opened them, much to their delight, they discovered hundreds of photographs that had been saved by Janet, as well as what seemed like every card and letter ever sent to her by her children. Jackie and Lee hadn't recognized just how sentimental Janet was about the past. In fact, when Lee tried to interview her for her book, she became prickly, not wanting to talk about Jack Bouvier, for instance. She said that what was done was done, the past was in the past, and there was no point in revisiting it.

Perched on dusty trunks in the attic, Jackie and Lee marveled at what they found there, including lengthy letters between Janet and her father, "Grampy Lee." As the sisters read them, they realized that almost every letter was unkind. Jim T. Lee criticized Janet in nearly all of the missives, calling her "stupid" and "lazy" and predicting that she would never come to any good in her life. He hated the man she loved, Jack Bouvier, and gave

555

chapter and verse as to why Janet was a fool to have ever married him. Reading this correspondence made them feel so bad for their mother. They had no idea how vicious Grampy Lee had been to her. She'd obviously never been good enough in his eyes, which may have reminded Lee of her relationship to Janet.

Jackie and Lee also found boxes of letters from their father, Jack, to Janet, long love letters in which Black Jack proclaimed his undying devotion to her. These letters were full of pain and anguish as he apologized for having affairs and for not being as devoted to her as he should have been. Again, Jackie and Lee were surprised. They couldn't believe they knew so little about Janet's hurt and sorrow. In one box, they found an old dog-eared photograph from 1934 of Jack, Janet, and a woman they didn't know (identified as "Virginia Kernochan" in pencil on the back of the picture). All three were sitting side by side on a split-rail fence at New York's Tuxedo Park Riding Academy. Jack was holding Virginia's hand while Janet was looking in the opposite direction. They had seen the photo before and often wondered about it.

Of course, none of the sisters' discoveries and ruminations about them had a thing to do with their summers in East Hampton — the subject of Lee's book. However, they came to view their mother in a new and more sympathetic light and realized they had a lot more in common with her than they'd thought. After all, how many times had Onassis been unkind to both of them over the years — and how many times had they gone back for more? However, when it came to Black Jack, it would always be difficult for them to take a completely pejorative view of him. The sisters agreed that his absence had created a void in their lives that would never be filled. Jackie didn't want to know anything more about him from these indicting letters; it was as if she couldn't bear it. She told Lee to take all of the correspondence, and to never show it to her again.

By the time the two women emerged from the attic, they had at least a dozen boxes of mementos. Lee said she would have a courier service pick them up in the morning and have them delivered to her apartment in New York. While Janet claimed to not be interested in the past, her reaction when she saw Lee's stash belied a different point of view. "I *need* that stuff," she said, alarmed. "You can't take it, Lee." She told her to put it all back just where she had found it. However, Philip Geyelin understood the importance of such research and told Janet, "Let her have it. It's history, Janet. *Family* history." When Lee then promised she would have it returned in less than two weeks' time, Janet reluctantly agreed to allow her to take the mementos, saying, "I

557

know I'll regret this. I can see it coming."

After all was settled about Lee's bounty, it was time for dinner. There were around twenty people present, some eating in the dining room at two tables — one oblong mahogany table in the middle of the expansive room on a plush gold carpet and under a large crystal chandelier, and another smaller rounded table closer to the deep bay window in what was considered a breakfast alcove. During dinner, Lee spoke about the memoir she was writing, and also about a television pilot she'd recently filmed — a series of interviews with Rudolf Nureyev; John Kenneth Galbraith, the economist; Halston, the designer; Gloria Steinem, the feminist journalist; Peter Benchley, the author of *Jaws;* and Dr. Robert Coles, the Harvard psychiatrist.

"My Lee is always telling me she wants to do more with her life," Janet told some of the guests over after-dinner drinks out on the porch. Glancing over her shoulder to make sure Lee wasn't in earshot, Janet then told Linda Murray's mother, Jane, "Lee has always somehow seen her destiny as being of a greater purpose than the rest of us."

At that moment, Lee happened to walk out onto the flowered terrace. She'd heard what Janet said and looked upset. "If you have something to say, Mummy," she told Janet, "just say it." At that, Janet threw both hands in the air and said, "In front of company, Lee? *Really?* I don't *think* so! The President has just been impeached," she added, all of a sudden referring to Richard Nixon, "and there are real problems facing our country, so stop being so self-involved." She then got up and walked away from her.

Lee stared at Janet in disbelief. Finally, she said to no one in particular, "I'm just trying to get through this day without *losing my fucking mind!*" She then donned a wool jacket and began to descend the steps from the porch to the front yard.

"At that moment, I saw Jackie meandering toward the house from the shore," recalled Linda Murray. "Apparently, she'd gone for a long walk on the beach. Quickly sizing things up, she seemed to sense Lee's angst. She stopped and, with a smile, beckoned for her sister. Once they were together, Jackie put her arm around Lee's shoulders. The two sisters then walked back down to the shore, Lee's head on Jackie's shoulder. It was so sweet. They stopped and stared at the majestic view of Jamestown and the harbor, as if they'd never seen it before. Then they sat out on one of the largest of a cluster of rocks and chatted until the sun began to set."

SOMETHING WRONG
WITH JANET?

March 15, 1975.

Jackie was in New York when she got the call. She was actually packing to return to Paris, where Ari had been convalescing due to complications of the myasthenia gravis from which he'd been suffering.

Since Ari had been hospitalized for some time, Jackie hadn't been able to make up her mind as to whether to stay in Paris to be with him or be with her children, who were in school in Manhattan. If not for his daughter, Christina, she probably would have stayed by her husband's side. However, Christina had made her life a living hell, accusing Jackie of not only being after Onassis's fortune but also of being unfaithful to him, which wasn't true. Having had her fill of Christina, Jackie said she needed to clear her head and return to the States, but with the intention of going back to Europe in about a week. However, then Ari took a sudden turn for the worse. Now Artemis sadly informed Jackie that he had died.

A distraught Jackie telephoned Janet to ask her to accompany her to Greece for the funeral. Of course, Janet was sorry Onassis was gone — not exactly devastated, but . . . sorry. However, she didn't want to pack up and go to Greece on the spur of the moment, as she had when Jackie got married. She said no, she wasn't going. Her mind was made up about it. Shortly after, Lee telephoned Janet, who told her that she was in the middle of packing to go to Greece. However, Lee said she had just spoken to Jackie, who'd said Janet had refused to go. Janet became irate. "*Of course* I'm going," she said.

A few weeks earlier, when Janet arranged a Mother-Daughter Tea with Jackie and Lee in New York City and didn't show up for it, the sisters knew for sure something was wrong. For Janet to forget such an important date on her calendar was completely unusual. As was often the case, Janet was staying with her friend Mary Whitehouse, two floors below Jackie at 1040 Fifth Avenue. When the sisters went there to make sure she was okay, she insisted that it was *they*, not her, who had gotten the date wrong.

"We were beginning to believe that something neurological was going on with Mummy," Jamie Auchincloss recalled. "Because they didn't have the tests they have today, nothing would come back pointing to anything specific. The doctors just said, 'It's probably just old age.' I remembered Mummy's drawer of mysterious prescription bottles and wondered if they were somehow responsible. She was becoming so forgetful."

In the end, Janet did meet Jackie for the

funeral; she and Marta Sgubin (Jackie's maid) brought Caroline and John with them to Greece for the service.

Lee didn't attend the service. In the past, it's been reported that the reason was that Jackie had specifically asked her not to go lest the public be reminded of Lee's past relationship with him. This isn't true. It was Lee's decision. Likely, her entire life would have been altered had she made different choices about Onassis along the way, as would have Jackie's. She just felt it was time to let it all go. His death was freedom for her; no longer would she need to wonder "What if?" Or . . . at least that was her hope at the time.

The funeral was difficult, of course, made even more so by virtue of the acrimony that existed between Jackie and Christina. Janet was displeased by the way her daughter was treated, conscious of the fact that so many of Onassis's friends seemed to somehow blame his widow for his death. Jackie had cursed the Kennedys, they said — echoing Ari's assertion after Alexander was killed — and now she had also done the same to the Onassises. Few seemed to understand that Jackie had always appreciated Ari's having rescued her and her children during the darkest time of their lives. In her own way, she did love him, and she had said that she knew in her heart that he felt the same about her.

The settling of the estate would, not surprisingly, also be trying for Jackie, especially when it was learned that complex Greek laws could influence how much a spouse might inherit, no matter a will's stipulation. Eventually, after a great deal of legal wrangling with Christina, Jackie agreed to a settlement of $25.5 million from Onassis's estate, $6 million of which would go to estate taxes and $500,000 for her attorneys, leaving her with $19 million. (Christina said she would gladly give Jackie the money "just to never have to lay eyes on you again.") Jackie would also receive $150,000 a year for the rest of her life. Her children would each receive $50,000 a year until they turned twenty-one. At that time, $100,000 a year would be added to Jackie's annuity. In return, Jackie gave up her interest in Skorpios and the *Christina*, as well as all of Onassis's homes.

To this day, most people believe that Jackie was left a wealthy woman when Aristotle Onassis died. However, when one considers that the shipping magnate was worth at least $500 million at the time of his death, $19 million and an eventual maximum of $250,000 annually for his widow doesn't seem like a large settlement. It would be the investments Jackie would make with that money, however, that ended up making her an extremely rich woman.

Unfortunately, Lee would not benefit in any

financial way from her tumultuous past with Ari. He had made no provision whatsoever for her in his will.

CRUSHING BLOWS

By the spring of '75, Lee Radziwill had been working on her memoir, *Opening Chapters,* for more than two years. It was due to be delivered to Delacorte in June; Lee eagerly sent off the manuscript and waited for a response. However, the letter she received from her editor, Eleanor Friede, indicated that there were serious problems with the writing. When Lee then later met with the publisher, it was suggested that she hire a ghostwriter. Lee balked. She wanted to write her own book, otherwise she felt it was duplicitous to call it a "memoir." When asked if she might consider adding personal stories about the Kennedys, she refused that request, too, saying she would never betray her sister's confidence.

Lee didn't want to write about the Kennedys because it wasn't her story to tell. It frustrated her that the angle that most interested her publisher was one that directly tied her to her sister. She didn't think it was fair, and it wasn't how she wanted to distinguish herself. In other words, she wasn't about to ride on her sister's coattails up the *New York Times* bestseller list.

In the end, Delacorte decided to cancel Lee's contract — another blow for Lee, but not the last one she'd suffer at this time. In the fall, CBS decided not to move forward with the pilot *Conversations with Lee Radziwill*. It wasn't because of Lee as much as it was simply because the network couldn't seem to find a slot for the show. Still, it felt to Lee as if nothing ever seemed to go her way!

At least Lee's relationship with Jackie seemed to be better. However, just when it seemed as if they had peace between them, Jackie made a decision that once again caused turmoil.

After Ari died, Jackie wanted to enter the workplace and, typically, figured out exactly what to do and then just did it. Unlike Lee, she didn't have numerous false starts and disappointments. In September of '75, she glided right into a job as an editor at the publishing house Viking Press, in New York, hired by Tom Guinzburg. Though she really had no skills as a book editor, she'd always had a great love of literature and was, obviously, well read. She'd also always enjoyed talking to authors and had a great appreciation for their craft. Moreover, she had undeniable clout as one of the most famous women in America. Viking really couldn't resist the idea of hiring her. "It was a good fit," recalled Tom Guinzburg. "Jackie was willing to do whatever it took to find complete fulfillment as a book editor."

The problem was that Jackie chose not to tell Lee about her new vocation. She felt that because Lee had been so upset by her failed book deal, this news of Jackie's job in publishing would hit too close to home. When Lee found out through mutual friends, she couldn't help but be disappointed and hurt.

Jackie said that she'd lived much of her life through her husbands' experiences and that, at the age of forty-five, the time had finally come for her to distinguish herself as her own woman. In other words, she had her own personal goals and desires that had nothing at all to do with upsetting her sister or causing her grief. In fact, Jackie had started seeing a psychoanalyst, Dr. Marianne Kris, who, strangely enough, considering JFK's much storied history with Marilyn Monroe, had once been Marilyn's therapist. In their sessions, according to what Jackie would tell her relatives, Kris delved deeply into Jackie's PTSD and helped her to understand that most of her decisions since 1963, as well as her behavior and interactions with loved ones, had been informed by trauma. "She told me, 'I've lived in a dark place for such a long time, I want out of it now,' " said one of the editors who worked with her at Viking. In other words, Jackie was on her own journey of self-discovery, just as Lee had been on one for years.

Yet no matter how hard Lee tried, it was always an uphill battle for her. Now she saw Jackie, who'd never worked after her job at the *Washington Times-Herald* almost twenty-five years earlier, hired right on the spot and then lauded as a huge success before she even started the job.

"Jackie O is just so amazing," opined a writer for *People* magazine. "She really *can* do it all! How in the world does she do it?" For Lee, this kind of commentary was understandably exasperating. Her longtime friend Chauncey Parker put it this way: "Jackie was still the star and everything always seemed to go so well for her. Lee was absolutely swamped by this."

LEE RADZIWILL, INC.

Now that Jacqueline Onassis seemed to have found her rightful place as a member of the workforce, what would be next for Lee Radziwill? After considering her options for a couple of months, she was clear about one thing: she wasn't going to give up until she found what she wanted. Despite recent disappointments, in some ways she remained a model of diligence and determination. She still felt the need to do something constructive to satisfy an urge not only to be creative but also to be taken seriously. However, one

567

of the great paradoxes of Lee's life was that, even given her ambition, whenever she faced disappointment, she would move on quickly from it. She would be too disheartened to continue trying. In the same way she quit acting after having received bad reviews, or didn't shop her documentary after having been betrayed by the Maysles brothers, she decided not to take her rejected manuscript to another publisher. Some in her life found it maddening that Lee would always seek to cut ties with any idea that wasn't immediately successful for her. They felt she might have been better served sticking to just one thing . . . and make that thing work. It was fine with Lee that others had such opinions. They didn't really matter to her. The way she saw it, she was adventurous and a risk taker, a woman never satisfied with the status quo, always eager for the next adventure, "and I just don't see anything wrong with that," she would say.

At about the same time that Lee was contemplating her professional future, she became involved in a new relationship with a noted New York attorney named Peter Tufo, whom she had met at a luncheon in Southampton in the fall of 1975. Tufo, who was thirty-seven at the time and, at five feet nine, considered by most to be more average-looking than dashing, was a Yale graduate. Lee was at his side in the fall when he was sworn in at City Hall as the pro bono chairman of the Board of Correction, the agency that runs the New York penal system.

Tufo was like Peter Beard in the sense that he didn't have great wealth, though he was certainly more financially secure. Lee again broke the mold set by her mother and sister of partnering up only for security. "Lee continued to like men who were actively and intellectually engaged, with an artistic bent," said Gustavo Paredes, Provi's son. "It still wasn't about money for her as much as it was about the way a man thought, his vision of things. She and my mother had many conversations about the men in her life, and my mother said that while Lee wanted stability she still, by the mid-seventies, was intent on finding it in her work, not in her men. This is something my mom felt people didn't know about Lee."

When Lee polled her friends about what they thought was right for her, a career as a professional interior designer often seemed to come up. Of course, Lee had always had a flair for design. She was widely known as a stylish woman, considered by many to be a tastemaker. She certainly had the networking skills to help make a design enterprise a great success. Lee also realized that she needed to be less reliant on other people to do right by her; she needed to make her own way. It was with this goal in mind that she started her own design firm. Rather than jump in without forethought, she wanted to take her time and strategize the best way into the business. She also decided not to tell many people outside of her close circle about it. "I have found that not everyone can be supportive of your dreams," she explained, "and that kind of negative thinking can influence you in ways you're not even aware of. It's best to keep your ambitions to yourself."

"Well, I guess it had to happen," Janet Auchincloss told Oatsie Charles one day at Hammersmith as they sat on the porch and talked things over. "Lee Radziwill, Inc., eh?" Janet was reading aloud a newspaper article about her daughter's latest venture. She noted that though Lee had always thought she was too hard on her, she'd just been worried about her. "She's so desperate to be someone she's not," Janet told Oatsie, "whereas Jacqueline is so desperate *not* to be someone she is." It was an astute observation on Janet's part, one that perfectly encapsulated the lifelong dilemma of both of her daughters.

Oatsie said that maybe it was a good idea that Lee would no longer be at the mercy of producers, editors, or others controlling her fate. Janet had to agree. "She has worked hard and no one has ever given her one goddamn thing," she said of Lee. "She has had to fight for every crumb, hasn't she?" Janet also noted that, in her opinion, Jackie's new job at Viking had somehow been influenced by Lee having made the first connections with publishers in New York, thereby introducing the literary world to the Bouvier sisters. Janet now took the view that Jackie had only encouraged Lee in her publishing venture so that she herself could scheme her way into that world. After all, Lee was the first one in publishing, not Jackie, Janet proffered, "and then Jacqueline just swooped right in as if she were made for it. Typical Jacqueline."

One of Lee's first commissions was to design a suite for the Americana Hotel chain's resort in Bal Harbour, Florida. She would also be hired to design the fiftieth-floor presidential penthouse suite of the Americana hotel in Manhattan. With these jobs in hand, her mind was made up about "Lee Radziwill, Inc." It was now in full swing. As soon as she made the official announcement in mid-February, she won another commission, a model room for Lord & Taylor, the Manhattan department store. When that model was unveiled on March 2, with its soft peach and green color scheme, rattan furniture, and straw rugs, the press showed up in droves for Lee's official debut as an interior designer.

"It's interesting that she's come full circle," Jackie said of her sister after the unveiling of the Lord & Taylor room. "Do you remember when she did Yusha's apartment in New York?" she asked Janet. They had gone to see Lee's unveiling with relatives. Janet, who was acting particularly chilly toward Jackie these days, said she had no memory whatsoever of Lee ever having remodeled Yusha's apartment. In fact, she insisted that it had never happened. "Of course it did," Jackie said, according to a witness to the conversation.

It was back when Lee was seventeen and Yusha was twenty-three. Yusha wanted something more modern than what he was used to at Merrywood and Hammersmith. He would recall, "The job Lee did was magnificent. She found pieces that were contemporary and did the apartment in blacks, whites, and splashes of red and purple. When it was finished, we invited my mother and father and Jackie over to dinner to see it." According to Yusha, Janet walked into the apartment, took a perplexed look around, said, "Oh dear, dear, dear," and that was about it. Lee asked Janet if she liked the modern décor, and Janet just said it was "certainly interesting." Jackie thought it was "just marvelous," though, took Lee by the arm, and asked her to show her around. The two sisters then walked about the apartment with Lee explaining why she had selected certain pieces and how she had decided on their placement. Later, at dinner at Le Pavillon, Janet kept changing the subject whenever anyone would mention Lee's work. Now, all these many years later, Janet said that none of this had ever happened. She became belligerent about it, too, according to the witness. "I said it didn't happen, Jacqueline," she insisted, her face darkening, "and I won't hear another word about it!"

Jackie was concerned. This kind of lapse in Janet's memory had been happening far too often.

"THE PRINCE IS GONE"

June 27, 1976.

"I'm sorry, but the princess is not available," Jamie Auchincloss was telling someone on the telephone. He always got a kick out of referring to his sister Lee as "the princess."

The entire family was in residence for the Bicentennial Celebration of 1976 in Newport. For the first time in history, so-called Tall Ships — which, as denoted by name, were large sailing ships with tall, majestic masts — would soon gather in Newport from all over the world to sail up Narragansett Bay. It was to be a July Fourth parade of international vessels from Argentina, Russia, Spain, England, and other countries. Thousands of people were expected to converge on Newport's shorelines to watch. Happily, the Auchinclosses had front-row seats. Nearly everyone came to the farm for the occasion, including Jackie and Lee and three of their children — Caroline, John, and Tina (Anthony was in London) — as well as Yusha, Tommy, and Nini and their broods, and even Janet Jr. and her husband, in from Hong Kong. Though Hugh was confined to a wheelchair because of his worsening emphysema, he, too, was in good spirits. Janet flitted around gaily, making certain that everyone was comfortable. That night, everyone prepared to attend a ball at The Breakers, the great Italian Renaissance–style mansion owned by the Vanderbilt family. It was to be the social event of the season.

"May I take a message for the princess?" Jamie asked the caller. Then, after a pause: "Oh, no. Not Stas!" He recalled, "Unfortunately, I was the one who had to tell Lee that Stas had suffered a heart attack in London, and had died."

Though many people questioned the way Lee and Stas sometimes treated each other, the divorce from Stas had actually been hard on Lee. He had been a part of her life for fourteen years; they had two children together. Afterward, she tried to continue a relationship with him. At first, he was unwilling to do so because of Peter Beard. However, he softened when, two years after the divorce, he also found happiness with a new love, Christine Weckert, just twenty-five. Apparently, Stas had proposed marriage to Christine only hours before he died. He was sixty-two.

Immediately after hearing the news, Lee and Jackie rushed off to England, along with John, Caroline, and Tina. "Anthony met them at the Ritz Hotel in London, where they all stayed," recalled Jamie Auchincloss. "Mummy didn't go because Daddy was too sick to travel. I know she went to church the next day and prayed for Stas, whom she had grown to love dearly. Jackie had also loved Stas like a brother; she was just as distraught as Lee."

The funeral took place in a church Stas had had built and dedicated to his mother, St. Anne's Church at Fawley Court near Henley-on-Thames, England. "The prince is gone," Lee tearfully told one of Stas's children from a previous marriage at the funeral. She was completely bereft. "We built a real life," she said. "There were ups and downs, but at least we were together. In many ways, Stas was my one sane relationship. I will always love him."

MAURICE TEMPELSMAN TRIES TO HELP

On a bright, sunny day in August of 1976, Jackie and Lee sat in the New York office of financier and diamond merchant Maurice Tempelsman. Jackie's attorney, Alexander

Forger, and two of Tempelsman's associates joined them for a meeting around a long mahogany conference table. The beige office was designed with classic antique furniture. Hundreds of books about international law and finance heavily lined two expansive walls, all alphabetically arranged on shelves custom-made in East Indian rosewood. Framed world political maps decorated the other walls. There were no windows; the room was like a dark and intimate study, with Maurice's desk in a corner. Maurice — about five-eight, balding, and wearing a tan double-breasted suit that seemed a little too big even for his potbellied frame — had a stack of documents before him. Thumbing through them, he shook his head in despair. As he sucked on a Dunhill cigar, he let out a plume of smoke and said, almost under his breath, "No money here. Not a dime."

"But how is that even possible?" Jackie asked. "Stas had so many holdings. Didn't he, Lee?"

"Well, things were tough" was all Lee had to say.

Stas had, for years, augmented his family's wealth from proceeds generated by a small private real-estate-developing firm he owned with a close friend, Felix Donovan Fenston. His and Lee's lifestyle remained fairly extravagant, with three homes — two in England and one in Manhattan — each of which was well staffed with butlers, cooks, maids, and all sorts of other people pulling a paycheck. At that time, money was never a problem for them; Lee was used to living well and Stas continued to make it possible for her to do so.

However, after Felix Fenstone died of a heart attack in 1970, things began to change. Stas was an aristocrat used to spending money, not making it. Fenstone had been the brains behind his and Stas's business whereas Stas was more or less a figurehead. People wanted to meet him not only because of his personal royal history but also because of his connection to the Kennedys. He could close a deal. However, he didn't know how to orchestrate one or how to compete for business. Therefore, his and Fenstone's small company was all but ruined within a year of Fenstone's death. There was no way Stas could keep up with all of his and Lee's spending. The pressure of such a demanding lifestyle weighed on him heavily.

After Stas's death, Lee was upset to learn that he had died broke. Jackie was disappointed as well. She actually couldn't believe it was true, which is why she wanted Maurice to review the paperwork. Maurice had joined Jackie in England for Stas's funeral, remaining at her side throughout the ordeal. He'd met the prince a few times in passing and always thought of him as a good fellow.

Maurice Tempelsman, a wealthy man who made his money in investments, especially diamonds, had been a friend of Jackie's and JFK's since the late 1950s, and he was the man she turned to immediately after Ari died. By the early seventies, theirs had become a romantic relationship, but certainly not one either wished to trumpet. Maurice was married with three grown children, but his wife, Lilly, refused to grant him a divorce; both were Orthodox Jews. When Jackie asked him to invest the millions she'd received from Onassis, he did a stunning job of increasing her capital. Because of his wise decisions and guidance, the future looked pretty rosy for her.

Maurice was a kind person who treated Jackie well. Unlike Ari, he was easygoing and affable, not a hothead. He would gladly acquiesce to Jackie's will and wouldn't have dreamed of being combative with her. In many ways, he was exactly the kind of man Jackie deserved at this time in her life. He didn't cheat on her, had money, was solicitous to her children, and shared the same interests in art, history, music, literature, and theater. She was completely happy, perhaps for the first time. She was also determined not to lose herself in this relationship the way she had with her two husbands. She was dedicated not only to her publishing job but to making certain she cultivated interests outside of anything having to do with Maurice.

"I'm sorry, ladies," Maurice said after he'd finished reviewing the papers before him, according to one of the others present for the meeting, "but there's nothing here." He said that Stas owed everyone with whom he ever did business. His debt far exceeded what he had in assets.

"The only thing I care about is my children's educations," Lee said, tears springing to her eyes. Jackie reached over and took her hand. "I'll set up trust funds for Anthony and Tina," she said. "I love you, Lee, and the kids, too. You know that, don't you?" Both women began to cry.

"I could see plainly how much Jackie cared about her sister," said one of the accountants present, who asked not to be identified since he still does business with Tempelsman. "The princess apparently had some money left from her divorce settlement. 'Stas was generous to me,' she said. Jackie agreed, saying, 'He was a good man. I hate to think of all the sleepless nights he must have endured.' It was a supportive, if also sad, meeting."

Jackie and Lee both rose, Lee taking Maurice's hand. She thanked him for his time, calling him "M.T." as did many of his friends and associates. Jackie kissed him on the cheek. "I'll call you later," she said. "I've got a little surprise for you," he told her with a twinkle in his eye. "See you tonight." As it happened, that same morning Maurice had made a substantial killing for Jackie in gold futures. He had invested while the price of gold was $100 an ounce. When it rose to $800 an ounce, he sold, resulting in millions of profit for Jackie. It was the surprise he planned to spring on her at dinner.

Turning to Alexander Forger, Jackie thanked him for coming to the meeting and said she would be in touch. Then, putting her arm around Lee, she walked her out of the office.

"Poor kid," Maurice said to the others after the sisters were gone. "Fourteen years of marriage to royalty and what does she get? Zip. That's a real kick in the pants for a princess, isn't it?"

EMERGENCY FAMILY MEETING

By September of 1976, the fiscal situation relating to Hammersmith Farm had become dire. Janet and Hugh could simply no longer afford it. Adding to the pressure was the fact that the Washington branch of Hugh's investment firm had recently been forced to close. Now the New York office was all that was left of his enterprise, but that branch was struggling, too, and would not last long.

The Auchinclosses had a firm offer for Hammersmith from a conglomerate of seven Massachusetts and Rhode Island businessmen, headed up by an attorney named Edward F. Sughrue. They would buy most of Hammersmith's nearly one hundred acres, including the Big House, the property around it, the pier, and eight other adjacent buildings, as well as the sixteen-horse stable. Janet and Hugh would be able to keep the Castle, to which they would relocate, and the Windmill, which would be for guests. The Faria family would still be allowed to continue to work at Hammersmith and live in the Caretaker's House, where they'd lived since 1967. The Caretaker's House garage — also known as the Carriage House — would still be theirs, as would guest quarters above it called the Palace. The investors' intention was to open Hammersmith as a tourist museum in May. Therefore, the family would have to leave behind all furnishings as well as memorabilia of President Kennedy's.

Janet called an emergency family meeting at the farm to discuss how to move forward. Present would be Janet and Hugh, of course, with Jackie, Lee, Yusha, forty-nine, and Tommy, thirty-nine. Hugh's daughter Nini (Tommy's sister) was invited but did not attend; neither did Jamie. Janet Jr. and her husband, Lewis Rutherfurd, also would not be present, both, of course, living in Hong Kong.

Garrett Johnston, Hugh's employee from Thomson & McKinnon, Auchincloss, was charged with taking the meeting's minutes for the firm. Another company associate, Candace Livingston, who worked in its finance department, was also there, as was Margaret Anne Kearney. Until recently, Margaret had worked for Hugh as the secretary of his Washington office and thus had knowledge of the Hammersmith situation. She and Janet had also forged a friendship over the years.

"There is an offer on the table," Janet announced, "for $825,000." She said it was "a pathetic proposal," but that the family seemed to have no other recourse.

"What was the asking price, again?" Jackie wanted to know.

"Nine hundred eighty-five thousand," Janet said, "and even *that* was low!"

Several developers had expressed interest in the property, Janet told the group, but their intention was to demolish the Big House and some of the other structures and build condominiums in their place. She and Hugh refused to allow that to happen. "Mrs. A. said that because the present interested buyers had a museum in mind, it seemed like a good idea to let them have the property," recalled Garrett Johnston.

"They're forming a conglomerate called Camelot Gardens and Associates," Janet explained. "You're joking, right?" Jackie asked. "No. I'm afraid not," Janet observed.

Of course, the new company was trying to exploit the mythological Camelot story of the Kennedy administration, which Jackie had spun in her grief for *Look* magazine back in 1963. Also, they were playing off the popularity of *Grey Gardens.* Jackie just shook her head sadly. "I guess I'm not surprised," she said.

"As the meeting went on, though, I noticed that everyone kept looking to Jackie, waiting, I think, for her to just offer up the money. I had the feeling they wanted her to put forth the $825,000 herself, or perhaps the entire asking price of $985,000. From her expression, though, I knew she was reluctant. Finally, she spoke up."

"If everyone chips in and this becomes a *family* investment, I *might* do the same," Jackie said with clear hesitation. Immediately, Yusha said he didn't have the money to invest. Tommy chimed in that he didn't, either.

In fact, if her relatives had wished to do so, Jackie's suggestion might have had merit. Hugh had earlier told Garrett Johnston that Tommy and Yusha had a significant amount of money stashed away. Also, Hugh said that Janet Jr.'s husband, Lewis, was doing well in Hong Kong as an investment attorney with his own venture capital firm, Inter-Asia Venture Management. The Rutherfurd family had substantial holdings in the States, too, and was well known. Not only that, Nini was now married to Michael Straight, deputy chairman of the National Endowment for the Arts, who was from a rich and prominent family. His father was a partner at J. P. Morgan. He and Nini had bought Jack and Jackie's old house on N Street and paid a bundle for it; they now had a huge place on Martha's Vineyard. (However, the fact that neither the Rutherfurds nor the Straights showed up for the family meeting suggested that they didn't want to have anything to do with Hammersmith's problems.)

Moreover, Hugh's older sister Esther Auchincloss Blitz had been married to real-estate developer Norman Blitz, one of the richest men in Nevada, for about the last forty-five years. He had committed suicide five years earlier, leaving Esther with a fortune. She had been loaning Hugh money all along, but even she wasn't interested in buying Hammersmith.

"In the end, though, the thinking, at least from what I could discern, was that none of the family members had the kind of money Jackie had — *Onassis* money," said Garrett Johnston. "So why should they be forced to maybe stretch their finances to the limit when Jackie could easily just write out a check and keep Hammersmith in the family? Or, at least that's what I believe everyone was thinking."

"I find it *quite* interesting," Janet finally

said, turning to Jackie, "that you would rather buy a bunch of *supermarkets* than save the home in which you were raised! The home that Jack loved so much."

"Who told you that?" Jackie demanded to know, her temper suddenly rising. "That is my *private business,* Mummy, and I do not appreciate it being announced to everyone in this manner." Janet told Jackie she had her ways of getting information. It didn't matter how she'd learned about it, she said, she just didn't think it was right.

It's not known how Janet found out but, in fact, Jackie had, that very same month, spent $800,000 on three Safeway stores, one in western Utah and the others in North Carolina. It had actually been a wise investment on her part, orchestrated by Maurice Tempelsman, and, if anything, was more a tax shelter for her than a source of income. "Yes, I admit, I am a very wealthy woman," Jackie told the others. "I make no apologies for that." Her relatives surely didn't know as much but, by 1977, Jackie's money from Onassis had grown from its approximate $20 million to at least $100 million, including her vast real-estate holdings. However, she told the group that she did not make such investments herself and that her "people" had specifically told her that investing in Hammersmith Farm was not prudent. That said, she reiterated that she would probably still contribute if others did the same.

"Well, that seems fair," Lee said of Jackie's offer. However, Lee certainly didn't have the money to even pitch in as part of any family effort. By this time, her children were finally reunited with one another when, after Stas's death, Anthony moved to Manhattan. He was boarding at Choate Rosemary Hall in Connecticut, which was pricy. She'd also spent what little money she had left from her divorce to buy a new beach home in Southampton for $329,000. Therefore, even though her design business was going well, Lee was tapped out. Jackie, as promised, had set up trust funds for both of Lee's children. "If we can't chip in like Jackie suggests, then I say we sell Hammersmith," Lee added. "What if we don't get another offer? Besides, look what it's doing to us!" she said as she nervously twisted her hands together. "We're at each other's throats!"

"We are *not* at each other's throats," Janet said, her tone sharp. She noted that they were just sorting things out as a family, and asked Lee to never again say that they were "at each other's throats." She added, "I don't like that kind of talk."

"I agree with Lee," Hugh finally said. "Let's just sell it, then." He was clearly tired of the discussion. This was the first time he had spoken during the entire meeting. He seemed beaten down and sick as he sat slumped over in a chair, an oxygen apparatus in his nose connected to a tank at his side. "We've all had our wonderful memories here, and maybe it's just time to let the ol' place go," he added. He said that, of course, he would rather keep Hammersmith Farm in the family, but if there was no way to do it, "the family is still the family whether we're sitting together at this table or at some other table. Let's not fight, please." Everyone looked sadly at Hugh. They loved him dearly and hated to see him so down and ill. "Yes, maybe it is for the best, then," Jackie said. Sitting next to her beloved stepfather, she rested her hand on his and looked at him with great warmth and sympathy.

Janet had heard enough. "*One of us* has all the money in the world," she said, seeming unable to look Jackie in the face. "And *one of us* has apparently made up her mind." After slamming both hands on the table, she then rose and stormed from the room, leaving everyone in stunned silence.

"GOOD-BYE, HUGHDIE"

By November, Hugh's declining health made things all the more bleak for the family. With his emphysema taking a great toll on him, he continued to be confined to a wheelchair with oxygen. "This was a tough time for the family," said Adora Rule. "Janet would wake up

587

every morning hoping he would be better, but he just kept getting worse. 'He's my rock,' she told me one day, 'and without him, I'm not sure how I can go on.' He meant the world to her. She would find him hobbling about aimlessly down by the shore, his medication also having a debilitating effect on him. Watching Hugh decline as he did was hard for her, especially since — though she wouldn't admit it — she was suffering from her own old age issues."

In November, Hugh accompanied Janet to the District of Columbia, where the couple wanted to cast their votes for the 1976 presidential election. Janet was voting for the Democratic candidate, Jimmy Carter, whereas Hugh was voting for the Republican, Gerald Ford. In a sense, as Hugh wryly noted, their votes would cancel each other out but, always the patriots, they were determined to do their civic duty. It was while in Washington, at the couple's O Street residence, that Hugh took a turn for the worse.

"On the morning of November 18, Janet called me and asked me to come to O Street immediately, saying that Hugh wanted to say good-bye to me," said Sherry Geyelin. "I lived in Bass Harbor, Maine, but took a plane to Washington as quickly as I could. By the time I got there, the next day, the nineteenth, poor Hughdie was already gone. I walked into the house and Janet was sitting on the couch with Oatsie Charles, crying. Hugh's former secretary, Margaret Anne Kearney, was also there, comforting Janet. She told me that Janet had summoned her the night before and that when she walked into Hugh's room, he said, 'Oh my God. I must be about to die.' His humor was intact until the very end.

"Poor Janet seemed so small to me, it was as if she had actually shrunk in stature and was just so tiny, so fragile and vulnerable, sitting there, crying."

"You know full well it's going to happen one day," Janet told Sherry through her tears, "but when it does, it's still such a shock. We were married for thirty-four wonderful years. I don't know what I will do without him."

Sherry sat next to Janet and held her hand. "He loved you very much," she said, now also crying. "He was such a loyal husband to you."

Janet looked up at her and softly said, "I know he did. That's true of him."

"We will always love him," Margaret said of her former boss, for whom she had worked for twenty-one years. "His suffering is over now, Janet. Maybe this is a blessing."

"Mummy was devastated when Daddy died," said Hugh and Janet's only son, Jamie. "Just absolutely devastated."

There would be two services for Hugh Auchincloss, one at Christ Church across from the O Street home and the second at Newport's Trinity Church. While Jamie and

Janet Jr. attended both services along with Yusha, Nini, Tommy, and many other relatives, including his grandchildren, Jackie and Lee attended only the Trinity service. The sisters arrived in separate cars; Janet Jr. accompanied Jackie. "We are here for Mummy," Lee told one relative. "But Jackie and I aren't really speaking to one another right now." When asked why, Lee shook her head sadly and softly said, "It's just more of the same. What can I tell you?"

About a week later, Janet and her young protégées, Linda and Joyce Faria, stood on the observation deck of the Windmill with its majestic view as far and as wide as the eye could see, all blue sky and sparkling Atlantic Ocean. "What a perfect day," Janet said as she took in the cool, crisp air. "Did you know that Uncle Hughdie was born right here at Hammersmith?" she asked, looking down at the girls. Nine-year-old Linda nodded. Janet said that Hugh "loved this place more than anything," which is why she had asked Mannie Faria for permission to bring his daughters to the Windmill to assist her in a solemn ceremony.

Janet held in her hands an ornate urn. Twisting off the top, she ran her fingers through the ashes — Hugh's ashes. "Now, I want you girls to grab a nice big handful of these ashes," she said, "and throw them out there as far as you can. Way, way out there.

Like this." She then took a fistful of ashes and scattered them off the observation deck with a wide gesture toward Narragansett Bay. The ocean breeze carried them out into the distance. With tears in her eyes but a soft smile on her face, Janet then watched as Linda took a handful of ashes from the box. In one motion as big as any that could be expected of a nine-year-old girl, she dispersed the ashes off the observation deck. They disappeared quickly. Seven-year-old Joyce did the same. Then another handful from Janet. "Good-bye, Hughdie," she said as the breeze carried the ashes toward the bay. "We love you." The Faria girls each took another handful of ashes and threw them toward the horizon. "Good-bye, Uncle Hughdie," Linda said. "We'll miss you."

Of course, Janet's first thought was to spread Hugh's ashes with Jackie or Lee, or Jamie, Yusha, or maybe Nini or Tommy. However, in thinking it over, she decided that she just didn't have the energy to try to get the family together, "what with this one being in one place, that one being somewhere else, and the other being who knows where," she said. She also said she thought it would be special for the Faria girls, a memory they would treasure forever. Maybe the emotionally charged moment was a little too much for Joyce, though, who began to softly cry. Janet knelt down before her. "Oh, no, no," she said, wiping her tears with her fingers. "This isn't a sad day, Joyce. This is a happy day. Hughdie is free, and thanks to you and Linda, he will always be a part of Hammersmith." She then reached into the box and put some more ashes into Joyce's hand. "Go on," she said, motioning out to the sea. Now with a big smile, Joyce threw the ashes off the side of the deck. "Good-bye, Hughdie," she said. "We love you. Me and Linda. Mommy and Daddy. And especially Mrs. A."

After the intimate ceremony at Hammersmith in Hugh's honor, Janet went to Trinity Church, where she met her good friends Oatsie Charles and Margaret Kearney. The three women then spent the next couple of hours in silence, lighting candles and praying for Hughdie.

■ ■ ■ ■

PART ELEVEN:
ENDURING

■ ■ ■ ■

CAMELOT GARDENS

"I am perfectly willing to cooperate," Janet
Auchincloss was saying as she poured hot tea
into a small cup, "but with one proviso: this
absolutely can *not* become a Kennedy museum," she added, handing the drink to her
guest. "That is not what I want, and not what
Jackie wants, either," she said. Janet was in
the living room of the Castle, not yet moved
into it from the Big House but comfortable
just the same. She was speaking to a young
brunette in a stylish woman's business suit
named Janet Crook. Crook represented Camelot Gardens and Associates, the new owners
of Hammersmith; her position was Director
of Hammersmith Farms. It was early 1977
and the deal had been finalized at last for
$825,000. "All my children hate it, and I hate
it," Janet would tell the press of the sale.
"Hugh and I wanted to keep the farm for
our descendants," she elaborated, "but it was
absolutely necessary to sell."

"You do have the presidential flag in the

foyer of the main house," Janet Crook noted. "You'll leave that there, won't you?"

Of course, Janet said. The two were referencing the framed presidential seal flag that Jack had long ago presented to Hugh; it had flown at the waterfront whenever the President was in residence. However, there should be no photographs of the Kennedy family on display, she added, clarifying her position. For Janet, it was a matter of family pride — *Auchincloss* family pride. "You see, this is our home, not theirs," she explained, "and so, there'll be no pictures of Rose, Ethel, Bobby, Teddy, and the others. Just a lovely wedding photo of Jack and Jackie, and maybe one or two other photos of Jack as President. But that's it. Do we have an understanding?" Crook agreed and assured Janet that the new owners would be respectful of her wishes.

The two then walked over to the main house so that Janet could show her guest some of the sights there. "Down in the basement, that's off limits, too," Janet said. She explained that the Secret Service had once been quartered there and that much of its equipment was still present, though no longer in working condition.

"There were no teary moments even though this was obviously all very difficult for Mrs. Auchincloss," recalled Janet Crook. "She was gracious and lovely, handling everything with the dignity that would be expected. I had

596

maybe four months to get the estate ready to be a tourist attraction. It would be open every May through October. So there was a lot to do, not the least of which was for Mrs. Auchincloss to move her personal treasured belongings into the Castle."

A few days later, Janet and Jackie rummaged through the enormous main house while giving dictation to an assistant. The secretary took frantic notes of furnishings and mementos that were still to be moved to the Castle.

For instance, on the third floor was a large walk-in cedar closet in which Janet's many riding trophies from her youth were displayed, as well as silver cups, red ribbons, and other mementos of Jackie's equestrian days. There was also a bulletin board covered with ribbons for the farm's prize cattle. Jackie thought that perhaps some of these keepsakes should be moved to the Castle so that they would be closer to her mother.

At the end of the emotional day, Jackie stood in the living room next to the golden marble fireplace and in front of the presidential seal flag. "Don't you think it's *marvelous* that people will be able to walk through here and experience Hammersmith just as we have all these years?" she asked Janet. While Jackie had made the decision to not purchase Hammersmith herself — and, in fact, was in the process of building her own estate on

597

Martha's Vineyard — she didn't like seeing her mother upset. She'd spent many tearful hours with Yusha trying to decide what was best, especially since he had promised his father he would always take care of Janet at Hammersmith. The decision was made, though, and now she was just trying to be encouraging.

Janet was never one to hide her true feelings, not in front of family anyway. Though someone like Janet Crook from Camelot Gardens would never know for sure how sad this time was, members of the family were well aware of it. "I suppose it will be nice," Janet answered, halfheartedly. She then turned and slowly made her way up the crimson-carpeted staircase — the same one on which Jackie posed in 1947 as "Debutante of the Year" and from which, six years later, she tossed her bridal bouquet when she married JFK.

As Janet gripped the wooden railing tightly, an assistant followed close behind making certain she wouldn't stumble. There actually was a small Elevette to the top floors, which had been installed back in '59 for Hugh because of his emphysema. However, maybe adhering to that great tradition of Lees and Bouviers when it came to high drama, Janet chose the more theatrical way up the stairs — one by one, very slowly, very deliberately. When she got to the top landing, she leaned

598

wearily against an enormous Dutch tall-case clock in the corner, twice her size. Then, gazing down to the floor below at her eldest daughter, she said simply, "You know your way out, Jacqueline. That will be all."

"A FAMILY THAT ENDURES"

"Okay, now how much do I owe you?" Janet Auchincloss asked little Joyce Faria. The young girl counted on her fingers. "Ten dollars," she answered proudly. Janet nodded. Joyce had delivered the newspaper to her door at the Castle for five days a week over a two-week period. So, yes, that was ten dollars. The girls were really growing up; Linda was ten and Joyce eight.

Janet was now moved into her new residence, the Castle. It wasn't so bad. The oldest building on the property, the Castle was a large farmhouse built around 1720 for the British admiral Jahleel Brenton. The name came from an old fable about a maid and butler who once lived on the property. They supposedly lived in the Brenton farmhouse because the Big House had no quarters for married servants. When children would go to visit the maid, she would always greet them by saying "Welcome to my castle" — thus its name.

The Castle was quite large, with a drawing room, library, dining room, kitchen, pantry, and maid's quarters all on the first floor, and on the second, two bedrooms including the master, two bathrooms, and two maid's quarters with another bathroom. There was also a garage, over which was the Palace, a three-bedroom apartment where Janet's trusty butler, Jonathan Tapper, would remain. Janet also still owned ten surrounding acres, including the Windmill. The Faria family continued to live in the Caretaker's House. Mannie remained as groundskeeper while Louise was re-assigned as manager of Hammersmith Farm's Gift and Garden Shop (formerly the Children's Playhouse). Meanwhile, the rest of Hammersmith — the Big House, the beach and pier, and about ninety more acres upon which sat a myriad of structures such as the stables would no longer belong to the Auchincloss family.

Within weeks, Janet had made herself comfortable in her new home, and she was especially happy to be in the company of her small charge, Joyce Faria. She sat down at her writing desk in the living room and took out her checkbook. The little girl was perched on a chair next to Janet, gazing up at her with her big brown eyes. "Now, you give this check to your daddy," Janet said as she tore it from her register, "and he'll cash it for you or maybe put it into a savings account. Okay?" The girl nodded.

"So, how are you doing in school?" Janet

wanted to know. As Joyce talked about her school projects, Janet listened and offered suggestions and advice about how to treat others. The two then went to the kitchen, where Jonathan Tapper served them both a heaping scoop of vanilla ice cream with some cookies. Finally, when they were finished, the little girl jumped up, kissed Janet on the cheek, and scampered outside. She then mounted her miniature donkey, Pedro, and was on her way back to the Caretaker's House. Janet watched from the door, smiled, and waved good-bye.

"In April of 1977, I joined Janet, Oatsie Charles, Margaret Anne Kearney, and another of Janet's friends, Ella Burling, on the patio of the Castle for a ladies' luncheon, an occasion we tried to organize at least once a month," recalled Adora Rule. "As we five women enjoyed the stunning view of ocean and sky, Janet's butler, Jonathan Tapper, served a French meal. 'This isn't a bad life, you have to admit,' I told Janet as we sipped mint juleps and whiled away the afternoon. She smiled and agreed. Janet then said that Jackie was coming for dinner that evening and bringing Caroline and John. Lee was also coming, she said, with Tina and Anthony. Yusha, Nini, and Tommy, along with their families, would also be arriving. She was expecting Jamie, as well. Some would be spending the night at the Castle, she said, while others would be in the Windmill. A couple of them would probably sleep up in the Palace. "We are nothing if not a family that endures," Janet said, proudly. "No matter what happens, we endure."

At least she didn't have to leave the property, though leaving the Big House had been quite the heartbreak for Janet. "I miss my house so desperately," she said, "and all of my lovely memories there. I can't believe that next month there will be people rummaging through my special things."

Ella Burling asked Janet if she was still angry at Jackie. "A little," Janet said, sadly. She added that she suspected Jackie's true reason for not wanting to help was that she'd never forgiven her for having objected so strongly to her marriage to Aristotle Onassis. She, therefore, made a decision that she wasn't going to use any Onassis money to bail out Hammersmith. Janet's guests were taken aback. "My God, Janet, can that be true?" Margaret asked. "Did Jackie tell you that?" No, Janet said, she didn't have to tell her, "but I know it's the case. We are known to hold grudges in this family," she added. Finally, she shrugged and concluded, "Look, it's Jacqueline's money and she has absolutely every right to spend it exactly as she pleases." Then, as Janet gazed longingly at her former home in the distance, she added, "But still . . . it sure would have been nice."

NEWTON COPE

In April of 1977, Lee began an exciting new design project in San Francisco at the estate of the millionaire industrialist William Hewitt and his wife, Patricia. While working on that project, she was invited to dinner at the home of the wealthy socialite and stylish bachelor Whitney Warren. His father had designed Grand Central Terminal in New York. Warren, who happened to be a close friend of Janet's, had known Lee for years and decided to try to set her up with a good friend of his, fifty-five-year-old Newton Cope.

Newton Cope had recently been left a real-estate fortune, including the landmark boutique Huntington Hotel, by his late (second) wife, Dolly Fritz MacMasters. The two had been a popular couple in San Francisco high society. Cope was also now the president of Nob Hill Properties Inc., a development firm and real-estate company. "We were seated next to each other at a dinner party," Newton Cope would recall, "and we talked about our children all night." (He had seven.) Cope was taken by Lee. He found her free-spirited, interesting, and also *interested* in the world around her. She was nothing like what he expected based on what he'd heard about her. When he told Lee as much, she said, "I'm not what people expect of me. And neither should you be." Cope was so taken by her, he panicked at the end of the evening thinking that perhaps he'd never see Lee again. Therefore, he drove her back to the hotel at which she was staying and, on the way, asked if she would take a look at his Huntington Hotel and see if she might decorate some of its rooms. "It was my way in," he said with a chuckle. Of course, she agreed.

By August, Lee found herself making periodic trips to the West Coast to work on the Huntington. In the meantime, she and Newton began to feel a certain chemistry. He was smart and funny, older than Peter Tufo by about twenty years, and wealthier. He was also relentless. He now had it in his head that he wanted Lee, and he was going to get her. To that end, Newton romanced her, swept her off her feet, and, to hear her tell it, "made me feel young and giddy."

At the end of '77, Lee and Peter broke up. With the unfolding of 1978, Newton Cope was at Lee's side as her new love interest. Lee was now spending more time with him on the West Coast, particularly at his home in Napa. One night, Newton asked her point-blank if she'd long felt in Jackie's shadow. It was a question that hit so close to home, Lee didn't feel entirely comfortable answering it. She said she was beginning to do some work for Giorgio Armani in New York as a director of special events and, of course, still had her own business. She was doing all she could, then, to once and for all distinguish herself. "But, to be honest, I don't know who I am if I'm not Jackie's sister," she said, really opening up.

"I do," Newton told her. He could see the pain and frustration in her eyes. According to his later memory, he stopped, took both her hands in his own, and, looking at her earnestly, said, "It's my turn to be honest now, Lee. I believe you'll be remembered for a lot more than just your relationship to Jackie. You have a destiny all your own." Lee had to have wondered what she'd ever done to deserve a guy like this one. Maybe the question of Jackie really was eating away at her after so many years because it was also at this time that friends noticed that she seemed to be drinking more than she had in the past. While it had actually started with the Rolling Stones tour, some felt her drinking was mostly a consequence of all of the cocktail parties and other functions she regularly attended. Others thought it had to do with the Jackie competition, constantly an issue. With her father an alcoholic, Lee had a genetic leaning toward the disease. Certainly Jackie did her own share of drinking, too, after JFK was killed. However, she seemed better able to control it. By the beginning of the new year, Lee wasn't yet ready to acknowledge that she had any sort of problem. However, it was becoming abundantly clear to others.

By the spring of '79, Lee had her mind made up: she wanted her future to be with Newton Cope. She had quickly become close enough to his daughters Marguerite and Isabelle to arrange private schooling for them, at Foxcroft in Virginia and Miss Porter's in Connecticut. She also made it possible for them to take an exciting chaperoned summer trip with her daughter, Tina, to Russia and Spain. "Lee was much more sophisticated than my father," recalled Isabelle Fritz-Cope. "For instance, she made my dad get rid of his eyeglasses to make him look more chic. My dad was more rugged. Think John Wayne — that was my dad.

"Lee did all of the decorating at our hotel — all of her rooms were always referred to as 'The Radziwill Rooms' — and completely redid my father's place in a much more extravagant way than he probably would have liked. She was always nice, though. None of us had any kind of conflict with her. We were actually quite fascinated by her, and a lot of that had to do with her connection to the Kennedys.

"She was super skinny — I don't think I ever saw her eat! — and always wore black, which was strange in sunny California in the 1970s. My brothers and sisters would joke and call her 'The Black Widow,' which probably wasn't nice but we were kids. My dad was completely smitten with her. She could say, 'Jump, Newt!' and he'd ask, 'How high, Lee?' He was crazy about her."

When Newton asked Lee to marry him, she said yes. This engagement seemed to signify a real turnaround of men in her life, and observers couldn't help but wonder about it. "As she was getting older, she was feeling a little desperate about the future," said one friend of hers from that time. "She was anxious to get on with her life with *someone.*"

Companionship was all fine and good, but Lee was still someone who'd been raised to at least consider wealth as a requirement of marriage, even if she pretty much never made decisions based on that criteria. It was no secret that the two men with whom she'd been most recently involved were not rich. Certainly Peter Beard didn't have any money. Peter Tufo was better situated but he was an altruistic person known for his pro bono work, and Janet and Jackie both felt that he had his limitations in terms of the kind of financial stability he could offer Lee. They weren't that disappointed when that relationship ended. However, when Lee made her plans relating to Newton Cope known to them, both mother and sister teamed up to make certain she knew what she was doing, and that she would be well taken care of in this new union.

Somehow, Lee was surviving, but barely. Her design firm ate most of its profits. The business was worth it to her, though, and she felt that if she just persevered, eventually her company would be in good shape. Still, every month she found herself in way over her head, her expenses always far exceeding her capital. Jackie and Janet still hadn't gotten over the fact that Stas left Lee with no money. They actually felt worse about it than Lee, who did what she always did, which was to look to the future, go on with her life, and hope for the best.

Because Newton Cope had such vast real-estate holdings, Janet and Jackie agreed that if he was going to marry Lee he should offer her some financial guarantees. In other words, they wanted an arrangement for Lee that resembled at least in intention (if not in actual figures) the kind of deal Jackie had struck when she married Onassis. When Janet, Jackie, and Lee discussed these matters over a Mother-Daughter Tea one day in New York at the Plaza, Lee was not at all open to the idea. She loved Newton, she said, and that was all that really mattered to her. However, she was torn. After all, she could at least appreciate her family's position that she should probably have *some* financial assurances, especially as she got older. However, Lee didn't want to appear to be mercenary. Also, she didn't want to be put into the position of having to discuss money with her fiancé directly. It was unseemly, distasteful, and she simply wouldn't do it. Janet didn't want to hear it. According to all accounts, her words to Lee were: "Now is not the time for soul-searching, Lee. Now is the time to take care of yourself."

A couple of days later, Newton Cope's telephone rang in his suite at the Carlyle. It was Alexander Forger, a partner with Milbank, Tweed, Hadley & McCloy and also one of Jacqueline Onassis's most trusted attorneys. Forger said he wanted to meet with Cope as soon as possible, that Jackie had asked him to talk to him about Lee. The meeting was arranged for that very afternoon at the Carlyle.

"What I am about to ask you should never leave this room," Forger told Newton Cope. "This conversation never happened, if you know what I mean." It didn't take him long to get to the point: would Cope be willing to sign a prenuptial agreement with Lee? Of course he would, Cope said. Whatever she brought into the marriage would be hers, and whatever he brought would be his. It was that simple. This, obviously, would not be the best deal for Lee, though, since Cope had a great deal more in assets than she did. However, it was fine with Forger and it was agreed that a document memorializing such an agreement would be drawn up. However, that would not be the end of it.

Forger said what was also needed was a

marital agreement that would specify how much Cope would be willing to give to Lee each month. Cope was immediately irate, snapping at Forger that it was none of his business. Forger wasn't intentionally trying to start trouble, he clarified. He was just trying to see to Lee's needs just as he had promised Jackie.

"How about $15,000 a month?" That seemed like a fair amount to Forger.

No, Cope said, he would not sign any agreement to that effect.

"Come on! It's not much," Forger said, "for you to just sign a simple agreement stipulating that you will pay this woman $15,000 a month in maintenance." (This would be the equivalent of about $50,000 a month today.) Cope was adamant that he wouldn't do it. He didn't want to be tied to an agreement he might later be forced to break if he had a reversal of fortune.

"I'm not buying an oil tanker," Cope finally said. "I'm not Onassis!" The suggestion that there'd been any sort of a deal made with Aristotle Onassis definitely rubbed Alexander Forger the wrong way. "You need to stop talking right now," Forger told him, his tone threatening, "before you say something you'll regret." He then put on his coat and stormed from the room.

LEE'S WEDDING
MISADVENTURE

The big day was set for May 3, 1979, Lee's wedding day. It was to be a civil ceremony at four P.M., performed by Justice E. Leo Milonas in the extravagant setting of Whitney Warren's Telegraph Hill estate, where Lee and Newton first met. Lee was so optimistic about her decision to marry, she said she now felt a real sense of destiny about it. "This is one of those rare moments," she said, dreamily, "when you sense that your life is about to change forever." No matter how tough Lee had it over the years, how much she had been kicked around by life and by love, she somehow never lost her romantic, idealistic attitude. She still believed that what was best for her, the thing she most deserved, was probably right around the corner.

At about one-thirty, Jackie called Alexander Forger to find out the status of the prenup. "Signed, sealed, and delivered," she was told. What about the marital contract with a monthly amount for Lee? No, she was told, that had not yet been signed. This wasn't good, Jackie said. In fact, she made it clear that Lee would not be able to marry Newton until the deal was finalized. She said she was determined to protect her sister in this regard and that Forger should do whatever necessary to finish the deal. He agreed.

At two, Newton Cope got a telephone call from Lee, who was at the Huntington Hotel getting her hair and makeup done for the ceremony. She said she had just gotten off the phone with Alexander Forger, who informed her that Newton was still balking at the monthly maintenance agreement. She seemed upset, her tone brisk and businesslike. Newton suggested that she tell Forger to call his [Newton's] San Francisco attorney, Yuen T. Gin, and take it up with him. He said it made no sense for the two of them to discuss such a thing on their wedding day. Lee agreed. A storm of telephone calls then took place between attorneys Forger and Gin during which Cope's position was reiterated: he would most definitely *not* sign any sort of maintenance contract with Lee Radziwill.

An hour before the ceremony, Lee called Newton, warning him that time was running out and that if he wanted to keep the peace, he really "should sign *something.*" He said, "Okay. Well, what if I offer you ten thousand a month, would you take that?" Her response: "But why not just give me the fifteen thousand and just get it over with?" The fact that she was now pushing so hard began to trouble him.

The fast and furious phone calls continued. Apparently, after Forger got off the phone with Lee, Jackie called her. According to all accounts, Jackie was adamant; if Newton refused to sign the agreement, Lee shouldn't marry him. Jackie felt that Newton's digging his heels into the ground suggested that there would be problems in the future with him, and she said she wanted Lee to avoid them. "In fact," Jackie reportedly decided, "the price just went up to twenty thousand!" Lee took a more reasonable position. She said she would be much better off financially as Newton's wife than she would be if she wasn't married to him at all. Should the marriage fail, *then* they could work out a settlement. No, Jackie told her. It would be better to get this matter straightened out now.

Forger then called Newton to tell him that the deal on the table was now for twenty grand a month. "What? It went up?" Newton asked, astonished. "Absolutely not!" he exclaimed. After Forger reported Newton's refusal back to Jackie, she called Lee and told her that the marriage shouldn't go forward. Crushed by this turn of events and feeling cowed by Jackie and her lawyer, Lee then called Newton and told him she was afraid the ceremony would have to be canceled.

Newton protested. Frantic, he reminded Lee that they were to be married in just an hour, the preparations all in order with guests already at the estate — though there were only a handful of them. Of course, this wasn't easy for Lee. She realized that canceling the wedding would make for scandalous newspaper headlines. She'd been raised to consider appearances, and these did not look good. More than that, though, she cared deeply for Newton. However, her mind was made up or, maybe more to the point, her *sister's* mind was made up. The guests were told that the wedding was going to be rescheduled for autumn when members of Lee's family would be able to attend.

Newton Cope's daughter Isabelle Fritz-Cope recalls her father telephoning her at boarding school to tell her that the wedding was canceled. " 'Jackie wanted me to sign a prenup,' he told me," she recalled. "I got the sense from talking to him that Lee had very little funds. He then said, 'There was no way I was going to sign a prenup.' I remember asking him, 'Um . . . Dad, what's a prenup?' "

Right before the ceremony was to take place, Janet Auchincloss telephoned Whitney Warren to ask if she could speak to Lee and wish her luck. She was told that Lee wasn't there. Dismayed, Janet managed to track Lee down at the Huntington Hotel. Lee then explained everything to her mother. Janet told Lee that it was a terrible shame that the wedding had to be canceled and that yes, it certainly did look bad and would no doubt generate no small amount of rumor and innuendo. However, she was proud of her for not buckling under pressure and marrying a man without a sound agreement in place. She also hastened to add that she was worried about Lee and recognized that none of what was going on could be easy for her. Lee said she was fine, though, that she'd done what she knew needed to be done.

After Lee got back to Manhattan, Newton Cope called and suggested that they go through with their honeymoon, anyway. It was all paid for, he reasoned, so why not? They still cared about each other, he allowed. After thinking it over, Lee agreed. The couple then went to St. Martin for two weeks. It was an extremely romantic time and, far away from her mother, her sister, and her sister's attorney and all of the pressures they'd brought to bear, Lee was light and easy and much more fun to be around, at least according to what Newton Cope would later recall.

Newton, to show his sincerity and good intentions in wanting to marry her, then shared with Lee his carefully considered wedding vows. He had them typed up on a sheet of paper and folded in his wallet for safekeeping. When she read them, Lee began to cry. Newton was absolutely eloquent and heartfelt in his feelings for her and in the promises he'd intended to make to always love and care for her as his wife. After hearing these promises that would now not be kept, Lee felt she'd been a complete fool. More than ever, she wanted to marry Newton. "How can I let you go?" she asked through her tears.

Lee then suggested she and Newton get married while on their vacation, telling him that she didn't require the signing of a formal agreement after all, that it had been something foisted upon her. She was sorry there had ever been a dispute about it. She said that she'd let her mother and her sister get to her, that she was not the kind of woman who cared only about money. Her first husband was completely broke, she explained, and her second died without a penny to his name. Her most recent paramours didn't have money, either — one lived in a tent in Africa and the other did pro bono work for the penal system! Janet and Jackie were the ones who married for money, "not me!" She felt misjudged and misunderstood. "I've never been this woman before," she reportedly said. "This is not who I am!"

Lee clearly felt that Janet and Jackie had mucked up her relationship with Newton, and she now wanted to fix it. After such an emotional plea, Newton believed that Lee probably wasn't as mercenary as her relatives. Still, considering everything that had transpired, he was uneasy about marrying her . . . and he decided against doing so.

BOOCH

October 25, 1979.

Janet Auchincloss smoothed down her beige silk dress as she stood before a full-length mirror in her bedroom. She was surrounded by a décor of cabbage-rose wallpaper and chintz, courtesy of her good friend, the late acclaimed interior designer Dorothy Draper. Draper's antique French furniture and expensive, original oil paintings gave Janet's bedroom a classic, austere feel. Lee didn't approve, though, feeling it was all just too gaudy. "Oh my God, the chintz in here makes me dizzy," Lee had said. Even Janet's headboard was upholstered and covered with the flowery fabric. There was also a comfortable floral-printed lounge in a corner, behind which was a gold-framed original oil painting of Janet. "Why is it that everyone thinks they have good taste," Lee had asked, looking around the room in dismay, "when, actually, very few people do."

"So how do I look?" Janet asked her son, Jamie.

"Beautiful, Mummy," he answered, "as always. Are you nervous?"

"As always," she said, turning around to face him. Janet was seventy-one now, seeming somehow smaller and more fragile than ever. Though still a spirited woman and as irascible as ever, a slightly confused expres-

617

sion often played on her face these days. She would try to disguise it, but Jamie could see it, as could her other children, Jackie, Lee, and Janet Jr., as well as her stepson Yusha. Janet often seemed to have trouble following conversations. She would forget the names of people she'd known for decades. She was also more sentimental. One day, Michael Dupree, Janet's head chef (who'd trained at La Varenne in France and thus specialized in French foods), caught her looking out the window of the Castle's library with tears in her eyes. When he asked why she was crying, she said, "I'm just looking at those poor cows out there and fearing for their future. I would hate harm to come to them."

While Jamie and Janet spoke, Jackie and Lee walked into the bedroom. "Oh, my! You look so beautiful," Lee exclaimed as she took both her mother's hands into her own. Jackie smiled and nodded her head. "Mummy, are you absolutely sure about this?" Jackie then asked. Janet shook her head in annoyance. "Yes, Jacqueline," she said. "As I have said a million times, I know *exactly* what I'm doing."

Nothing could have surprised or disturbed Janet's daughters more than her decision to marry for a third time. However, when one thought about how happy she'd been with Hugh for almost forty years, it made sense that Janet would want to continue to have a partner in her life. About a year earlier, she'd heard from an old friend, someone she had briefly dated almost fifty-five years ago, that he'd just lost his wife. Janet was only thirteen when she first met this gentleman. "She hadn't thought about him or his wife, Mary Rawlins — who had been a bridesmaid at her wedding to Jack Bouvier — for decades," recalled her son, Jamie. "However, she remembered that he'd always been a nice, amiable fellow. They had dated when she was a teenager at St. George's School. She was a friend of the woman he went on to marry, and in fact was a bridesmaid at their wedding. This man called to tell Mummy that his wife had died, after having been an invalid for many years with diabetes that had resulted in the amputation of her legs. The newspapers had been on and off strike at this time and Mummy thought maybe he hadn't heard that Hugh died. So they commiserated over their late spouses. His name was Bingham Willing Morris. Soon they were enjoying meals together at the Castle prepared by her waitstaff."

Bingham Willing Morris, born on June 23, 1906, in New York, was educated at St. George's and Harvard. He was also a member of the Native American confederacy and the Iroquois, as well as the Racquet and Tennis Club and the Harvard Club of New York. He and Janet had a great many common interests; both were fascinated by Civil War history, for instance. Like her, he also enjoyed music and dancing. When Janet told him that she was related to Robert E. Lee, he just accepted it with no questions asked. Janet felt comfortable in his presence. "The fact that he was from a distinguished and influential family in Philadelphia helped a lot," said Jamie.

Nicknamed "Booch," Bingham Morris was an eccentric character, always appearing slightly disheveled and nothing at all like someone Janet Auchincloss might consider as a companion. He wore T-shirts, casual slacks, floppy straw hats, and always had a towel wrapped around his neck because, apparently, he perspired a great deal. His appearance caused Yusha to proclaim, "That man looks absolutely ridiculous." At seventy-three, Morris owned a nice home in Southampton on Edge of Woods Road called Pra-Qua-Les. He also had a little money put away. He'd been lonely for a long time, he explained, especially since he and his late wife didn't have any children.

Even at the age of seventy-one, Janet was still desirous of physical intimacy. The longing for passion she felt when she gave up sexual attraction for financial security by marrying Hugh Auchincloss had never really dissipated over the passing of so many decades. The entire time she was married to

Hugh, she never found sexual fulfillment. "Daddy, suffering for twenty-three years with emphysema, had his limitations in the bedroom, but that was the case even before he was sick," said Jamie Auchincloss. "After Daddy died, Mummy wanted to date," recalled Jamie. "She still felt young and vital. However, the men she came across always seemed to be widowers who didn't want to reattach or were gay. Booch offered a heterosexual lifestyle to Mummy that she craved. He was good-looking, an outdoorsman who liked dogs and long walks, and they were compatible in every other way, too. They were also lonely. So, on paper, it seemed to work."

In August of 1979, Bingham asked Janet to marry him. She agreed. Understandably, some members of her family were concerned. Who was this man, and what did he have up his sleeve?

Jackie flew to Newport with her daughter, Caroline, now twenty-one, to try to talk her mother out of the marriage. The three of them sat down in the library of the Castle — Janet behind Hugh's enormous desk and Jackie and Caroline seated in front, as if in a business meeting — and tried to hash it all out. It was always so dark in there — no windows, low lighting — they could barely see one another. However, Janet was adamant. At one point, she became upset enough at them to storm from the room and out to

621

the adjoining courtyard. Jackie went to join her and was astonished to find Janet smoking; she hadn't smoked in years. Jackie bummed a cigarette from her. The two then sat at a bistro table enjoying their smokes and trying to come to terms. A week later, Lee tried as well. She also got nowhere. Janet Jr. was in Hong Kong and talked with her mother on the phone, but she, too, also made no progress. Yusha tried; no luck. Jamie, now living in Washington, knew better than to even bother. "Booch was a tough nut to crack," he said. "He hated the Kennedys. He hated Democrats and liberals. He was gruff and, in my eyes, maybe not very kind. Luckily," he laughed, "it was not I who had to marry him."

Despite her bouts of confusion, Janet's thought process around Bingham Morris seemed clear. She was going to marry him, and no one was going to talk her out of it. "I am the mother and you are the daughters," she told Jackie and Lee one evening at the Castle when they gave it one last try. "*I* tell *you* what to do. Not the other way around." It had all happened so fast, Janet Jr. didn't even have time to make plans to fly home from Hong Kong for the wedding!

"Maybe it won't be so bad," Jackie finally decided. Her feeling was that at least there would be someone at the Castle to watch out for Janet because the rest of the family obviously couldn't be there all the time. Jamie now lived in Washington and was working as a photojournalist. Lee was spending less and less time at Hammersmith. Tommy and Nini had their own families and were barely around. Yusha divided his time between Hammersmith and his own apartment at Eighty-ninth and Park in Manhattan. Jackie thought it would be best if someone was with Janet full-time.

If Janet's family was worried about her money, they didn't have to be concerned. Janet had a prenuptial agreement in place with Bingham. After her insistence that Lee do the same with Newton Cope less than six months earlier, there was no way that she would ever do otherwise, if only to lead by example. Whatever she and Bingham brought into the marriage would be considered theirs and theirs alone, and anything they acquired during their union would then be considered community property — except anything having to do with Hammersmith Farm. If any changes were made to the property during the course of their marriage — for instance, if another portion of it was to be sold — that money would be Janet's alone. Alexander Forger had worked out the agreement; Jackie, Lee, and Yusha had read it and all three were satisfied with it. (There was no need for Bingham to give Janet a monthly maintenance fee, as had been requested of Newton Cope.) So why shouldn't Janet marry Bingham Morris? One reason: Jackie didn't trust him. There was just something about him she didn't like, and she couldn't put her finger on it. When she raised her suspicions to other family members, they thought she was being either too cautious or protective, or maybe too controlling. "But she had good instincts, and we all knew that about my sister," said Jamie. "So we were sort of on high alert from the very beginning."

Before they could get started with the ceremony, Jackie pulled Yusha aside and had a word with him. "Yusha, you need to talk to him and make sure he knows who's boss around here," she told him, motioning to Bingham Morris. Yusha did what Jackie asked; he took Bingham Morris down to the Windmill to have a heart-to-heart with him. Years later, in a letter to Bingham, Yusha would remind him of what he had said to him at that time: "I told you at the Windmill before the marriage of the deep devotion I felt toward her [Janet], both as a stepmother and friend, ever since I had been best man in her wedding to my father," he wrote, "and the promise I had made to my father before he died, that I would watch over her at Hammersmith." After the two men finished talking, they shook hands and walked back up to the Castle where Janet was waiting, ready to get married for the third time.

Janet and Bingham Marry

"The deed is done," said the priest as he finished the brief ceremony between Janet and Bingham. Everyone applauded as the newlyweds gave each other a quick kiss on the lips. There was then a lovely reception on the grounds. Jackie took a quick look around at the few friends and family members in attendance and noticed someone she didn't recognize. "Him, *over there,*" she said to one of the ushers sent over by the Trinity Episcopal Church to assist in the ceremony. She pointed to a sheepish-looking man in a corner. She said she'd seen him earlier, nosing around the premises. Sure enough, the man turned out to be a writer for the *National Enquirer* who had somehow snuck onto the property. He was immediately ejected.

"Let us welcome Bingham Morris to our family," Yusha said as he raised his glass of champagne, and everyone followed suit. "And let us welcome him to Hammersmith on a" — he paused for a moment before adding — "more . . . permanent basis," he concluded. It was awkward. Still, everyone clinked glasses.

"So I imagine you'll be moving into the Castle here with Mummy," Jackie later said to Bingham as she tried to make small talk. By this time, the little party had moved out to the bluestone courtyard behind the Castle.

In the distance, on the other side of a wooden fence, could be seen a herd of Black Angus steers as they grazed in the bucolic green hills. Janet was sitting at the small dining set, trying to prevent her dogs from jumping up onto her lap and mussing her dress. Yusha was at the table with Janet, as was Jamie. At another nearby table sat Louise Faria drinking a cup of coffee, along with her daughters, Joyce and Linda.

"We'll see," Morris said to Jackie in answer to her question about his moving into the Castle. From his lackadaisical expression, he was not at all impressed to be having a conversation with Jacqueline Kennedy Onassis. It wasn't as if Jackie *expected* to be treated with deference. However, people who didn't know her well were inevitably excited and impressed to be in her presence. She'd gotten used to the public's reaction to her many years ago. Being in the company of someone who clearly didn't care who she was or what she meant to the world bothered her a little. Booch's nonchalance was off-putting and just served to add to her discomfort about him.

Morris took a swig of beer from the bottle in his hand and, looking around, added, "This place is pretty big, don't you agree?"

"Yes. But Mummy's *comfortable* here," Jackie said, according to one witness to the conversation. "I would hope that you two

626

would stay here, and at O Street, too."

"O Street's also too big," Bingham said. "Look, we're two old farts, Jackie. We can't climb all of those stairs."

"Well, that's what the *elevator* is for, Mr. Morris," she said, now truly annoyed.

"I love your mother," Bingham said, equally irritated. "I'll do what I think is best. And by the way, call me Booch," he suggested, offering his nickname.

"Indeed," Jackie said as she studied him with cold eyes. "*Mr.* Booch," she muttered as she walked away.

The job had fallen to Jamie, the family's resident photographer, to take pictures of everyone on this momentous day. At one point, Janet said to her son, "You should get in a picture, too, Jamie!" He then handed off the camera to someone else and stood with the family for a group photo. As the photographer instructed them all to "say cheese," Jamie threw out his arms dramatically as if to say '*Ta-da!*' In the resulting photograph, everyone is smiling broadly except for Jackie, who is glaring at her half brother.

As it happened, Jackie was unhappy with Jamie at this time for having cooperated with the author Kitty Kelley in the writing of an unauthorized book about her. Of course, Kelley would go on to have quite a reputation as a scandalous biographer, but when she asked Jamie for an interview (around 1977), she

627

hadn't yet written a book. No one knew anything about the "Kitty Kelley" brand at that point, but the world would learn about it soon enough with the publication of *Jackie Oh!* Even Janet and Yusha gave interviews for the book, which shows that they really didn't understand the magnitude of what they were doing. One would have thought they would have known how Jackie felt about these things, though. After all, when JFK's good friend Paul "Red" Fay Jr. wrote a book about his friendship with Kennedy, *The Pleasure of His Company,* in 1966, Jackie was upset about it. When the author sent a check from the book's proceeds to the Kennedy Library as a donation, Jackie sent it right back! (Years later, though, she would have a change of heart about this particular book, telling Fay she felt it was probably the best of the books ever written about Jack.)

Among the revelations in Kitty Kelley's book Jackie later blamed on Jamie was the fact that the blood-stained pink suit she'd worn in Dallas in '63 had been stored for safekeeping in the attic of Janet's George-town home, next to another box containing her trousseau for her wedding to Jack. After Kelley's book was published, the treasured mementos had to be relocated to the National Archives because the family was so afraid someone would break into the house and steal them. Lee was also angry at Jamie for inadvertently confirming for Kelley that Anthony had been conceived out of wedlock. (It's not as if Kitty couldn't have done that arithmetic for herself, though — Lee and Stas married in March and Anthony was born in August.) Therefore, it was tense between the siblings, which was why Jackie was in no mood for Jamie's humor.

After the reception, Janet and Bingham were off on their honeymoon by automobile across New England, visiting sights Bingham had planned out for them in advance. "Things were off to a rocky start because Mrs. Morris was used to wearing evening gowns every night, without exception," said Michael Dupree, her chef along with Jonathan Tapper. "So she packed all of her gowns and all of her white gloves only to find that, for their first night together, Bingham had taken her to a little log cabin in the middle of the woods. She was shocked. 'No dancing? No fine dining? No . . . *people*?' It was a surprise, all right."

"She later told me she got dressed for dinner anyway," said one relative of Janet's. "In my mind's eye, I saw poor Janet in her lovely evening gown and gloves sitting at a simple metal card table in the middle of a dusty log cabin across from Booch, in his jeans, flannel shirt, and floppy straw hat."

Things only got worse when, before bed,

Janet knelt down to say her prayers — which she'd done for many years — and was inadvertently kicked in the face by her new husband, who was already sound asleep. Of course, it was an accident, but Janet was still upset about it and would later say she viewed it as "a bad sign."

"They drove through Vermont, New Hampshire, and Maine in November when there were no longer any leaves on the trees, there was snow on the ground, it was just miserable," said Jamie. "Mummy came back from the two-week honeymoon frigidly cold and rather shell-shocked, wondering what the hell she'd gotten herself into."

Upon her return, Janet said she woke up one night, took one look at Bingham, and decided then and there that she didn't want to be with him.

"Making things a little worse, Mummy couldn't find anything appealing about Booch's completely masculine home in Southampton," said Jamie. "His home was like a shrine to his dead wife. He even had her old Karmann Ghia still in the garage. So, as his wedding present to Mummy, Booch offered to allow Lee to completely redecorate the house to Janet's taste, and then send him the bill. Lee went to town, of course, so much so that, soon, Booch didn't even recognize his own house. He also didn't like it. Finally, he told Mummy and Lee, 'Look, this is my den. Let me at least have it the way I like it, and you can have the rest of the house for yourselves.' After the job was done, Lee sent him an enormous bill. By this time he felt she'd completely ruined his house, and he was now banished to its den."

One day soon after Janet and Booch returned from their honeymoon, Jackie went to the Castle for a fitting; Janet had a dressmaker who, every week, came to the house to alter evening gowns. This week, Janet had one in mind for Jackie and asked her to come by. Jackie showed up in blue jeans with a sweatshirt, her hair pulled back, saying she wanted to be a "blank slate" for the dressmaker.

As she was being fitted, Janet confided in Jackie that the marriage hadn't been consummated. Somehow, Jackie wasn't surprised. Janet wondered if it was grounds for annulment. Jackie certainly hoped so; she said she would have Alexander Forger look into it. Meanwhile, Janet decided to talk to a priest at Trinity Church. He, apparently, told her that, under the circumstances, an annulment would be not only appropriate but understandable. Because she was a churchgoing woman, the priest said he felt the decision to marry had been made prayerfully, not carelessly. Afterward, when Janet also talked to Yusha about it, he said he felt an annulment was probably for the best. "But Janet thought it would look bad," Oatsie Charles recalled, "and, she told me, 'I don't want people to think I have lost my marbles.' Rather than have people talk about her, she was willing to stay in the marriage and make the best of it." Also, Janet just didn't want to be alone. She'd been married for most of her life, was used to the companionship, and was frightened by the prospect of being on her own. Therefore she said she'd do her best to just learn to live with Bingham Morris, faults and all. "That *is* what marriage is all about," she concluded. In the end, Booch wasn't so bad, she decided. He just wasn't Hughdie.

"JED CLAMPETT"

"Just wait until you see what *I* have," Bingham Morris exclaimed to Jonathan Tapper one morning. "You'll be so excited," he promised. "Wait right here!" He then left for a few moments and returned to the kitchen carrying an enormous bushel of lima beans. "After you shell these babies, I guarantee you'll never have lima beans quite like these," he told the butler. He had a towel wrapped around his neck, as he often did to absorb perspiration. "I picked them myself exactly four weeks after the last frost when the soil temperature was about seventy degrees." Jonathan rolled his eyes. He didn't care about the details, all he cared about was the work he anticipated would be involved in shelling a mountain of lima beans. "Get to it right away," Morris suggested, "because me and the missus will want them for dinner." That was typical Bingham Morris, the new, strange, and somewhat maddening presence at Hammersmith Farm.

"He had the house in Southampton," recalled Adora Rule of Morris, "so, Mrs. A. would go there on some weekends, and then he'd be at the Castle during the weekdays. Or, he would be gone for two weeks and then suddenly reappear like a bad penny. But they talked every single day while they were apart; they could talk for hours on the phone. She was with him for the companionship. There was also a sense that maybe he was a manifestation of her growing confusion; the 'old' Janet would never have had someone like Mr. Morris in her life.

"Jackie would come to visit and there would be Booch out on the porch in his shorts, T-shirt, and big floppy straw hat. You could see the hackles rise on her. He'd be drinking beer, listening to sports on his loud transistor radio. She was so chagrined by the sight of him. 'I see that Jed Clampett has returned,' she would say. She didn't understand how Janet had gone from a sophisticated man like Hughdie, with his expensive tweed suits, to Booch, with his tattered shorts and straw hats. I told Jackie he was okay, just different. 'Can I tell you something?' she said, pulling me aside. 'I don't trust that man as far as I can throw him. Make sure everyone here keeps an eye on him.' I thought, well, she's just being Jackie, protective of her mother, as well she should be. Booch seemed harmless to me."

"He loved to tease Janet," recalled Janet's chef, Michael Dupree. "He would pull up in his car and he'd have at least ten hats stacked up in the rear window, straw hats and different kinds of summer hats. He'd try on all of these hats for her, and she really hated them all. But he made her laugh. There was something sweet about it."

Despite his eccentricities, Bingham Morris did have a certain charisma that sometimes even Lee couldn't resist during those rare times when she came to visit. At first, Lee didn't want to know anything about him. She had said, "I'm sorry but I will *not* talk to a man whose name is *Booch*. Now, if that makes me a bad person, so be it." In time, though, Lee began to see Bingham Morris in her mother's life in the same light as Peter Beard had been in hers — an unconventional man who had, against all rhyme or reason, somehow won a place in the life of an entitled woman. "There's something extraordinarily appealing to me about people who aren't quite in tune with the world," she would say. "It's a quality of being slightly lost, slightly out of step. I don't know why I understand it so well." She would recall Peter's clothing as "an extraordinary costume that only he could get away with." That would certainly also describe Bingham Morris's daily wear.

One day, Oatsie Charles happened by to check on Janet and found Lee and Bingham lying on two chaise lounges on the deck, his transistor radio blaring as the two of them spoke to each other. He was telling her that, prior to his marrying her mother, he'd sailed around the world more than once. She seemed fascinated. "Looks like we got us a coupla' empty bottles over here," Morris told Oatsie. "Be a sweetheart and go get us some cold ones, will you?" Oatsie went into the kitchen and retrieved two chilled beers from Jonathan Tapper. She then brought them out on a silver tray, handing one to Bingham and the other to Lee. Lee popped off the cap with a stainless-steel bottle opener and then handed it to Bingham to do the same. "Be a dear and bury these bottles out there in the sand, won't you, dear Oatsie?" Lee then asked, giggling. She was obviously a little tipsy. As an annoyed Oatsie bent over to pick up the empty bottles, her ear was right next to Lee's mouth. "If you ever so much as breathe a word of this to another soul," Lee whispered, referencing the fact that she was getting along so well with Booch, "I will deny it to my grave!"

MAURICE TEMPELSMAN

"Are you happy, dear?" Janet asked Jackie in January of 1980. She and Jonathan Tapper were visiting Jackie at her home on Fifth Avenue. Janet was in the city to do some shopping, and since she did not like to travel alone these days, she'd asked her butler to accompany her. They had lunch at Tavern on the Green, and then went to Jackie's for afternoon tea. When they arrived, Jackie was just saying good-bye to her friend and former personal assistant Provi Paredes, who had stopped in to say hello.

"I *am* happy, Mummy," Jackie said with a bright smile.

"He's a nice man," Janet said. "Even though he's still married," she added, not able to resist the little dig.

Jackie smiled and, ignoring the comment, said. "Let's have a nice afternoon. I'm just so happy you're here, Mummy!" Janet nodded; she seemed in no mood for an argument, anyway.

After Provi left, Jackie sat down with her mother while Jonathan assisted her cook, Marta Sgubin, in the kitchen. The topic of discussion was still Maurice. As Janet had pointed out, he had not yet been able to obtain a divorce from his wife. The irony was not lost on mother and daughter. After all, for years they had campaigned against Lee ever having extramarital affairs and now here was Jackie, in her fifties, finding herself in the strange position as "the other woman." However, Maurice and his wife had been separated for some time. She knew about his relationship with Jackie. It would be about four more years, though, before he moved into Jackie's home.

The times Jackie and Maurice spent with Lee were few and far between. By 1980, the sisters didn't seem to even want to share their friends with each other. Lee was in Maurice's company only a handful of times during the approximately seventeen years he would be Jackie's companion. Maurice didn't want to get in the middle of Jackie's complicated relationship with her sister. There were a few times when Lee needed money for one thing or another and Jackie took care of it through Maurice. The money was never enough to really set things straight for Lee, though. Jackie would take care of certain bills, give Lee a little extra for this or that, "but in terms of giving her a few million to really straighten things out," one relative observed, "no, this did not happen."

By this time, Jackie was working for the publishing company Doubleday after having departed from Viking on bad terms when its publisher, her friend Tom Guinzburg, decided to publish a novel by Jeffrey Archer called *Shall We Tell the President?* about an assas-

sination attempt on Ted Kennedy. At Doubleday, she was encouraged to use her clout to
bring in new authors and was after major
celebrities to write their memoirs. Eventually,
she would nab Michael Jackson for his, called
Moonwalk. She was well liked in publishing
circles, respected not only for her exquisite
taste but for her lack of pretense when it
came to the people with whom she dealt on a
daily basis. She enjoyed being a "working
girl," and took her job seriously, as well as
the colleagues with whom she worked.

"When Maurice came and joined Mrs. A.
and Mrs. O. for tea, I had a chance to see
Janet's reaction to Maurice," recalled Jonathan Tapper. "I was nervous because of what
I knew had been her feelings about Onassis.
However, it was different with Tempelsman.
First of all, he was a gentleman, and Madam
always appreciated that. He also looked the
part, if you know what I mean. He was atten-
tive to her and there was warmth between
them. Madam approved. She felt that Jackie
had finally found someone worthy of her.
Now, she only hoped that Lee could get
herself sorted out, as well."

"I'M LEE AND I'M AN ALCOHOLIC"

It was Monday evening, June 8, 1981. A black
town car slowly drove down James Lane in

East Hampton past the historical sites of Mulford Barn, Mulford House, Pantigo Windmill, and Home Sweet Home to its destination, St. Luke's Episcopal Church at 18 James Lane. It was a large, traditional-looking stone structure with stained-glass windows and a small peak at its arched front entrance upon which had been placed a stone cross. The car wound around the driveway to the back of the church and stopped at a small ancillary building in front of which a small crowd of people milled about, chatting. Once the car stopped, the small group ceased talking and turned its attention to it. The driver got out and opened one of its doors. A high-heeled foot emerged from the vehicle and touched onto the brick pavers. Suddenly, a sense of anticipation surged. *"Who's this?"* Then, a woman rose from the car, someone who was instantly recognizable in a black skirt and white silk blouse. Maybe it was the hair and sunglasses that gave her away, though — a jet-black coif cascading to her shoulders, oversized dark glasses hiding almost half her face even though it was evening. "It's Jackie O," someone exclaimed loud enough for her to hear. She stiffened and turned her back to the small group as another woman exited the car, this one smaller, thinner, and seeming more delicate. She, too, was wearing large sunglasses, her brownish hair pulled into a sleek chignon. "Is that her sister?" someone was overheard asking. Now side by side, the two women locked arms and, heads held high, walked past the small, staring group, nodding and smiling as they passed, into the meeting room. "Welcome to Alcoholics Anonymous," said a woman behind a table as she handed Jackie and Lee a pamphlet. Jackie said, "Thank you," but Lee, a searching expression on her face, said nothing. They then took a seat in a corner in the back of the small room.

No matter their problems, no matter their disagreements, no matter what had happened in the past, Lee Radziwill and Jacqueline Kennedy Onassis were still sisters. They had a long storied history that was theirs, and theirs alone. Though they wouldn't always admit as much, they did treasure their relationship even if they had so often been careless in nurturing it. It would be Jackie who would take Lee to her first AA meeting that warm summer night in June of '81 at St. Luke's.

When one considers Lee's life and times and the behavior of alcoholics as described by professionals, it seems to make sense that she might need help. Ruth Fowler, who has written in depth about alcoholic thinking — which she calls AT — seems to describe Lee in defining the term. "AT is the conviction that we need external validation to fill a hole deep inside and that in the event that our own impossible demands are not met, we must drink to fill the hole," she notes. She has never discussed the matter with Lee and doesn't know her, but her analysis of the condition certainly seems to apply to her. " 'If only I had a boyfriend, my life would be perfect,' the thinking may go," says the author. "Or, 'If only I had more money, I wouldn't be unhappy.' And then there's: 'If only I had a drink, my life would be bearable.' Which all leads to: 'I don't have these things and that's evidence that the world is pitted against me. I called my sponsor to complain, but he didn't call back. It's because he — like the world, like God, like the universe — is against me."

Jackie helped Lee get settled in the back of the meeting room, and then waited there with her as several people spoke. Finally, Lee stood up and walked to the podium and announced, in the tradition of AA, "Hello. I'm Lee. And I'm an alcoholic." At that moment, Jackie discreetly rose and left the building, likely for two reasons. First of all, she probably didn't want to pull focus from Lee during her talk. And also, she likely didn't want to embarrass her sister by hearing whatever it was she had to say. Instead, Jackie waited in the car until Lee exited about a half hour later, and then the two sisters were driven off into the night.

Janet Comes to Terms

It was September 1982. Janet was seated at her writing desk in the Castle with Mannie Faria standing before her. She had asked to speak to him about an urgent matter. By this time, Mannie and his family had lived at Hammersmith Farm for almost fifteen years. His daughters, Joyce and Linda, were now teenagers, thirteen and fifteen. Janet loved them as much as she would have if they'd been her own grandchildren. "I wanted to make an offer to you," she told Mannie. "I would like to leave you a significant amount of money in my will." He was stunned. A proud man, his first response was to protest. However, "Mrs. A." wouldn't hear of it. "I want to leave you a lump sum to pay for Linda's and Joyce's college educations," she elaborated. "I'm thinking about sixty thousand dollars."

"No, I couldn't let you do that, Mrs. A."

"Oh, but you have no choice," Janet said with a smile, "because I have already made up my mind."

Mannie said he would have to talk to his wife, Louise, about it. As he left Janet's side, though, he was completely choked up. The next day, when he returned he said that he and Louise would very much appreciate the assistance. Neither had been able to afford higher education, so for Janet to make it possible for their daughters to have it was more than the Farias could ever have hoped for. He said that they couldn't be more grateful. Janet was thrilled. "Wonderful," she exclaimed. "I will have my will amended then."

"I've been so upset in the past when I've read about Mrs. A. and the way she's been depicted," said Joyce Faria Brennan. "She'd been old-fashioned in her youth and came from a different time, raising daughters in the 1940s alone before she married Hugh. I'm sure it was difficult for her. I'll bet she had good reason to be tough. To be strong, powerful, and assertive. But what I saw during her older years was a gracious, elegant, and generous woman."

"It was as if Janet was tying up loose ends," Adora Rule recalled. "She had a similar conversation with me about my daughter, Janine." Today, Rule says she doesn't feel comfortable revealing particulars of the gift Janet provided her daughter, but others have said it was along the same lines as what she did for the Faria girls. Though Janine never lived at Hammersmith, she spent much of her childhood there when Adora worked for Janet. Janet was quite close to her, as well. By 1982, Janine was twenty and attending college.

"Are you well, Mrs. A.?" Janine asked Janet at the end of the season at Hammersmith in '82. She had come to the Castle to have tea with her, along with a scoop of vanilla ice cream, as she did at least once a week. Before their tea, Janet had enjoyed a massage from a masseuse who visited the Castle thrice weekly. While Jonathan Tapper dutifully served them on the patio, Janet answered Janine's question with surprising bluntness. "I'm ready to die, dear," she said. She made the statement not with anxiety or distress, but just as a simple matter of fact. When Janine told her she had many more years left, Janet shook her head. "I'm seventy-five," she said. "It's my time." She said that she'd had "such a good life" and that she didn't want to end up a burden to her children. "That would kill me," she said.

"As we sat with our tea, I asked her if she had any regrets," Janine Rule recalled. "She said she'd lately begun to feel that she'd been too hard on Lee. 'I must make it up to her,' she said. She also said she was worried about how Jamie would feel about her once she was gone. She and Hughdie had sent him away to boarding school, she said, as early as the fourth grade. Now she feared he would think they'd just been trying to get rid of him when, actually, she said, 'We only wanted the best education possible for him.' She said she loved her son with all her heart and just hoped he knew it. Then, she firmly concluded, 'I think I was a good mother to all of my children, though. I did all the right things.

I tried my best, anyway.' "

After another long moment of thought, Janet then surprised Janine by suddenly admitting that her biggest regret was that she hadn't been able to protect her daughters from Aristotle Onassis. She said she considered the fact that she'd been unsuccessful at keeping him out of their lives to be one of her only failings as a mother. "Did you know that I actually slapped Jackie right after she married him?" Janet asked. Startled, Janine said no, she hadn't heard about it. Janet paused for a second. Judging from the pensive way she stared out at the sunset and the sense of repentance in the air, Janine thought Janet was about to add that particular mother-daughter moment to her list of regrets. Instead, with a wicked grin, Janet concluded, "I sure did. And she deserved it, too, let me tell you!"

With that, "Mrs. A." dissolved into gales of laughter.

Maybe one of the reasons Aristotle Onassis was on Janet's mind was because she recently had been reminded of a gift he'd given her. A few months earlier, she and Bingham had decided to put the O Street home on the market. They then purchased a three-bedroom condominium at the Watergate apartment building in Washington, putting the house in Janet's name since it was bought with her money. She said she and Bingham would then split their time between that location, the Castle at Hammersmith, and his home in Southampton.

"The move from O Street to Watergate was hard on Madam," recalled Jonathan Tapper. "I would follow her from room to room and she would pick up something and try to recall its origins. Sometimes, she was sharp. 'Jackie bought me this tea caddie in '67,' she would say, or, 'I remember when Lee picked out this 1750 mahogany stool.' Other times, she would stare at an item and have absolutely no idea where it had come from. Her mind was slipping more and more with each passing day. I made a list as she handed me the items and decided, 'Watergate' or 'Newport' or 'Weschler's' because she was auctioning off a great deal of it [266 items were auctioned by Adam A. Weschler & Son]. It was as if her whole life was being picked over. It was sad."

At one point, Jonathan opened a drawer and found an obviously expensive set of canary diamonds — a necklace, bracelet, and drop earrings. Janet groaned. "I got those old trinkets from Onassis," she said. "He gave them to me for one reason or another, I can't remember. Maybe a birthday."

"What shall I do with them?" Jonathan asked.

"Throw them out," Janet said curtly.

"But Madam," he protested, "these must

be worth almost fifty thousand dollars!"

She shrugged her shoulders and changed the subject. Jonathan decided to put the jewels in a red box, and then deposit them in a locked safe off the kitchen in the new Watergate apartment. A few months later, he and Janet went to fetch jewels for her to wear to a special occasion. While going through the contents of the safe, she found the red box. "What's in here?" she asked. He said it was the Onassis jewels. "I thought I told you to throw these into the trash!" she said, upset. She had a good memory for certain instructions, that much was clear. Jonathan promised he would do as he was told. Instead, he got the jewels out of the house and stored them in a safe-deposit box at a bank.

A DEVASTATING DIAGNOSIS

"What's wrong with me?" Janet Auchincloss asked Jonathan Tapper one day in January 1983. She reached for his arm, her fingers tightening on it, her eyes pleading. "I haven't been right for years," she said, "and I don't know why. I'm just so darn forgetful!" Placing his hand reassuringly on hers, Jonathan told her that she was fine. She pulled away from him. "No, I'm not," she said, irritated. Knowing there was nothing to be gained by alarming her, the butler smiled and said, "Trust me. You are fine, Madam. Nothing has changed. You're still completely impossible." She smiled and nodded her appreciation. As Jonathan rose and walked away from her, he turned to make sure she was not too upset. He was saddened to see her just staring blankly into space. An hour later, she walked up to him and, this time much more urgently and with tears in her eyes, asked, *"What's wrong with me?"* as if they'd never had the previous conversation.

At the beginning of 1983, numerous medical evaluations finally resulted in the terrible confirmation that Janet was suffering from Alzheimer's disease. At last, her family members began to fully understand what had been going on with her. Looking back, it seemed to them that the onset of the disease may have been as early as 1974, when they first noticed Janet began behaving differently. There were many instances over the last nine years or so that, when reviewed and analyzed, certainly seemed to point to the onset of Alzheimer's.

Obviously, accepting such a devastating diagnosis was difficult for everyone, each of Janet's loved ones handling it in his or her own way. "What can one say about such a conclusion?" asked Jamie. "When the doctor told us, we thought, 'Oh my God, this is terrible. What do we do?' Five minutes later, we asked the exact same question. Nothing registered."

Of the Bouvier sisters, Jackie was always the more pragmatic, realistic one. She had seen so much tragedy in her lifetime and, as a result, bore the battle scars of days often lived in great despair. By the time she was in her fifties, she had learned to accept the unpredictable unfolding of life with resignation. Within weeks of Janet's diagnosis, after its immediate shock subsided, Jackie went into caregiver mode, doing the research necessary to find out as much about Alzheimer's as possible. She became active with the Alzheimer's Association, donating $250,000 to the organization for research immediately upon Janet's diagnosis. (Not only would she continue to grant that same amount every year thereafter, she would also serve on the association's benefit committee.) Planning for an uncertain future, she arranged with Maurice to create a one-million-dollar trust fund to handle all of Janet's care not covered by medical insurance. Janet may have felt let down by Jackie over the years — certainly she'd never gotten over the crushing disappointment of the Hammersmith sale — but in her declining years, whether she fully understood it or not, her eldest daughter would come through for her. Chief among Jackie's concerns now was Janet's marriage to Bingham Morris. While she hadn't been able to do anything about it in the past, she hoped that now she might have a little more latitude, especially if she was able to enlist Janet's doctors in the effort.

It was harder for Lee to accept her mother's diagnosis. "Unlike Jackie, Lee didn't want to know what to expect from Alzheimer's," said one person close to her. "She needed time alone, not with professionals, to grieve what she suspected was the end of her mother as she knew her. I don't believe she had the tools available to her to come to terms with the diagnosis. Lee told me, 'I don't want to wake up tomorrow and find that there's no hope for my Mummy.' Unfortunately, she and Jackie weren't close enough to process it together."

Despite the diagnosis, Janet was still in good enough health to continue her regular life. Things would become bleak with time and she knew it, but meanwhile she insisted on keeping her schedule, including board meetings with her favorite charities, such as the Newport Jazz Festival, the Redwood Library, and Stratford Hall, where she was still on the board. Jackie came to Hammersmith to attend one meeting with her mother relating to her philanthropic activities, and was amazed to see Janet in near perfect form. "She could camouflage any memory loss," said Michael Dupree. "She was still graceful and wonderful, and still a stickler for orderliness and cleanliness. For instance, after that meeting as she left the parlor, she tossed a Kleenex into the trash can just to see how long it would take for one of the maids to find it and dispose of it. It was still there the next morning. 'Not acceptable,' she told one of the maids. 'Not *at all* acceptable.' That was *very much* like Madam."

■■■■

PART TWELVE:
"WELL, HAPPY, AND
LOVED . . ."

■■■■

Janet Jr.'s Life in Hong Kong

In the spring of 1983, Janet and Jamie took a cruise ship to China on a vacation to visit Janet Jr. and her husband, Lewis Rutherfurd, to see their boys, Lewis Stuyvesant and Andrew Hugh, and also to meet the new granddaughter, Alexandra. Janet Jr. had built quite a life for herself in Hong Kong since she and Lewis moved there back in 1966. Lewis had gone on to be the cofounder and managing director of Inter-Asia Venture Management, a venture-capital investment firm; his wife was a shareholder and adviser. Janet Jr. had taught French at the Chinese University for two years, just as planned. Meanwhile, she and Lewis had Lewis, Andrew, and, now, baby Alexandra.

"Janet and Lewis had a happy, satisfying marriage," said Dawn Luango, who, with her husband, James, often socialized with the Rutherfurds in Hong Kong. "He took a lot of pride in being married to Janet, always complimented her on her intellect as well as her beauty. Janet was private, though. I had first met her in 1966. Sometime in 1970, I was in a store with her when we noticed a magazine on the newsstand with Jackie's picture on it. I said, just in passing, 'Oh, she's lovely, isn't she?' Janet responded, saying, 'Yes, she is. She's my sister, you know?' I was speechless. I said, 'What? Since when is Jackie Onassis your sister?' She laughed and said, 'Pretty much since the day I was born.' "

"To me, it made a lot of sense that Janet Jr. didn't want people to know about her relationship to Jackie," said her brother, Jamie. "After all, what good had it done Lee? It was a cross she had to bear for her entire life, wasn't it? The comparisons, the competition. Janet recognized it as a problem she didn't want in her own life. I understood it, as did Jackie."

It's worth noting that Janet may have been the one female family member who actually *chose* politics as an endeavor. Jackie was rather forced into it by virtue of her marriage to Jack (though Jamie opines that she probably would have married someone in politics eventually simply because of her attraction to power). Janet Sr. became involved because of Jackie (though she was always a patriot). Lee was never that politically minded at all. However, Janet Jr. was an expatriate who actually sought out politics when she founded the first overseas chapter of the League of

Women Voters in 1979 in Hong Kong. "She was smart and well read, a quiet sort of political animal," recalled Mary Leventhal, the league's secretary under Janet. "In '84, Janet was elected president of the Hong Kong chapter," she added. "She was lively, intelligent, and keenly interested in world affairs.

"The League of Women Voters was affiliated with the American Club in Hong Kong, consisting of expats who would meet regularly to discuss social and business concerns and, also, tactics to stay involved in American politics while living abroad," Mary Leventhal explained. "A major component of the league's activity was the implementation of a voter registration drive designed to allow Americans living in China to vote on important American issues. We also ran debates at the American Club. For instance, during one memorable night, Janet encouraged two men with different views to debate gun control. Of course, gun control was something she cared deeply about because of her brothers-in-law. It was contentious, as one might imagine, but Janet was the perfect moderator. Actually, now that I think of it, she was a terrific debater herself. 'I got that from my mother,' she told me. She called her mother 'the original politician in our family.' "

During her visit, Janet Sr. was quite happy about how well Janet and Lewis were living on Lugard Road in an exclusive neighborhood on Victoria Peak, the highest point on Hong Kong Island. Janet Sr. and Jr. spent many hours gazing out at the spectacular Hong Kong cityscape and talking quietly about the past, present, and future. Fluent in both Mandarin and Cantonese, Janet would try to teach her mom a few words to keep her mind active. "She's so different," she told Jamie one day, "and it's as if she doesn't have that fire she'd always had." Jamie had to agree. "Every day, she seems just a little more subdued," he added with concern.

Shortly after Janet and Jamie returned to America, Janet Jr. and Lewis went to Hammersmith for a visit. While there, Janet Jr. began complaining of severe backaches and joint issues. "It didn't seem very serious," Yusha Auchincloss would recall. "I suggested she see a chiropractor, thinking she'd probably hurt herself while playing with the kids." However, within weeks, the family would be devastated by a surprising and terrible diagnosis: Janet had lung cancer. "Since she had never smoked a day in her life, this was completely unbelievable," Jamie recalled. "We all had to spring into action as a family. Quick plans had to be made, and among them was the decision that Janet and Lewis and the kids would stay in the States for as long as necessary so that Janet could have the best possible treatment available."

Janet Sr. was beside herself with worry

about her daughter, fearful for the future. "Who will care for my grandchildren if my daughter dies?" she asked Jonathan Tapper through her tears one day. She was, these days, much more emotional than ever before. He tried to tell her not to worry while reassuring her that Janet was going to make it. "But it's just not fair," Janet said, crying. "It should be me. Not my Janet. I'm *ready* to go. *It should be me.*"

TRANSFUSION

January 1985.

Jacqueline Kennedy Onassis was sitting in a small white plastic chair next to her half sister, Janet Jr., who was lying on her back in a bed at the Dana-Farber Cancer Institute in Boston. Three times a week, it would be the same routine. Jackie would have her right arm punctured so that blood could be drawn and then passed and filtered through what she called "a god-awful machine of some kind" — actually, it was a sophisticated cell-separating apparatus. The machinery would collect platelets from Jackie's blood and return the remaining blood components, along with saline, back into Jackie's system. The platelets would then be transferred to Janet as part of an aggressive treatment to battle her cancer. Since a platelet transfusion from just a single donor would reduce Janet's exposure to germs from multiple donors, it was decided that Jackie and only Jackie would give blood. Though it was known that Janet Sr. shared the same blood type as her daughters, this process would have been too much of an emotional ordeal for Janet Sr. to handle. "This is my responsibility," Jackie had said, and so she devoted herself to it entirely. She was able to sneak in and out of the hospital through a back entrance; few would ever know of her devotion to her half sister.

"Terribly weakened as a result of her treatment, Janet Jr. would spend the hours chatting away with Jackie about their lives, their children, and, of course, their mother," recalled Sylvia Whitehouse Blake, who had known Janet Jr. all of her life. "Jackie remained committed to Janet's recovery, especially after Janet underwent a painful bone marrow transplant at Dana-Farber in the hopes of keeping the cancer at bay."

When Yusha brought Janet Sr. to her daughter's bedside in early March, the senior Janet seemed older and much more fragile. Jackie held her mother's arm tightly as they spoke to Janet Jr., steadying her. Not only was Jackie extremely worried about her mother, she didn't want Janet Jr. to realize the great toll her illness had taken on "Mummy." As doctors and nurses dutifully came and went from the room, Janet and Jackie tried to keep Janet Jr.'s spirits up. It all felt hopeless, though.

VIGIL

"Oh Lord, help me now. Continue your heal-
ing. Make me strong for this. Please cure
me so I can be a mother and a wife again
— soon; so I can be with my family and
friends, and so I can find something to do
to help others. Thank you."
— Prayer by Janet Jennings Auchincloss
Rutherfurd as she began her last
chemotherapy treatment on March 7, 1985

March 11, 1985.
Winthrop Rutherfurd III was behind his
desk at his estate-planning firm in New York
when he got the call. His sister-in-law, Janet
Jr., had just a few more days to live. Shaken,
he called his wife, Mary, to tell her he was
flying immediately to Boston to be with his
younger brother, Lewis, and the rest of the
family. He also called his sister, Linda, who,
he learned, was already rushing with her
husband, Gordon, to be at Janet's side.
Jamie Auchincloss had seen his sister a
week earlier. At the time, Janet Jr.'s son
Andrew was suffering from such a bad cough,
there was concern about his mother possibly
catching something from him. However, Janet
Jr., now wearing a wig after having lost her
hair due to chemotherapy, insisted on seeing
him one last time. It was his birthday; he and
his uncle Jamie shared the same natal day.

After it became clear that Janet's lung cancer had spread to her brain and pancreas, many of her old friends — such as her old beau, John Kerry — called Jamie wondering if they could see her. Jamie told them he thought it best if they all just waited for the memorial. As for himself, Jamie just couldn't bring himself to go back to the Dana-Farber Cancer Institute after his and Andrew's birthday. He couldn't bear it. It was also decided that "Mummy" shouldn't go back, either. It was too much for her.

When Winthrop Rutherfurd finally arrived at Dana-Farber on the 11th, he raced to his sister-in-law's room. There he found Jackie seeming completely bereft. She was standing at Janet Jr.'s bedside with Lewis and their two sons, Andrew and Lewis. "For the next three days and nights, we stayed with Janet," Winthrop recalled. "We never left her side, not for a second. Jackie slept on a couch. None of us were able to bathe or make ourselves presentable. She could have been 'Mary Smith,' or anyone else, that's how anonymous, if you will, and low-key Jackie was; she was just Janet's sister, and that was it. Looking back on it, I can't help but think how extraordinary it was that this woman, one of the most famous, celebrated in the world, sat with the rest of us for three days and nights as part of our family. That's just who Jackie was, though, to us — family.

That's why she was there, holding Janet's hand. She cared for her deeply. There was a quiet strength about her, a sort of bravery, which, of course, we had all read about — Dallas, and all of that — but I don't think we'd actually experienced it prior to this time.

"There was a solarium outside the room, and sometimes we would go out there and sit and talk and cry. For those three days, though, there was actually nothing we could do but just wait. Jackie would go into Janet's room, hold her hand, talk softly to her, and say good-bye, as we all did. The boys would leave at night, and then come back the next day. We just waited and waited for the inevitable."

Finally, on March 13, with the family all holding hands in a prayer circle around her bedside, Janet Auchincloss Rutherfurd took her last, labored breath. She was just thirty-nine. "When she flatlined," recalled Winthrop Rutherfurd, "the doctor turned to us and said, 'She's gone. I'm very sorry. She put up a brave fight, but it's over.'"

"You can rest now," a tearful Jackie said as she gently placed her hand on her half sister's forehead. "My sweet, sweet Janet."

BRAVE

On March 19, 1985, Janet Auchincloss sat in a pew at Trinity Church in Newport next to her only son, Jamie. She looked small and frail, not at all the formidable presence of days gone by. The terrible occasion was Janet Jr.'s funeral. "Are you okay, Mummy?" Jamie asked, concerned about her. She nodded yes. "Is there anything I can do for you?" he pressed. She shook her head no. Staring straight ahead, she showed no emotion, seeming somehow paralyzed by her terrible grief. Jamie took her hand and held it tightly. As he studied her face, it suddenly occurred to him that his mother might never get over this tragedy. Janet Jr.'s decline had taken a serious toll on her; the traumatic ordeal seemed to have caused Janet's Alzheimer's to somehow overcome her. She was now more forgetful, distant, and vacant than ever. In fact, Jamie had to wonder whether or not his mother even knew what was going on around her.

As Janet sat staring blankly, her eldest daughter, Jackie, gave a eulogy at a lectern in the front of the church. "Knowing Janet was like having a cardinal in your garden," she said. "She was bright and lovely and incredibly alive." She then read a number of poems, including one Janet had written: Jackie said that Janet wrote it back in 1966 when she first got to Hong Kong. " 'I am the richest person in the world!' " Jackie read. " 'I always own the view from my window. All my windows.' Then, this last part," Jackie explained with a soft smile, "you really had to know my sister to understand. 'I'm tired,' " Jackie read, " 'hot . . . and my baby toe tickles.' " The mourners laughed. "That was very Janet," Jackie said. "She always had such a whimsical view of things."

While he and his mother sat through the service, Jamie couldn't help but fear for her future. In fact, Michael Dupree, Janet's chef and a registered nurse who worked with Alzheimer's patients, observed, "Many times, the disease is hastened by trauma, and I definitely believe her daughter's illness and then death accelerated the disease in Mrs. Auchincloss. She loved her children, I always knew it. At Janet Jr.'s funeral, she told me, 'A mother losing a child is a terrible thing, and my poor Jackie lost two. I can't imagine the strength she must have had to be able to survive that. I don't think I have it in me. I'm not Jackie.' "

Of course, everyone who loved Janet Jr. was completely devastated by her death; those who worked at Hammersmith were at the funeral, including Mannie and Louise Faria and their kids, Joyce and Linda, both of whom were close to Janet's boys, Andrew and Lewis. "Mrs. A. was overwhelmed with sadness," said Joyce Faria. "You could see it all over her face that day, her heart completely broken."

Lee did not attend the service. While some

665

thought she should have been present to support her mother through the ordeal, she chose not to do so. Winthrop Rutherfurd III noted, "I don't think I saw Lee more than maybe a couple times in my entire life. I'm not suggesting anything negative, I just never saw her." Jamie added, "She never clicked with Janet Jr. for some reason. I always thought maybe having one challenging relationship with a sister was more than enough for Lee to handle." Lee may have found the service meaningful, though, especially given that a poem by Robert Frost read by Jackie from the lectern sounded like a nod to Lee's own belief system: "The utmost reward of daring should be still to dare."

Bingham Morris was also not present at the service. Apparently, there was some tension between him and Jackie on this day — no one quite remembers what was at issue, only that the family was afraid it would further upset Janet to have "Booch" at the service in Jackie's company. Therefore, in what some viewed as a magnanimous gesture, Bingham decided to absent himself from the funeral rather than take a chance on further troubling his wife.

After the service, Janet was taken back to Hammersmith Farm by Michael Dupree. Meanwhile, Jackie waited for her own car in the parking lot, nervously smoking one Pall Mall after another. "I tried not to be too maudlin," she told Jamie as she reflected on her eulogy. "Ari used to always say, 'There should never be a wedding without some tears or a funeral without some laughter.'" The two then remembered that at JFK's private service in the East Wing at the White House, Jamie, who was then sixteen, remained at the Communion railing in front of the casket for a very embarrassing few moments hoping for wine, only to find out that none would be forthcoming. Janet didn't think it was at all funny, but everyone else did. All these years later, Jackie still got a charge out of the memory of her half brother solemnly on his knees with his eyes closed, waiting patiently for his wine. "I don't know if you realize this, but I was even a little tipsy at your wedding to Jack," he now told her. "But, Jamie, you were six!" she exclaimed. *"I know!"* he said. After they shared a laugh, Jackie became serious again. "Janet was so brave," she remarked. "I'm not sure I could be that brave in the face of all she went through."

"But you *have* been brave, Jackie," Jamie reminded her. "The whole country admires you for your bravery."

Jackie smiled. "My God, that was *so* long ago, Jamie," she said. "I was a completely different person back then. I can barely remember that dreary woman in black."

"Well, *I* remember," Jamie said as he began

to walk her to her arriving car. He tried to put his arm around her, but she pulled away. "Everyone in America remembers," he continued. They then talked a little about the second planned service for Janet, which would take place at the Church of the Heavenly Rest in New York City on April 15. Jackie wasn't sure she would be able to attend, saying she didn't know if she could possibly go through it again. She brought up Janet's daughter, Alexandra. "She's only two," Jackie said, shaking her head in despair. "She will never know how wonderful her mother was and how much she loved her."

"We'll make sure she knows," Jamie said.

"Yes, we will," Jackie agreed. In fact, Alexandra's aunt Jackie would make a special effort to remain an important part of her life as she grew up. She would even leave her the sum of $100,000 in her will. Her daughter, Caroline, is very close to Alexandra to this day.

The half siblings then stood and stared at each other without words, maybe wondering why their rapport was so often interrupted by such incredibly awkward moments. Jamie realized, though, that Jackie really didn't trust him, not after the Kitty Kelley book. Though he loved her deeply, he would just have to accept it. Of course, as par for the course with his family, he and Jackie never actually discussed the problem. He had sent her what he thought was a sincere letter of apology; she didn't respond. Therefore it wasn't as if they had a full airing of things. Instead, they just tried to go on with their lives despite this unresolved issue between them, never again feeling truly at ease with each other.

COMPARTMENTALIZATION

One warm day in the spring of 1985, Jackie had dinner with her old friend Roswell Gilpatric (JFK's former deputy secretary of defense) at Sardi's in New York City. After Ari died, she said, she never imagined she'd ever be in another serious relationship. While she'd had a brief flirtation with the noted writer Pete Hamill, it never materialized into anything because Maurice Tempelsman seemed to always be in the wings. "I'm fifty-five," Jackie exclaimed, tossing back her thick fall of hair. "I'm *old*, Ros," she added. The two friends laughed. "And I'm so *stubborn*. You know me. I'm quite fussy, aren't I?" Rather than answer the question and state the obvious, Roswell smiled at her and assured her that these were her best years and that it was fun to sometimes throw caution to the wind. "But must I do it for another man who smokes cigars?" Jackie asked, laughing.

Since being with Maurice, Jackie had experienced a renaissance, of sorts; she had a very nice, satisfying life at home and at work.

However, most people were unaware of the tension that sometimes existed between her and her immediate family members. She'd always been adept at compartmentalizing things, but never more so than during the period of time her mother was suffering from Alzheimer's. Jackie recognized her duty where her mother was concerned and she rose to the occasion with diligence, but also great discretion. It was as if she had two distinct, very different lives: the one in New York as a publishing executive with Maurice Tempelsman and her children at her side, and the one in Newport with Janet and the other Auchinclosses and, occasionally — and becoming more rarely than ever — with Lee. She tended to keep people from one another, maybe as a way of controlling things: Jamie, for instance, never once even met Maurice!

In fact, if one really considers the notion, Jackie actually had yet *another* life, didn't she? The one she still shared with the Kennedy family. There was always some cataclysmic drama unfolding in their lives, and Jackie remained an integral part of each story. For instance, she was vital to Joan Kennedy's support system as Joan struggled to maintain her sobriety; important to Joan's husband, Ted, as he rehabilitated his political career after the drowning of Mary Jo Kopechne at Chappaquiddick. She and Rose, Ethel, Eunice, and all of the Kennedy women were still close, contrary to what a lot of people said and wrote about them. (Don't forget that she took Aristotle Onassis to meet Rose and the family at the Kennedy compound in Hyannis Port *before* she took him to meet her own mother at Hammersmith!) However, her life with the Kennedys pretty much never intersected with the one she had with the Auchinclosses.

Whenever Maurice asked Jackie how Janet was faring, Jackie would usually respond vaguely that she was "as well as could be expected." She did complain to him once in front of an associate that she'd recently dropped in at Hammersmith without warning and, much to her dismay, found all of the employees out of their uniforms. "Mr. Dupree was wearing an Oxford shirt and *khakis,*" she exclaimed. She said she now suspected the staff only dressed formally when they knew she was coming. Maurice told her to leave the workers alone, that the last thing she needed to do was alienate them, especially given the tension that existed between her and Bingham Morris. "You need them a lot more than they need you," he warned her. "As long as they are taking care of things over there, you'd better not make trouble for those people." Jackie listened to his advice.

671

"Your background is phony, Janet, and you know it," Bingham Morris was telling his wife over dinner. As the staff waited on them, he began to rail at her. "You have been lying about it for years," he said, "and you know it. Your kids know it. Everyone knows it!"

"That is not true," Janet said, crying. "Why are you being so mean to me, Booch?"

"Oh, don't give me that," he told her, annoyed. "It's time for you to face the truth. You're *Irish,* Janet. Deal with it. Jesus Christ! There's nothing wrong with being Irish."

Janet stood up and rushed out of the room in tears. One of her servants raced after her.

Something had definitely switched in Bingham Morris's personality by the spring of 1985. Frustrated by his wife's debilitating disease, he had become difficult and argumentative. While he'd started out as an amiable, almost comical presence at Hammersmith — maybe even a breath of fresh air — by the middle of '85, he was disliked by pretty much the entire staff. Needless to say, when these household workers reported back to Jackie certain upsetting exchanges they'd witnessed, she was concerned.

According to what Jackie told a colleague, who was also an editor at Doubleday, it all came to a head one day when she was visiting Janet and noticed black-and-blue marks on her arm. "What is that, Mummy?" she asked as she rolled up the sleeve to Janet's dress. Surprise then immediately turned to horror. The marks on Janet were clearly an imprint of a hand. Janet quickly reached over and pushed down the sleeve, saying she didn't want to discuss it. Jackie then called Yusha into the room and showed him the markings. He was shocked, so much so that tears instantly sprang to his eyes. The two then had one of the servants track down Bingham, who was listening to the radio out on the pier.

Leaving Janet in the kitchen, Jackie and Yusha went down to the pier to interrogate Bingham about what they'd discovered. Naturally, he was irate and defensive. He explained that Janet had almost slipped down the stairs and that he'd reached out to catch her just in time. They should be *thanking* him, he said, not indicting him. He was so convincing, Yusha tended to believe him. He actually had seen Janet nearly stumble from time to time; it was not unusual these days. Jackie didn't buy it, though. "How *hard* did you grab her?" she demanded of Bingham. "Those black-and-blue marks are a distinct impression of your hand!" He didn't want to discuss it any further, saying he would never win with Jackie, so why try?

When Jackie and Yusha then went back to the Castle to question Janet, she said she had no memory of how she got the marks. She also didn't remember almost falling down any stairs. Her whole demeanor was skittish and fearful. Was she really just too embarrassed to admit that Booch had been violent with her? Was Jackie just now discovering abusive behavior that had been going on for years? With so many questions unanswered, Jackie was, at first, heartbroken that her mother had had to endure even a moment of suffering. Then, of course, she became quite angry. "She, basically, didn't know what to do," said her colleague at Doubleday. "She said to me, 'I know I am not imagining things. What is going on here? I need to get to the bottom of this!' Her protective instincts went into overdrive, I think that's maybe the best way to describe it."

"Pretty much overnight, Jackie felt we had a big problem on our hands with Booch," confirmed Jamie. "She wanted it solved by, basically, evicting him from the Castle. It was at around this time that we decided we'd better have Yusha move into the Windmill to keep an eye on things. It was the only sensible thing to do under the circumstances. From this point on, Yusha would split his time between his apartment in New York and the Windmill."

In a subsequent letter to Yusha after he was settled into the Windmill, Jackie laid it on the line: "Booch's visits to [Janet] must be limited

674

to the minimum at one weekend a month. These visits to her should be planned to *include* [her emphasis] holidays, anniversaries, etc. . . . Those events should *not* be supplementary weekends." In other words, she didn't want Bingham to use special occasions to, as she put it, "fit more weekends in." Furthermore, she wanted someone to be with him and Janet *"at all times"* when he was at the Castle, and that someone should sleep in the house with them. And when they went for walks, she wanted a caretaker to follow them. When he called on the telephone, she wanted someone standing right next to Janet during the entire conversation. Jackie added that she was worried that Bingham's mistreatment of the staff, had them "on the verge of leaving and if Mummy should lose any of the devoted people who care for her, who are irreplaceable, she will have a terrible relapse."

When Yusha relayed Jackie's terms to Bingham, he was furious and demanded to talk to Jackie, himself. A couple of days later, the two had angry words. While he recognized that "these walls have ears," Bingham told her he felt that he and Janet still deserved their privacy. He accused Jackie of being overprotective and controlling. He reminded her that he was still Janet's husband. How dare she tell him to leave? "We're *married,* Jackie," he said. "You don't get to tell us how to live our lives." Undaunted, Jackie said her decisions were final, and that if he didn't adhere to them, she would call the police on him. "I promise you that I will protect my mother from you if it is the last thing I ever do," she told him in front of witnesses.

"Mrs. O. had come to believe that Booch was mistreating her mother and she wasn't going to tolerate it," said Janine Rule. "When she asked Janet about it, sometimes Janet would say yes, and sometimes she would say no. She was confused. Because of her disease, it wasn't easy to get a straight answer from her. Jackie wasn't going to take a chance, though. The 'yes' was all she needed to hear to take action. But then Booch didn't adhere to her demands. He kept showing up when he wasn't supposed to, and Jackie kept getting calls from Michael Dupree and Mannie Faria that Booch was there when he wasn't supposed to be.

"I was with my mother [Adora Rule] at Jackie's home when a call came in from Michael, and Jackie became very, very upset. 'Why is he there?' I overheard her ask. 'He shouldn't be there!' Finally, she said, 'Goddamn that Booch! I'm coming up tomorrow and I'll take care of it.'

"She slammed down the phone, furious. 'If he stuck to the rules, even *then* I would be upset and I'd want him out altogether,' she said. 'But he doesn't. He shows up whenever the hell he wants. I always knew this man was trouble. I always knew it!' "

JANET'S SURPRISING GIFT TO LEE

"Is there anything I can do for you?" Janet would ask Jamie more than a couple of times a day. "For instance, do you need any money?" This was certainly a gentler, maybe it could be said more benevolent, Janet Auchincloss, now often asking her children if she could be of financial assistance. "No, Mummy, I'm just fine," Jamie would say. However, he would find his mother's persistent question a little troubling. If Janet were taken advantage of, he feared, who knew what she might do in her current state? His concern was prescient; in the end, Janet's offer of money would come between her daughters, Jackie and Lee.

Shortly after buying the condominium she owned at the Watergate complex, Janet had decided to sell it. Of course, again, this sale made no sense to most people. However, Janet was supposedly making her own decisions, even though everyone felt that Bingham was controlling things. She then bought a small town house at 3224 Volta Place in Georgetown.

In December of 1986, there was a fire in

Janet's new home. Though she was at Hammersmith at the time, the blaze was still quite upsetting to Janet. "These days, she just couldn't handle any kind of upheaval in her life," recalled Jamie. "We all did our best to step in — Jackie kept up with Mummy's correspondence, for instance." For example, Jackie wrote to Dr. John Lattimer, one of the doctors who had treated Janet Jr., to thank him for a letter he had written to Janet Sr. (on May 13, 1986). "Thank you for your thoughtful letter about Janet," she wrote. "She was brave and courageous throughout her illness. We will never cease to think of her or miss her. Sadly, my mother has a bad memory problem and while I know she would be happy to hear from you, I thought I should tell you about her condition, as I do not believe she will be able to answer you."

Under the circumstances, Jackie didn't think Janet should make major decisions about her finances. Janet disagreed, and vehemently. She may not have had a memory for names, but she still felt she knew what she wanted to do with her money.

After the fire damage was repaired at the Volta Place residence, Janet decided to sell it, as well. Jamie Auchincloss recalled, "My mother then asked Lee the question she often asked us: 'What can I do for you? Do you need any money?' Apparently, Lee said yes and explained that she was having some financial difficulties."

At around this same time, Lee decided to abandon her designing business. It had become too costly for her to run and she never seemed able to turn a profit with it. Though as optimistic as ever, Lee actually had no idea what she was going to do next. From critiquing fashion, to acting onstage and then on television, to producing a documentary, to hosting a talk show, to writing a book, to running her own design firm . . . she'd certainly done a lot with her life. If not for the fact that she was Jackie's sister, she might not have had so many opportunities. Being related to one of the most famous women in the world had to have helped. However, no matter the field, Lee's great efforts somehow always turned to ashes before her.

After she sold her Park Avenue penthouse to raise cash, Lee moved into a rental town house on East Seventy-third Street. Though it was nicely appointed, she was tired of the flux. It felt to her as if she'd been working most of her life and was still always concerned about money. While she had enough to continue an entitled lifestyle — she still had her Southampton beach house, after all, and many people in her life would have been astonished to know she had any financial concerns — it was a strain. "Therefore, my mother decided that she wanted to give Lee the proceeds from the sale of the Volta house, about six hundred and fifty thousand dollars," said Jamie. "I think she felt guilty that she'd been so hard on Lee in the past; she'd been expressing as much lately. She wanted to do something nice for her."

It sometimes happens in families that the child who does the least is reframed in the needy parent's mind as the one most appreciated. That was the case here. Jackie was the daughter who was always present for Janet, yet Lee had now become the favored one. "Jackie was on the phone every single day," Jonathan Tapper recalled, "or at the Castle, always involved every step along the way. But if that phone would ring and it would be Lee, maybe once a month if that, oh my, Madam would light up! She would say it outright, 'Lee is my favorite.' By this time, Jackie and Jamie both knew it and would have to live with it. Madam was always quite critical of Jackie, but never of Lee. She would glow when talking about Lee and all the things she had done — the acting and writing and designing. But when you would ask about Jackie, she would shrug and say, 'She was a very good First Lady, I'll give her that much. But then Jack died and she married Onassis and it was all over for her.'"

Jamie confirms, "Mummy had two eleven-by-fourteen photos of Jackie and Lee side by side in a scrapbook, each picture taking up a whole page. One had the simple caption written in my mother's handwriting: 'Jackie.' The other: '*My* Lee.' "

"This has been going on since we were kids," Jackie told one relative. Of course, back then it was Jackie who was the favored daughter. "Yes, it's hurtful when you can't seem to do enough for your mother," Jackie continued, "when she is always asking about the daughter who's not present. It drives me up a wall, actually."

At the beginning of 1987, Janet asked Lee to come to the Castle for a Mother-Daughter Tea. Whereas these family moments used to always take place at one of the best hotels in New York — usually the Plaza — now it was just easier for Janet to host her daughters at her home. Jackie wasn't present, it was just Janet and Lee. After they caught up with each other's lives, Janet reportedly slid the check across the table. "This is for you, dear," she said. According to a later recollection, Lee didn't know what to say. "I'm sorry," Janet then told her. She said she had been thinking about it for some time and that she had regrets about the way she had raised Lee. "For any time I ever let you down, I'm very sorry," she said. "Maybe this small gift will make your life a little easier. I love you, Lee."

We don't know Lee's reaction; she's never discussed it and only she and Janet were in the room at the time the gift was presented.

Sisterly Dispute
Over Money

"We didn't know a thing about Mummy giving Lee money until my mother's secretary told us about it," Jamie Auchincloss recalled. "Suffice it to say, while I was a little surprised, Jackie was *very* surprised. Jackie didn't think it at all appropriate for Mummy to give Lee the proceeds from the sale of the Washington real estate. Something about it seemed suspect to Jackie and, to be honest, me, too. We weren't sure how it had happened that Lee ended up with the money."

At the very least, Jackie told Janet, the gift should have been split evenly between Lee and Jamie — $325,000 each. Janet disagreed, saying that it was her money and that she would do with it what she pleased. Moreover, if Jamie needed money, she said, he would ask her for it and she would then be more than happy to give it to him. At this time, Jamie was working as a photographer in Washington and doing well; he also had a trust fund from "Grampy Lee." He'd led somewhat of a bohemian lifestyle for years, not spending much time at home. He is gay, which complicated things for him. "It would be difficult for me to imagine that my sisters didn't know about my sexuality, though," he said. "I was fine with whatever they thought,

682

though we never once discussed it. I was living my life. It was good." In fact, he'd recently returned from India, where he'd purchased a painting for Jackie, which she said she loved "more than anything." In a letter to him, she wrote, "How lucky you were to have spent such a long time in India. I'm jealous! Thank you, dear Jamie." She wished him "all my best wishes" and signed it "Love, Jackie."

Lee was bewildered as to why Jackie would even care about the money gift. After all, Jackie had millions in the bank. Why begrudge her sister this small amount? Lee was upset about it, and she didn't care who knew it. "What is *wrong* with her?" she asked one of her relatives, speaking of Jackie. "Does she not have enough money?" This was also one of those rare moments when Lee's life-altering decision about Aristotle Onassis from so many years earlier came back to haunt her. After all, had she chosen to be with him in '63 instead of renewing her vows to Stas, she most certainly wouldn't have needed Janet's $650,000. "She didn't live in regret" is how one of her friends put it, "but if you think what she did in order to keep Jackie free of scandal back when she was First Lady didn't sometimes vex Lee, you'd be wrong."

Typically, the sisters didn't have a discussion about Janet's gift to Lee, at least no one that anyone remembers.

An Alarming Accusation

By the spring of 1987, Janet Auchincloss was slipping terribly. As the family made plans for her to be moved from Washington to Newport for the spring/summer season, they suspected that it might be her last time at Hammersmith.

The season got off to a rocky start when, shortly after moving back into the Castle, on May 18, Janet was found wandering around in the middle of the night, somehow locked outside. Her knee was bleeding; apparently, she'd taken a fall. Jackie couldn't help but blame Bingham, who was sound asleep in the Castle at the time. She wanted answers. How did her mother end up locked outside? Had there been an argument? And why was she bleeding? Mannie Faria, who'd found her, said Janet told him Bingham had kicked her out of the house after a fight. However, when Jackie later asked Janet about it, she denied it, saying she had locked herself out. It was just impossible to get a straight answer! The next day, Jackie was dismayed to learn that Bingham had melted down the prized sterling cups Janet had won in hunting competitions during her youth. He wanted to sell them as silver. "But who gave you permission to do that?' Jackie demanded. He hemmed, hawed, and stammered but, in the end, didn't really have an answer.

"We were all pretty much at the end of our ropes with this man by this time," is how Jamie put it.

On May 20, an agitated Janet came down to the kitchen, where Yusha was having breakfast. Something had happened between her and Bingham in their bedroom, she said. She wouldn't explain what it was, only that she wanted him out of the house, and immediately. Of course, Yusha went up to talk to Bingham. All he did, Bingham explained, was slip into bed with Janet and be there when she awakened, "and she just went completely ape-shit when she turned over and saw me," he said. Maybe it made sense. Janet and Hugh had always slept in twin beds, never in the same one. (Yusha was actually the one Auchincloss with a double bed in his room, back in the Big House.) Janet was probably frightened when she awoke to find Booch next to her. Still, Yusha couldn't help but wonder if there was more to the story. In the end, he didn't care; if Janet wanted Bingham out, he had to leave. Fine, Bingham told Yusha, "I'll leave, then. Don't get all bent out of shape over it." He left.

When Yusha called Jackie to tell her about the incident, she was frantic. She actually blamed Yusha. Why couldn't he keep a better eye on things? The two had angry words; Jackie even threatened to send her son, John, to live at the Castle to keep an eye on things.

He was studying to take the bar exam, so, she reasoned, perhaps the time alone would be worthwhile. Yusha said no, he could handle things on his own. Jackie would later say she deeply regretted ever being cross with Yusha about the matter; it was as if Bingham's actions were somehow turning them against each other.

In a missive to Bingham at this time, Yusha wrote: "As you surely must realize, your constant complaining, abusive language, and derogatory accusations about her [Janet's] children, grandchildren, staff, and dogs deeply disturbs as well as disrupts her staff . . . and disgusts me."

Jackie canceled her entire day of meetings at Doubleday and got to Hammersmith as quickly as possible. She then spoke to Janet, who said that she didn't know what in the world Yusha was talking about, claiming that he had imagined the whole thing. Not only that, she wanted to know where her husband was and she demanded that he be returned to the Castle at once. Now, as was becoming par for the course, Jackie didn't know what to think. "I actually feel like I'm losing my mind," she later told one of her colleagues at Doubleday. "I just can't seem to get a handle on what's going on!"

Less than a week later, Jackie went back to Hammersmith to check on things. She found Janet walking hand in hand with Bingham on the beach as Jonathan Tapper followed them while holding an umbrella over their heads. Jackie took a seat on a wicker chair on the porch and watched the pleasant scene. One can only imagine what was going through her mind as she studied her mother enjoying the day with her troublesome husband while a dutiful functionary shielded them from the sun with a large parasol. Certainly, Janet seemed content with Bingham, at least in this moment.

After about an hour, the threesome ambled back up to the Castle. Janet was delighted to find her daughter on her way down to the beach to greet her. "What in the world are *you* doing here?" she asked as she made her way toward Jackie with uneasy footing. She embraced her tightly, so very pleased. "Will you be staying for dinner?" she asked. Jackie said that she would be happy to do so. "Is Lee coming, too?" Janet asked, hopefully. "No," Jackie said. "Goody-goody," Janet exclaimed as she put her arm around her eldest. "It'll just be you, me, and Booch, then. Just family." She turned to Jonathan Tapper and said, "Set another place at the table, will you? Right next to me, for Jacqueline." She said she wanted to "change for dinner." Every night, Janet wore an evening gown for dinner; it had been that way for years and would not change until she was unable to do so.

Jackie took her mother's arm and the two

of them walked slowly up to the Castle, Jackie steadying Janet every step along the way. As they made their way, they began chatting in French to each other, just the way they used to so many years earlier when they didn't want others to know what they were saying. Much to Jackie's delight, despite her failing mind and health, Janet's French was still absolutely flawless. As Bingham and Jonathan made their way more quickly up the hill to the Castle, Janet turned to Jackie and, now in plain English, said the words that would change everything for everyone at Hammersmith. "That man wants to do bad things to me I don't like," she said.

"Who?" Jackie asked, alarmed.

"Booch."

JACKIE AT WAR

Now Jackie was really on the warpath. What exactly did her mother mean when she said that Bingham Morris wanted to do "bad things" to her? The next day, while Janet was down at the Windmill napping, Jackie had it out with Bingham. He claimed to have no idea what Janet was talking about, insisting that there was no issue between them. Upset, Jackie didn't want to hear another word about it. "I want you to, once and for all, stay away from my mother! Do you hear me? Stay away from my mother!" she screamed at him,

688

this according to stunned witnesses in the household.

Bingham raised his voice as well, becoming completely incensed. "Why don't you stop being such *a little bitch,* Jackie," he hollered at her.

Jackie looked as if she couldn't believe her ears; no one may have ever spoken to her like that before, not in her entire lifetime! "How dare you?" she demanded to know. *"How dare you?"* Bingham again reminded Jackie that he was still Janet's husband and thus had "certain rights." Jackie said she didn't want to hear it. In full attack mode, she insisted he leave the Castle at once, and said she wasn't going anywhere until he was gone. If he refused, she would call the police. She added that there were any number of household staff members who would eagerly testify against him, "and you're going right to jail, Mr. Morris. In fact, by the time I finish with you," she threatened, "you'll be sorry you were ever born. Now, get the hell out!" She then stood at the front door with her arms folded and waited for him to go upstairs and pack his bags. A half hour later, Bingham finally came downstairs with a suitcase. "Mannie, please escort this . . . *person* . . . off the property," Jackie said. "And don't you dare come back," she told Bingham.

After she was sure Bingham Morris was gone, an upset Jacqueline Onassis left Hammersmith and took a flight back to New York.

It had been a terrible scene; Jackie later said she couldn't believe how completely unhinged Bingham had become during their altercation. Of course, she had not been a model of decorum, either. Things were definitely getting out of control. "He is an angry and disturbed man," Jackie wrote to Yusha about the incident. She was afraid that whatever they did to fix the situation could make things worse. "He will be momentarily checked but his anger will be boiling inside," she wrote, "and after a while I believe it will erupt again."

The next day, Jackie was at work at Doubleday juggling a full day of appointments and responsibilities. She was in a conference room with a team of editors when a call came for her. She excused herself and took the call in her office. When she didn't return, one of the editors went to get her. She found her sitting at her desk, crying. Rarely did anyone ever see Jacqueline Onassis cry, and likely if the editor had given her ample time, Jackie would have composed herself and this colleague wouldn't have seen it, either. She recalled, "I was stunned. It was upsetting. She was shaking, seeming very . . . traumatized I guess would be the word. I asked her what was wrong and she said, 'It's my mother. I have to leave and go back to Hammersmith. Something's going on there with her husband.' I asked if I could help and she said no. Maybe I should go with her? No. She said she was going to make the four-hour drive herself so that she would have time to think. She then sort of pulled herself together and stood up, and I saw this transformation come over her. 'That fucking man,' she exclaimed as she gathered her things, angrily. She got her coat and purse and stormed out of the office."

Booch was back.

SADIST?

What happened between Jacqueline Onassis and Bingham Morris when she got back to Hammersmith after the phone call at Double-day is unknown. For the rest of 1987, Jackie would continue to wage war against Bingham Morris, enlisting in it Dr. Dennis Selkoe, Janet's doctor from Harvard Medical School Center for Neurologic Diseases at Brigham and Women's Hospital, in Boston. Referring to the possibility of sexual abuse, Jackie wrote at this time that she recognized it as "a delicate matter," but that she was sure Dr. Selkoe would know how to handle it. Jackie noted, "We don't know what goes on in the bedroom, but Mummy has said, 'That man wants to do bad things to me.'" She further noted that her mother had re-located to the guest room when Booch was in residence at

Hammersmith. "Booch is torturing Mummy and he cannot hide behind the rights of a husband!" Jackie further noted, adding that she felt they had no choice but to try to protect Janet from him.

Jackie added that she felt Dr. Selkoe should let Booch know that her family, her staff, and her lawyer were all well aware of how much Booch antagonized Janet, and that they were all cognizant of "the details of his psychological [and perhaps physical] torture of Mummy." She concluded that, given all that was going on in the household, she was more certain than ever that Booch posed "a greater danger" to Janet than even her Alzheimer's!

At Jackie's request, Dr. Selkoe went out to Hammersmith to investigate. He specifically asked Janet whether or not Bingham Morris was being abusive to her and she said no, absolutely not. She didn't show any outward signs of physical abuse, either. He asked about sexual abuse, and she said, again, no. Selkoe then called a meeting for the staff, which was conducted in the living room at the Castle, without Janet's and Bingham's presence. Jackie was there, as were Yusha, Jamie, Mannie and Louise Faria, Michael Dupree, and a number of others. Some people felt Janet was being abused — others did not. Michael Dupree, for instance, sided with Morris, as he does today: "I saw no signs of physical or verbal abuse," he would say in

2017. "I had a high esteem of Booch. The problem as I saw it was that he didn't understand Alzheimer's and, as a result, was impatient with Janet. He wanted her to be what she had been before, and she wasn't. So, he would lose his patience. But abusive? No."

At the general meeting, the physician reiterated what was already known, which was — just to be on the safe side — that Janet should not leave Hammersmith, "except in extraordinary circumstances." Jackie had already said that she didn't want Janet going to Southampton with Bingham, so at least the doctor was now ratifying that wish.

The biggest problem Jackie now faced, though, was that, based on his interviews with the staff and his personal observations, Dr. Selkoe wasn't so sure that Janet was being abused. "I didn't see any sign of it," he would say in 2017. "I continued to see Janet after my visit to Hammersmith. She would come to my office at Brigham Hospital. I would also visit her at the Castle. She was usually gay, bright, and still intelligent, though clearly forgetful. Mrs. Onassis would call me at home to discuss her mother's care. She had clearly done her research and read up on all of the information available at that time. I know she had serious concerns about Mr. Morris. But he accompanied his wife to my office every time and he always seemed pleas-

693

ant and genuinely concerned. In my presence, there was nothing but warmth and affection between the two of them. I saw no evidence, no signs of trouble."

"Even though Yusha was on the same page as Jackie, I think maybe he was now beginning to wonder if he and Jackie were overreacting," said Jamie. "I mean, you had to wonder, especially about Jackie, given everything she had been through."

One of Janet's doctors went so far as to theorize that Jackie's fears about Bingham Morris were somehow informed by her PTSD. Was it possible that she was still so traumatized by what had happened to Jack and Bobby, and her powerlessness in both incidents, that she was now trying to exert control over the possibility of something terrible happening to her mother? "This was my guess," said one of Janet's doctors at that time. "I had to agree with Dr. Selkoe that there was no clear-cut evidence of physical or sexual abuse. However, emotional abuse? Maybe. You'd have to be in the house to know for sure, and no doctor was in the house. Emotional abuse is bad enough, though, and reason for Mrs. Onassis's concern, obviously. However, there was a growing concern that she was overreacting, and that her state of mind was perhaps somewhat influenced by her own tragic personal history. She couldn't protect Jack. She couldn't protect Bobby. She couldn't protect her children who died. She was going to protect her mother, though. She was *definitely* going to protect her mother."

For her part, Lee had begun to agree with Dr. Selkoe. "I spoke to Lee personally," he recalled. "We had conferences and I told her my opinion, yes."

Lee had been around Jackie's PTSD for years and well knew the havoc it had played on her life and that of the entire family's. If Dr. Selkoe didn't believe Janet was being physically abused, Lee would also not believe it. She didn't spend much time at Hammersmith, though — and everyone agrees on that point. "I don't think I ever saw her," says Michael Dupree, who worked at Hammersmith from 1986 through 1989, "though she did call from time to time. She could have slipped in and out. I wasn't standing guard over her mother. But did I see her? No."

It didn't matter what other people thought, though; Jackie said she had to listen to her *own* reason and it continued to tell her that Bingham Morris was a real threat. "She finally laid down the law," recalled Jamie, "and banished Booch to the Palace — and it was anything *but* a Palace. It was a real shoddy apartment up a steep stairs over the garage next to the Castle. We couldn't get rid of him, but at least we got him out of the Castle. He would visit Mummy in the Castle, she would get upset, he would then leave.

695

Then he would telephone Mummy from the Palace. She would say she missed him and wanted to see him, and the vicious cycle would repeat."

In a letter to Yusha, Jackie made an equivalency between her mother and the needs of a child who fears desertion. In her opinion, Janet longed for Booch every time she talked to him on the telephone, forgetting how angry and upset she'd been with him the last time she saw him. Then she'd want to see him again. When that occurred, she would only end up being tormented by him once again. Jackie wrote that she was certain Booch was "a sadist," that "tyrannizing" the entire household staff was what he most enjoyed, and that "doing worse" to Janet is what made him truly happy. She concluded by saying that the Hammersmith employees firmly believed that Booch was "sick" and that he played "sick games" with Janet.

JANET'S EIGHTIETH

December 3, 1987.

"Are you happy, Mummy?" Jackie asked as she watched Janet thumb through a leather-bound scrapbook called "Janet's Birthday Letters," full of handwritten memories and personal family photos. The book had been compiled by Jackie and Yusha for the occasion of Janet's eightieth birthday. Janet smiled and nodded as she turned each page.

In the last few months, Janet's physical and emotional condition had worsened. "It was just the natural course of the disease that it got worse," explained Dr. Dennis Selkoe, "and sometimes that happens all of a sudden."

"There was a period of time when she began to suffer from Sundowner's Syndrome," said Michael Dupree. "It is common with Alzheimer's patients. Janet would become irritable, confused, and nervous when the sun went down. I would always go around and close all of the curtains and turn on all of the lights just so that she wouldn't notice the coming of nightfall."

These days, Janet spent most of her time in a hospital bed in a guest room in the Castle. However, on this day, she was seated on a couch in the Deck Room, back at the Big House at Hammersmith, which she had loved for so many years. Her head-of-staff nurse, Elisa Sullivan, had made it possible for Janet to celebrate her eightieth birthday here, with a surprise party. Dressed in a black sweater with a long gold necklace and pendant, Janet looked as if she couldn't really move, her rail-thin body purposefully and carefully arranged among pillows and comforters. Though propped up on the long wood-edged sofa, she was in great spirits.

Along with Jackie, Yusha, and Yusha's

daughter, Maya, surrounding Janet on this special day were, of course, Lee and Jamie and a gaggle of close friends, such as Oatsie Charles and Eileen Slocum, as well as long-time employees, like Janet's majordomo, Jonathan Tapper; her former assistant, Adora Rule, and Adora's daughter, Janine; current chef, Michael Dupree; and, of course, Elisa Sullivan. Bingham Morris was present, too. Jackie had her eye on him the whole time, not letting him have even a second alone with her mother. Others caring for Janet were also there, including her nurse Sally Ewalt. "My father [Mannie Faria] was at her side the entire time," recalled Joyce Faria Brennan, who also was present, as were her mother and sister. "Janet was especially surprised that they'd flown in her grandchildren Lewis and Andrew [Janet Jr.'s sons] from Hong Kong. So it was a wonderful day for all of us."

"The memories this must bring back to you," Oatsie Charles said as she watched Janet turn the pages. A few weeks earlier, Yusha had sent a form to each family member and friend on which they were to explain what they were up to these days, and share a special thought about Janet. "I have too many lovely memories to fill this small space," wrote Lee, "but enough to fill books. I love you very much." She also mentioned some of their wonderful times together, including driving all over Italy one summer. Jackie remembered how much she used to love to hear Janet sing to her and Lee the old Harry Lauder song "I Just Can't Make My Eyes Behave" and "Comin' Through the Rye." She noted of Janet's eightieth that it was "the greatest day in the history of Hammersmith." She also wrote the words to the "Happy Birthday" song on a decorative sheet of paper, along with the comment: "I think it is better to read this than to hear me sing it. I love you, Jackie."

Making the keepsake all the more memorable were handwritten reminiscences by Yusha and Jamie, as well as Caroline, John, Anthony, and Tina, friends such as Oatsie Charles and Nancy Tuckerman, and employees such as the Farias and their daughters.

"Are you staying for supper?" Janet suddenly asked Michael Dupree, her chef. He said yes, he was. In fact, he would be preparing it. Janet said, "That's nice." She then leaned into Jackie and said, "I don't know who that nice man is, but he's making us supper." Jackie patted Janet's knee to assure her that everything was all right. By this time, Oatsie had placed a scrapbook she'd made on Janet's lap, pictures she had taken of good times in the past. Turning a page, Janet came upon a newspaper clipping about the President and First Lady's tenth wedding anniversary spent at Hammersmith in 1963.

"Oh, look, Mummy," Jackie exclaimed. "That's me and Jack."

Janet stared at the newspaper clipping, running her index finger over it. She stopped at each word in the headline and paused as if her memories were flooding her fully, taking her back. She smiled to herself and nodded. A moment passed, and then another. Finally, Jackie took her mother's hand into her own. "You *do* remember, don't you, Mummy?" she asked, hopefully.

Janet nodded. "Yes, I do," she said, softly. Then, fixing Jackie with an earnest expression, she paused for a second. A frown crossed her still-smooth brow as she asked, "So, tell me, dear. Who is this President Kennedy?"

HERBERT ROSS

In January of 1988, Lee Radziwill met a man who would change the course of her life in many ways. He was someone with whom she felt she had a great deal in common, for he, too, had experimented with many different career aspirations. The difference was that he was enormously successful in everything he touched, whether in dance, choreography, theater, television, or film. Lee felt a connection to his wanderlust and admired not only his versatility but also his spirit. Though he'd been largely criticized in his life and career, he still pushed forward despite what people said or thought about him, much like Lee.

Herbert David Ross — known professionally as "Herb," though his friends and family called him "Herbert" — was born in New York in 1923 and started his career as a chorus boy in no less than fifteen Broadway shows in the 1940s. After breaking his ankle at the age of twenty-three, he changed course and became a successful choreographer. Soon, he was choreographing for the Broadway stage, twenty-six shows in all, including *A Tree Grows in Brooklyn* and *House of Flowers.* He then began to work at staging ballet for Broadway shows, including *On a Clear Day You Can See Forever* and Barbra Streisand's debut, *I Can Get It for You Wholesale.* After that, he found his way into directing musical numbers for movies, including *Funny Girl.* He then went on to a successful career as a director with a string of memorable films such as *Goodbye, Mr. Chips, The Owl and the Pussycat, Funny Lady, The Sunshine Boys, The Turning Point, Footloose, The Goodbye Girl,* and, just as he and Lee began to know each other, *Steel Magnolias.*

Ross was a man who lived life on his own terms, refusing to be pigeonholed or stereotyped, again something Lee felt she had in common with him. He spent most of the 1940s into the 1950s living as a gay man in a

701

committed relationship with a dancer named John Ward. He then married another dancer, ballerina Nora Kaye, in 1959, choosing to then live his life as a straight man. This choice fascinated Lee; he truly did not care what people thought of it, and there was something about his audacity that intrigued Lee. She had always been a fan of his movies — *The Turning Point* and *Pennies from Heaven* being personal favorites — and so when she had the opportunity to get to know him, she was excited to pick his brain. Within three months, she began to fall for him. Soon she found herself in Louisiana with him, scouting locations for *Steel Magnolias.*

At sixty-five, Herbert Ross was distinguished-looking, intelligent, engaging, and, happily enough, quite wealthy. He'd accumulated a decent-size nest egg from his many decades in show business and was also now commanding more than $2 million per picture with a healthy percentage of profits. When Lee met him, he had just buried his wife of twenty-eight years, Nora Kaye.

"Herbert missed Nora terribly," said his goddaughter, Leslie Browne. "He'd been so devastated by her death, some feared he'd never recover! I actually think he would have died if he had to be on his own, without a wife. Therefore, when Lee came into his life, a woman with whom he had such a great rapport, it was as if he'd found salvation. She was classy, educated, and came from a prestigious family. There was a hint of the Kennedys about her, too, so that was fun for him, as well. He immediately fell into a rhythm with her that felt comfortable and made him happy again."

For her part, Lee admired the fact that Herbert had been married so long and had demonstrated a capacity to be so committed to a relationship. He shared her love of art, design, fine dining, and travel. He was also a great raconteur with so many fascinating stories about his life in show business. She really couldn't get enough of him. "I love our life together," she said, happily, "and I never want it to change." Did she have questions about his sexuality? Not really. She'd had complex relationships in the past with men with ambiguous sexual identities — she was even said to have had a one-night stand with Rudolf Nureyev — and, in her mind, sexuality was fluid. She made no judgments about any of it. She fell for him hard, as was Lee's fashion.

By this time, Lee had sold her Southampton beach home, another necessity in order to make ends meet. The fact that she'd now met someone wealthy, a man to whom she was attracted and who seemed to feel the same about her, gave her some hope that maybe her long romantic drought might be over — and along with it, her financial problems as well.

Still, going on in the background of Lee's life, of course, was her mother's ongoing illness. "Have you seen my sister?" Jackie asked Garrett Johnston, Hugh's former business colleague, when he came to visit Janet at the Castle. When Garrett said he hadn't, Jackie nodded and said it was "hard" and that it was "everything I can do to come here, myself." She noted that it was in dealing with situations such as the one in which they now found themselves "that you really find out what you're made of." When Garrett told Jackie that he'd heard Lee was dating a film director, and that the two of them were out of town on the set of a movie together, Jackie was surprised. It seemed clear that the sisters hadn't spoken. "Okay, well, look, I hope this works out for her," Jackie said. "I don't want Lee to be alone. It's no good being alone." When Garrett told Jackie that he would pass a message on to her if he saw Lee, Jackie shook her head no. "I think we need our space," she said, without explanation.

DISTANCING HERSELF

On an early September morning in 1988 two vehicles made their way to Hammersmith Farm, one a shiny black limousine, the other a dirty old station wagon. The vehicles came upon two driveways, one that wrapped around the property in the direction of the Big House and another that veered off to the right eventually ending in the vicinity of the Castle. The latter driveway was mostly used by household employees. "That's *her*," a paparazzo shouted out as the limousine turned onto the main driveway. "That's gotta be her. Jackie O!" At that warning, a fleet of motorcycles pulled out of the brush, each with a photographer mounted on it. This coterie of photographers slowly followed the limousine as far down the path as possible before the car got to a small gatehouse. As it slowly pulled past the guard shack, the photographers jumped off their bikes and began setting up their long lens equipment. They wanted to be ready to take pictures of the limousine's passenger exiting the vehicle and then walking up to the front door of the Big House. Meanwhile, the station wagon made its clunky way down the other road, followed by no one.

Once the station wagon was in front of the Castle, Jacqueline Kennedy Onassis, huddled in the back seat of the vehicle, threw off the blanket covering her. Mannie Faria then jumped out of the front seat, ran around the car, and opened the passenger door. Jackie stood up and faced him with a smile. They had once again been able to evade the paparazzi, as they did at least two or three times a week.

Today there was a certain amount of urgency to Jackie and Mannie's gamesmanship. *The National Enquirer* had reported that Janet was ill, possibly with Alzheimer's. As a result, the press had been at Hammersmith's front entrance all week waiting for some sort of confirmation. Jackie's presence at the farm would be all they would require to run with a story about Janet's illness. They didn't realize that Jackie's being at Hammersmith wasn't really that unusual. She was there almost every weekend, staying at the Castle with her mother and seeing to her care. However, the fewer pictures of her entering or leaving the premises at this time, the better. Mannie was a trusty accomplice in Jackie's comings and goings, always one to dream up a clever way of camouflaging her activities.

"Mrs. O. called my father all the time to check on Mrs. A.," said Joyce Faria Brennan. "No matter how many years we knew her, my mom was in complete awe of her. Mrs. O. would call and Mom would whisper, 'It's *Mrs. Onassis* on the phone,' and everyone in the room would be still and silent as my dad gave her the update on Mrs. A."

As Janet's disease progressed, the desperate situation regarding Bingham Morris seemed to subside. The sad truth was that Janet just became too sick for him to be viewed as much of a threat. Jackie still had her eyes on him, though. It had been about a year and a half of true worry and anxiety relating to him. If it had gone on maybe even a few months longer, Jackie likely would have been better able to get to the bottom of it, whatever it was. She was in the process of establishing a conservatorship for her mother. She remained uncertain, though, overwhelmed even, especially as Janet became more ill. There was no time to continue her war against Booch. Her focus now had to shift from dealing with him to coordinating the caregiving of her mother. Still, as far as Jackie was concerned, Bingham Morris would always be the enemy on the premises she'd not been able to banish. "I know something bad was going on," she told one household employee. "I know it. Even if I can't prove it. I know it."

As Janet became less aware of her surroundings, there were days she didn't even remember the important people in her life. "Do you remember Janet Jr.?" Jamie once asked his mother. She shook her head no. "She was a good friend of yours," Jamie said, not wanting to upset Janet by saying she was her daughter. "She died about three years ago." Janet looked sad. "Was she very young?" she asked. "Yes," Jamie answered. "Just thirty-nine." Janet thought it over. "What a shame," she said. "I'm sure she was a wonderful girl. Was she?" Jamie took his mother's hand. "Yes," he said sadly. "Janet was wonderful. We all loved her very much."

Janet's entire life was being swept away by the disease — all of her memories, her history, her very identity. However, she was sweet, mellow, and pleasant. "From her expression and the way she was with people," recalled Jamie, "it was actually as if she had opened her heart to more love."

This would be an important time in Jackie's relationship with her mother. Who knows what they discussed in their many private moments together? However, Jackie would tell intimates that she would never forget the final year of Janet's life, that it had "meant the world to me." She told Yusha, "We were so busy being angry with each other, we forgot how to be mother and daughter. I'm trying to get back to that with her."

One day, according to what Yusha would later remember, Jackie asked Janet, "Mummy, are you scared?" Janet smiled and asked, "Of what, dear?" She seemed just fine, lost in her own little world.

Once, Jackie walked into the kitchen and found Janet sitting alone humming the obscure Christmas song she and Lee used to sing to her during their Christmas plays when they were young, "One Night, When Stars Were Shining." She had tears in her eyes, as she always did when the girls sang it for her. Jackie went over to her mother, sat next to her, and held her hand as they hummed the song together. Sometimes the two would sit in the living room and just watch television, no words necessary between them. Often they would enjoy *Jeopardy!* together and Yusha recalled, "Jackie would provide all the answers in her famous whisper so that her mother felt she was winning thousands of dollars." Once, Yusha walked in on them while they were in the midst of gales of laughter. Jackie exclaimed, "My sides are starting to hurt, Mummy!" Yusha didn't know what they were laughing about; it was private between mother and daughter. However, Jackie kept saying, "No, Mummy! You *didn't*! That can't be true!"

"Jackie was beyond extraordinary the last years of our mother's life," Lee Radziwill would say. "She really focused on her. She called her every single day. It was very difficult to deal with her a lot of the time and then, of course, it became most of the time. I don't know too many children who would have behaved better and been more certain of her comfort, attention, and care."

In fact, one of Jackie's biggest disappointments during this time was that Lee couldn't bring herself to spend much time with her mother at the Castle. "I don't really have a memory of Lee during this time," said Joyce Faria Brennan. "It's not good or bad, I just draw a blank. She wasn't around. We never thought about it, or wondered about it. It was always Mrs. O. or Jamie or Mr. Yusha, that's all we knew."

Today, when Jamie is asked if Lee helped out, his succinct answer is the same as everyone else's: "No."

Though Janet's accelerating illness had definitely been hard on Lee for the last few years, she may have had specific reasons for her absence at Hammersmith that didn't have to do with Janet. "There was a sense that Lee didn't want to get sucked into another one of Jackie's PTSD psychodramas," said one person who knew them both well. "Lee had to agree with Dr. Selkoe that Booch wasn't abusing her mother, and I think she wondered if Jackie had been imagining the whole thing. Was Jackie just being dramatic? She didn't know. Look, she always thought Jackie was sort of over the top. I think it's safe to say she believed the doctor, not her sister. Whatever was going on, she'd had enough of it and didn't want to be a part of it."

Making things even more complicated for Lee was that her son, Anthony, had recently been diagnosed with testicular cancer. Lee was coping with it all as best she could, but it was difficult. Anthony would be in and out of remission for the next twelve years. One of her friends recalls running into her in New York. Lee had just gotten back from Natchitoches, Louisiana, where she'd been with Herbert on the set of *Steel Magnolias*. After having an amiable conversation about her experiences on set, this friend — who also

710

knew Janet — asked Lee, "Have you seen your mother?" Lee's eyes filled with tears. She put her hand to her mouth, as if stifling a cry. She shook her head no. So overwhelmed was she, she couldn't even speak. Finally, she said, "I'm sorry but I must go. If you do see Mummy, tell her I love her." With that, she rushed off.

Jackie's sympathy for Lee only went so far. Lee's decision to absent herself from Janet's caregiving was something Jackie couldn't easily reconcile, according to people who knew her best back then. The fact that Lee had sided with Dr. Selkoe in believing that Janet was not being abused couldn't have made Jackie feel any better about things.

Meanwhile, Jackie began to make arrangements to have Janet moved to a nursing home where she could be taken care of by a staff that specialized in late-stage Alzheimer's. When she gently told Janet that she might have to leave the Castle soon, Janet became emotional. She didn't want to go anywhere, she said. She was happy just where she was, at Hammersmith, where she'd lived for more than forty-five years. "Do you remember what I told you many years ago about Edie Beale?" she asked, according to one account. Jackie knew what she was talking about, though she was stunned that Janet had memory of it. "I said that when I become old I don't want anyone to put me in a home,"

Janet said, tearfully. "Please don't do it, Jacqueline. I'm begging you." What a burden this must have been for Jackie. In the end, she said she understood and she promised Janet that she would be able to stay at the Castle. However, she must have wondered for how much longer.

At the beginning of October 1988, just as Hammersmith Farm was being closed for the season and Janet was about to be relocated to Washington for the harsh winter, Jackie went to visit her mother. She found her sitting in a wooden Adirondack chair out on the expansive lawn in front of the Castle, all bundled up in a sweater under a blanket. She was crying. As the Hammersmith workers watched with heavy hearts, Jackie knelt down beside her on the grass and gently rested her head in her mother's lap.

LEE AND HERBERT MARRY

On the evening of September 23, 1988, a beaming Jackie stood in the library of her Fifth Avenue apartment holding both of Lee's hands. "I'm so happy for you," she said in front of a small group of friends. "Herbert is wonderful," Jackie exclaimed. "He's perfect for you, Pekes." Though she had just met him a day earlier, Jackie had immediately approved of Herbert Ross. He was successful, worldly, and wealthy and he treated her sister well. He had just purchased a four-hundred-acre ranch in the Santa Ynez Valley, outside of Santa Barbara, California, where he planned to raise cattle. Lee was excited about moving in and spending as much time as possible on the "other" coast with him. Jackie could see no reason to be disapproving, even if there was a nagging question of Herbert's sexuality. "Isn't he homosexual?" Jackie had asked her and Lee's friend Karen Lerner, the former wife of Alan Jay Lerner. With the greatest of social diplomacy, Karen answered, "Well, I never heard that he wasn't."

Though Karen's response gave Jackie pause, she decided not to pursue it. After all, Lee was fifty-five years old, old enough to know what she was doing. Moreover, Jackie and Lee were more and more superficial with each other these days. They seemed to not be as personally involved in each other's life choices. Given what was going on with their mother, they'd pretty much lost the will to keep their sisterly bond intact, as if each had unilaterally decided it wasn't worth the effort, or maybe the drama. Jackie agreed to host a wedding reception for Lee, but people in their lives felt it was more out of duty than anything else.

Lee looked stunning in her two-piece blue silk Giorgio Armani outfit — she'd lately been employed by the designer, orchestrating special events for his company — her dark hair pulled back from her angular face. "Thank you for doing this for me," Lee told Jackie. Jackie had cleared out her library and transformed it into a lovely dining area — round tables draped in canary-yellow silk with tall, tapered candles, delicate rose arrangements, and pink-and-gold Versace Byzantine china. "This is beautiful," Lee exclaimed. As the two exchanged embraces, any observer could sense their holding back. "Frozen smiles and false interactions" is how one witness described their rapport.

Though it hadn't even been a year since Lee met Herbert, marrying him was, as Lee would later put it, "probably the easiest decision I'd ever made." She knew he was serious about her when, a month earlier, she'd taken her annual vacation to Sardinia and he missed her so much he dispatched a private jet to bring her back home early. When he then asked her to be his wife, she eagerly accepted. There was practically no time to plan their wedding, but she didn't care.

The civil ceremony took place in the living room of Lee's new Upper East Side apartment, with Rudolf Nureyev, who'd flown in from Paris to be Lee's witness. Her daughter, Tina, was present, though Anthony was in Korea on assignment for NBC News. Then it was off to Jackie's for the reception, which was attended by about thirty people, including friends of Herbert's such as Ray Stark,

714

Bernadette Peters, Steve Martin, and Daryl Hannah (whom Ross had recently directed in *Steel Magnolias* and with whom John Kennedy Jr. would soon become romantically involved). Jackie's daughter, Caroline, and her husband, Ed Schlossberg, were also present, but they had left their three-month-old infant — Jackie's first grandchild, Rose — at home with the nanny.

"WE'LL BE JUST FINE . . ."

Saturday, July 22, 1989.

"Have you been able to find Lee?" Jackie asked her stepbrother Yusha Auchincloss. She was sitting next to a hospital bed that had been set up in the living room of the Castle. In it, her eighty-one-year-old mother, Janet, was comfortably laid on her back, her head turned to face her daughter. She gazed at Jackie with a serene expression, a soft smile, and sad eyes. "No" was the answer from Yusha. Jackie then wondered about Jamie's whereabouts. Yusha said Jamie had just seen his mother about a week or so earlier. Now he was back in Washington, where he was working as a photographer. "I'm trying to reach him," Yusha said. As the two spoke, they could hear loud music blaring from a bedroom upstairs. Exasperated, Jackie shook her head in disbelief. "Oh my God," she exclaimed. Why was Booch in the Castle? He was supposed to be in the so-called Palace! She asked Yusha to go upstairs and tell him to turn down his music. No sooner had Jackie given the order than the music suddenly went off; Michael Dupree had already run upstairs to handle Booch.

Janet had actually been physically strong until the previous March, when she took a nasty fall at the Castle and broke her hip. That accident was the beginning of a steady decline. Following it, Janet wasn't physically well enough to even be a candidate for the nursing home Jackie had been considering for her. Therefore, she would stay at the Castle, just as she'd always wanted.

For the last couple of weeks, Janet had been so medicated it was difficult to know, especially given her advanced Alzheimer's, how much she was able to comprehend. "She knew Jackie, though," recalled Michael Dupree. "I know for a fact that she knew her daughter."

"She's doing as well as can be expected," Jackie wrote to one of Janet's friends. "There's no need to see her," she added. "Just know that she is well, happy, and loved."

Especially in the last year, Jackie had felt a great sense of injustice where Janet's condition was concerned. It had been excruciatingly painful to watch her decline. The ordeal would leave her concerned for the rest of her life that, one day, the same thing might happen to her, especially since both of Janet's sisters suffered from the same disease; Marion had died from it and Winifred was presently battling it. She said she could never put her children through it.

On this day, July 22, Jackie had been preparing to go to Hyannis Port to celebrate with the Kennedys the family matriarch Rose's one hundredth birthday when Yusha called her to tell her that her mother had taken a turn for the worse. Jackie arrived within two hours to find Janet lying in her bed on a morphine drip. Even now, there was still something regal about her. Her makeup had been applied with great care by Yusha. Her gray short-cropped coif came to a striking widow's peak above her elongated face with pronounced cheekbones. When she opened them, her brown eyes were still large and deep-set. Jackie told Yusha she looked beautiful, and thanked him. Most everyone had already been to her bedside: Mannie Faria, his wife, Louise, and their daughters, Joyce and Linda; Jonathan Tapper; Michael Dupree; Elisa Sullivan; Oatsie Charles; Adora Rule and her daughter, Janine. "I held her hand and told her how much I loved her," Adora recalled. "We had known each other for thirty-six years. I went to work for her right before Jack married Jackie! It was difficult to fathom the passing of the years and how much Mrs. A. had seen in her lifetime."

Exhausted from the emotion of the day, Yusha felt the need to take a nap. Jackie told him to go, saying she would wait with Janet just a while longer. "We'll be just fine," she said. Less than an hour later, while the sun began to set over Narragansett Bay, Jackie watched as her mother took her final breath. With her firstborn daughter at her side tenderly holding her hand, Janet then passed from this world to the next, finally at peace.

THE SERVICE FOR JANET

Jamie Auchincloss wasn't sure how he would feel about his mother's death. More precisely, he wasn't sure how he *should* feel. After all, he had been raised in a family where loving emotions were usually suppressed. While combustible feelings were often at the fore, warm ones were pushed aside. Making matters more complex for him, his sexual identity was not known to any of his family members. "Therefore, I have never been an emotionally available person," he confessed. However, he was also raised by Janet to place a premium on appearances. "How things looked mattered," he recalled. "I was so afraid that I might appear cold and detached at my own mother's funeral."

Janet had died of a disease that had robbed her of all memory of Jamie and just about everyone else. Her death was a blessing, as

718

far as he was concerned. He was relieved that her suffering was over, not devastated. He found good in her passing. Still, he knew he would be in sitting in a pew at the service between his two famous sisters, Jackie and Lee. The conundrum for him was that he felt an overwhelming sense of anxiety about how he would react during the service. He felt he needed a trigger, something that might help him elicit the deep emotion he'd need for appearance's sake.

At this same time, Jamie's fourteen-year-old Norwegian elkhound named Carioca would soon have to be put down because she wasn't well. He knew that the dog would not survive the drive from Washington to Newport. Therefore, he decided to put her to sleep right before leaving for his mother's funeral, thinking, "Maybe if I did, I could feel some sorrow in the church." Though it was a sad, and arguably strange, way for him to generate what he felt he needed in terms of emotion for his mother's funeral, his decision spoke volumes about the way he was raised, his disconnect from true feelings.

The service for Janet Lee Bouvier Auchincloss Morris took place at Trinity Church, the Episcopalian parish in which she had worshipped for so many years, on July 27, 1989, the day before Jackie's sixtieth birthday. Though all of the family was present, of course, Jackie was the focus of attention. As she stepped from a silver limousine into the mass hysteria of paparazzi angling to get that one great shot of the daughter in mourning, she seemed resigned to just get through the day. More than a thousand onlookers, who had begun to gather three hours earlier, pressed forward to take a closer look at her in her simple, short-sleeved, knee-length black dress. Lee followed with her husband, Herbert, in their own limousine, a jet-black one. Then Jamie, Yusha, and all the rest arrived in town cars. Janet's good friend Eileen Slocum held court with the press, telling the reporters that even though Janet had suffered from Alzheimer's for so many years, "her memory failure was graceful, and even at the end she never became disoriented or inappropriate."

There were Kennedys scattered throughout the church, most notably Ted Kennedy and his son Patrick, Ethel Kennedy and many of her children, as well as Sargent Shriver, all of whom obviously attended out of respect for Jackie. Of course, Jackie's children, John and Caroline, and her son-in-law, Ed, were all present, as were Lee's children, Anthony and Tina. (True to Jackie's unique compartmentalization of things, Maurice Tempelsman was not at the funeral.) In the rear of the church was a grieving Bingham Morris, all alone. Everyone rose as a tearful Mannie Faria, so handsome and stately looking in a black suit, walked down the center aisle of the church carrying in his hand an ornate box of Janet's ashes. How fitting it was that Mannie was selected by the family for such an honor, considering how much he, his wife, and their children had meant to Janet. "Nothing will ever go wrong," Janet always used to say, "because Mannie is here. And he'll take care of it."

As Mannie walked slowly toward the church's triple-tiered pulpit, he approached the hand-painted stained-glass window depicting Cornelius Vanderbilt. Mannie's wife, Louise, and their children, Joyce and Linda, sat watching in pews in the front on the right side of the altar. What an interesting study in contrasts: a hardworking, middle-class estate manager carrying the ashes of his wealthy high-society employer in a church that featured in one of its stained-glass windows one of the richest Americans in history, Commodore Vanderbilt.

It would be just a thirty-minute service, during which some of the letters written by loved ones and included in the scrapbook given to Janet on her eightieth birthday were read from the pulpit. There were also familiar psalms and hymns as well as a bagpipe rendition of "Amazing Grace."

In a wedged box in the front of the church by the lectern — pews in which President George Washington, Queen Elizabeth of

England, and South Africa's Bishop Desmond Tutu had all once worshipped — were seated Janet's three biological children, Jackie, Jamie, and Lee. "It was a triangular box," Jamie recalled, "with its own little, waist-high door. I was a large man. Jackie was tall. Lee was more normal-sized. So we were squeezed in there tightly, the three of us, and it was extremely uncomfortable." As Jamie feared, many of the mourners were fixated on him and his sisters. The siblings would have more on their minds, though, than just appearances. Sadly, it would seem that old grudges and bitter resentments could not be set aside, even on this mournful day. It was as if the mere presence of a sibling could conjure up bad feelings; each had an ax to grind with the other. The three of them weren't even speaking to one another.

Unfortunately for Jamie, there was only one prayer book in the box and he had to hold it up for his sisters to refer to throughout the service. They did so without so much as even a nod of thanks, or a word of liturgy. "I felt like saying to them, please, it's our mother's funeral, can't we just at least *act* like siblings on this one day, please?" Jamie recalled.

In the church's vestibule following the service, Jackie finally broke down. Crying, trembling, and smoking nervously, she was completely distraught. Her mother's illness had really taken a toll on her. Standing in a corner by herself while mourners consoled one another all around her, it was as if Jackie was all alone in her sadness, which is maybe how she'd felt for some time while caring for Janet.

From the other side of the vestibule, Jackie's breakdown caught Lee's eye. It also caught the attention of Oatsie Charles. After hesitating a moment, Lee walked over to Jackie, followed by Oatsie. As Oatsie waited her turn, the sisters embraced. While pulling away from each other, whatever anger Jackie felt toward Lee seemed to momentarily vanish. "You and I, we've been down a long road together, haven't we, Lee?" she asked. Lee seemed overcome by the question. "I love you," Jackie added, crying. "You know that, don't you?" Lee nodded, kissed Jackie on the cheek, and then rushed away, her hand to her mouth. While their mother's illness seemed to have made Jackie more in touch with her emotions, it had, at the same time, made Lee even more protective of her own.

After witnessing the exchange, Oatsie approached Jackie. "I am *so* sorry," she said, reaching out and embracing her. Jackie was stiff in her arms. "She pulled away and looked at me as if she didn't even know who I was," Charles recalled. "She was in total shock, not herself. I saw such pain in her eyes. But, then, I also saw a steely resolve come over her. She knew there was no way she could go out to the front of the church until she collected herself. She was Jacqueline Lee Bouvier, after all, her mother's daughter."

Once in front of the church, there was a mix-up about the transportation that was to take the family to Island Cemetery. In the confusion of the moment, Jamie was about to get into the limousine with Jackie, Yusha, and Bingham. Jackie abruptly grabbed Jamie's arm. "No, Jamie," she said, holding him tightly. "Please go and find another car," she said, her voice shaking.

"Sure, if that's what you want, Jackie," Jamie said. He looked at Yusha. He looked at Bingham. Then back at Jackie. From their expressions, he had a strong feeling that some sort of confrontation was in the offing. Jackie either didn't trust him enough to have him witness it or simply didn't want him to get involved. "Still, I found it very harsh," recalled Jamie, "that the only son of Janet Auchincloss had to hitch a ride with someone else to get to the cemetery."

Jamie's intuition was correct: There *would* be a confrontation.

Bingham Morris got into the front seat with the driver, while Jackie and Yusha made themselves comfortable in the back. Once they pulled away, according to Yusha's later memory, Jackie made her position clear, speaking to, basically, the back of Bingham's head. "I would appreciate if you would return any of Mummy's belongings that may be left at your house in Southampton to the Castle," she said in a level tone. "And also," she added, "I would like for you to be out of the Castle by the time the sun sets tonight."

Bingham, appearing a little disoriented, turned around to face his stepdaughter. "But, Jackie, I was planning to spend the night," he protested.

Jackie shook her head, no. "Absolutely not," she said. "I want you out. By the time the sun sets. Tonight, Mr. Morris. Do we have an understanding?" Furthermore, she said he would be entitled to just $25,000 from Janet's estate, "and don't you dare try to contest it," she warned him, because if he did so, she threatened, Alexander Forger would see to it that he'd end up with absolutely nothing. Then she reiterated that she wanted him out of the Castle. "Not tomorrow. Tonight, Mr. Morris. *Tonight!*"

Bingham Morris nodded his head. According to Yusha, there was no further discussion about anything else on the way to the cemetery. "I got to the cemetery at around the same time as the family car pulled up," Jamie recalled. "As they all filed out of the car, I could tell that something upsetting had happened in that vehicle. I remember thinking, I may have been kicked out of the family car at my own mother's funeral, but maybe it was for the best. I was just glad I didn't have to witness another big scene."

A Blaze of Glory

"You want things to work out," Lee Radziwill Ross was telling Adora Rule as they left the Island Cemetery, where some of Janet's cremains were buried in a simple wooden box swathed with one of her favorite scarves. "But I'm a practical person," she allowed. "In the real world, things are not so easy." As she spoke, she was walking next to her husband, Herbert, holding his hand. Jackie was in front of them, making her way with Yusha toward their gleaming silver limousine. While Lee studied her sister, she noted that "people just are who they are," and said that there was no changing them. She also said that Janet had never tried to change who she was, that she'd always lived her life on her own terms. "I hope I have, too," Lee concluded.

"Your mother would so love it if you and Jackie could be closer now that she's gone," Adora told Lee.

Lee shook her head. "I can't imagine that happening," she said frankly. "We'll see, I guess." She didn't seem hopeful, though.

Eight small boxes of ashes had been set aside for Jackie, Lee, Jamie, and Yusha as well as for Yusha's grown children, Cecil and Maya, and Hugh's offspring, Tommy and

726

Nini, each with the intention of being distributed on the grounds of Hammersmith Farm, the place where Janet had always found limitless peace. Once back at the farm, Lee and Herbert, along with Adora and her daughter, Janine, walked with Michael Dupree through the rock garden, where Michael then spread some of Janet's ashes. They were followed by Jackie, along with Caroline and John Jr. and Tina and Anthony. Trailing behind were the rest of the family members as well as friends, employees, and relatives, including Bingham Morris, who tried to make himself scarce after Jackie's dressing-down of him. Also present, of course, were Mannie and Louise Faria

Because the Faria daughters, Joyce and Linda, had to return to college after the funeral, they were not present for the spreading of ashes at Hammersmith. However, thanks to Janet's largesse, both would be able to have all of their college expenses paid for from her estate. As well as bequeathing Mannie and Louise $30,000 in her will, Janet set aside $60,000 for the Faria girls' education, as promised. Linda Faria would go to Providence College in Providence, Rhode Island, graduate with a degree, and become a mathematics teacher. Today she is the assistant superintendent of schools in Middletown, Rhode Island. Joyce Faria would go to Northeastern University and graduate with a bachelor of science degree in journalism. She presently works in public relations. Other employees also benefited from Janet's will; she left Jonathan Tapper, for instance, $8,000. Booch got the $25,000 Jackie had told him about and a gold watch. Each of Janet's grandchildren and stepgrandchildren was bequeathed $3,000.

Janet's real-estate holdings, including the Castle and the Windmill, were divided into sevenths — six shares to her living children and stepchildren, Yusha, Nini, Tommy, Jackie, Lee, and Jamie, with the remaining seventh bequeathed to Janet Jr.'s three children, Andrew, Lewis, and Alexandra.

"The Black Ships Festival is tonight," Jamie told Yusha, Tommy, and Maya. "You know how much Mummy loved those annual fireworks."

The Black Ships Festival was an annual event that paid homage to Commodore Matthew C. Perry, USN, of Newport, Rhode Island. "Black Ships" is the American translation of *kurofune*, the Japanese term for the foreign ships that were excluded from Japan for two hundred years. In 1854, Commodore Perry negotiated the Treaty of Kanagawa, the first treaty between the United States and Japan, thus ending two centuries of Japanese isolationism. Every year, the Black Ships Festival celebrates the signing of this treaty. Part of the festivities is a fireworks display at sunset, which Janet used to love to watch from the Deck Room of the Big House, and later from her porch at the Castle.

As the small group walked along, they stopped and spread Janet's ashes about the property's many elegantly designed lush gardens. Finally, when they got to a lovely sitting area at the center of which was an enormous sundial, they dispersed more of Janet's ashes in the same spot where Janet Jr.'s ashes had once been spread. "Mummy is with Janet for all eternity," Jackie said to Yusha as she approached. "I think she'd like that."

Yusha, Tommy, Maya, and Jamie then headed around to the back of the Big House along a paved road — passing a blind corner and Mannie's hand-painted sign that said "Honk Horn" — down a long grassy pathway to a dirt road that led toward the pier at the end of the property. Once at that pier, Jamie walked to the end of it by himself, his head bowed at the exact place where, years earlier, his father, Hugh, used to sit and fish for mackerel. He then scattered some of his mother's ashes to the wind. Stepping back, he allowed Yusha, Tommy, and Maya to do the same. The four then turned around and began the long walk back up the rolling and manicured hills toward the Castle, passing Jackie and Lee on their way but with a great distance between them.

As twilight set in and the night breeze picked up, Jackie and Lee slowly made their way down to the pier together, each with her own small box of ashes. The two sisters stopped at the end of the wooden dock. There was no railing in this spot, just the flat surface of timber, pockmarked with bird droppings. The sisters stood inches away from the pier's edge, very close to the undulating waves beyond it. As the other mourners watched from a distance, Lee emptied the contents of her box into the sparkling water. She lowered her head as if in prayer. A moment later, Jackie, with a dramatic, wide flourish of her hand, sowed her mother's ashes up and outward toward the blue sky.

As the daughters of Janet Lee Bouvier Auchincloss stood together in private tribute to the headstrong but devoted woman who'd given them life, a series of loud popping noises interrupted their reverie. They looked up in surprise to see the sky filled with unexpected starbursts of fiery red, golden yellow, and emerald green. Putting her arm around Lee, Jackie drew her close, so close that Lee was able to put her head on Jackie's shoulder. The sisters then watched the streaking fireworks in a state of wonderment as their beloved "Mummy" went out in what was nothing less than a fitting blaze of glory.

EPILOGUE: PASSAGES

At their mother's funeral, Lee doubted that she and Jackie would find their way back to each other. Not surprisingly, she was right. The next five years found the sisters leading their own lives, coming together only at special family occasions such as the birthday celebrations of their now-grown children. While there was no obvious acrimony between them, there also wasn't much warmth.

Once Janet was gone and Jackie finally had time to really think about the difficulty of the last few years, she realized she was quite angry at Lee for having made herself so unavailable. "She was *not* okay with Lee having abdicated her role as a caretaker" is how one of her friends put it. "She still hadn't reconciled in her mind whatever had been going on between Janet and Booch, and she felt she'd been abandoned by her sister during a very tough time," continued the source. "She needed time and distance from Lee to come to terms with it." Moreover, Jackie said she now realized that the real reason she didn't want Lee to have Janet's gift of $650,000 back in 1987 was because she felt her sister didn't deserve it. She was probably being petty, she said, but she couldn't help it. That's just how she felt.

During this time, Jackie stayed in touch with her half brother, Jamie, and stepsiblings Yusha, Tommy, and Nini. However, she also decided to relegate Hammersmith to her past while becoming attached to her own estate on Martha's Vineyard. Everything was different for her at Hammersmith, she said, especially after Mannie Faria died on the property about a year after Janet. Jackie made sure to keep Janet Jr.'s husband, Lewis, in her life, though, and remained close to her nephews Andrew and Lewis and especially her niece Alexandra. Meanwhile, Jackie continued to dote on her adult children, John and Caroline, as well as her grandchildren from Caroline — Rose, Tatiana, and John, who, as he got older, began to answer to "Jack." She also remained happy in her relationship with Maurice Tempelsman while continuing her rewarding work at Doubleday.

Meanwhile, Lee almost entirely broke with the past. She sold her share in Hammersmith back to her siblings, and then rarely, if ever, spoke to them again. She and Jamie lost touch completely. "Mummy was the only thread holding the two of us together, and it was tenuous at best," said Jamie of his relationship with Lee. "After Mummy was gone, it completely unraveled."

Lee built a very happy life for herself with her husband, Herbert Ross, and her children, Anthony and Tina. She became immersed in Herbert's successful film career while on the sets of his movies, forging new and exciting friendships in the world of show business. It was her choice, the way she had decided to live her life. Perhaps it was also her way of avoiding certain emotional triggers that might have jeopardized her continued sobriety.

This détente was acceptable to both sisters. However, as often happens in estranged families, serious illness would precipitate a rapprochement. At the beginning of 1994, Anthony's cancer came back again, with a vengeance. At this exact same moment, his aunt Jackie was diagnosed with cancer, too.

Jackie's non-Hodgkin's lymphoma was so fast-moving, she and Lee barely had time to settle old scores. In fact, they didn't even try. The last thing either wished to do, especially during such a critical time, was review their troubled history and try to come to terms with it. Instead, Lee was simply present for Jackie as she battled the disease. As much as possible, Jackie tried to also be present for Lee as she dealt with her only son's aggressive cancer, now discovered in his abdomen. Still, there was a troubling undercurrent between them. No doubt it was the awkwardness that occurs when complex life circumstances make the venting of suppressed hurt and anger feel somehow inappropriate. In other words, they needed to sit down and have a good talk and, once and for all, make themselves completely vulnerable to each other and tell each other the *truth* about how they felt. Unfortunately, even after all these years, they still weren't able to do so.

Jackie did have the love and support of her close circle, people such as Maurice and, of course, her children and other family members, like Yusha and Jamie. She wrote to Jamie in February to tell him not to "worry," saying that the reports about her illness had been "exaggerated" by the media. He happened to be moving to Ashland, Oregon, at the time. "Moving to Oregon sounds like a wonderful idea," Jackie wrote to her half brother in the last letter he would ever receive from her. Shortly thereafter, she wrote to Yusha: "You know how much I love you — as always, XO Jackie." That would also be the last note Yusha would ever receive from his stepsister, ending over a half-century of special correspondence between them.

Then, of course, there was always Jack.

Jack Warnecke, now divorced for more than twenty years, had never gotten over Jackie. He continued to send her Valentine's Day cards every year and see her whenever he was in New York, which was quite often. For a number of years, he didn't believe Maurice would be permanent in Jackie's life — wishful thinking, perhaps, because he hoped he'd have another chance with her. She always wondered, too; he was such a good man, had she made the right decision in choosing Ari over him? Somewhere along the line, though, they reconciled themselves to the reality of their relationship. "Wouldn't it be the craziest thing in the world if, after all this time and all we've been through, we became just friends?" he asked her. Jackie said, "Why, Jack, we already are!"

In March of 1994, Jackie discussed with Jack a new treatment plan now that the cancer had spread to her brain. This process involved the insertion of a stent in her skull through which chemotherapy would be introduced into her system. As she explained it with customary pragmatism, he couldn't help but be just a little shocked. They had to laugh; after everything Jackie had been through in her lifetime, he knew she could handle this new horror. She said that he should not spend even a moment worrying about her. "I am too young to die," Jackie said. "Why, I'm only sixty-four! I refuse to go," she concluded.

Years later, Jack Warnecke would wish to keep private other details of what he and Jackie discussed in this, their last phone call.

He did share one moving memory. "How are you dealing with it all?" he asked her. "I do cry from time to time," Jackie said, lowering her voice. "In the shower, Jack. Where no one can hear me. I think that's best."

Jackie's health declined so quickly, her friends and family couldn't believe it. On Wednesday morning, May 18, 1994, she was given the last rites of the Roman Catholic Church in her Manhattan apartment, the same one on Fifth Avenue in which she had started life anew after President Kennedy's assassination. Soft Gregorian chants filled Jackie's home as a procession of friends, family, and loved ones held vigil throughout the day and into the evening, Auchinclosses, Bouviers, and Kennedys among them. The group of loved ones became hushed and seemed to part in the middle as Lee walked out of the elevator and into the parlor. Appearing small and frail, she had Anthony at her elbow in place of Herbert, who was shooting a movie in California. After embracing John and Caroline, Lee took a deep breath to compose herself and then stepped into Jackie's bedroom and closed the door.

Jackie looked peaceful in her large canopied bed, partially under a blanket with an intravenous tube connected to one arm. She had earlier decided that she wanted to die at home on her own terms. In order that she might hasten her own death, she wished to be injected with more morphine than would have been legally permitted at any hospital. By this time, she was in a deep coma.

After about a half hour, at just before midnight, Lee emerged from Jackie's room. Her face seemed ashen, her eyes reddened. "My sister looks so beautiful," she told John, according to witnesses. "Do you know how much she loves you?" John asked as he embraced his aunt. Choked up, Lee put her hand to her mouth and just nodded.

Shortly thereafter, Lee steeled herself once again and went back into her sister's room, followed by John, Caroline, Anthony, and his new fiancée, Carole DiFalco. Ted Kennedy and his wife, Vicki, as well as his sister-in-law Ethel, were now there as well, as was Yusha. They all gathered around Jackie's bed, holding hands and praying. On his knees, with his hands folded in prayer before him, Anthony said to his beloved aunt, "I hope I can face this disease with as much dignity and courage as you have." Rising from her knees, Lee then walked from the foot of the bed to its head. Standing next to Jackie, she rested her hand on her sister's cheek. "I love you so much," she said. "I always have, Jacks," she concluded as she gently kissed her sister on the lips. "I hope you know it," she added, barely able to get the words out.

Finally, Lee left Jackie's apartment. With

her head bowed, she made her way through the bustling crowd of admirers, mourners, and reporters, all of whom had nosily congregated in front of Jackie's building waiting for word. As she did so, she cried shamelessly and without restraint.

The following night, May 19, 1994, Jacqueline Kennedy Onassis passed away. A few days later, she was buried next to her first husband, President John F. Kennedy, at Arlington National Cemetery.

"I have made no provision in this my Will for my sister, Lee B. Radziwill, for whom I have great affection, because I have already done so during my lifetime."

Jackie's decision to leave no money to Lee was a big surprise to the outside world but not so much to those who actually knew the sisters. In her will, which was signed in March of 1994, Jackie left most of her estate to Caroline and John and a half million dollars each to Anthony and Tina — but nothing for their mother. "Figured" is how Jamie put it, who wasn't even mentioned in the will. "At least Lee got her name in it," he said. "For some, it was as if I didn't exist. However, I always knew the parameters and limitations of the relationship I had with my sister, and I also knew her character and personality. I'm comfortable with all of it, all of our history. I certainly didn't expect anything from her in

738

her will. I knew how we felt about each other, and that's what sustained me."

While Jackie had helped Lee out on occasion over the years, to say she gave her money freely and with abandon would not be true. Though Lee had somehow lived a rich and entitled lifestyle, it was never easy for her. The sisters' dynamic had become so familiar it was, by this time, almost a caricature: Jackie always had it so good while Lee . . . didn't. Some in the family thought it would have been a loving gesture for Jackie to finally alter that situation once and for all, especially given that Aristotle Onassis chose not to bequeath any of his money to Lee, either, so many years earlier. Unfortunately, though, behavior that had been so true in life also held in death.

Two years after Jackie's death, on May 28, 1996, Bingham Morris — Booch — passed away quietly at his home in Southampton. He was eighty-nine and had no survivors. Almost twenty years later, on June 13, 2015, Hugh D. Auchincloss III — Yusha — would pass away at the age of eighty-seven, survived by many loved ones, including his two grown children, Cecil and Maya.

"Fine. Since I can't make up my mind," the woman was saying, "I'll just take one scarf in each color."

Adora Rule hadn't heard that voice in ten years, not since Janet Auchincloss's funeral. It was June 1999 and she was in the Bergdorf Goodman department store on Fifth Avenue in New York City. "Lee," she exclaimed, walking up to a woman examining herself in a mirror. The lady whirled around to face her. "Oh my God! Adora!" she exclaimed. "My God! It's been *ages*."

Adora would say that Lee looked "wonderful," even though, secretly, she was a little taken aback by how thin she was at the age of sixty-six. "She seemed incredibly frail," she would recall many years later.

Standing there in the aisle at Bergdorf's, the two women tried to catch up on the unfolding of the last decade. Anthony had been working as a producer for HBO, Lee said, and his wife, Carole, had the same job at ABC. Tina had just become engaged to a research doctor named Ottavio Arancio. John was publishing a new political magazine called *George* and was now married to a former publicist, Carolyn Bessette.

"I read about Anthony," Adora finally said. She reached out to take both of Lee's hands. As Lee nodded, she tried to choke back emotion. "We're at the end," she said sadly. "Three weeks. Maybe." She leaned against the counter, her body seeming to go slack. "Not many people in my life would understand this," she then said, lowering her voice to a whisper, "but you would. This is Mummy," she added, dropping her head. "This is Jackie. This isn't me. I can't do this. This isn't me."

Adora reached out and took Lee in her arms; she would remember the feel of her spine just under the skin on Lee's back. "Lee, you are so much stronger than you ever knew," she said. She reminded her that she'd always been her own woman. She always took chances. She pursued each and every one of her dreams with everything she had in her, no matter the consequences. If there was one thing Lee Radziwill always had, it was the courage of her convictions, "and that takes *strength*," Adora told her. "You have it, Lee. In fact, I always thought you were the strongest of the three. You will get through this . . . for your son."

"Thank you for saying that," Lee said as she reached into her purse for a handkerchief. They then talked a little about Janet and Jackie. Lee said that when she looked at herself in the mirror while putting on her makeup, she saw both of them staring back at her. She missed them, she said, especially these days. She then laughed and asked, 'How in the world did *I* become the matriarch, Adora? First of all, I'm too young," she observed. "And secondly, I'm still too goddamn irresponsible to be anyone's matriarch!"

For years, they had all been prepared for Anthony's death. But then, in July of 1999, in a twist all too tragically familiar to the Kennedys, the unthinkable happened: John was killed in a plane crash, along with his beautiful wife, Carolyn, and her sister Lauren Bessette. Three weeks later, Anthony died. "Loss upon loss" is how Lee had once put it when speaking of the dual tragedies of John and Bobby Kennedy.

Anthony was cremated wearing a crisp white starched shirt that had belonged to his uncle President John F. Kennedy, with its the collar stamped "1600 Pennsylvania."

After Anthony's death, Lee's marriage to Herbert began to crumble. For about ten years, they had been happy. However, after they grew apart and decided to separate, their bond was all but destroyed, ironically, by negotiations about money. After all, Lee had always been the Bouvier to disregard wealth when choosing a mate, often much to her mother and sister's dismay. She had to admit, though, that as she got older she wished she hadn't completely ignored their advice. It would have been much easier for her if she didn't have to worry about her finances in her advancing years. While she wouldn't change anything about the past, she realized now that she needed to look to the future. She felt the time had finally come for her to be practical, not idealistic. She could probably still hear Janet's admonition from years earlier relating to Newton Cope: "Now is not the time for soul-searching, Lee. Now is the time to take care of yourself." Perhaps that's why her divorce from Herbert, which was finalized in 2001, was so contentious. In the end, it was estimated that Lee wound up with in excess of $20 million.

Some felt that with her divorce, Lee, as one observer put, "finally joined her mother and her sister on the dark side." However, Lee was married to Herbert for twelve years. At the time of their divorce she was sixty-eight. Perhaps at one time in her life she might have walked away from the marriage with her future unsecured and the hope that something better might be right around the corner — maybe a new career . . . who knows? A book? A documentary? But not at sixty-eight. At sixty-eight, she decided to take care of herself. Maybe Janet and Jackie would have been proud.

Herbert Ross died shortly after his and Lee's divorce was finalized.

Lee's daughter, Tina, divorced in 2005. Presently single and with no children, she divides her time between America and Europe.

Today Lee Radziwill is eighty-four and lives

in Paris and New York. She says she is very happy, continues to work on her sobriety, and has "not one regret" about a life that has been nothing if not well lived.

SOURCE NOTES

A NOTE ABOUT MY SOURCES

When a historian spends years writing about a specialized interest, as I have the Kennedys, he and his team of researchers will inevitably contact and interview a wide range of sources. Very often, these sources will provide information that will not be used in the book for which they were been interviewed but will, instead, be utilized later in another work along the same lines. For instance, some who were interviewed for my first book about the Kennedys, *Jackie, Ethel, Joan: Women of Camelot* (2000) did not see their stories come to light until my next Kennedy book, *After Camelot* (2012). For *Jackie, Janet & Lee,* as well as having conducted scores of new interviews, I and my team drew from the research of both of my previous Kennedy books. Therefore, stories not utilized for those books (usually for space reasons and sometimes for storytelling purposes) have found their way into this one.

It's also worth noting that the stories of many people interviewed for *Janet, Jackie & Lee* did not make it into this book but, if history is any indication of things to come, they will probably appear in another Kennedy book down the line. In that regard, I want to especially thank Gustavo Paredes, the son of Jackie's trusted assistant, Provi, for the many hours he spent being interviewed. His insight will, no doubt, find its way into a Kennedy book I have planned for the future, as will the stories of, for instance, Katia Bede, the widow of Settimio Garritano, who took the famous nude photos of Jacqueline Kennedy Onassis in the 1970s. The stories of another invaluable source, Herbert Ross's attorney Stanford Lotwin, also did not make this edition, not because they weren't riveting but simply because of space concerns. There are many others who were interviewed for this work whose stories also do not appear in it. I am sure their memories will be included in books of mine in the future, however. I want to thank them; they know who they are. In particular, I want to acknowledge Vince Palamara, one of the world's leading experts on the Kennedy Secret Service detail, who has written several books about the subject, was interviewed a number of times for this work, and who assisted me in many ways. I urge you to visit his fascinating blog at vincepala mara.blogspot.com.

In writing about families as beloved and as controversial as the Auchinclosses, the Bouviers, the Kennedys, and the Radziwills, a historian always encounters sources who would like to speak but not for attribution. As I have often stated over the years, it is sometimes not easy for a source to come forward. Many times, that person has nothing to gain other than just the opportunity to tell his or her story for the sake of history and to, hopefully, illuminate the character of the subjects of the book. Cooperating with a biographer such as myself can often put a person at odds with someone he or she has known for many years. Sometimes, it makes more sense to ask for anonymity, and when a source of mine does so, I always grant it — but only after carefully reviewing that person's history with my subjects and the memories that are being shared to make certain they are aboveboard and not in any way compromised. I appreciate and value all of the people from so many walks of life who spoke to me and to my team of researchers for *Janet, Jackie & Lee,* whether specifically named in these notes or not.

I would like to especially thank the family of John Carl Warnecke — Jack — for sharing their memories of their dad and of his romance with Jackie Kennedy, augmenting what Jack told me back in 1998 and 2007. This includes his daughter, Margo Warnecke

Merck, and his son, Fred. I so appreciate their trust and hope they agree that their father, a truly great man and historical architect, is accurately portrayed in these pages.

Special thanks to Joyce Faria Brennan for all of her assistance, her memories of her family as she grew up at Hammersmith Farm, the wonderful photographs she shared with me, the videos she lent me, and all of the many other ways she helped bring her story and that of her family's — Mannie, Louise, and Linda — to life in this book. I hope she is happy with the portrayal of Janet Auchincloss, one of the most influential people in the lives of her and her family.

More than five hundred friends, relatives, politicians, journalists, socialites, lawyers, celebrities, business executives as well as foes, classmates, teachers, neighbors, newspeople, and archivists were contacted in preparation for *Jackie, Janet & Lee.* It should be obvious to most people that in my research, I and my team also carefully reviewed, as secondary sources, the many books that have been published over the last fifty years about assorted Kennedy, Bouvier, and Auchincloss family members, as well as thousands of newspaper and magazine articles written about them. I'm not going to list all of them in the Source Notes that follow, though I will acknowledge the ones I think are most necessary in understanding my research.

The following notes and source acknowledgments are by no means comprehensive. Rather, they are intended to give you, the reader, a general overview of my research. Also, I've provided a little more information here and there that did not make it into the book but may still be of interest.

GENERAL RESEARCH

Jackie, Janet & Lee would not have been possible without the assistance of many organizations that provided me with articles, documents, audio and video interviews, transcripts, and other material that was either utilized directly in this book or just for purposes of background, especially the John F. Kennedy Presidential Library.

Thanks to Maryrose Grossman, Nadia Dixson, and Kyoko Yamamoto at the John F. Kennedy Presidential Library. Much of the source material used in this book is now online, so please do avail yourself of the opportunity to read for yourself, for instance, the oral histories of Janet Auchincloss, which I utilized — go to jfklibrary.org. What the hardworking staff at the JFK Library has done in making their extensive archives available to the public is an outstanding service. Take advantage of it, especially if you are a Kennedy enthusiast.

I would also like to express my gratitude to

the following institutions: Academy of Motion Picture Arts and Sciences; American Film Institute Library; Ancestry.com; AP Images; Associated Press Office (New York); Association for the Preservation of Historic Natchitoches; BeenVerified.com; Beverly Hills Library; Boston Herald Archives; Corbis Gamma Liaison; Corbis Getty Images; *East Hampton Star;* Fairfield (Connecticut) Museum and History Center; Globe Photos; Hedda Hopper Collection in the Margaret Herrick Library, Academy of Motion Picture Arts and Sciences, Beverly Hills; Heritage Auctions, Hong Kong; Institute of Heraldic and Genealogical Studies, Kent, England; Kobal Collection; League of Women Voters; Lincoln Center Library of the Performing Arts, Lincoln Center, New York; Los Angeles Public Library; *Los Angeles Times;* Margaret Herrick Library; MPTV Images; Museum of Broadcasting, New York; MyRoots.com; Natchitoches Parish Tourist Commission; Natchitoches Tourism Bureau; New York *Daily News; New York Post; New York Times;* New York University Library; Newport Chamber of Commerce; Newport Country Club; *Newport Daily News;* Newport Garden Club; Newport Historical Society; *Newport Mercury;* Occidental College, Eagle Rock, California; *Philadelphia Daily News; Philadelphia Inquirer;* Philadelphia Public Library;

Polish Institute and Sikorski Museum, London; Preservation Society of Newport County; Rex Features; *Shreveport Times;* Southampton Historical Museum; *Southampton Press;* St. Clare–Newport Senior Center; Time-Life Archives and Library, New York; Tour Natchitoches; University of California, Los Angeles.

Special thanks to the following people, who assisted me in tangible and intangible ways: Alan Shayne, Alexandra Lee Rutherfurd, Barbara Doyle, Benno Graziana, Beth Hall, Brian Quigley, Carter Faria Savastano (Mannie's grandchild, Linda's son), Cecil Auchincloss, David Nash, Don Johnston, Douglas Cramer, Ed Pisoni, Edgar Ammaguer, Elios Petrionakis, Ella Auchincloss (Tommy's daughter-in-law), Harold Adams, Isabel Fritz-Cope, Jackie Rogers, James Kalafatis, Jerica Michaud (Oatsie Charles's assistant), Jill Blumer (Peter Beard's assistant), Jocelyn Brennan (Mannie's grandchild, Joyce's daughter), Joe T. Mullen, John Cope, John Llewellyn Moxey, John Radziwill, Jonathan Tapper, Katia Bede, Linda Faria Savastino, Lisa Gunning, Louise Jaffe (Herb Ross's niece), Mandolyna Theodoracopulos (Taki's daughter), Marguerite Joy Savastano (Mannie's grandchild, Linda's daughter), Marta Sgubin, Mary Barelli Gallagher, Mary Leventhal, Maude S. Davis, Maya Auchincloss, and Michael Okowita.

751

ORAL HISTORIES

I utilized many oral histories in the writing of this book, again most provided by the John F. Kennedy Presidential Library. Without exaggeration, hundreds of thousands of pages of material have been archived by the library, which is so invaluable to researchers and historians such as myself. When I wrote *Jackie, Ethel, Joan* back in 1998, I actually had to go to the library and sit there for weeks looking for nuggets of information. Today much of the material is online — not the special collections, though (maybe one day!) — and available at jfklibrary.org.

I want to thank the following staff members of the JFK Library who assisted me and my researchers with oral histories: William Johnson, Ron Whealon, June Payne, Maura Porter, Susan D'Entrement, Kyoko Yamamoto, Allen Goodrich, and James Hill.

As I do with all of my Kennedy-related books, I must also acknowledge David Powers, former special assistant to President John F. Kennedy, the first curator of the JFK Library. I was lucky enough to interview him back on January 11, 1996, and a lot of that material is used in this book, if only for background. Certainly, no mention of the JFK Library is complete without a nod to Mr. Powers, who died in March 1998 at the age of eighty-five.

I am also grateful to Marianne Masterson

and Delores DeMann for assisting me in the reading and analyzing of these many transcripts.

See the specific "Sources and Other Notes" section below for how the oral histories were utilized.

A WORD ABOUT JAMIE AUCHINCLOSS

James Lee Auchincloss is the only son of Janet Auchincloss and Hugh D. Auchincloss, half brother of Jacqueline Bouvier Kennedy Onassis and Lee Radziwill. Given his first-hand proximity to the story, there is simply no way to write a book about Jackie, Janet, and Lee — his mother and his sisters (and he never refers to Jackie and Lee as "halfs," by the way) — without his assistance and cooperation.

In 2009, twenty years after the death of his mother, Jamie got in trouble with the law after admitting to possessing child pornography. He was sentenced to thirty days in jail and three years' probation.

It's my view that this unfortunate turn in Jamie's life in no way impacts his standing in history or his memories of growing up with his parents, Janet and Hugh, and siblings — Jackie, Lee, Janet Jr., Nini, Tommy, and Yusha — or his brothers-in-law, Jack, Bobby, and Ted Kennedy. The times I spent with Jamie were memorable; I appreciate him so much. He also provided many photographs for this book.

Jamie paid his debt to society. Today he spends much of his time researching his family as well as the families of other presidents of the United States at presidential libraries across the nation. He also gives lectures on American history.

James Lee Auchincloss was interviewed more than forty times for this book. Since he has never written his own memoir, I feel honored that he saw fit to share so many details of his life and times with me for this work. Rather than list the dates of his interviews in these source notes, it's more expedient to clarify here the dates of the ones that provided the most information: May 18, 2016; May 19, 2016; May 22, 2016; May 26, 2016; May 27, 2016; June 12, 2016; June 14, 2016; June 19, 2016; September 7, 2016; September 9, 2016; and December 2, 2016.

CATHY GRIFFIN

I am extremely fortunate to have been associated with the same private investigator and chief researcher for the last twenty-eight years, Cathy Griffin. As always, for this book, Cathy managed to locate people who had never before talked about the Auchinclosses, Bouviers, and Kennedys and then conducted many interviews with each of them, going back to them repeatedly for the sake of detail and accuracy. Since Cathy was also the primary researcher on *Jackie, Ethel, Joan* and *After Camelot,* she has a great grasp of the subject matter and was able to hit the ground running with *Jackie, Janet & Lee.* Though I have expressed as much to her many times over the years, I just want to once again go on record as saying that not only is Cathy the ultimate professional in every way, but she is also a close and valuable friend. Long after we are gone from this earth, the work she has done on all of my books will stand as testimony to how much she cares not only about me and my work, but also about the very people who trust us to tell their stories. In all of the years I have been publishing books, I have never had a disgruntled source, and that's largely due to the respect Cathy shows each and every one of them. So, again, I thank her.

SOURCES AND OTHER NOTES
Prologue
Jackie's dinner for Lee at the White House and Janet, Jackie, and Lee in the Oval Office:

Interviews: Adora Rule, August 1, 2016; Oatsie Charles, May 5, 1998, October 18, 2016; Ben Bradlee, October 1, 1995; Philip Geyelin, March 1, 1998; Oleg Cassini, June 5, 1998, March 5, 2004.

Documents: File: "March 15, 1961 Private Dinner," JFK Library, including photographs, menus, planned and finalized guest lists, correspondence (from Janet Auchincloss) and other research material.

Volumes: *Designing Camelot* by James A. Abbott and Elaine M. Rice; *In the Kennedy Style* by Letitia Baldrige; *The Kennedy White House* by Carl Sferrazza Anthony; *Life in Camelot — The Kennedy Years* by *Life* magazine.

Oral Histories: Janet Auchincloss/JFK Library (September 5, 1964, September 6, 1964); Letitia Baldrige/JFK Library.

Note: For years, it's been said that on this night in question, March 15, 1961, Stas was not able to be at Lee's side, as planned. Oleg Cassini told me in an interview that he was a stand-in for the prince, whose transatlantic flight was delayed by bad weather. Cassini's presence at Lee's side was a little ironic because he and the prince looked so much alike they could have been brothers. In fact, later in the evening, a large poster of the two posing side by side would be produced by the President and displayed to the guests as a joke. "Here's to Stas," Jack said, raising his glass to the poster, "wherever you are. And to Oleg, who stands here in your place." Oleg repeated this story in his book, *A Thousand Days of Magic*. In fact, though, the JFK Library, in our research into the evening of March 15, helped us determine that the night Oleg refers to in which he stood in for Stas was actually February 9, 1962, at a dinner given in the State Dining Room in honor of Jack's sister Jean and her husband, Stephen Smith. (In Oleg's defense, there are certainly worse things than getting your White House state dinners mixed up because you've attended so many of them!)

Part One: The Beginning

Lee at *Harper's Bazaar* and lunch with Jackie and Janet:

Interviews: Deena Atkins-Manzel, August 5, 2016, September 8, 2016, November 1, 2016; Anna DeWitt, September 1, 2016, November 5, 2016, January 2, 2017.

Articles: "Lee Radziwill: In Search of Herself" by Charlotte Curtis, *McCall's,* January 1975; "Lee" by Andy Warhol, *Interview,* March 1975.

Volumes: *The Kents* by Audrey Whiting; *Edward VIII* by Frances Donaldson.

Photographic Evidence: I referred to photographs taken by Deena Atkins-Manzel for descriptions of the ladies' wardrobes on the day of Janet's visit to *Harper's.*

Lee's early days with Michael Canfield and subsequent marriage:

Interviews: Terrance Landow, May 3, 2016, June 17, 2016, October 14, 2016; Jamie Auchincloss; Blair Fuller (for a profile on Eunice Kennedy for *Redbook* in 2002);

Deena Atkins-Manzel; Chauncey G. Parker III, October 5, 2005; Thomas Guinzburg, March 6, 2005; Adora Rule, April 1, 2016, May 1, 2016.

Volumes: *In Her Sister's Shadow* by Diana DuBois; *Up & Down & Around: A Publisher Recollects the Time of His Life* by Cass Canfield; *The Windsor Story* by J. Bryan and Charles Murphy; *White Mischief* by James Fox; *King Edward VIII* by Philip Ziegler; *The Reluctant King* by Sarah Bradford.

Articles: "Revealed: The Secret Illegitimate Brother of the Queen's Cousin Who Never Got Over the Pain of Not Knowing His Real Parents," by Christopher Wilson, *Daily Mail,* July 2013; "Scandal of Forgotten Prince George . . ." by Adrian Lee, *Express,* July 15, 2013; "The Complicated Sisterhood of Jackie Kennedy and Lee Radziwill" by Sam Kashner, *Vanity Fair,* April 26, 2016; "War of the Poses" by Michael Gross, *New York,* April 27, 1992.

Oral History: Cass Canfield/Columbia University.

Jackie's and Lee's childhoods:

Interviews: Lavinia Jennings, July 8, 2016, August 5, 2016; Oatsie Charles; Hugh "Yusha" Auchincloss, October 12, 1998; Nini Auchincloss Strait, October 11, 1998.

Articles: "First Lady Was a First-Class Rider Here" (no byline), *East Hampton Star,*

November 17, 1960; "How The Remarkable Auchincloss Family Shaped the Jacqueline Kennedy Style" by Stephen Birmingham, *Ladies' Home Journal,* March 1967; "Lee Radziwill: Girls Who Have Everything Aren't Supposed to Do Anything," by Jane Howard, *Life,* July 14, 1967; "Daddy Didn't Want His Little Girl to Be a Kennedy," by Harriman Janus, *Photoplay,* May 1969; "Opening Chapters: Enchanting Memories and Photos of Her Early Life with Jackie" by Lee Radziwill, *Ladies' Home Journal,* January 1973; "And Starring Lee Bouvier! A Nonfiction Television Play" by Gloria Steinem, *McCall's,* February 1968; "Jackie Kennedy's Girlhood Home for Sale," by Jack Friedlander, *The Connection* (McLean, Va.), November 6, 1995; "The Public and Private Lee" by Henry Ehrlich, *Look,* January 23, 1968; "Revealed: The Secret Illegitimate Brother of the Queen's Cousin Who Never Got Over the Pain of Not Knowing His Real Parents," by Christopher Wilson, *Daily Mail,* July 2013; "Scandal of Forgotten Prince George . . ." by Adrian Lee, *Express,* July 15, 2013; "The Complicated Sisterhood of Jackie Kennedy and Lee Radziwill" by Sam Kashner, *Vanity Fair,* April 26, 2016; "Lee Radziwill's Search for Herself," by John J. Miller, *The Column,* December 17, 1972; "Stay Tuned for the Princess," by Terry Coleman, *New York Post,* June 24, 1967.

Volumes: *One Special Summer* by Lee Bouvier and Jacqueline Bouvier; *Black Jack Bouvier: The Life and Times of Jackie O's Father* by Kathleen Bouvier; *To Jack with Love; Black Jack Bouvier: A Remembrance* by Kathleen Bouvier; *Janet & Jackie* by Jan Pottker; *A Woman Named Jackie* by C. David Heymann; *Jacqueline Bouvier Kennedy Onassis: A Life* by Donald Spoto; *Jacqueline Bouvier Kennedy* by Mary Van Rensselaer; *Palimpsest* by Gore Vidal; *The Bouviers* by John Davis; *The Auchincloss Family* by Joanna Russell Auchincloss and Caroline Auchincloss; *Our Forebears* by John Vernou Bouvier, Jr. (privately printed).

Articles: "James T. Lee," *National Cyclopedia of American Biography,* vol. 54; "Northern Irish Ancestry of Rose Anna Cox Fitzgerald, Great-Grandmother of a President" by R. Andrew Pierce, *Nexus: The Magazine of the New England Historic Genealogical Society,* October/November 1994.

Private Papers: "Growing Up with Jackie: My Memories 1941–1953" by Hugh D. Auchincloss, JFK Library; Auchincloss Family Tree, Joanna Russell Auchincloss and Caroline Auchincloss Fowler, Salem (Massachusetts) Library, 1957; courtesy of Hugh D. Auchincloss III: Auchincloss family Bible, family records from 1730 to the present time inscribed therein, Auchincloss genealogy wall chart, and maps of Hammersmith Farm and the Castle.

Speeches: "Mud Wrestling with History: Snapshots of My Life as a Brother-in-Law to John F. Kennedy" by James Auchincloss.

Oral History: Janet Auchincloss/ JFK Library.

Jackie's relationship with John Husted:

Interviews: John Husted, April 1, 2008; Jamie Auchincloss; Gore Vidal, June 2, 1998, November 7, 1999, May 2, 2008, May 3, 2008; Trina Lloyd, September 4, 2016, October 5, 2016.

Volumes: *A Woman Named Jackie* by C. David Heymann; *Jacqueline Bouvier Kennedy Onassis: A Life* by Donald Spoto.

Background of Jack Bouvier:

Interviews: Barry Davis, October 15, 2016; Danine Barber, November 11, 2016, November 12, 2016; Oatsie Charles; John Davis, September 13, 1998, September 14, 1998, September 15, 1998.

Volumes: *Black Jack Bouvier: The Life and Times of Jackie O's Father* by Kathleen Bouvier; *To Jack with Love; Black Jack Bouvier: A Remembrance* by Kathleen Bouvier; *Janet & Jackie* by Jan Pottker; *A Woman Named Jackie* by C. David Heymann; *Jacqueline Bouvier Kennedy Onassis* by Donald Spoto; *Jacqueline Bouvier Kennedy* by Mary Van Rensselaer; *Palimpsest* by Gore Vidal; *The Bouviers* by John Davis; *The Auchincloss Family* by Joanna Russell Auchincloss and Caroline Auchincloss; *Our Forebears* by John Vernou Bouvier, Jr. (privately printed).

Article: "Daddy Didn't Want His Little Girl to Be a Kennedy" by Harriman Janus, *Photoplay,* May 1969.

Jackie's courtship with Jack Kennedy:

Interviews: John Davis; Jamie Auchincloss; Senator George Smathers, October 5, 1998, December 12, 1998.

Articles: "An Exclusive Chat with Jackie Kennedy" by Joan Braden, *Saturday Evening Post,* May 12, 1962.

Volumes: *The Good Son* by Christopher Andersen; *An Unfinished Life: John F. Kennedy, 1917–1963* by Robert Dallek; *Profiles in Courage* by John F. Kennedy; *JFK: Reckless Youth* by Nigel Hamilton; *In Her Sister's Shadow* by Diana DuBois; *Reporter* by Maxine Cheshire; *A Woman Named Jackie* by C. David Heymann; *Times to Remember* by Rose Kennedy.

Video: "Hugh [Yusha] Auchincloss: Remembering Jackie O," NBC 10/WJAR, November 20, 2013.

Oral Histories: Janet Auchincloss/JFK Library (Janet and Jackie's conversation about JFK, ["You're too *available* to him."] and her suggestion that Jackie go to London to attend the coronation of Queen Elizabeth and other conversations they had about JFK are recalled in detail by Janet); Charles Bartlett/JFK Library; Cardinal Richard Cushing, Roman Catholic Archbishop of Boston/JFK Library; Paul B. Fay Jr./JFK Library; Dun Gifford/RFK Oral History Project; Roswell Gilpatric/JFK Library; Louella Hennessey/JFK Library; Robert Francis Kennedy/JFK Library.

Correspondence: Jacqueline Bouvier to Rev. Joseph Leonard, July 1952, writing of JFK: "He's like my father in a way — loves the chase and is bored with the conquest — and once married, needs proof he's still attractive, so flirts with other women and resents you. I saw how that nearly killed Mummy."

Janet's difficult times after Jack Bouvier and courtship with and marriage to Hugh Auchincloss:

Interviews: Trina Lloyd, June 18, 2016; Jamie Auchincloss; John Davis; Lavinia Jennings; Yusha Auchincloss; Nina Auchincloss Strait; Gore Vidal, April 8, 1998, May 1, 2010.

Volumes: *Black Jack Bouvier: The Life and Times of Jackie O's Father* by Kathleen Bouvier; *To Jack with Love: Black Jack Bouvier: A Remembrance* by Kathleen Bouvier; *Janet & Jackie* by Jan Pottker; *Palimpsest* by Gore Vidal; *America's Secret Aristocracy* by Stephen Birmingham; *Top Drawer: American High Society from the Gilded Age to the Roaring Twenties* by Mary Cable; *Louis Auchincloss: A Writer's Life* by Carol Gelderman; *Fifth Avenue: The Best Address* by Jerry Patterson; *Smithsonian Stories: Chronicle of a Golden Age 1964–1984* by Wilton S. Dillon.

Articles: "The Garden of Hammersmith Farm" by Rose Machado, *Country Life in America*, June 1916; "Hugh Auchincloss Dies," *New York Times*, April 12, 1913; "Bouvier Estate Goes to Widow," *New York Times*, January 19, 1926; "James T. Lee Buys East 48th St. Site," *New York Times*, January 22, 1928; "Dr. James Lee Dies at 75," *New York Herald Tribune*, May 15, 1928; "Mrs. Auchincloss Hit by Propeller," *Washington Evening Star*, July 16, 1929; "Hugh Auchincloss Marries in Capital," *New York Times*, May 8, 1931; "Mrs. H. D. Auchincloss Asks for Reno Divorce," *New York Times*, May 24, 1932; "Newport: There She Sits," by Cleveland Amory, *Harper's*, February 1948; "Mrs. Janet Bouvier Weds Liet. Hugh Auchincloss," *East Hampton Star*, June 24, 1942; "Hugh D. Auchincloss Weds Janet Bouvier at Virginia Estate," *Newport Daily News*, June 23, 1942; "How the Remarkable Auchincloss Family Shaped the Jacqueline Kennedy Style" by Stephen Birmingham, *Ladies' Home Journal*,

March 1967; "Lee Radziwill: Girls Who Have Everything Aren't Supposed to Do Anything" by Jane Howard, *Life,* July 14, 1967; "Opening Chapters: Enchanting Memories and Photos of Her Early Life with Jackie" by Lee Radziwill, *Ladies' Home Journal,* January 1973; "And Starring Lee Bouvier! A Nonfiction Television Play" by Gloria Steinem, *McCall's,* February 1968; "The Public and Private Lee" by Henry Ehrlich, *Look,* January 23, 1968; "Vanished Opulence," by Suzanna Andrews, *Vanity Fair,* January 2001; "Quality Developer with a Legacy" by Christopher Gay, *New York Times,* March 12, 1995; "Lee Radziwill: In Search of Herself" by Charlotte Curtis, *McCall's,* January 1975; "Lee" by Andy Warhol, *Interview,* March, 1975; "Lee Radziwill's Search for Herself" by John J. Miller, *The Column,* December 17, 1972.

Private Papers: "Growing Up with Jackie: My Memories 1941–1953 (original unedited manuscript) by Hugh D. Auchincloss, JFK Library; "I Remember . . . Reminiscences of Hammersmith Farm" by Esther Auchincloss Blitz, Newport History (Newport Historical Society), spring 1994; "Original Manuscript of Esther Auchincloss Blitz: My Life," Newport Historical Society; "Hammersmith Farm" by John T. Hopf, Camelot Gardens, Inc., 1979; "In Living Memory: A Chronicle of Newport, Rhode Island, 1888–1988,"

Newport Savings and Loan Association, 1988;

Video: Lee Radziwill's interview with Sofia Coppola for *T* magazine, February 7, 2013 ("I was left alone at this enormous house . . ."); Hammersmith Farm Tour Video, Camelot Gardens, Inc., 1979.

Correspondence: Emma Jennings Auchincloss to Mrs. James T. Lee, July 3, 1942.

Additionally: Marriage certificate, New York City, of Thomas Merritt and Maria Curry, June 6, 1875; Newark, New Jersey, census: 1860, 1870, 1880; St. Patrick Pro-Cathedral, Newark, New Jersey, baptismal records for James Lee, born December 23, 1852; baptism, January 1, 1853.

Janet's unconventional pregnancy:

Because of the sensitive nature of this chapter, my interviewed sources asked to remain anonymous.

Volume: *Palimpsest* by Gore Vidal

Additionally: Birth certificate of James Lee Auchincloss, March 4, 1947, The Doctors Hospital, Inc; Invitation to Jackie's debutante party and Jamie's christening: "Mr. and Mrs. Hugh Dudley Auchincloss, Miss Jacqueline Lee Bouvier, Master James Lee Auchincloss, At Home on Friday, the first of August from five until seven o'clock, Hammersmith Farm, Newport, Rhode Island."

Part Two: A Mother's Duty

Jackie's marriage to JFK and Janet's involvement:

Interviews: Robert Westover, May 2, 2016; Jamie Auchincloss; Janine Rule; Adora Rule.

Volumes: *Jacqueline Bouvier Kennedy Onassis* by Barbara Leaming; *America's Queen* by Sarah Bradford (Lee's quotes about her mother's intrusion in the marriage are culled from this book); *Janet & Jackie* by Jan Pottker; *Jackie Oh!* by Kitty Kelley; *Jacqueline Bouvier Kennedy Onassis: A Life* by Donald Spoto.

Speech: "Mud Wrestling with History: Snapshots of My Life as a Brother-in-Law to John F. Kennedy" by James Lee Auchincloss.

Lee's marriage to and divorce from Michael Canfield:

Interviews: Lois Aldrech, August 5, 2016, August 6, 2016; Terrance and Betty Landow, September 2, 2016, September 8, 2016, October 15, 2016, and, also, email exchanges in November 2016 clarifying details; Jamie Auchincloss; Eileen Gillespie Slocum, May 5, 1998, June 6, 1998; Chauncey Parker III, May 6, 2008; Blair Fuller; Nini Auchincloss Strait; Tom Guinzburg.

Articles: "Miss Bouvier Is Wed Here," *Washington Evening Star,* April 19, 1953; "Miss Caroline L. Bouvier Married to M. Canfield," *East Hampton Star,* April 23, 1953;

"Jacqueline Kennedy Onassis — A Tribute," *People,* various writers, Summer 1994; "Jackie's Childhood Friend Tells All" by Judy Stone, *Movie Mirror,* July 1968; "Revealed: The Secret Illegitimate Brother of the Queen's Cousin Who Never Got Over the Pain of Not Knowing His Real Parents" by Christopher Wilson, *Daily Mail,* July 2013; "Scandal of Forgotten Prince George . . ." by Adrian Lee, *Express,* July 15, 2013; "The Complicated Sisterhood of Jackie Kennedy and Lee Radziwill" by Sam Kashner, *Vanity Fair,* April 26, 2016; "Lee Radziwill's Search for Herself" by John J. Miller, *The Column,* December 17, 1972.

Volumes: *In Her Sister's Shadow* by Diana DuBois. (Lee's affair with David Somerset was first written about in this book.); *Palimpsest* by Gore Vidal; *Up & Down & Around: A Publisher Recollects the Time of His Life* by Cass Canfield.

Oral History: Alastair Granville Forbes/ JFK Library ("Well, Michael, I think the best thing for you is to get her some real money."); Cass Canfield/Columbia University.

Jackie's early marriage to JFK:

Interviews: Julian Balridge, October 11, 2016, December 10, 2016; Jamie Auchincloss; Senator George Smathers; Eileen Gillespie Slocum.

Volumes: *The Other Mrs. Kennedy* by Jess

Oppenheimer; *The Patriarch: The Remarkable Life and Turbulent Times of Joseph P. Kennedy* by David Nasaw; *Sins of the Father* by Ronald Kessler; *The Founding Father: The Story of Joseph P. Kennedy* by Richard Whalen and Joan Whalen; *The Nine of Us: Growing Up Kennedy* by Jean Kennedy Smith; *Jacqueline Kennedy: Historic Conversations on Life with John Kennedy* by Caroline Kennedy and Michael Beschloss; *My Life with Jacqueline Kennedy* by Mary Barelli Gallagher; *Those Few Precious Days: The Final Year of Jack with Jackie* by Christopher Andersen; *Mrs. Kennedy: The Missing History of the Kennedy Years* by Barbara Leaming; *Jacqueline Bouvier Kennedy* by Mary Van Rensselaer Thayer; *Hostage to Fortune* by Amanda Smith; *Jackie After Jack* by Christopher Andersen; *Jacqueline Kennedy Onassis* by Lester David.

Articles: "Senator Kennedy Takes Wife Amid Pomp of Newport," *Boston Globe*, September 12, 1953; "Jack Kennedy: The Senate's Gay Young Bachelor," *Saturday Evening Post*, June 18, 1953; "Jacqueline Bouvier, Senator Kennedy to Wed," *East Hampton Star*, July 16, 1953; "Kennedy-Bouvier License Issued," *Newport Daily News*, September 4, 1953; "Kennedy-Bouvier Nuptials Held at St. Mary's Church Before 700 Invited Guests," *Newport Daily News*, September 12, 1953; "Kennedy-Bouvier Rites

Colorful," *Danbury News-Times,* September 14, 1953, "Traffic Curbs Set for Kennedy-Bouvier Wedding," *Newport Daily News,* September 11, 1953; "Wedding Principals Enter St. Mary's Church This Morning," *Newport Daily News,* September 12, 1953; "What Jackie Kennedy Has Learned from Her Mother," *Good Housekeeping,* October 15, 1962; "Lee Radziwill: In Search of Herself" by Charlotte Curtis, *McCall's,* January 1975; "An Exclusive Chat with Jackie Kennedy" by Joan Braden, *Saturday Evening Post,* May 12, 1962.

Correspondence: Rose Kennedy to Janet Auchincloss, September 1953. Maud Shaw to Janet Auchincloss, December 28, 1960; Rose Kennedy to Janet Auchincloss, North Ocean Boulevard, Palm Beach Florida, undated; Jackie to Jamie, undated, Christmas note with money gift: "I hope you can turn this into a Christmas present for yourself — with all love, Jackie."

Additionally: Social Files/Senator's Wedding/JFK Library: including letters to Janet Auchincloss from John F. Kennedy (July 28, 1953) and Evelyn Lincoln (August 7, 1953, and September 3, 1953); "Suggested Lists for Jack's Wedding," for "Mrs. Auchincloss and Bobby," August 4, 1953.

Oral Histories: Janet Auchincloss/JFK Library; Jacqueline Kennedy Onassis (interview conducted by the Lyndon Baines Johnson Library, 1974, as well as the newly released oral histories for the JFK Library in 2011); Charles L. Bartlett/JFK Library; Edward Berube/JFK Library; Rose Fitzgerald Kennedy/Herbert Hoover Library Foundation; Laura Bergquist Kriebel/RFK Oral History Project; Frank Mankiewicz/ RFK Oral History Project; Esther Newberg/RFK Oral History Project; Joan Braden/JFK Library; Maud Shaw/JFK Library; Nancy Tuckerman/ JFK Library; Kenneth O'Donnell/Lyndon Baines Johnson Library; Pierre Salinger/RFK Oral History Project; George Smathers /U.S. Senate Historical Office; Charles Spalding/ JFK Library.

History of Prince Stanisław Albrecht "Stas" Radziwiłł:

Interviews: Jan Stanislaw Albrycht Radziwill, September 29, 2016; Terrance Landow, Betty Landow; Chauncey Parker III; Blair Fuller; Tom Guinzburg.

Note: By now it is accepted wisdom that Lee was married to Michael Canfield when she began her affair with Stas Radziwill, also confirmed by his son John.

Articles: "Princess Lee Radziwill" by Peter Evans, *Cosmopolitan,* March 1968; "Country House in Flower" by Polly Devlin, *Vogue,* July 1971; "Lee Radziwill" by Leslie Field, *Daily Mail,* November 16, 1971.

Volumes: *The Radziwills: The Social History*

of a Great European Family by Tadeusz Nowa-kowski; *Mrs. Kennedy* by Barbara Leaming; *America's Queen* by Sarah Bradford; *Jackie Oh!* by Kitty Kelley; *Palimpsest* by Gore Vidal; *Away from the White House* by Lawrence L. Knudson; *The Property Boom* by Oliver Marriot.

Jack Bouvier's death:

Interview: Jamie Auchincloss.

Volumes: *Black Jack Bouvier: The Life and Times of Jackie O's Father* by Kathleen Bouvier; *To Jack with Love; Black Jack Bouvier: A Remembrance* by Kathleen Bouvier; *Janet & Jackie* by Jan Pottker; *A Woman Named Jackie* by C. David Heymann.

Articles: "John Bouvier 3rd, 66, Dies," *New York Times,* August 4, 1957; "John V. Bouvier 3rd," obituary, *East Hampton Star,* August 8, 1957; "Lee" by Andy Warhol, *Interview,* March, 1975.

Documents: Last will and testament of John Bouvier III.

Part Three: Heady Times
Lee's courtship and marriage to Stas:

Interviews: John Radziwill; Julian Balridge; Jamie Auchincloss.

Volumes: *In Her Sister's Shadow* by Diana DuBois; *The Radziwills: The Social History of a Great European Family* by Tadeusz Nowa-kowski.

Jackie's early days as wife of JFK presidential candidate:

Interviews: Julian Balridge; Jamie Auchincloss.

Volumes: *The Fitzgeralds and the Kennedys: An America Saga* by Doris Kearns Goodwin; *Rose Kennedy's Family Album: From the Fitzgerald Kennedy Private Collection* by Caroline Kennedy; *Jacqueline Kennedy: Historic Conversations on Life with John Kennedy* by Caroline Kennedy and Michael Beschloss; *John Fitzgerald Kennedy: As We Remember Him* by Joan Meters and Goddard Lieberson; *My Life with Jacqueline Kennedy* by Mary Barelli Gallagher; *Those Few Precious Days: The Final Year of Jack with Jackie* by Christopher Andersen; *Kennedy: The Classic Biography* by Ted Sorensen; *Mrs. Kennedy: The Missing History of the Kennedy Years* by Barbara Leaming; *Jacqueline Bouvier Kennedy* by Mary Van Rensselaer Thayer; *Sons of Camelot* by Laurence Leamer; *Torn Lace Curtain* by Frank Saunders; *The Kennedy Case* by Rita Dallas; *The Kennedy Men* by Laurence Leamer; *The Kennedys: A Chronological History* by Harvey Rachin; *Our Special Summer* by Lee Bouvier and Jacqueline Bouvier.

Articles: "Mrs. Kennedy Improving After Loss of Child" *Boston Globe*, August 24, 1956; "Mrs. Kennedy Learned Politics by

'Osmosis,' " *New York Times,* July 15, 1960; "Lee Radziwill: In Search of Herself" by Charlotte Curtis, *McCall's,* January 1975; "Ahhh Paris" by Lee Radziwill, *McCall's,* November 1962.

Correspondence: Rose Kennedy to Janet Auchincloss, December 30, 1960.

Oral Histories: Janet Auchincloss/JFK Library (for all of Janet's memories of stumping for JFK, early Jackie and Jack homes, etc.); Jacqueline Kennedy Onassis (interview conducted by the Lyndon Baines Johnson Library, 1974, as well as the newly released oral histories for the JFK Library in 2011); Joan Braden/JFK Library; Charles L. Bartlett/JFK Library; Edward Berube/JFK Library; Rose Fitzgerald Kennedy/Herbert Hoover Library Foundation; Cardinal Richard Cushing/JFK Library; Paul B. Fay Jr./JFK Library; Dun Gifford/RFK Oral History Project; Roswell Gilpatric/JFK Library; Louella Hennessey/ JFK Library; Robert Francis Kennedy/JFK Library.

Additionally: "Hugh D. Auchincloss Personal Papers"/JFK Library: personal correspondence with Jacqueline Bouvier Kennedy Onassis, a memoir of their relationship, and mementos from President John F. Kennedy's inauguration and trip to Paris in 1961.

Speech: "Mud Wrestling with History: Snapshots of My Life as a Brother-in-Law to John F. Kennedy" by James Lee Auchincloss.

Lee's bout with postpartum depression:

Note: This subject was first broached in *In Her Sister's Shadow* by Diana DubBois. Also, Lee alluded to it in her letter to Pope John XXIII, July 18, 1961: "Faith and hope in justice gave me unquenchable strength and saved me twice in my lifetime. I was *gravely* ill, *mortally* ill [her emphasis] in these last two years. Perhaps my faith was the miracle that saved me."

Articles: "Lee Radziwill: Reluctant Princess" by Eddy Gilmore, Associated Press, July 5, 1960; "Lee Radziwill's Search for Herself" by John J. Miller, *The Column,* December 17, 1972; "Princess Lee Radziwill" by Peter Evans, *Cosmopolitan,* March 1968.

Volumes: *Janet & Jackie* by Jan Pottker; *In Her Sister's Shadow* by Diana DuBois; *Jacqueline Bouvier Kennedy Onassis* by Barbara Leaming; *Upstairs at the White House* by J. B. West; *The Bouviers* by John Davis; *Nothing to Declare* by Taki.

Details of Stas's affair of 1960:

Told to the author by an anonymous family source.

Part Four: The White House Years

Jackie's romance with Jack Warnecke:

Beginning with the chapter "A New Love for Jackie?" and throughout this book, details of this relationship are culled from interviews with John Carl (Jack) Warnecke, March 1, 1998, April 1, 2007; Fred Warnecke, June 25, 2016; Margo Warnecke Merck, June 25, 2016; Harold Adams, July 29, 2016; Bertha Baldwin, July 8, 2016; Don Johnston, June 26, 2016.

Articles: "Jackie Kennedy — World's Most Eligible Widow, Will She Marry Again?" by Lloyd Shearer, *Detroit Free Press,* December 4, 1966; "Jackie Aloha: When Jacqueline Kennedy Lived in Hawaii for Seven Weeks," by Carl Anthony, CarlAnthonyOnLine.com, June 5, 2012.

JFK's inauguration:
Interviews: Jamie Auchincloss, Adora Rule.
Oral History: Janet Auchincloss/JFK Library; Letitia Baldrige/JFK Library; Charles Bartlett/JFK Library; Luella Hennessey/JFK Library; Maud Shaw/JFK Library.

JFK's visit to Hammersmith:
Interviews: Jamie Auchincloss; Eileen Slocum; Chauncey Parker III; Stelio Papadimitriou, June 8, 1998; Taki Theodoracopulos, June 20, 2016, July 15, 2016, September 8, 2016, October 22, 2016; Agnetta Castallanos, June 4, 2016, July 5, 2016, October 5, 2016, September 15, 2016.
Oral Histories: Janet Auchincloss/JFK

Library; Joan Braden/JFK Library; Maud Shaw/JFK Library; Jacqueline Kennedy Onassis/LBJ Library.

Private Papers: "The First Lady as a Leader of Public Opinion," PhD dissertation, Norma Ruth Holly Foreman, University of Texas at Austin, May 1971.

Articles: "Mother-in-Law for Kennedy," *Boston Globe,* November 3, 1960; "Mrs. Kennedy Says Criticisms of Her Wardrobe Are Unfair," *New York Times,* September 15, 1960.

Volumes: *The Kennedy Legacy* by Theodore Sorensen; *With Kennedy* by Pierre Salinger; *Upstairs at the White House* by J. B. West; *Diamonds and Diplomats* by Letitia Baldrige; *Power at Play* by Betty Beale; *Ethel Kennedy and Life at Hickory Hill* by Leah Mason (unpublished manuscript); *The Kennedy Women* by Laurence Leamer; *Jack and Jackie* by Christopher Andersen; *All Too Human* by Edward Klein; *The Sins of the Father* by Ronald Kessler; *Seeds of Destruction* by Ralph C. Martin; *First Ladies* by Carl Sferrazza Anthony; *Jacqueline Kennedy* by Gordon Langley Hall; *The Kennedy White House Parties,* by Ann H. Lincoln; *Jacqueline Kennedy: La Première Dame des États-Unis* by Peter Peterson; *Jackie: The Exploitation of a First Lady* by Irving Shulman; *Reporter* by Maxine Cheshire; *Jackie Oh!* by Kitty Kelley;

The Bouviers by John Davis; *Jacqueline Kennedy: Beauty in the White House* by William Carr; *Jackie: The Price of the Pedestal* by Lee Guthrie; *The President's Partner: Beaton in the Sixties* by Cecil Beaton and Hugo Vickers; *Janet & Jackie* by Jan Pottker; *Aristotle Onassis: The Fabulous Onassis* by Christian Cafarakis; *The Onassis Women* by Kiki Feroudi Moutsatsos; *Maria Callas* by Anne Edwards; *JFK: Day by Day* by Terry Golway and Les Krantz; *Rose Kennedy and Her Family* by Barbara Gibson and Ted Schwartz.

Correspondence: Jackie Kennedy to Janet Auchincloss, October 1, 1960; Jackie Kennedy to William Walton, 1962.

Janet's work with the National Cultural Center:

Interview: Jamie Auchincloss

Articles: "Drive Set for Fall for Cultural Center," *Washington Evening Star,* July 14, 1962; "5000 Pay Half Million to Put Culture in Capital Letters," *Washington Post,* November 30, 1962; "Civic Group Seeks to Shift Location of Cultural Center," *Washington Post,* February 15, 1964; "President to Wield Historic Spade" by Tom Kelly, *Washington Evening Star,* November 21, 1964; "Culture Was Seen but Not Always Heard," *Washington Daily News,* November 30, 1962; "Kennedy Cultural Center Washington's Home for the Arts," *The Georgetowner,* November

19, 1964; "Labor Pledges to Aid Culture Center Telecast," *Washington Evening Star* by Jerry Landauer, November 3, 1962; "Cultural Center Staff Has Impressive List of Likeliest Donors," *Washington Post,* September 18, 1960; "Mrs. Auchincloss Aids Cultural Center Drive," *Washington Evening Star,* March 25, 1962; "Groundbreaking Ceremonies Are Held for the Kennedy Cultural Center," *The Georgetowner,* December 10, 1964; "Ground Breaking Ceremony, December 2, 1964," *Footlight,* December 22, 1964; "Shape of Cultural Center Is Changing" by Marjorie Hunter, *Washington Post,* January 7, 1962; "Mrs. Eisenhower Visits Redecorated White House," *New York Times,* June 23, 1962. "Mrs. Auchincloss Rallies Cultural Center Interest," *Washington Evening Star,* April 25, 1962; "Time Is Now on the Center," *Washington Post,* November 18, 1962; "Cultural Center Campaign Begins 'Arm-Twisting' Phase," *Washington Evening Star,* November 3, 1962; "Cultural Center Drive Advances on 3 Fronts," *Washington Post,* June 11, 1963; "Cultural Center Post Goes to J. C. Turner," *Washington Post,* February 19, 1963; "Cultural Center Site," *Washington Evening Star,* March 13, 1962; "Dig D.C. Wallets," *Washington Post,* March 22, 1962; "Downtown Site for Cultural Center, Not Foggy Bottom, Urged by Builders," *Washington Post,* February 22, 1962; "Drive-in Culture," *Washington Post*, December 9, 1962; "First Lady Leads Drive for Center," *Washington Evening Star*, February 25, 1962; "Capital's Culture Gets Lift from Gifts," *Washington Post*, May 6, 1962; "Franklin Square Urged as Site for Kennedy Cultural Center," *Washington Post*, March 7, 1964; "Mrs. Auchincloss Heads Cultural Center Drive," *Washington Post*, March 23, 1962; "Mrs. Kennedy Unveils Cultural Center Model," *Newport Daily News*, September 12, 1962. "Planners Find Flaws in 6 Cultural Center Sites," *Washington Post*, March 12, 1964. "President Names 3 to Arts Group," *Washington Evening Star*, May 31, 1962. "Stone Says Center Site Is Close to Social Hub," *Washington Evening Star*, April 30, 1964. "The John F. Kennedy Center Location Plans Are Defended," *The Georgetowner*, April 16, 1964. "12 Named to Center's Art Group," *Washington Post*, September 16, 1960; "Mrs. Hugh D. Auchincloss," *Vogue*, November 15, 1962.

Oral History: Janet Auchincloss/JFK Library.

Speeches: Janet Auchincloss, Merrywood, January 1962 re: The National Cultural Center; Janet Auchincloss, The Elms, Newport, February 1962 re: architectural model of the Arts Center; Janet Auchincloss, Merrywood (undated) re: Cultural Center plans.

Additionally: A pictorial scrapbook compiled by Janet for Hugh when the Auchinclosses sold Merrywood, entitled "Hugh D. Auchincloss, Merrywood, 1960," and inscribed: "For Hugh D. — A Souvenir of 18 Years Together at Merrywood, with all my Love, Janet, June 21, 1960."

Video: Jackie and Lee on a boat cruise on Lake Pichola, Udaipur, March 17, 1962; Lee Radziwill on *Larry King Live,* March 27, 2001, including this interesting anecdote of being at the White House during the Cuban Missile Crisis: ". . . it was the most memorable, extraordinary time of the White House years that I knew, because I was staying there at the time of the Cuban missile crisis. And there was one moment nearing the end, when we — that's Jackie, the President, and myself — were in their private rooms upstairs, and the phone rang and it was McGeorge Bundy saying that there was extreme trouble ahead. And then, when the President put down the phone, he said, 'In three minutes, we'll know if we're at all-out war or not.' And I can't tell you how long those three minutes seemed. I'm sure you can imagine, but you pictured missiles rising all over the world, submarines submerged . . . And then the phone rang and the President had an extraordinarily tense expression on his face and hung up and said, 'The Russian ships turned back.' And there was such relief."

Part Five: Trouble Brewing

Interviews: Agnetta Castallanos; Karina Brownley, May 1, 2016, November 11, 2016; Adora Rule, October 11, 2016; David Powers, January 11, 1996; Lt. Nancy Lumsden, October 1, 1998; Taki Theodoracopulos; Robert Wentworth, June 11, 2012 (for my book *The Hiltons: An American Dynasty*); Patricia — (Trish) Skipworth Hilton, February 27, 2012 (for *The Hiltons: An American Dynasty*); Stelio Papadimitriou; Chauncey Parker III; Sherry Geyelin, October 6, 1998.

Articles: "An Exclusive Chat with Jacqueline Kennedy" by Joan Braden, *Saturday Evening Post*, May 8, 1962; "Women Who Make World Fashion" by Robin Douglas-Home and Wilhela Cushman, *Ladies' Home Journal*, October 1961; "Ahhh Paris" by Lee Radziwill, *McCall's*, November 1962; "Lee Radziwill" by Leslie Field, *Daily Mail*, November 16, 1971; "A Princess Writes a Story and That Makes It a Party" by Charlotte Curtis, *New York Times*, December 20, 1972.

Volume: *Of Diamonds and Diplomats* by Letitia Baldrige.

Oral History: Joan Braden/JFK Library.

Correspondence: Truman Capote to Cecil Beaton, February 2, 1962: "My God, how jealous she is of Jackie . . ."

Lee Radziwill's annulment:
Details were culled from the cover story

about the proceedings found in the Italian magazine *ABC* (published in Milan), November 12, 1967. The Italian police confiscated all newsstand copies of that issue when it was discovered that documents from the ecclesiastical tribunal of New York had been used to generate the report. Also, I referenced Lee Radziwill's letter to Pope John XXIII, July 18, 1961. I also referenced White House records of Jackie's and Lee's visit to the Pope, March 11, 1962.

Stas's affair with Charlotte Ford:
    This subject has been written about in the past, most notably in *In Her Sister's Shadow* by Diana DuBois.
    Volume: *Princes, Playboys & High-Class Tarts* by Taki.

The death of Patrick Bouvier Kennedy:
    Interviews: Clint Hill, January 4, 1998, March 5, 2010, June 4, 2010, April 3, 2011; Jack Walsh, March 9, 1998; Joseph Paolella, September 11, 1998, September 17, 1998; Anthony Sherman, September 29, 1998; Robert Foster, August 11, 1999; Larry Newman, September 29, 1998, September 30, 1998, October 7, 1998.
    Volumes: *Patrick Bouvier Kennedy: A Brief Life That Changed the History of Newborn Care* by Michael S. Ryan; *The Kennedy Baby* by Steven Levingston and the *Washington Post;*

Mrs. Kennedy and Me by Clint Hill; *Sons of Camelot* by Laurence Leamer; *The Kennedy Women* by Laurence Leamer; *The Kennedy Women* by Pearl Buck; *Among Those Present* by Nancy Dickerson.

Articles: "Mother Cool, Calm in Crisis," *Boston Globe,* August 9, 1963; "Mrs. Kennedy Awaits News on Discharge," *Boston Globe,* August 13, 1963; "Mrs. Kennedy 'Fine,' " *Boston Globe,* August 8, 1963; "Mrs. Kennedy Gets News of Death from Doctor," *Newport Daily News,* August 9, 1963; "Bibs and Bootees Flood White House" by William Blair, *Boston Globe,* July 12, 1963; "2nd Son Born to Kennedys; Has Lung Illness," *New York Times,* August 8, 1963; "Funeral Mass Said for Kennedy Baby," *New York Times,* August 11, 1963; "President at Wife's Bedside" by Kenneth D. Campbell, *Boston Herald,* August 10, 1963; "Mrs. Kennedy to Have Baby at Walter Reed," *Boston Globe,* June 5, 1963; "News Stirs Cleveland Daughter," *Boston Globe,* August 8, 1963; "Tragic Reunion for Kennedys," *Boston Globe,* August 9, 1963; ". . . Waits in Grief," *Boston Globe,* August 11, 1963; "Washington's Best-Kept Secret," *Boston Globe,* April 16, 1963; "Wexford Sends Silver Cup to Baby Kennedy," *Boston Globe,* February 12, 1961; "Onassis Eased Jackie's 3 Tragedies" by Frank Falacci, *Boston Globe,* October 20,

1968; "JFK Gift to Wife? CIA Not Told," *Boston Globe,* July 29, 1963; "Most Kin on Cape During Blessed Event," *Boston Globe,* August 8, 1963; "Family Rejoins Mrs. Kennedy," *Boston Globe,* August 10, 1963; "Happy Days for Jacqueline," *Boston Globe,* May 28, 1963; "3rd Baby Due for JFKs," *Boston Globe,* April 16, 1963; "It Started Out as Cape Outing," *Boston Globe,* August 9, 1963; "Jackie May Have Her Baby on Cape," *Boston Advertiser,* June 9, 1963; "Jackie Wants Another Baby, and Would Like It at Otis," *Boston Herald,* August 17, 1963; "Jacqueline Ordered to Curb Activities," *Boston Globe,* August 15, 1963; "Jacqueline Plans Quiet 34th Birthday Fete Today," *Boston Globe,* July 28, 1963; "Mrs. Kennedy Given Blood," *Boston Globe,* August 8, 1963; "Mrs. Kennedy Has Visitors," *Boston Globe,* August 12, 1963; "Mrs. Kennedy Never Knew Pat Worse 'Til JFK Said He's In . . . ," *Boston Globe,* August 9, 1963.

Oral Histories: Janet Auchincloss/JFK Library; Luella Hennessey/JFK Library; Maud Shaw/JFK Library.

Private Papers: Dr. Samuel Levine, Professor of Pediatrics at Cornell University (1938–1971), Medical Center Archives of New York Presbyterian/Weill Cornell.

JFK's relationship with Janet Jr.:
Interviews: Jamie Auchincloss; Yusha

Auchincloss, October 12, 1998.

Oral History: Janet Auchincloss/JFK Library.

Articles: "Janet Jennings Auchincloss Presented in Newport," *New York Times,* August 18, 1963; "Newport Debut Revelry Carries Over to 2nd Day," *Boston Globe,* August 19, 1963; "John Kerry: A Privileged Youth, a Taste for Risk" by Michael Kranish, *Boston Globe,* June 15, 2003.

Speech: "Mud Wrestling with History: Snapshots of My Life as a Brother-in-Law to John F. Kennedy" by James Lee Auchincloss.

Jackie and Jack's anniversary at Hammersmith:

Interviews: Adora Rule, November 11, 2016; Ben Bradlee, October 1, 1995; Sylvia Whitehouse Blake, January 2, 1998, November 13, 2016; Yusha Auchincloss, October 12, 1998.

Oral Histories: Janet Auchincloss/JFK Library; Maud Shaw/JFK Library.

Volumes: *A Good Life* and *Yours in Truth,* both by Ben Bradlee; *With Kennedy* by Pierre Salinger.

Articles: "Kennedys Come Here for 10th Anniversary," *Newport Daily News,* September 12, 1963; "City, Navy Prepare for Kennedy Vacation from September 22 to October 4," *Newport Daily News,* September 18, 1961; "Kennedy Is Facing a Busy Weekend Before

786

Leaving Newport on Monday," *Newport Daily News,* September 30, 1961; "Kennedy Swears in Customs Official at Hammersmith Farm," *Newport Daily News,* September 29, 1961; "Kennedys Devoting Time to Rest and Relaxation," *Newport Daily News,* September 28, 1961; "Kennedys Go Yachting in Summer," *Newport Daily News,* March 18, 1961; "Kennedys Go on Cruise after Visit to Beach," *Newport Daily News,* September 14, 1963; "President Plans for Vacation Here," *Newport Daily News,* September 16, 1961; "President Ends Visit Here," *Newport Daily News,* October 9, 1961; "President at Hammersmith Farm for Weekend with His Family," *Newport Daily News,* October 2, 1961; "Mrs. Kennedy in Newport with Caroline and John Jr." *New York Times,* June 28, 1961; "Sunset Days of Camelot: An Interview with Cecil Auchincloss" by G. Wayne Miller, *Providence Journal,* September 8, 2013; "Lee Radziwill: In Search of Herself" by Charlotte Curtis, *McCall's,* January, 1975.

Jackie and Lee's trip to Greece:
Interviews: Mari Kumlin, September 8, 1998; Stelina Mavros, October 8, 1999; Clint Hill.
Note: I also interviewed a Secret Service agent for this section who asked for anonymity.
Volumes: *Nemesis* by Peter Evans; *Mrs.*

Kennedy and Me by Clint Hill; *The Fabulous Onassis* by Christian Cafarakis; *The Onassis Women* by Kiki Feroudi Moutsatsos; *Maria Callas* by Anne Edwards; *The Kennedy Women* by Laurence Leamer; *Jack and Jackie* by Christopher Andersen; *All Too Human* by Edward Klein; *Jacqueline Kennedy* by Gordon Langley Hall; *The Kennedys: America's Emerald Kings* by Thomas Maier.

Articles: "Jackie's Maid Tells All" by Grethe Nilsen, *Screenland,* November 1970; "Jackie: Her Loneliest Battle," *Vanity Fair,* October, 2009; "Jacqueline Plans Trip to Greece," *Boston Globe,* September 17, 1963; "Love Letter from Camelot," New York *Daily News,* February 27, 1998; "Mrs. Kennedy's Blunt Answers," *Boston Globe,* January 20, 1963; "JFK Children Romp in Park with Mother," *Boston Globe,* June 1, 1963; "Kennedy Baby to Be Born at Otis Hospital," *Boston Herald,* July 24, 1963; "Love Letter from Camelot," New York *Daily News,* February 27, 1998; "Princess Lee Radziwill" by Peter Evans, *Cosmopolitan,* March 1968.

Part Six: The Assassination
Assassination of JFK:
Interviews: Jamie Auchincloss; Adora Rule; Clint Hill; James Ketchum; Yusha Auchincloss; Taki Theodoracopulos; Janine Rule.

Volumes: *White House Nannie* by Maud Shaw; *The Kennedys* by Peter Collier and David Horowitz; *The Kennedys in Hollywood* by Laurence Quirk; *President Kennedy* by Richard Reeves; *A Lady, First* by Letitia Baldrige; *First Ladies* by Carl Sferrazza Anthony; *Maria Callas* by G. B. Meneghini; *The Christina* by January Jones; *In Search of History* by Theodore White; *Just Enough Rope* by Joan Braden; *The Dark Side of Camelot* by Seymour M. Hersh; *Palimpsest* by Gore Vidal; *All Too Human* by Edward Klein; *Jack and Jackie* by Christopher Andersen; *Beaton in the Sixties* by Cecil Beaton and Hugo Vickers; *Greek Fire* by Nicholas Cage; *Janet & Jackie* by Jan Pottker; *Death of a President* by William Manchester; *A Good Life* by Ben Bradlee.

Article: "Lee" by Andy Warhol, *Interview*, March, 1975.

Oral Histories: Janet Auchincloss/JFK Library; Maud Shaw/JFK Library; Charles L. Bartlett/JFK Library; Luella Hennessey/ JFK Library; Lord Harlech (David Ormsby-Gore)/JFK Library; Jacqueline Kennedy Onassis/Lyndon Baines Johnson Library, 1974, as well as the newly released oral histories for the JFK Library in 2011; Joan Braden/JFK Library; Edward Berube/JFK Library; Rose Fitzgerald Kennedy/ Herbert Hoover Library Foundation; Cardinal Richard Cushing/JFK Library; Paul B. Fay Jr./ JFK Library; Dun Gifford/RFK Oral History Project; Roswell Gilpatric/JFK Library; Louella Hennessey/JFK Library; Robert Francis Kennedy/JFK Library; Laura Bergquist Kriebel/RFK Oral History Project; Frank Mankiewicz/RFK Oral History Project; Esther Newberg/RFK Oral History Project; Nancy Tuckerman/JFK Library; Kenneth O'Donnell/Lyndon Baines Johnson Library; Pierre Salinger/RFK Oral History Project; George Smathers /U.S. Senate Historical Office; Charles Spalding/ JFK Library.

Additionally: "Biography of Mrs. Hugh D. Auchincloss," file library, Washingtoniana Division, Martin Luther King Jr. Memorial Library, Washington D.C., March 21, 1962.

Video: Clint Hill interview with C-SPAN, May, 2012.

Part Seven: Recovery

Jack Warnecke's relationship with Bobby Kennedy:

Interviews: Harold Adams; Fred Warnecke; Margo Warnecke Merck.

Volumes: *Just Enough Rope* by Joan Braden; *Nemesis* by Peter Evans.

Oral History: Joan Braden/ JFK Library.

Janet's mission to disinter "Arabella" as per Jackie's request:

Interviews: Jamie Auchincloss; Gerald

Monroe, May 15, 2016, not acknowledged but a close friend of Edward Zimny, the late pilot; Rev. Philip Hannan, October 22, 2009; Janine Rule; Oatsie Charles.

Articles: "My Life with the Kennedys" by Archbishop Hannan, *Daily Beast,* June 1, 2010; "Former N.O. Archbishop Philip M. Hannan, Confidant of JFK, Dies at 98" by Peter Finney Jr., *Clarion Herald,* June 18, 2014; "Private Camelot" by Sally Bedell Smith, *Vanity Fair,* May 4, 2004.

Volumes: *The Archbishop Wore Combat Boots* by Rev. Philip Hannan; *Just Jackie: Her Private Years* by Edward Klein.

Additionally: "Most Holy Trinity Church, 1894–1969," pamphlet, East Hampton, New York, 1969.

Correspondence: Jackie Kennedy to Bishop Hannan, December 20, 1963: "If only I could believe that he could look down and see how he is missed and how nobody will ever be the same without him. But I haven't believed in the child's vision of heaven for a long time. There is no way now to commune with him. It will be so long before I am dead and even then I don't know if I will be reunited with him. Even if I am I don't think you could ever convince me that it will be the way it was while we were married here."; Jackie Kennedy to Bishop Hannan, June 1, 1964: "You must know how grateful I am to you every day — for believing in and being a friend of John Kennedy when he was alive — and for bringing meaning out of the despair at his funeral and birthday Masses — and for the night in Arlington with our two children — and for your work now at the Kennedy Center. You will always be working for all the things he believes in — and I will always know that and be comforted. I will try so hard to recover a little bit more myself — so that I can be of more use to my children — and just for the years that are left to me — though I hope they won't be too many. And maybe one day soon I will feel strong enough to come and talk to you."

Janet's advice to Jackie:
Interview: Jamie Auchincloss.
Articles: "Jacqueline Kennedy, Part 1," *Ladies' Home Journal,* February 1961; "Jacqueline Kennedy, Part 2," *Ladies' Home Journal,* March 1961; "Jacqueline Kennedy, Part 3," *Ladies' Home Journal,* April 1961.
Speech: "Mud Wrestling with History: Snapshots of My Life as a Brother-in-Law to John F. Kennedy" by James Lee Auchincloss.

Lee's concern about Jackie's state of mind:
Interviews: Oatsie Charles; Janine Rule.
Private Papers: Diaries of Father William McSorley, S.J, Georgetown University Library, Special Collections.

Articles: "The McSorley Connection," by Colman McCarthy, *Washington Post,* October 16, 1992; "McSorley and His Famous Friend Go Way Back" by Arthur Jones, *National Catholic Reporter,* July 28, 1995.

Jackie's cemetery:
Interviews: Jack Warnecke; Fred Warnecke; Margo Warnecke Merck; Jamie Auchincloss.
Volume: *Just Jackie: Her Private Years* by Edward Klein.

Part Eight: Transition
Jack and Jackie in Hawaii and then back to Hammersmith:
Interviews: Jack Warnecke; Fred Warnecke; Harold Adams; Bertha Baldwin; John Nash, August 8, 1998; Don Johnston, July 3, 2016; Yusha Auchincloss, describing the relocating of the Windmill.
Note: The Warnecke children were extremely impressed that both John and Caroline received handwritten notes from President Johnson for their November birthdays. For John, the President wrote: "When I was six, I wanted to be sixteen. At sixteen, I couldn't wait to be twenty-one. But today I wish I was six again, like you!" To Caroline, he wrote, "I remember when my own girls were nine. It is such a pleasant memory that I just wanted to add my happiness to you on

this special day. May you have a life of days just like it." He signed both notes, written on White House stationery: "Lyndon Johnson." Both can be found at the Lyndon Baines Johnson Library.

Janet Jr.'s wedding:
Interviews: Jamie Auchincloss; Virginia Guest Valentine, July 22, 2016; Sylvia White-house Blake; Winthrop Rutherfurd III, October 14, 2016, November 19, 2016.
Articles: "Miss Janet Auchincloss in Church Nuptials Here Becomes Bride of Lewis Rutherfurd," *Newport Daily News,* July 30, 1966; "Auchinclosses Host at Daughter's Dinner," *Newport Daily News,* July 30, 1966.
Volume: *Jacqueline Bouvier Kennedy Onassis* by Stephen Birmingham.

Janet's relationship with Onassis:
Interviews: Jamie Auchincloss; John Radziwill; Adora Rule; Delores Goodwin, June 5, 2016, July 10, 2016, August 8, 2016.
Article: "Union Everyone Said Couldn't Last" by Fred Sparks, Associated Press, August 1, 1969.
Volumes: *In Her Sister's Shadow* by Diana DuBois; *Nemesis* by Peter Evans.

Jack's confession to Jackie about finances; Jackie's decision to be with Ari:
Interviews: Jack Warnecke; Bertha Bald-

win; Harold Adams.

Volume: *Jackie: Her Private Years* by Edward Klein.

Lee's acting aspirations: *Philadelphia Story* and *Laura:*

Interviews: Jack DeMave, June 9, 2016; John Llewellyn Moxey, October 16, 2016; Garrett Johnston, October 11, 2016; Jamie Auchincloss.

Articles: "How the Remarkable Auchincloss Family Shaped the Jacqueline Kennedy Style" by Stephen Birmingham, *Ladies' Home Journal,* March 1967; "Lee Radziwill: Girls Who Have Everything Aren't Supposed to Do Anything" by Jane Howard, *Life,* July 14, 1967; "And Starring Lee Bouvier! A Nonfiction Television Play" by Gloria Steinem, *McCall's,* February 1968; "Opening Chapters: Enchanting Memories and Photos of Her Early Life with Jackie" by Lee Radziwill, *Ladies' Home Journal,* January 1973; "The Public and Private Lee" by Henry Ehrlich, *Look,* January 23, 1968; "The Complicated Sisterhood of Jackie Kennedy and Lee Radziwill" by Sam Kashner, *Vanity Fair,* April 26, 2016; "Princess Lee Radziwill" by Peter Evans, *Cosmopolitan,* March 1968; "A Princess Writes a Story and That Makes It a Party" by Charlotte Curtis, *New York Times,* December 20, 1972.

Volumes: *Capote* by Gerald Clark; *In Her*

Sister's Shadow by Diana DuBois; *Double Life* by Alan Shayne and Norman Sunshine.

Correspondence: Email from Nicky Haslam to Cathy Griffin, November 24, 2016.

Janet's relationship with the Farias:

Interviews: Joyce Faria Brennan, July 16, 2016, September 12, 2016; Gustavo Paredes, September 20, 2016, October 9, 2016; Oatsie Charles.

Jamie's twenty-first birthday with Jackie:

Interview: Jamie Auchincloss.

Correspondence: Jackie to Jamie, undated note: "Happy birthday dearest Jamie — I am so happy that you are spending your 21st birthday with Caroline and John and Me — Love Jackie."

Speech: "Mud Wrestling with History: Snapshots of My Life as a Brother-in-Law to John F. Kennedy" by James Lee Auchincloss.

Document: "The Last Will and Testament of James T. Lee."

Part Nine: Onassis

Jackie's cruise with Onassis, May 1968:

Interviews: Joan Thring, March 15, 1998; Johnny Meyer, April 25, 1998; Jamie Auchincloss.

Volumes: *Maria Callas* by Anne Edwards; *The $20,000,000 Honeymoon* by Fred Sparks; *The Spectator* by Taki Theodoracopulos.

Correspondence: Jackie to Janet, undated, from 1040 Fifth Avenue: "I thought you'd like the pictures of when Caroline and I went hunting in Virginia in March . . ."

RFK's assassination:
Interviews: Jamie Auchincloss; Richard Goodwin, May 11, 1998.
Oral History: Joan Braden/JFK Library.
Article: "Lee" by Andy Warhol, *Interview,* March, 1975.
Volumes: *Beaton in the Sixties* by Cecil Beaton and Hugo Vickers; *Jackie, Ethel, Joan* by J. Randy Taraborrelli; *After Camelot* by J. Randy Taraborrelli.
Document: "Tribute to Senator Robert F. Kennedy by Senator Edward M. Kennedy, St. Patrick's Cathedral," New York City, June 8, 1968.

Onassis at Hammersmith:
Interviews: Jamie Auchincloss; Adora Rule; Janine Rule.
Volumes: *Janet & Jackie* by Jan Pottker; *The Fabulous Onassis* by Christian Cafarakis; *Onassis* by Willi Frischauer; *Heiress: The Story of Christina Onassis* by Nigel Dempster; *Onassis: An Extravagant Life* by Frank Brady; *Destiny Prevails* by Paul J. Ioannidis.
Document: Hammersmith Farm Guest Book.

Janet's fiction about her family history:

Interviews: Jamie Auchincloss; Adora Rule; Janine Rule; Oatsie Charles.

Private Papers: "Our Forebears: From the Earliest Times to the First Half of the Year 1940," by John Vernou Bouvier.

Documents: Robert E. Lee Memorial Foundation, Stanton, Virginia: Fortieth Annual Council Minutes, October 13–17, 1968, including Board of Directors Roster and Appendix 28; "Report of the Records and Research Committee" Letter from Mrs. Randolph C. (Mary H.) Harrison to Mrs. John B. (Florence) Hollister, July 6, 1968; Janet Auchincloss Memo File, Robert. E. Lee Memorial Foundation; miscellaneous files relating to activities at Stratford Hall, October 1968.

Janet's dismay over Jackie's decision to marry Onassis:

Interviews: Jamie Auchincloss; Agnetta Castallanos; Garrett Johnston; Mary Tyler Freeman Cheek McClenahan, January 11, 1998; Nancy Tuckerman, March 10, 2007; Mona Latham, May 4, 2009, April 3, 2010, January 11, 2011; Margaret Kearney, March 11, 1998.

Volumes: *Ari* by Pete Evans; *Maria Callas: The Woman Behind the Legend* by Arianna Huffington; *Aristotle Onassis* by Nicholas Fraser, Philip Jacobson, Mark Ottaway, and Lewis Chester.

Lee's dismay over Jackie and Ari both before and after the wedding:

Interviews: Jamie Auchincloss; Janine Rule; Adora Rule; Agnetta Castallanos.

Volumes: *Capote: A Biography* by Gerald Clark; *Jacqueline Bouvier* by John Davis; *The Deadly Sins of Aristotle Onassis* by Stuart Speiser; *Happy Times* by Lee Radziwill.

Articles: "Sued by Gore Vidal and Stung by Lee Radziwill, a Wounded Truman Capote Lashes Back at the Dastardly Duo" by Mary Vespa, *People,* June 25, 1979; "The Complicated Sisterhood of Jackie Kennedy and Lee Radziwill" by Sam Kashner, *Vanity Fair,* April 26, 2016; "Lee Radziwill: In Search of Herself" by Charlotte Curtis, *McCall's;* March 1975; "Lee" by Andy Warhol, *Interview,* March, 1975; "Lee Radziwill's Search for Herself" by John J. Miller, *The Column,* December 17, 1972.

Video: Truman Capote's appearance on Stanley Siegel TV show, June 1979.

Janet's reaction to Jackie's wedding to Ari:

Interviews: Marie-Hélène de Rothschild, May 15, 2016; Jamie Auchincloss; Adora Rule; Janine Rule.

Articles: "Jackie's Mother Says Newlyweds to Come to New York Within Three Weeks" by Betty Beale, *Lubbock Avalanche-Journal,* October 23, 1968. *Note:* Beale, a close friend of Janet's, asked her, "Is Jackie happy?" Janet responded, "I hope she will be. But everyone is so tired. I didn't have any idea I was going [to Greece] until the night before I came, and I was at Stratford Hall. I had no idea about any of it! Jackie called and said, 'Could you get on a plane tomorrow afternoon, Mummy? So I very nobly did. I obviously had no clothes to wear. I wore a white wool dress and a coat." She said that Ari's wedding gift to Jackie was "a lovely ruby ring." When asked about a popular rumor at the time, Janet said, "And if he gave her a tiara as reported, I certainly don't know about it."

Video: Footage of Jackie Kennedy in the days before the wedding on Skorpios, October 18 and 19, 1968.

Aftermath of Jackie's marriage to Ari:

Interviews: Kiki Feroudi Moutsatsos, July 12, 2016; Jamie Auchincloss; Garrett Johnston; Gustavo Paredes; Letitia Baldrige, May 11, 1998.

Articles: "Onassis Mother-in-Law Denies Divorce Claim," *Boston Globe,* April 19, 1975; "Onassis: Memories of an Insomniac," *Washington Evening Star,* March 17, 1975; "A Dream Realized" by Jacqueline Kennedy Onassis, *Ladies' Home Journal,* September 1971.

Volumes: *The Onassis Women* by Kiki Feroudi Moutsatsos; *Jackie, Ethel, Joan* by J. Randy Taraborrelli; *After Camelot* by J. Randy

Taraborrelli.

Correspondence: Jacqueline Kennedy Onassis to Richard Nixon (undated but sent in February 1971).

Note: In 1970, Janet Auchincloss was one of twenty-two socialites from all over the country who gathered to judge an annual home-decorating contest sponsored by Burlington House, the textiles company. She told Judy Klemesrud of *The Fresno Bee* (on October 25, 1970): "I think we will help raise decorating standards because when people see pictures of homes that have won the prizes, they will set higher standards for themselves." Klemesrud described Janet as "a painfully shy woman who kept fumbling with her purse and her sunglasses as she was being interviewed." She quoted Janet as saying, "Eighteenth century is my favorite [period.] But then, that's almost everybody's favorite, isn't it?"

Part Ten: Shifting Tides

Lee's relationship with Peter Beard:

Interviews: Audrey Cheaver, July 17, 2016; Thomas Cheaver, July 19, 2016; Richard DuPont, August 28, 2016; Peter Beard, May 11, 1998.

Note: Lee has publicly confirmed that her romance with Peter Beard commenced before she was divorced from Stas.

Volumes: *Happy Times* by Lee Radziwill;

In Her Sister's Shadow by Diana DuBois; *America's Queen* by Sarah Bradford. *Note:* Of Jackie and Ari, Peter Beard told Sarah Bradford, "I saw the biggest fights between them. He would blow up all the time — tantrums about everything. Yelling and screaming at her . . . what Ari hated most was any kind of mess. I remember once we had all gotten haircuts on the *Christina* from Marta, the very nice governess. And Ari was stomping around the deck, just exploding with anger at the fact that these little hairs were in the bathroom — John and I hid in the shower bath. When he was mad at Jackie he used to say how he'd given up 'an artistic cultural international background' for 'this American.'"

Janet's appeal to Jackie and subsequent upheaval relating to the saving of Hammersmith:

Interviews: Garrett Johnston; Oatsie Charles; Adora Rule; Janine Rule; Eileen Slocum.

Lee's original desire to make a documentary and subsequent *Grey Gardens:*

Interviews: Eva Marie Beale, August 16, 2016, August 27, 2016, August 29, 2016, and an extensive Q and A on August 29, 2016, about her relatives, the Beales, including a comprehensive family tree. Please visit her excellent website about her family at https://greygardensofficial.com; Adora Rule; Jamie Auchincloss; Sherry Geyelin, October 6, 1998.

Volumes: *Andy Warhol: A Biography* by Wayne Koestenbaum; *The Philosophy of Andy Warhol* by Andy Warhol; *The Andy Warhol Diaries* by Andy Warhol and Pat Hackett; *Holy Terror: Andy Warhol Close Up* by Bob Colacello; *Life and Death of Andy Warhol* by Victor Bockris; *Edith Bouvier Beale of Grey Gardens: A Life in Pictures* by Eva Marie Beale and Anne Verlhac; *I Only Mark the Hours That Shine* by Edith Bouvier Beale and Eva Marie Beale; *Letters of Little Edie Beale* by Walter Newkirk; *Grey Gardens* by Sara Maysles and Rebekah Maysles.

Articles: "For Lee Radziwill, Budding Careers and New Life in New York" by Judy Klemesrud, *New York Times,* September 1, 1974; "The Complicated Sisterhood of Jackie Kennedy and Lee Radziwill" by Sam Kashner, *Vanity Fair,* April 26, 2016; "A Princess Writes a Story and That Makes It a Party" by Charlotte Curtis, *New York Times,* December 20, 1972.

Jackie and Lee coming to terms:
Interviews: John Radziwill; Jamie Auchincloss; Karen Lerner, May 5, 1998.
Volumes: *In Her Sister's Shadow* by Diana DuBois; *Jacqueline Bouvier Kennedy Onassis*

by Barbara Leaming; *Mrs. Kennedy: The Missing History of the Kennedy Years* by Barbara Leaming.

Articles: "Daddy Didn't Want His Little Girl to Be a Kennedy" by Harriman Janus, *Photoplay,* May 1969; "Lee Radziwill: Girls Who Have Everything Aren't Supposed to Do Anything" by Jane Howard, *Life,* July 14, 1967; "Lee Radziwill's Search for Herself" by John J. Miller, *The Column,* December 17, 1972. "Opening Chapters: Enchanting Memories and Photos of Her Early Life with Jackie" by Lee Radziwill, *Ladies' Home Journal,* January 1973. "Nobody Wants a Part Time-Marriage: Interview with Prince Stanislaw Radziwill" by George Carpozi, *Photoplay,* April 1973.

Video: Lee Radziwill interview with Sofia Coppola, *T* magazine *(NYT),* also broadcast on Vimeo and YouTube, Spring 2013.

Lee's breakup with Peter Beard:
Interview: Barbara Allen Kwiatkowska, August 21, 2016, September 20, 2016.
Volume: *Capote: A Biography* by Gerald Clark.

Lee's divorce from Stas and introduction to the publishing community:
Interviews: John Radziwill; Tom Guinzburg.
Volume: *Happy Times* by Lee Radziwill.

Article: "Opening Chapters: Enchanting Memories and Photos of Her Early Life with Jackie" by Lee Radziwill, *Ladies' Home Journal,* January 1973.

Raiding Janet's attic:
Interviews: Linda Murray, July 15, 2016; Sherry Geyelin; Philip Geyelin.
Articles: "Lee" by Andy Warhol, *Interview,* March, 1975; "Luncheon with Jamie Auchincloss" by Gwen Dobson, *Washington Evening Star,* December 22, 1972; "Kennedy Center Bows to Jackie Onassis" by Mary Anne Dolan, *Washington Evening Star,* June 6, 1972.

Aristotle Onassis's death and Janet's reaction to it:
Interviews: Jamie Auchincloss; Eileen Slocum; Oatsie Charles.
Volumes: *Nemesis* by Peter Evans; *After Camelot* by J. Randy Taraborrelli.

The cancellation of Lee's book contract:
Interview: Tom Guinzburg.
Volume: *In Her Sister's Shadow* by Diana DuBois.

Lee Radziwill, Inc.:
Interviews: Gustavo Paredes; Oatsie Charles; Jamie Auchincloss; Linda Murray.
Volumes: *In Her Sister's Shadow* by Diana

DuBois; *Happy Times* by Lee Radziwill; *Lee* by Lee Radziwill; *Janet & Jackie* by Jan Pottker.

Articles: "Lee Radziwill As Decorator: A New Step Confidently Taken" by Lisa Hammel, *New York Times,* February 20, 1976; "A Question of Power: What Makes Peter [Tufo] Run" by Judy Klemesrud, *New York Times,* March 7, 1977; "Jackie's Shadow: 'I'm Nobody's Kid Sister,' Snaps Jackie's Kid Sister" by Lee Wohlfert, *People,* November 1, 1976 (Interesting passage: "Her decision at 43 to join the ranks of the working rich is not dictated — Lord knows — by any need to make money, or simply to follow in the footsteps of Jackie, 47, who took a job as a book editor last year. 'Don't be silly,' says Lee icily. 'I never even conferred with her.' ").

Stas's death:
Interviews: R. Couri Hay, November 17, 2016; Jamie Auchincloss.

Article: "Stanislas Radziwill Dies; Brother-in-Law of JFK," *Washington Evening Star,* June 29, 1976.

Maurice Tempelsman tries to help Lee (and background of Tempelsman):
Note: The source present at this meeting asked for anonymity.
Volumes: *A Woman Named Jackie* by C. David Heymann; *Jackie as Editor: The Liter-*

ary Life of Jacqueline Kennedy Onassis by Greg Lawrence; *Jackie Style* by Pamela Clarke Keogh; *Remembering Jackie: A Life in Pictures* by *Life* magazine; *As We Remember Her: Jacqueline Kennedy Onassis in the Words of Her Family and Friends* by Carl Sferrazza Anthony.

Video: Interview with Marta Sgubin, ABC News, March 12, 2013.

Emergency family meeting at Hammersmith:

Interviews: Garrett Johnston. There were also several people present at this meeting who asked for anonymity.

Articles: "Auchincloss Says He Isn't Surprised on Farm Rejection," *Providence Journal-Bulletin,* May 8, 1976. "Auchincloss Tells of Wish to Save Family Estate," *Newport Daily News,* April 23, 1976; "Exclusively Yours: Historic Hammersmith" by Betty Beale, *Washington Evening Star,* November 28, 1971; "Committee Endorses Plan," *Providence Journal-Bulletin,* March 27, 1977; "Cultural Center Proposed for Hammersmith Farm," *Providence Journal-Bulletin,* August 10, 1977.

Volumes: *After Camelot* by J. Randy Taraborrelli; *Jacqueline Bouvier Kennedy Onassis: The Untold Story* by Barbara Leaming; *Jacqueline Bouvier Kennedy Onassis: A Life* by Donald Spoto.

Hugh Auchincloss's death and the spreading of his ashes:

Interviews: Adora Rule; Joyce Faria Brennan; Sherry Geyelin; Jamie Auchincloss.

Articles: "Hugh Auchincloss of Newport Dies," *Providence Journal-Bulletin,* November 22, 1976; "Hugh Auchincloss Sr., Stockbroker, Dead," *New York Times,* November 22, 1976; "H. D. Auchincloss Death Notice, Thomson & McKinnon Auchincloss Kohlmeyer Inc.," *Wall Street Journal,* November 24, 1976; "Hugh Auchincloss Dies, Prominent D.C. Banker," *Washington Evening Star,* November 22, 1976.

Part Eleven: Enduring

Hammersmith Farm transition by Camelot Gardens:

Interviews: Janet Crook, December 27, 2016; Adora Rule; Janine Rule; Oatsie Charles; Jamie Auchincloss.

Articles: "Hammersmith Farm Will Open to the Public Starting May 1" by Brian C. Jones, *Providence Journal-Bulletin,* January 28, 1978; "Tourists Flock to the Green," *Providence Journal-Bulletin,* November 19, 1978; "Tour Provides Close-up of 'The Way We Were' at Hammersmith Farm" by Fritz Koch, *Providence Journal-Bulletin,* July 14, 1977; "Seasons in the Sun: Mrs. Hugh D. Auchincloss's Historic Newport Home" by Valentine Lawford, *Architectural Digest,* July 1985;

"Hammersmith Farm Owner's Death Clouds State Acquisition Plans" by John F. Fitzgerald, *Providence Journal-Bulletin,* April 15, 1977; "Hammersmith Farm Sold to Consortium, Will Become Museum," *Providence Journal-Bulletin,* August 17, 1977; "Hammersmith Farm to Be Sold," *Providence Journal-Bulletin,* August 16, 1977; "Historic Houses: Hammersmith Farm" by Avis Berman, *Architectural Digest,* August 1991.

Brochure: "English Furniture and Decorative Arts, Including the Property of the Heirs of Janet Auchincloss," Christie's East, Sale no. 8427, October 10, 2000.

Documents: Sales documents and subsequent tourism brochures and videotapes relating to the Camelot Gardens acquisition of Hammersmith Farm.

Janet and her new life at the Castle, her relationship with the Faria girls, and her decision to make provisions for them in her will and talk of "regrets":

Interviews: Jonathan Tapper, April 25, 2016, April 27, 2016, May 3, 2016; Ella Burling, May 23, 2016; Joyce Faria Brennan; Oatsie Charles; Adora Rule; Janine Rule.

Article: "Butler Shares Look Behind Family of Jackie O." by Ryan Neal, *Review Atlas,* August 9, 2010.

Lee's relationship with Newton Cope, including their engagement and interrupted wedding:

Interviews: Newton Cope, April 6, 1998; Isabella Fritz-Cope, August 21, 2016; Marion Cope, September 15, 2016.

Articles: "Truman's True Love" by Liz Smith, New York *Daily News,* September 23, 1984; "Lee Radziwill's Interior Life" by John Duka, *Vogue,* April 1985.

Volume: *In Her Sister's Shadow* by Diana DuBois.

Janet's early relationship with and marriage to Bingham Morris:

Interviews: Michael Dupree, September 27, 2016, January 3, 2017; Jonathan Tapper, April 25, 2016, April 27, 2016, May 3, 2016, May 13, 2016, December 4, 2016; Jamie Auchincloss; Yusha Auchincloss; Adora Rule; Janine Rule; Oatsie Charles.

Articles: "Jackie Spots Paparazzi at Mother's Wedding," Associated Press, *Baltimore Sun,* October 27, 1979; "Hot Blood — and Gore, Chapter Two" by Sally Quinn, *Washington Post,* June 7, 1979; "Mrs. Auchincloss to Marry for the Third Time," *New York Times,* August 21, 1979; "Mrs. Onassis Is the Witness at Her Mother's Wedding," *New York Times,* October 26, 1979. "The Kennedys Gathered for Ceremony" by Gloria Negri, *Boston Globe,* September 20, 1980; "Her Famous Family Gathers at Wedding of Mrs.

Auchincloss" by Marialisa Calta, *Providence Journal-Bulletin,* October 26, 1979.

Volume: *Janet & Jackie* by Jan Pottker.

Correspondence: Yusha Auchincloss to Bingham Morris, undated.

Jackie's relationship with Maurice Tempelsman:

Interviews: Jamie Auchincloss; Jonathan Tapper; Gustavo Paredes; Tom Guinzburg; Roswell Gilpatric, 1990 (for my book *Michael Jackson: The Magic, The Madness, The Whole Story 1958–2009* relating to Jackie's work as editor to Jackson but wide-ranging in scope).

Volumes: *Cooking for Madam* by Marta Sgubin; *John and Caroline: Their Lives in Pictures* by James Spada; *Jackie: Her Life in Pictures* by James Spada.

Lee's alcoholism:

Because of the sensitive nature of this topic, our interview subjects asked for anonymity. However, to read more about Lee's battle with alcoholism, see *In Her Sister's Shadow* by Diana DuBois.

Onset of Janet's Alzheimer's:

Interviews: Jonathan Tapper; Jamie Auchincloss; Michael Dupree; Yusha Auchincloss.

Part Twelve: "Well, Happy, and Loved . . ."

Janet Jr.'s life in Hong Kong:

Interviews: Dawn Luango, September 12, 2016; Jamie Auchincloss; Mary Leventhal, June 7, 2016.

Article: "Janet Rutherfurd Active in Women's Group," *Boston Globe,* March 19, 1985.

Documents: Various brochures, publications, and other material relating to the Hong Kong League of Women Voters.

Janet Jr.'s illness and subsequent death and funeral:

Interviews: Winthrop Rutherfurd III, October 14, 2016, November 10, 2016; Yusha Auchincloss; Jamie Auchincloss; Mary Leventhal; Jonathan Tapper; Joyce Faria Brennan; Sylvia Whitehouse Blake; Michael Dupree.

Documents: Mass cards, programs, and other handout materials from the funeral Mass and services for Janet Jennings Auchincloss Rutherfurd at both Trinity Church in Newport (March 19, 1985) and Church of the Heavenly Rest, New York City (April 15, 1985).

Bingham Morris's alleged mistreatment of Janet:

Interviews: Dr. Dennis J. Selkoe, January 2, 2017; Jamie Auchincloss; Jonathan Tapper; Michael Dupree; Adora Rule; Janine Rule.

Note: Because of the sensitive nature of these accusations, many of my sources requested anonymity, including my source who worked at Doubleday & Company at the time.

Article: "VIP: The Auchincloss Family's Missing Silver" by Maxine Cheshire, *Washington Post,* April 7, 1980.

Volumes: *Janet & Jackie* by Jan Pottker; *In Her Sister's Shadow* by Diana DuBois.

Correspondence: Jacqueline Onassis to Yusha Auchincloss, August 25, 1989; Yusha Auchincloss to Bingham Morris (undated).

Janet's gift of money to Lee and Jackie's reaction to it:

Interviews: Jamie Auchincloss; Jonathan Tapper.

Volume: *Janet & Jackie* by Jan Pottker.

Correspondence: Jacqueline Onassis to Dr. John Lattimer, May 13, 1986.

Janet's eightieth birthday party:

Interviews: Dr. Dennis Selkoe; Michael Dupree; Jamie Auchincloss; Oatise Charles; Eileen Slocum; Jonathan Tapper; Adora Rule; Janine Rule; Joyce Faria Brennan.

Documents: "Janet's Birthday Letters" (scrapbook compiled by Yusha Auchincloss for Janet's birthday celebration). A few highlights from the scrapbook, notes to Janet:

From Jackie: "You used to sing to me an

old Harry Laud song, 'I Just Can't Make My Eyes Behave' and 'Comin' Through the Rye.' I loved it when you sang them. We will all be with you on the 80th birthday and it will be the greatest day in the history of Hammersmith Farm!"

From Lee: "I have too many lovely memories to fill this small space but I have enough to fill books. I love you very much . . ."

From Jamie: "I will be coming back here for Christmas to give you the videotape of last night's wonderful celebration. I hope it shows how really splendid it was. You were beautiful and always the center of admiration and great love."

From Caroline Kennedy: "Happy Birthday Grandmere: I remember all the Thanksgivings we spent at Hammersmith Farm. We used to have oyster soup which Mummy said we had to eat because it was a delicacy . . . and it tasted yummy!"

From John: "Dear Grandmere: I send you lots of love on your birthday. I won a mock trial at law school so I'm happy about that. I'm going skiing over Christmas and fox hunting with my mother and Caroline over Christmas . . ."

From Anthony: "Happy, happy birthday! I miss you!"

From Yusha: "You and I have shared many special celebrations over the last 46 years . . . usually with vodka, caviar and champagne . . ."

From Mannie and Louise Faria: "We will never forget your concern and thoughtfulness to us and our daughters — Linda and Joyce — over the years. If we had few words to describe you we would say, a gracious lady who has always given us the feeling that we were family. Over the years we have shared the happiness and sorrows with you and will keep those precious years in our memories forever."

From Joyce and Linda Faria: "Through the years to know you has been a pleasure. For the joy and happiness you have spread, there is no measure."

From Oatsie Charles: "I have been thinking of all the happy times I have had at Merrywood and Hammersmith — the picnics, the debuts, the weddings, the birthday, and particularly the daiquiris with Hugh D on the terrace watching the sun set over Narragansett Bay."

Lee's courtship with and marriage to Herb Ross:

Interviews: Leslie Browne, December 11, 2016; Garrett Johnston. We also interviewed Ed Pisoni, set decorator for *Steel Magnolias* (though his commentary was not used in the book for space reasons), December 12, 2016.

Articles: "That Hollywood Touch" by Leo Janus, *New York Times,* November 12, 1978;

"Herb Ross at the Turning Point" by Stephen Farber, *Film Comment,* January 2, 1978; "Serious Director of Funny Hits" by David Sterritt, *Christian Science Monitor,* January 30, 1978.

Volumes: *In Her Sister's Shadow* by Diana DuBois; *Janet & Jackie* by Jan Pottker.

Lee's distancing herself from Janet and Jackie's reaction:

Interviews: Jamie Auchincloss; Joyce Faria Brennan; Adora Rule; Janine Rule.

Article: "Blaze Damages 3 Georgetown Town Houses," *Washington Post,* December 3, 1986.

Jackie evading paparazzi with Mannie's help:

Interview: Joyce Faria Brennan.

Additionally: *Stratford Journal* newsletter, "Coaching Day Honoring Mrs. Hugh D. Auchincloss," Stratford Hall Plantation, March/April 1987 — 473rd Installment; Invitation: Coaching Day Honoring Mrs. Hugh D. Auchincloss, Sunday, April 16, 1987.

Janet's decline in health and then death:

Interviews: Jamie Auchincloss; Robert Westover; Jonathan Tapper; Michael Dupree; Joyce Faria Brennan; Adora Rule; Janine Rule; Dr. Dennis Selkoe; Yusha Auchincloss; Oatsie Charles.

Articles: "Jackie Onassis's Mother, 81, Injures Hip" by Jim Seavor, *Providence Journal-Bulletin,* March 20, 1989; "Spectators Flock to See Celebrities at Funeral," *Providence Journal-Bulletin,* July 28, 1989; "Janet Lee Auchincloss Morris, 81," *New York Times,* July 24, 1989; "Janet Lee Auchincloss, Mother of Jacqueline Onassis, Dies," *Washington Post,* July 24, 1989; "Janet Auchincloss Dies, Wealthy Mom of Jackie O." by Ken Fireman, *Newsday,* July 24, 1989.

Volumes: *Janet & Jackie* by Jan Pottker; *America's Queen* by Sarah Bradford; *In Her Sister's Shadow* by Diana DuBois; *Just Jackie: Her Private Years* by Edward Klein; *Jackie Oh!* by Kitty Kelley; *What Remains: A Memoir of Fate, Friendship and Love* by Carole Radziwill.

Janet's funeral service and the spreading of ashes at Hammersmith:

Interviews: Jamie Auchincloss; Jonathan Tapper; Michael Dupree; Joyce Faria Brennan; Adora Rule; Janine Rule; Oatsie Charles; Yusha Auchincloss.

Documents: "Last Will and Testament of Janet Lee Auchincloss," Newport, Rhode Island, March 9, 1984; "Codicil to the Last Will and Testament of Janet Lee Auchincloss," Newport, Rhode Island, June 29, 1984.

Epilogue: Passages

Interviews: Jamie Auchincloss; Jack Warnecke; Fred Warnecke; Bertha Baldwin; Oatsie Charles; Adora Rule; Harold Adams;
Stanford Lotwin, October 7, 2016 (Herbert
Ross's attorney in his divorce from Lee;
anecdotes not utilized because of space concerns).

Articles: "Jacqueline Kennedy — Her
Personal Photos," Countrywide Publications,
January 1963; "Woman About Town" by
Christopher Andersen, *New York,* February
16, 1998; "Jackie Kennedy's Sister, Lee
Radiziwll, Gives Rare Peek at Her Life Beside
the Icon: 'You Have to Walk Three Steps
Behind' " by Sandra Sobieraj Westfall, *People,*
December 3, 2015; "Lee Radziwill's Interior
Life" by John Duka, *Vogue,* April 1985;
"Herb Ross" by Hillel Italie, Associated
Press, April 8, 1991; "A New Balance: Lee
Radziwill Finds Serenity in Paris" by William
Norwich, *New York Times,* October 22, 2000.

Volumes: *What Remains* by Carole Radzi-
will; *In Her Sister's Shadow* by Diana DuBois;
Janet & Jackie by Jan Pottker; *Happy Times*
by Lee Radziwill; *Just Jackie: Her Private
Years* by Edward Klein; *America's Queen* by
Sarah Bradford; *Jackie, Ethel, Joan* by J.
Randy Taraborrelli; *After Camelot* by J. Randy
Taraborrelli.

Correspondence: Jacqueline Onassis to
Jamie Auchincloss, February 1994. Jacqueline

Onassis to Hugh D. Auchincloss III, (undated, 1994.)

Documents: "The Last Will and Testament of Jacqueline K. Onassis," March 22, 1994.

ACKNOWLEDGMENTS

This is actually my second book for St. Martin's Press, my first being a biography of Cher more than thirty years ago, in 1986. It's great to be back!

I want to thank my editor, Charles Spicer, for his encouragement and for his great interest in the subject of Jacqueline Kennedy Onassis, her mother, Janet Auchincloss, and sister, Lee Radziwill. It's certainly rare to come up with an idea about a Jackie-related book that has not yet been done — and, I dare say, this is probably the last of them. I am honored to have it edited by Charles and published by St. Martin's Press. Thanks also to Charles's assistant, April Osborn, and to Kim Lewis, who did a wonderful job copyediting this manuscript.

I would also like to acknowledge my domestic agent, Mitch Douglas, for almost twenty years of terrific representation. Mitch is a good friend as well as my agent, and I am eternally grateful to him.

And I would like to acknowledge my foreign agent, Dorie Simmonds of the Dorie Simmonds Agency in London, who not only represented me for more than twenty years but is a trusted friend.

I would like to thank my very good friend Andy Hirsch, for reading this book before publication for his point of view. My close friend Jillian DeVaney also read it in manuscript stage and offered invaluable insight, and so I thank her as well. Barb Mueller read it in its infancy, too, and I thank her, as well as my sister, Roz Barnett, who also pored through many early drafts to render important and useful opinions.

My thanks to Jonathan Hahn, a brilliant writer, my personal publicist, and good friend.

Special thanks also to Michael Horowitz, Jo Ann McMahon, and Felinda Adlawan of Horowitz Zaron McMahon as well as Stephen Breimer and Candice Hanson of Bloom, Hergott, Diemer, et. al.

Thanks to: Andy Steinlen, George Solomon, Jeff Hare, Samuel Munoz, Bruce Rheins, Dawn Westlake, Jeff Cook, Brandon Schmook, Richard Tyler Jordan, John Passantino, Linda DiStefano, Hazel and Rob Kragulac, Andy Skurow, Brad Scarton, Brian Newman, Scherrie Payne, Freda Payne, Susaye Greene, Barbara Ormsby, David Spiro, Billy Masters, Marlene Morris, Kac

Young, Yvette Jarecki, Robin Roth, Sammy Roth, Mary Downey, Felipe Echeri, Laura Fagin, Corey Sheppard, Rita Bosico, Deb Armstrong, Susan Kayaoglu, Sal Pinto, David Gunther, Eric Edmonds, Michael Coleman, Rob Kesselring, and Howard Field.

I also want to acknowledge my television producing partners and colleagues: my very good friend Keri Selig along with Jonathan Koch, Steve Michaels, Stanley Hubbard, Michael Prupus, Stephen Kronish, Joan Harrison, Sherryl Clark, Eva Miller, and Kimberly Current.

I have always been so blessed to have a family as supportive as mine. My thanks and love go out to: Roslyn and Bill Barnett and Jessica and Zachary; Rocco and Rosemaria Taraborrelli and Rocco and Vincent; and Arnold Taraborrelli. A big smile, also, for Spencer Douglas Taraborrelli.

I must also acknowledge those readers of mine who have followed my career over the years. I am indebted to each and every reader who has stuck by me. I am eternally grateful to anyone who takes the time to pick up one of my books and read it. Thank you so much.

This book is dedicated to my late parents, Rocco and Rose Marie Taraborrelli. Both encouraged a young kid from Morton, Pennsylvania, to not only reach for the stars but to do so with the knowledge that they'd be there for him whenever he fell short of the mark, which was often. I miss them.

ABOUT THE AUTHOR

J. Randy Taraborrelli is the author of nearly 20 biographies, most of which have become *New York Times* bestsellers, including: *Call Her Miss Ross*, *Sinatra — Behind the Legend*, *Madonna — An Intimate Biography*, *Jackie, Ethel, Joan — Women of Camelot*, *Elizabeth*, (a biography of Elizabeth Taylor); *The Secret Life of Marilyn Monroe* and *After Camelot — A Personal History of the Kennedy Family 1968 to the Present*, which has been adapted as a mini-series for Reelz.